$\mathcal{A}$MERICAN
EMPRESS

NANCY RUBIN

iUniverse Star
New York Lincoln Shanghai

AMERICAN EMPRESS

THE LIFE AND TIMES OF

MARJORIE

MERRIWEATHER

POST

For my parents,
Ethel and Stuart Zimman

Foreword

"The queen is back—long live the queen!" announced the syndicated newspaper columnist Suzy in December 1969. The woman she was referring to was the handsome silver-haired Marjorie Merriweather Post, who had just arrived in Palm Beach to open her renowned estate Mar-A-Lago for the first time in years.

Indeed, to a crowd of curious men and women who gazed at the eighty-two-year-old Mrs. Post as she stepped off her Viscount jet and climbed into a custom Cadillac that whisked her to the pink-towered Mediterranean estate on South Ocean Boulevard, she must have seemed as close to royalty as one can come in America. Marjorie, like a true monarch, was accompanied by an entourage of advisers and servants. Once settled at Mar-A-Lago, she would entertain dignitaries from foreign countries—in this instance, ambassadors from Washington's Embassy Row. Every year they were part of a select group of men and women Marjorie invited as her guests to Palm Beach's annual American Red Cross International Ball.

To millions of Americans, the face of the still-beautiful heiress had long been a symbol of social grace, wealth, and magnanimity. For decades photographs of her, resplendent in ball gowns, ermine capes, and sable coats, her delicate features and snow-white skin enhanced by jeweled tiaras, forty-carat sapphires, and the pear-shaped diamond earrings that once belonged to Marie Antoinette, had appeared in the press. Nearly as familiar were pictures of Marjorie in tailored suits, business dresses, and hats as she presided over charity luncheons, benefits, and other fund-raisers at her homes in Washington and Palm Beach.

Less public was Marjorie's role as a member of the board of directors of the General Foods Corporation—the conglomerate that had evolved from the Postum Cereal Company, the breakfast food empire of her father, C. W. Post. Although Marjorie was heiress to the Post Toasties cereal fortune, her contribution to General Foods was far from nominal. Hers had been the insistent voice that had demanded the incorporation of Birds Eye Frosted Foods into the old Postum company and transformed it into the General Foods Corporation.

Marjorie's various surnames from her marriages—Close, Hutton, Davies, May—have also floated through the public consciousness. Whatever her surname, she was always linked with social and charitable causes: the American Red Cross, the soup kitchens of the Depression, Soviet War Relief of World War II, the Boy Scouts of America, and the National Symphony Orchestra. To these and other charitable organizations Marjorie donated millions of dollars. Privately she also supported widows, orphans, and impoverished students, often without their knowledge of their benefactor. "While she has always lived like a queen," observed *The New York Times*, "she has always given like a philanthropist."

Typically it was anonymity that the publicity-shy benefactor sought for her contributions. Marjorie anonymously donated one hundred thousand dollars toward the creation of the Kennedy Center for the Performing Arts. A half century earlier, during World War I, she outfitted an American Army hospital ship with equal modesty. At age twenty-seven, when Marjorie inherited her father's fortune, she already understood that great wealth could be as much a curse as a blessing. "Let's not make too much about my sponsorship because that has a tendency to drive money away," she once warned a publicist for the National Symphony Orchestra.

It was no secret that Marjorie was one of the wealthiest women in the world. While her blue eyes blazed angrily when reporters confronted her with the "richest woman" label, Marjorie hardly lived in a modest manner. The castles of conspicuous consumption she built in Palm Beach, Washington, and New York were famous for their opulence and fairy-tale luxury, legendary in their creature comforts and attention to the details of daily life. Perfection was the order of the day. The position of table place settings was measured with a ruler to assure uniformity.

Outside, every lawn had to be weed-free, every tree and flower a prize specimen. Inevitably the mansions Marjorie built and her lifestyle within them attracted the attention and awe of the press.

To be Marjorie Merriweather Post was to be the best and to do the best for others, but that conviction was never spoken aloud. Instead it was expressed through the philanthropist's perfectionistic zeal, her persistent efforts to create a flawless and flower-filled world where all the ills of humanity—want, evil, sickness, and death—could be at least temporarily forgotten. With that sense of personal mission, Marjorie played fairy godmother, queen, empress to the world.

Those who were guests at Marjorie's homes witnessed that perfectionism for themselves. They approached Mar-A-Lago through thick steel gates and a majestic bank of bowing coconut palms leading to a porte cochere and elegant entranceway. Then, passing beneath a beamed hand-painted Spanish ceiling, past coats of arms, Dresden vases, and Roman busts, they walked through carved double doors into a visual splendor so rich that it took hours to absorb.

Money, millions of dollars of it, had been spent creating the estate. Built at the height of the Roaring Twenties by the heiress and her second husband, E. F. Hutton, the palace on seventeen acres between Lake Worth and the Atlantic had been the inspiration of Florenz Ziegfeld's set designer, Joseph Urban. Marjorie had furnished it with the same gaily plumed abandon as a *Ziegfeld Follies* stage set, filling it with furniture, tapestries, and paintings from decaying ducal palaces and stone carvings reminiscent of ancient Greece and Egypt.

The parties held at Mar-A-Lago were equally fabulous. Guest lists often exceeded two hundred and included some of America's most celebrated tycoons, moguls, and movie stars, as well as European aristocrats. At the hour indicated on Marjorie's engraved invitations, her guests appeared in Mar-A-Lago's shimmering drawing rooms or upon the crescent-shaped patio beneath the mansion's artificial "blue moon." The men arrived in black or white ties, tuxedos, and pince-nez, and the women were draped in flowing gowns and trains, aglitter with gems, and trailed by feather boas.

To entertain her guests, Marjorie once imported a three-act comedy produced by her friend the Broadway showman Charles Dillingham. Another time she brought the Ringling Bros. and Barnum & Bailey Circus to her Florida estate. On innumerable occasions her friends Florenz Ziegfeld and Billie Burke provided costumes and set designs for amateur-night benefits. For the more "ordinary" costume balls of the twenties Marjorie's guests arrived in hand-sewn, beaded, or jeweled costumes representing the most glorious cultures of the past—eighteenth-century France, Arabia, the Orient, and the Italy of the Renaissance.

Royalty, in the flesh as well as the spirit, always fascinated her. Among Marjorie's friends were kings and queens, princes and dukes, lords and ladies. In imitation of the royal courts of Europe, Marjorie's parties were flawlessly elegant, attended by teams of liveried footmen, chauffeurs, and maids. Her dinner table—whether for groups of fifty, one hundred, or two hundred—glistened with antique china from the royal houses of France, Germany, and Britain. Flatware and serving pieces were fashioned from silver and, especially, gold. Even the fixtures in Mar-A-Lago's guest powder room were plated with gold. Their advantage, Marjorie explained to friends, "was that they didn't lose their luster."

In the heyday of the Roaring Twenties, Marjorie's home on Long Island and her apartment in New York were no less lavish. Within her fifty-four-room Fifth Avenue triplex apartment were Gainsboroughs, Boucher tapestries, and French antique furniture. At Marjorie's Tudor mansion Hillwood—a sprawling 177-acre country estate on Long Island's "Gold Coast"—were greenhouses, nurseries, horse stables, and even a racecourse.

In the summer, Marjorie and her family enjoyed a 207-acre camp in the Adirondacks on Upper St. Regis Lake. Surrounded on all sides by water, Camp Hutridge had eighteen guesthouses, each with its own fireplaces, baths, and sitting rooms. There were fleets of pleasure boats, water skis, and canoes. Every house that Marjorie built was centered on a collection. At Hutridge the main lodge contained a rare assembly of Indian artifacts, including Apache playing cards, beaded moccasins, Sitting Bull's tomahawk, and Geronimo's war bonnet.

By the mid-thirties Marjorie had married Washington lawyer Joseph Davies, who then became ambassador to the Soviet Union during the Stalin regime. On the eve of World War II, after residing in Soviet Russia and Belgium, the couple returned to Washington. There the former ambassador and "ambassadress" settled into Tregaron, a sprawling mansion that they filled with the Russian imperial treasures purchased in the warehouses and commission shops of the USSR.

In the late fifties, following her divorce from Joe Davies, Marjorie established another majestic monument, a huge Georgian Colonial on twenty-four acres of land overlooking Washington's Rock Creek Park. For the second time in her life, Marjorie named her home Hillwood. In the spring, the title seemed especially fitting as Hillwood's sloping site blazed with vibrant hues from four thousand varieties of azaleas, dogwoods, and other shrubs Marjorie ordered for the grounds.

Had she lived in a different era, Marjorie Merriweather Post might have exercised her power differently. Perhaps she would have been president of the giant General Foods Corporation, ambassador to a foreign country, or head of a major cultural institution. But Marjorie was a product of the nineteenth century, born and bred in the pre-suffrage era, at a time when wealthy young women were "finished" and wed to become wives, mothers, and hostesses.

Marjorie faithfully fulfilled those three roles, but her keen business mind, natural organizational skills, and vast wealth seemed to hinder her. In spite of Marjorie's personal assets, all four of her marriages failed. As she once confided to a friend, "I had many beautiful things, but choosing a husband, I never had much luck."

In between husbands she carved out an independent life. While never an avowed feminist, Marjorie often behaved like one. In 1936, after a heart-wrenching divorce from the love of her life, E. F. Hutton, she became one of the first women to serve on the board of directors of a major American corporation. In 1955, exasperated with the trail of ex-husbands' names attached to hers, she legally resumed her maiden name of Marjorie Merriweather Post. In 1964, at the end of her marriage to Pittsburgh executive Herb May, she once again embraced her maiden name. This time she kept it for good.

At her worst Marjorie had an imperious streak that jibed poorly with the modern democratic world. In the mornings, after a maid had removed the breakfast tray from Marjorie's bed, Marjorie would rattle off instructions for the day to her butler, secretary, and children. "We used to call her the train dispatcher," said her daughter the actress Dina Merrill.

Nor did Marjorie expect anything but exemplary behavior from her three daughters. Among her most cherished rules was that a sense of propriety, punctuality, and good posture must be maintained. Throughout her life Marjorie exemplified these principles herself. Marjorie even as an octogenarian stood so erect that it was said "her ramrod posture would have delighted a Marine sergeant."

In Marjorie's lofty view, there were absolutes. The rules of social decorum were simple and inviolate. Guests who drank too much, flirted across the table, or failed to talk to those sitting on either side of them were reprimanded by one of Marjorie's footmen. Should a guest refuse an invitation more than twice in a row, he was usually not invited again.

As a result, some who encountered Marjorie only at dances and parties found her forbiddingly formal. Society writer Stephen Birmingham, who met Marjorie late in life when she was nearly totally deaf, was one of them. Her Thursday night square dances, he recalled, were "universally dreaded, although attending them was a must." Guests had to arrive exactly on time, and no one was served more than two drinks. The dance itself was carried out with "paramilitary precision, with Mrs. Post barking out the orders in her loud midwestern twang." Said *The New York Times Magazine* in 1971 of the eighty-four-year-old Marjorie: "Mrs. Post, who is often described as regal, or even imperious . . . happens to like to square dance. Social Palm Beach would, by and large, just as soon skip it, but each Thursday night in the season . . . 100 or so turn out for a couple of hours of hoe-downs."

To the young and politically ambitious, Marjorie was a fourteen-karat symbol of social supremacy. Her vast wealth was intimidating, despised, and feared as much as it was admired. Even as a younger woman, as Marjorie's stepdaughter Emlen Davies Evers explained, "she was so extraordinarily beautiful and had such lavish jewels and clothes and lived in such a grand style that people were awed and frightened. But to those who knew her well, Marjorie was a very warm, intelligent person, very loving and human."

High expectations for herself and for others were the centerpiece of Marjorie's life. Her philanthrophic deeds, glittering public appearances, positive can-do attitude, and absolute decorum made Marjorie an unofficial standard for American excellence. Besides all this was a personal romanticism that captivated others. Life was to be enjoyed; pain and trouble were to be pushed aside or forgotten. She would not tolerate a house that was dark, a movie that ended sadly, or a life that was without hope.

As one of the richest, most privileged and capable women in the world, Marjorie felt it was incumbent upon her to bring hope to others. She was truly an American empress.

Contents

A
MIDWESTERN
MILLIONAIRE'S
DAUGHTER

1

"A Healthy, Hearty, and Handsome Girl"

*O*n a chill desolate day in February 1891, a gaunt man lay on a stretcher in a compartment of the Michigan Central Railroad as it steamed into the Battle Creek depot. The invalid Charles William Post, his wife, Ella, and their young daughter, Marjorie, made the journey to that snow-covered city out of sheer desperation.

Illness was common to many of the travelers who descended the sooty steps of the train at Battle Creek that mid-February day. Some of them were white with pain; others wheezed with catarrh, trembled with ague, or were swollen with dropsy; still others slumped in their seats with melancholy or shook with nervous tics. Invalids traveled to the "health" city of Battle Creek to be cured at the famous sanitarium run by Dr. John Harvey Kellogg.

Ultimately Charles Post—or C.W., as he became known to his personal and professional associates—would not only triumph over his disease but bring hope to millions of Americans that they could live healthier lives through a proper diet. In time C. W. Post would create the nation's first breakfast food industry, inspired in part by the tasteless cereals fed him at Dr. Kellogg's sanitarium and in part by the zeitgeist of the age: from a new interest in mesmerism, spiritualism, psychology, and mental therapeutics that was changing the thought of middle-class citizens. Most of all, C.W.'s cure would arise from the deep recesses of his inventive mind, his entrepreneurial spirit, and his indomitable will to live.

So powerful were these drives that few who met C.W. forgot him. Poet Walt Whitman, who had known C.W. a decade earlier, wrote to him, in the early twentieth century Samuel Clemens praised his ideas, and politicians like Teddy Roosevelt cultivated his friendship. That C.W. was charming, handsome, and brilliant was indisputable to his contemporaries. His tall frame, immaculately groomed appearance, quick wit, and soft-spoken demeanor inevitably inspired respect and admiration from many quarters. C.W.'s vibrant personality left an indelible imprint upon his daughter, Marjorie, who would spend her life searching for his double among the men who were to become her beaux and husbands.

In February 1891 few people traveling to Battle Creek could have imagined that the invalid C. W. Post would one day create a new American industry. Least among these was his wife, Ella, whose most fervent desire was to have her husband restored to health.

Initially, C.W.'s case may not have seemed unusual to Dr. Kellogg. Hundreds, indeed thousands of well-to-do men and women in the late nineteenth century suffered from a similar cluster of symptoms: insomnia, digestive difficulties, headaches, and nervous exhaustion. Like many of his Gilded Age peers, C.W. suffered from a relentless anxiety, an excessive dissipation of energy, the illness of an affluent but frightened generation. The prevalence of these nervous symptoms suggested to later historians that Americans were ambivalent about postbellum "progress." If they were grateful for innovations like the railroads, the steam engine, and the incandescent lightbulb, they were also unnerved by boom-and-bust business cycles, industrialization, new waves of immigration, labor unions, and land speculation.

In 1869, a decade after the publication of Darwin's *Origin of Species*, America's mysterious nervous disease was dubbed "neurasthenia" in the medical literature. It was an affliction thought caused by the overly rapid advance of industrialization upon refined people. In 1881 George M. Beard, M.D., a leading proponent of the neurasthenic theory, proclaimed: "American nervousness is the product of American civilization." Modernity, as expressed in such inventions as the telegraph, steam power, the sciences, journalism, and feminism, had taken a terrible toll upon Americans—and particularly those of wealth, intelligence, and artistic sensibilities.

By the time C.W. was admitted to the Battle Creek Sanitarium, neurasthenia was a popular affliction. Often, after following Dr. Kellogg's vegetarian diet, coupled with an abstinence from coffee, tea, and alcohol and combined with a regimen of fresh air, exercise, and hydrotherapy, patients improved. Sometimes they recovered completely.

The hospital C. W. Post was entering was markedly different from the fashionable spas of that era like Saratoga, Newport, and White Sulphur Springs. The sanitarium was a no-nonsense institution owned by the Seventh-Day Adventist church. Dr. John Harvey Kellogg, a medical doctor trained at New York's Bellevue Hospital, supervised with a dictatorial hand and insisted that his patients follow a unique regimen of health care practices.

The Seventh-Day Adventist church had been established in the early nineteenth century by the upstate New York farmer William Miller. By mid-century, nearly a decade after Miller's erroneous prediction that the world would come to an end in 1843, the Adventist religion was revitalized by "Sister" Ellen White and her husband, James. A tenet of the Adventist faith was the union of spiritual and physical health. Devotees were to eat no more than two meals a day. They were also to refrain from stimulants like tobacco, tea, and coffee. The consumption of animal flesh was strictly forbidden; in its place Adventists were to eat natural grains and vegetables. They were also encouraged to seek the "remedial value of water treatments, pure air, and sunshine."

To promote their ideas, the Whites began a journal called the *Health Reformer*. They also enlisted a physician in their congregation, Dr. Russell Trall, to advocate vegetarianism in a medical column. In addition, Dr. Trall criticized the ill effects of tobacco smoke, salt pork, and tight corsetry in his writings.

Despite broad circulation of the *Health Reformer* and its advocacy of the water and vegetable cures of the Western Health Reform Institute, the Whites' little hospital failed to attract a steady following of paying patients. To do so would require a well-trained, publicity-minded medical doctor who could help them gain an affluent clientele.

John Harvey Kellogg, son of another congregationalist, soon became a likely candidate. His first act was to change the name of the Western Health Reform Institute to a more important-sounding one, the Battle Creek Medical and Surgical Sanitarium. By so doing, he made the new institute sound as if it epitomized the latest advances in medicine. Although the term *sanatorium* had been in use since the late 1830s, Dr. Kellogg's newly coined word *sanitarium* cleverly capitalized upon the new medical concept of sanitation and its importance to personal health.

Dr. Kellogg then launched a building campaign for a larger health facility. He demanded that the *Health Reformer* have its name changed to *Good Health*, a name the magazine still retains. When patients at the "San," as it came to be called, grumbled about its tasteless vegetarian fare, Dr. Kellogg developed new recipes by experimenting with nuts and vegetables. One result of these tinkerings was the creation of peanut butter around the same time that George Washington Carver was conducting his own experiments with it. Although Dr. Kellogg eventually held a U.S. patent for the product, he never marketed it commercially.

At the San, patients were routinely encouraged to eat granola, a granular cereal composed of wheat, oatmeal, and cornmeal, a product suspiciously similar to an earlier wheat product called Granula served to patients at Dr. James Jackson's Water Cure spa in Dansville, New York. Since the Adventists avoided tea and coffee, sanitarium patients drank Dr. Kellogg's substitute, which was called Caramel Coffee and made from burned bread crumbs, molasses, and bran.

By 1878 the feisty "little doctor" had a new four-story building on twenty acres of lawn and forest, where patients not only followed a regimen of dietary reform, exercise, water therapies, electric vibrations, and massage but were watched with professional medical scrutiny.

The San expanded steadily and by 1881 had a staff of eighty, including medical doctors, nurses, cooks, bath attendants, and masseurs who cared for upwards of four hundred patients. A key member of the staff was Dr. Kellogg's younger brother, W. K. Kellogg, a bespectacled, taciturn man who officially served as his assistant and the San bookkeeper but was unofficially the doctor's personal servant. Thanks to Dr. Kellogg and W.K., the Battle Creek Sanitarium grew rapidly and by 1885 was said to be "the largest institution of its kind in the world." Word about the San's success with invalid patients—particularly those with digestive complaints, like Marjorie's father—began to spread, reaching states as distant as California, Massachusetts, and Texas.

But C.W. was different from most of the other patients who received treatments at Dr. Kellogg's Sanitarium. To start with, he seems to have lived at the hospital only intermittently. Although he may have stayed initially at the San while Ella and Marjorie took rented rooms at the Haddock boardinghouse, all three of them lived in a furnished cottage in Battle Creek during the summer of 1891. According to local legend, Ella Post pushed C. W. Post in a wheelchair up West Van Buren Street to the San for treatments.

C.W. had other distinctions as well. In contrast with many of the wealthy citizens who came to the San for treatments, Marjorie's father had not yet been successful in business. Yet within him beat the heart of a hard-driving, ambitious man with twenty years of experience as a salesman, an inventor, and an entrepreneur. Already by thirty-six years of age C.W. had broad life experience. As a youth he had been a cowhand in Kansas and Oklahoma, opened a hardware store in Independence, Kansas, peddled farm implements in Iowa and Nebraska, and traveled as far west as Dodge City.

Moreover, C.W. was mechanically gifted and over the years had created a long list of inventions. Among his devices were several models of cultivators, a harrow, a haystacker, an electric paddle, a player piano, a safety bicycle, a new kind of suspenders, and a sulky plow. Some of those inventions—especially the sulky plow—were so successful that C.W. received revenue from their patents. By 1891 C.W. was thus a seasoned man who had tasted life in the exploding western territories of postbellum America and had become intoxicated by its seemingly endless possibilities.

Yet at the time of his visit to the Battle Creek Sanitarium, C.W. and his wife, Ella, had little to show for their union of seventeen years other than their one child, Marjorie. That, and several packing crates containing blankets and samples of C.W.'s newfangled suspenders.

The Posts had met as children in their hometown, Springfield, Illinois. At first Ella Letitia Merriweather, the shy gray-eyed daughter of merchant John Hood Merriweather of Maryland and Elizabeth Hummel of Ohio, had seemed the perfect complement to C.W.'s bombastic temperament. By the time Ella was ten her prosperous father had died. Even less is known about Ella's mother except that she, too, had passed away by the girl's fifteenth year. As an orphaned adolescent with a comfortable inheritance, young Ella went to live with her uncle in Pawnee, Illinois. Although a full year older than C.W., Ella seems to have sensed in him an ambitious, inherently protective figure.

In contrast, C.W. came from a family of vibrant Vermonters. His father, Charles Rollin Post, a tall, bright-eyed young man, had crossed the Great Divide by mule team with his brother and arrived in California during the gold rush of 1849. There Rollin quickly found an opportunity for himself not in the prospecting pans and dusty terrain of the California hills but in the provisioning of supplies to fortune hunters. By 1852 Rollin had accumulated enough capital to return to Illinois. That year he settled in Springfield and opened a grain and farm implement business.

Boosted by throngs of energetic young men and women from back East who hoped to carve new family homesteads out of the flat, fertile prairies, farming was a major activity in Illinois at mid-century. In 1853 Rollin married a young widow from Connecticut named Carolyn Cushman Lathrop. From her private poetry and letters, Carrie, as Rollin's bride was called, was a devout, sentimental woman whose tendencies were tempered by a strong dose of common sense.

On October 26, 1854, Carrie gave birth to a baby boy whom the Posts named Charles William, or C.W. In short order there were two other male children, Carroll and Aurrie. As his three sons grew to young manhood, Rollin became prosperous enough to be considered one of Springfield's most prominent citizens. Well into his dotage, he proudly talked about his youthful acquaintance with a local lawyer named Abraham Lincoln. In 1865 Rollin's stature in Springfield was heightened when he was asked to be part of the honor guard for President Lincoln's funeral.

Most of the time, however, life in Springfield proceeded at a laconic pace. C.W. and his brothers were educated in the public schools. To his parents' delight, their eldest son had a gift for words and an outstanding mechanical ability. The latter talent led C.W.'s parents to enroll him at thirteen in the Illinois Industrial College at Urbana, the future University of Illinois. But C.W. was restless. After two years at the college he begged to drop out and try his fortune out West, as his father had done before him.

Four years later, after a dizzying series of adventures that included Governor's Guard service in the Chicago fire, the fully grown, now six-foot-one-inch-tall C.W. returned to the family homestead to marry his childhood sweetheart, Ella Letitia Merriweather. The wedding took place on November 4, 1874, in Pawnee, Illinois, at the home of Ella's uncle.

At first, as was then the custom, the newlyweds lived in a local boardinghouse. After a few months C.W. left his petite, reticent bride at the Post family homestead on the corner of Sixth Street to try his luck as an agricultural salesman in the West. In 1883, after nine years of marriage, Ella became pregnant, and in December of that year, she gave birth to a stillborn boy.

It was not for another three years, on March 15, 1887, at ten in the evening, that Ella finally produced a healthy baby. C.W. and Ella named their pretty seven-and-a-half-pound baby girl Marjorie Merriweather Post.

. . .

Early pictures reveal Marjorie to be a well-formed, intelligent-looking baby who soon grew into a cherubic, blue-eyed, blond-haired child. Marjorie not only had a strong physical resemblance to C.W. but even as an infant seems to have favored him. And the feeling was returned in kind. One of the most famous baby pictures of Marjorie shows her cuddled comfortably in C.W.'s arms, while he peers tenderly at the camera from behind her fine baby hair.

Much was made of little Marjorie as the first surviving Post grandchild. Not only was she surrounded by doting parents and grandparents, but soon she became the favorite of her aunt Mollie, the wife of her uncle Carroll (also called Cal or Callie). Having recently lost her own six-month-old daughter to croup, Aunt Mollie cherished little Marjorie as her own. Thus it was that three loving women—her mother, grandmother, and aunt—hovered over Marjorie from the moment of birth.

At that time the Post family fortunes were in serious jeopardy. In fact, plans were already under way for the entire family to pull up their roots in Springfield. No one had anticipated that the family would suffer such financial reversals. The Posts had prospered in Springfield for nearly three decades. In 1881, six years before Marjorie was born, Rollin, his three sons, and several silent partners had established the Illinois Agricultural Works, Inc. The new company manufactured cultivators and grew so quickly that it was soon turning a handsome profit. Then somehow—and here the details get murky—the funds were seized by an unscrupulous banker who had helped underwrite the business. To C.W.'s horror, his well-meaning, naïve parents had quietly and without their sons' knowledge assigned a mortgage on the family homestead in Springfield, Illinois, to secure the loan.

By the time of Marjorie's 1887 birth, the Posts had been forced to liquidate their holdings in the Illinois Agricultural Works, Inc. They planned to sell their now heavily mortgaged home and move to Fort Worth, Texas. Possibly the move was postponed until after Marjorie's christening in August 1887. Within a few weeks the elder Posts had moved to a two-hundred-acre Fort Worth ranch, where they were soon joined by Aurrie, Carroll, and Mollie. According to family records, a long lawsuit against the Springfield banker, C.W.'s ongoing feelings of fury and frustration, and the subsequent strain of a Fort Worth real estate venture precipitated the decline of his health in 1890 and 1891.

This was not C.W.'s first such illness. During the earlier years of his marriage to Ella, C.W. had collapsed from nervous exhaustion during a business venture. Long before his wedding C.W.'s parents had known that their son was high-strung. Family legend suggests that it may have been for that reason that they had excused C.W. from continuing his education at the Illinois Industrial College.

At nearly four years of age Marjorie may not have understood how ill C.W. was when he first came to Battle Creek or exactly how it was that he regained his health. C.W.'s health had been precarious almost from the moment of his daughter's birth. Before Marjorie was a year old, her parents had taken her to California in hopes that a mild climate would improve C.W.'s health. Later they had journeyed to the East Coast. Only after that did the little family join their relatives in Fort Worth. For a few months C.W.'s health seemed stable, and in September 1891 Ella took Marjorie back to Springfield to visit relatives. Soon Ella got word that C.W. was again seriously ill, and she hastened with Marjorie back to Fort Worth.

In contrast to her father, Marjorie was a resoundingly healthy child. By her first birthday she weighed twenty-one pounds. At two and a half years of age, her mother noted, Marjorie had become a "healthy, hearty, and handsome girl."

Nevertheless, the psychic anguish of C.W.'s illness—and his subsequent steps toward recovery—may have led to Marjorie's preoccupation with her own health throughout her life. No matter where she traveled or whom she entertained, Marjorie remained a strict advocate of three meals a day, regular exercise, and eight hours of sleep each night. Routinely at the stroke of 11:00 P.M. Marjorie left her own dinner parties whether or not her guests had already departed.

The actual course of C.W.'s treatment at the Battle Creek Sanitarium remains a matter of conjecture. Old-timers at the San recalled C. W. Post as a gloomy, depressed patient who lay about the hospital grounds reflecting upon the short time he had left to live. Yet Horace B. Powell, W. K. Kellogg's official biographer, reports that C.W. made rapid progress under Dr. John Harvey Kellogg's care at the San, gained forty or fifty pounds between February and November 1891, and was restored to health by the end of 1891.

The Post family insists that by November of that year C.W. had become alarmingly weak and that his weight had dwindled to ninety pounds. Finally, Dr. John Harvey Kellogg told his wife that he had little hope for C.W.'s recovery. There is, in fact, an entry in Ella's hand in

Marjorie's baby book that "Papa down again and had to return to Sanitarium. Remained there until November 9, 1891 when supposed to be near the end of mortals. . . ."

By then one of Ella's cousins had written about a friend who had been cured by Christian Science. After her meeting with Dr. Kellogg, Ella asked the cousin for more information. An answer was relayed by telegraph. There was an Elizabeth Gregory, a Christian Scientist living in Battle Creek, who was reputed to have worked miracles with invalids. Perhaps she could do something for C.W.

Ella soon had her husband transported to Mrs. Gregory. Although the Christian Science church had been temporarily dissolved by its founder, Mary Baker Eddy, in 1891, Mrs. Gregory was still a member of its lay ministry. That ministry, composed of Christian Scientists skilled in the practice of spiritual healing, was called practitioners.

The Christian Science movement had begun with Mrs. Eddy's 1875 publication of *Science and Health.* Among her teachings were the beliefs that God was good and all-powerful and had created man in His own image. Anything that deviated from His essential goodness—illness, injustice, grief, and evil—had no basis in spiritual reality. Although human beings only imperfectly understood that reality, their efforts at prayer and biblical learning helped them experience it more clearly.

Illness was thus considered not so much a condition of the human body as a reflection of a doubting or ailing spirit. Its cure, Eddy and her followers maintained, did not lie in the pills, powders, and surgical treatments of conventional medical doctors, but rather in prayer and spiritual growth.

In her first meeting with C.W., Mrs. Gregory talked about the power of the divine spirit to cure the body. Before long C.W. was fascinated, so much so that he was soon insisting that he had no intention of returning to the Haddock boardinghouse that night. "Mrs. Gregory, I am staying right here under your care," he announced. In fact, he intended to stay with Mrs. Gregory overnight so as to understand Christian Science better and apply it to his own life.

Mrs. Gregory protested, pointing out that she had five children of her own to look after and no place to house C.W., but ultimately he prevailed. Sensing the man's earnestness and despair, Mrs. Gregory relented. The children were asked to double up, and C.W. took one of their bedrooms. Then he ate dinner with them—the first real food he had eaten in months. As C.W. began to pick at his food, Mrs. Gregory said, "Mr. Post, go ahead and eat your dinner. There is nothing here that will harm you except fear. Eat slowly, eat anything you want, it is what you need, you have been without food far too long."

Mrs. Gregory insisted that there was nothing physically wrong with C.W., that it was within his power to cure himself if he would only change his negative attitude. C.W. finished his meal. Before retiring, Mrs. Gregory reminded her guest that if he got hungry during the night, there was cold chicken and other snacks in the icebox. To his surprise, C.W. awakened during the night with hunger pains. He raided the refrigerator, then returned to sleep. The next morning Marjorie's father awoke feeling better than he had in months.

For three weeks he stayed at Mrs. Gregory's, where he received a copy of Mary Baker Eddy's *Science and Health*. When it seemed certain that C.W. was on the mend, Ella took Marjorie to Toledo to visit relatives. By that time C.W. was gaining a pound a day. Soon he was walking brightly down the same streets where Ella and Marjorie had pushed him in a wheelchair. Within a few months C.W. had gained back all of his weight. Battle Creek natives were amazed at C.W.'s seemingly miraculous return to health. Word of his recovery soon reached the Battle Creek Sanitarium. By then C.W. and Ella had become enthralled with the powers of "mental healing" and begun to integrate Christian Science concepts into their daily lives. They also read *Science and Health* regularly. Before long their new beliefs were put to a test.

That winter Marjorie was stricken consecutively with scarlet fever and the mumps. Both diseases, but especially the former, were serious illnesses for any nineteenth-century child. As Marjorie's symptoms became more pronounced, Ella and C.W. prayed, assiduously applying the principles of Christian Science to their daughter's recovery.

The subsequent course of Marjorie's illnesses was mild, so innocuous that Ella penned in her daughter's baby book that the child "hardly knew any disease was about her." That mind-set became an important part of Marjorie's legacy. When Marjorie was confronted with problems or illness in later years, her first instinct was to play them down. A positive attitude and a belief in the greater good, she maintained, could ameliorate many of her own ills. Christian Science, as Marjorie wrote to her friend the Greek ambassador Aleco Matsas some seventy-two years later, "has been my strength and comfort all my life."

2

"There's a Reason"

*B*y early 1892 C.W. had regained not only his health but his old zest for life. Entrepreneurial schemes, stifled by years of harrowing illness, began to sprout anew. The idea of a ready-made breakfast cereal like the ones created by the Kellogg brothers fascinated C.W. So did the concept of a hot drink without the ill effects of caffeine.

C.W.'s physical recovery had also spiritually humbled him. It had imbued him with a new sense of responsibility toward his fellowman. Suddenly he felt it was his duty to help others as he had been helped by Christian Science. Brotherly love and business ambitions were integrated into one common goal: the creation of a product that would help heal others.

Years later C.W. explained his motive for creating a breakfast food industry thus: "I thought it over . . . and came to believe it would be cowardly to quit then, with so much to do and so much responsibility and . . . made up my mind I would not quit, but would finish the work I ought to do. I supposed I was a sight, but the only way I knew to get well was to BE well, however ill I looked and I began walking around like a man who had business to attend to."

Exactly when C.W. first discussed his idea for a commercial breakfast food industry with the Kellogg brothers is not known. He may well have broached the idea while still at the Sanitarium. Or he may have returned to the Sanitarium to talk with the Kelloggs after his recovery. Whenever it was, the Kelloggs rejected C.W.'s idea. By late 1891 Dr.

John Harvey Kellogg was in no mood to deviate from his current line of duties at the San. Although he and W.K. were continually developing new food products under the auspices of the Battle Creek Sanitarium Health Food Company, those products were sold primarily to San patients and nearby residents. To do otherwise, Dr. Kellogg insisted, would have been unprofessional. In reality, some of the doctor's treatments, such as intestinal bypass surgery for obesity, were being sharply criticized by members of the American Medical Association, and Dr. Kellogg did not want to jeopardize further the status of his medical license.

Nevertheless, Battle Creek was an ideal environment for an entrepreneur like C.W. In 1891 the city was thriving. Smart two-horse cabriolets and thick-rimmed country carts clogged the streets. The high school was coeducational and boasted a fine staff of teachers. Streetcars were jammed with workers on their way to and from jobs. At dawn, wagons arrived in Battle Creek with shiny containers of fresh milk from nearby dairy farms. In the summer, farmers brought crops of fruit and vegetables to market. On clear mornings, black swirls of smoke twisted lazily over Battle Creek from factories, foundries, and mills.

For a decade the San had contributed to this bustle with a steady stream of paying patients and their families. Earlier in the nineteenth century Battle Creek, situated between Detroit and Chicago at the confluence of a creek and the Kalamazoo River, had been a pioneer settlement. In 1835 Sands McCamly dug the first canal and established a sawmill. Other pioneers, lured by Michigan's fertile farmlands, tallgrass prairies, and access to waterpower, homesteaded farms. In 1845 the Michigan Central Railroad chugged into town, bringing tools, dry goods, and settlers. As early as 1850 oil was discovered in Battle Creek; before long mills were pumping the precious fluid out of the ground. These, combined with the commercial activity generated by Battle Creek's flour and sawmills, not only contributed to the city's boom at mid-century but also helped it rebound from the precarious post–Civil War economy.

By the late 1870s merchants were conducting more than a million dollars' worth of business annually, and by 1884 Battle Creek had a population of ten thousand. Even by eastern standards Battle Creek was a thoroughly up-to-date city in 1884 with telephones and electric lights. A year later its residents had streetcars, and by 1887, running water.

Battle Creek also had an extraordinary tolerance for liberals and eccentrics. No one is sure exactly why. Perhaps it was due to the peculiar mix of settlers who had migrated from New England and western New York State. The early arrival of Quaker pioneers, like Erastus Hussey of the Underground Railroad, may also have encouraged a flow of free-thinkers. Possibly memories of cooperative pioneer life in the Indian-filled settlement of the 1820s were still too fresh for Battle Creekers to discourage diversity.

The Quakers, with their fierce admonitions against slavery, had arrived in Battle Creek in the 1830s but were largely dispersed by mid-century. In 1844 three hundred Michigan pioneers, spellbound by a freethinker named Dr. Henry R. Schetterly, participated in a communal living experiment called the Adelphia Society. The experiment failed in 1848 but was soon replaced by a community of Swedenborgians. Other nonconformists, like the universalists and the spiritualists, also settled in Battle Creek.

In the 1850s spiritualism, with its séances, table tippings, Ouija boards, and visitations, had been popularized by the Fox sisters. Those colorful, publicity-conscious women, who were allegedly disturbed by restless spirits in their Hydesville, New York, home, eventually settled in the Battle Creek community of Harmonia. Their choice was hardly coincidental, for Harmonia was already tolerant of spiritualism. Not only was its name derived from spiritualist doctrine, but a seer named Reynolds Cornell and his son managed a spiritualist academy there. By mid-century spiritualism was firmly entrenched in Battle Creek.

In 1858 the popularity of Battle Creek's spiritualist community was underscored by the theatrical appearance of the Reverend James M. Peebles. This self-appointed "spiritual pilgrim" Peebles, who alternately portrayed himself as a spiritual minister, a medical doctor, a temperance leader, and an anti-vivisectionist, shocked an audience of Battle Creekers by hypnotizing a nonbeliever. Before an incredulous audience, Peebles's subject became "possessed" with the spirit of a man killed a few hours earlier in a train accident. The next day news of that accident shocked Battle Creekers when it was reported in the newspapers. Spiritualism had such a hold on the community that in August 1881 hundreds of followers converged at Battle Creek's Goguac Lake for a state convention.

In 1857 another notable figure appeared in Battle Creek. This was Sojourner Truth, a former slave and a prominent social reformer. Shortly after her arrival the outspoken six-foot black celebrity purchased land in nearby Harmonia. Although Sojourner Truth was not a spiritualist, she had chosen Harmonia because she knew Quakers there who came from her native Ulster County in New York. In 1860 Olive Gilbert published Truth's widely circulated biography, *Narrative of Sojourner Truth*, with a Battle Creek imprint upon it. Thus was the town's reputation for freethinking impressed upon citizens far and wide.

In a community less tolerant of eccentrics and the flow of new ideas, an unusual newcomer like C.W. might have felt uncomfortable. But in the heady 1890s anything seemed possible in Battle Creek. If a doubting man could be possessed by the spirit of another who was recently killed, if an ex-slave could write a best-seller, if a patient could be cured of a wasting disease by the power of positive thinking, what was to stop any man from becoming a millionaire?

By early 1892 C.W. was already experimenting. While the Posts were still living at the Haddock boardinghouse, C.W. often walked downtown to visit the Osgood jewelry store. As it happened, a young man named Harry Burt, who lived next door to the Haddocks, worked at that jewelry store, where he eventually became a partner.

For weeks C.W. had been intrigued with an old popcorn roaster in the jewelry store basement, and before long he was tinkering with it for his cereal experiments. The course of those first trials was not recorded, but they must have been encouraging. C.W. soon realized he needed a kitchen of his own, as well as a home for Ella and Marjorie.

By March 1892 C.W. had liquidated his shares in his Fort Worth real estate venture. Most of them had been financed with funds from Ella's inheritance. On the twenty-third of that month C.W. and Ella jointly purchased the ten-acre Charlotte Beardslee farm on the eastern outskirts of Battle Creek. On one side stood a small white barn surrounded by cornfields and hills covered with woods. On the Marshall Street side was a brick farmhouse that was to be the Post homestead. But the family would use only part of that house, one section of which was set aside for a health institute. Because it was dedicated to curing invalids through Christian Science, the use of positive thinking, and healthy foods, C.W. named the institute La Vita Inn. Its establishment typified C.W.'s obsessive nature: Once possessed with a dream, he had to bring it to fruition in an immediately concrete and theatrical form.

Ella's reaction to the new institute has not been preserved. Certainly it must have been an imposition on her privacy. But things had not gone well for her and C.W. for some time. Their economic situation was fragile, and while C.W. had only recently recovered his vigor, he had withdrawn from his wife. In 1892 Ella was still a young woman and may well have clung to the hope that if C.W. could achieve his dreams, his coolness toward her would change. For many years they had been drifting apart.

Marjorie was blissfully unaware of her parents' disaffection. For her the move to the farm was simply a great adventure. At last she would have a bedroom of her own. No longer did she have to sleep, as was then the custom, on a thin rollaway trundle in her parents' room. Moreover, the farm had chickens, cows, and eventually dogs and cats. There were apple, pear, and cherry orchards, grape arbors, and several varieties of berries. To help with the chores, the elder Posts also acquired a hired hand.

Inevitably the move to the farm required some adjustments. Marjorie's mother, Ella, was a skilled and inventive cook, and one of her best desserts was tutti-frutti, a combination of fresh fruits and brandy. Being a thrifty sort, Ella dumped the remainder of that dessert into the chicken feed in the barnyard one morning. An hour or two later the hired man appeared at her door. "Oh, Mrs. Post, come out and see, something awful is the matter with the poor chickens, they are cackling, crowing and they are dropping onto the ground like they are dead," he lamented. Immediately an alarmed Ella and Marjorie dashed to the barnyard to watch the chickens' strange behavior. Only then did Ella realize that the tutti-frutti she had thrown in the feed must have made the fowl drunk. "Sure enough, you never saw such confusion, we didn't know what they were doing," Marjorie recalled with amusement seventy years later. "After a certain amount length of time [sic] they got over it, they sort of slept it off. . . ."

Soon after C.W. settled on the farm, he established La Vita Inn as a business corporation from which he issued stocks. Since most of the investment came from Ella's money, 98 percent of the shares were put in her name. Admittedly it was a gamble. But C.W. still had money from the sale of his Fort Worth property. Additional revenue came in from his Texas woolen mill and from his old patents on his farm machinery inventions.

C.W. was obsessively thrifty. Like Ella, he never liked to see things go to waste, and in his case, that included his inventive ideas. He believed, for example, that there was money to be made from his improvement on suspenders. In the late nineteenth century men wore suspenders that fastened in the front, on the sides, and crossed in the back. To hide that unsightliness, men were forced to wear vests, even in the summer months. A year or so before his last illness C.W. had devised a solution:

suspenders that attached only at the side and crossed in the back. Now men could wear suit jackets without vests and their suspenders would remain hidden.

Capitalizing on the era's zest for scientific progress, C.W. accordingly dubbed his invention "Scientific Suspenders." Soon after the Posts moved to the Beardslee farm, C.W. established a special workroom in the farmhouse. Every morning a small team of hired girls arrived to sew suspenders in a variety of colors: For weddings they were made out of white satin and embroidered with orange blossoms; for formal occasions they were in black with cherry designs. Before long C.W.'s suspenders were selling rapidly in Battle Creek.

With that encouragement C.W. began to advertise in national magazines. Prices began at thirty-five cents apiece. To give his "Scientific Suspenders" additional credence, Marjorie's father modeled them in photographs coordinated with the ads. "Do you see them?" asked the caption line for the suspenders. Above it appeared a photo of a dapper C.W., carefully dressed in a jacket, shirt, and cummerbund, with no sign of suspenders. Requests started to arrive by mail order. Eventually the suspenders netted C.W. an income of ten dollars a day.

C.W.'s dreams were slowly being realized. In that same period invalids living in or near Battle Creek who had heard about C.W.'s case of instantaneous healing began to arrive at La Vita Inn. Many were refugees from the Battle Creek Sanitarium who, like C.W., had languished for months and hoped he could help them recover through other means. In contrast with Dr. Kellogg's rigorous program for a return to health, C.W. had a more leisurely approach. During the day patients were free to amuse themselves as they wished: to exercise, read, play games, or hear music in the farmhouse parlor on C.W.'s Pianola. Nor were there restrictions on meat or other kinds of food. Only alcohol, tea, and coffee were prohibited.

A key factor in the La Vita treatment was C.W.'s lectures on the "mind cure." That cure, as the entrepreneur expostulated to his audience, was a combination of the principles of Christian Science and his own theories on the powers of positive thinking. The early results were heartening. About 95 percent of the patients, Ella privately noted, were cured of their complaints.

In spite of a constant flurry of guests, the inn never treated more than ten or twelve people at a time. C.W. gradually lost enthusiasm for expanding La Vita Inn. He believed there was more to the mind-body connection to be learned, and he began to read voraciously and eclectically in medical books, on neurology, nutrition, and dietetics, and in the psychological sciences on hypnotism.

C.W. simultaneously pursued his newest business idea. Knowing that coffee kept many people up at night and interfered with their digestion, he was determined to develop a hot drink substitute that could be marketed commercially. It would seem that his imagination had been kindled by Dr. Kellogg's "Caramel Coffee." Years later, when asked about his new products, C.W. emphatically denied having stolen the idea. He had been considering it, he insisted, long before his arrival in Battle Creek. The idea had come from his youthful travels out West, from his observation of frontier wives who, lacking easy access to coffee beans, roasted wheat berries with chicory as a substitute beverage.

What is certain is that in early 1892 C.W. began experimenting with wheat and grains in the kitchen at La Vita Inn. The roasting process for wheat was tricky and so time-consuming that it soon became obvious that he could not continue his experiments indefinitely in the farmhouse kitchen. The operation was moved to the white barn, and C.W. hired a Swiss chemist to continue the experiments. For eighteen months the chemist labored unsuccessfully. C.W. grew increasingly frustrated.

When he was not worrying about his coffee substitute, C.W. spent his waking hours delving into the intricacies of the "mind cure." By 1894 he had penned a book of his own theories entitled *I Am Well.* The treatise, subtitled *The Modern Practice: Natural Suggestion, or, Scientia Vitae,* implored those who were ill to think of themselves not as body but rather as spirit. Through an understanding of the "Higher Mind," or godly spirit, the reader could be cured.

To assure readers of his sincerity, C.W. revealed the agony of his own battle with physical illness. "I come to your side, with the deep compassion of a mother for her helpless child. I have been through the seven times heated furnace (seven years) of physical disease and mental distress . . . " he wrote. ". . . Kill off the old man (self) and let the new Being come up. Know yourself as Spirit, Mind, and not body. . . . When you read the written thoughts . . . join me fully, *heart and soul.* You thereby get at once into the state of *Health and Harmony."*

The work was an amalgam of C.W.'s broad reading. *I Am Well* borrowed not only from Christian Science but also from the Scriptures, geological theory, and the works of Henry Ward Beecher, Ralph Waldo Emerson, and other nineteenth-century thinkers. Although C.W. was still devoted to Christian Science, his readings in medical theory, Eastern religions, and current philosophy led him in new directions. One of the most intriguing was his study of hypnotism. If pain or discomfort was merely a flaw of the spirit, could not hypnotism—the ultimate in mind control—serve to relieve human ills?

To a sensitive child like Marjorie, C.W. was a captivating father. When she was five or six, Marjorie used to run into her parents' bedroom at sunrise and climb on C.W.'s knees to hear Indian stories spun out of his western experiences. C.W. often took Marjorie fishing with him; at other times they tramped through the woods together. They shared adventures, secrets, and jokes. He even made her do calisthenics at an early age.

In the summer C.W. urged Ella and Marjorie to go out on the lawn with him and make shadows in the moonlight. For Marjorie these were simply childhood excursions. But strange currents ran through C.W.'s mind. Shadow play fascinated him and may well have been part of his studies on metaphysics and mental perceptions of "reality." For all of his paternal protectiveness, C.W. was far more than a conventional father figure; he was at once Marjorie's friend, confidant, and companion. In her eyes, he epitomized masculinity itself—adventurous, dashing, and unpredictable. Mysterious things could happen in his presence—and often did.

In 1892 or 1893 C.W.'s interest in hypnotism became so compelling that he went to Paris to study with the French neurologist Jean-Martin Charcot. His new knowledge had a price. Gradually, Marjorie recalled, C.W. lost his ability to heal. It was, she said years later, because of his eclectic studies and the resultant "diversion of thought" from Christian Science that he lost his ability to heal others.

After his trip abroad C.W. began to hypnotize Marjorie. He did so with the help of a special machine that had a shiny device on it. From everything he read and studied, C.W. knew that hypnosis was a dangerous psychological tool that was to be used gingerly. Once, at the dentist's office, though she had been hypnotized three times, Marjorie persisted in coming out of her trance. When she begged her father to hypnotize her a fourth time, C.W. refused. "Now, goddamn it, you've just got to stand it!" he insisted. "I wouldn't put you under again for anything in the world. Now, you just sit there and stand it."

C.W. also used his family as subjects for his experiments with the powers of mental suggestion. On snowy mornings and nights he shed his socks and boots and urged Marjorie and Ella to do the same. The three of them then walked into the deep Michigan snow barefoot. These excursions rarely lasted more than five minutes. Afterward Marjorie insisted that her father's experiments enabled her to play for hours with friends in the snow without getting cold feet.

Marjorie, like most middle-class nineteenth-century youngsters, was carefully reared. Ella, who was a strict disciplinarian, found her daughter's high spirits a particular challenge. An abiding if uneasy love flowed between mother and daughter, and though Ella and Marjorie did not openly clash, their instincts and reactions were often at odds.

At forty Ella's hair had already turned white. Her posture was excellent, and that, in combination with her delicate health and proper midwestern clothes, gave her a somewhat stern appearance. Temperamentally, too, Marjorie's mother seemed somber and tending toward silence. Constantly brooding about her husband's health and their unhappy marriage, she rarely vented her feelings openly. Nor did Ella engage in even occasional frivolity; while C.W. and Marjorie often played parlor games like checkers, backgammon, and cards, Ella never joined in. Such habits made her seem at times like a strict, even unapproachable parent, especially in comparison with the effusive C.W.

Occasionally Marjorie caught glimpses of her mother's inner vitality, the kind that must have first attracted C.W. In her teens Ella had been an outstanding dancer. Sometimes at night, dressed in her robes, Ella whirled young Marjorie around the parlor. She also had a lovely singing voice and might, on a particularly beautiful morning, burst into song. Despite her reticent demeanor, Ella was an artful mimic who, to Marjorie's and C.W.'s amusement, could imitate anybody—a meddlesome neighbor, a gruff shopkeeper—with deadly accuracy.

Still, Ella was so heavily imbued with a sense of decorum, so stiffened by it that she did not always see the lighter side of life. One memorable night when she came into Marjorie's room and sat on her bed, a miller moth flew out of Ella's voluminous pantaloons. Horrified, Marjorie's mother began to jump wildly around the room so as to rid herself of the insect. Years later Marjorie recalled the incident gleefully, but she also remembered that Ella had not seen the humor in it. Instead, Marjorie recalled, her mother was "perfectly furious" at the indignity of the situation.

Like most energetic children, Marjorie occasionally got into mischief. Once Ella walked into a room to find Marjorie cutting the pigtails off her black nurse's head. Apparently the child had convinced her good-natured caretaker that it would be a good idea to trim her hair.

Another time when Marjorie was to be punished, Ella went to fetch the hickory stick, the favored instrument of punishment for nineteenth-century children. To her surprise, it had been snapped in two. When confronted, Marjorie admitted she had deliberately broken the stick. Ella was neither fazed nor amused. Without skipping a beat, she pulled off her brown leather slipper and gave Marjorie a spanking.

C.W. used a different approach. He never spanked Marjorie. Nor did he ostensibly forbid her anything. Should Marjorie ask for an untoward privilege, C.W.'s tactic was to throw the situation back in her hands. "Marjorie, I would prefer if you would not," he would say. Or, "Well, Marjorie, I wonder about that. What would you do if such-and-so happened as a result of my saying yes?"

In the spring of 1893, around the time of Marjorie's sixth birthday, she entered the first grade at Battle Creek's Franklin School. Even at that tender age Marjorie was a bright, eager youngster with effervescent energy that sometimes exploded into fanciful flights very much like those of her father. Ella fretted about those tendencies in her daughter. Perhaps that was why she made such a concerted effort to bring the girl up with a strict sense of right and wrong.

By November 1893 Ella was beginning to believe that she had succeeded. Marjorie, she wrote in her daughter's baby book, has become a "full-fledged school girl" who "reads some, writes and figures well . . . a loving and loveable little girl, heady perhaps from pre-natal motives, but with great good sense & a quick keen desire to do the right and sensible things. . . ."

The following March grandmother Carrie Post confirmed Ella's observation about Marjorie's dynamic disposition. After a visit from her granddaughter, Carrie wrote from Fort Worth that Marjorie was a "bright, winsome . . . little creature, restless . . . never quiet for any length of time." But there was no need for concern. "That wonderful exuberance of spirit will settle down after awhile when she comes into the reality of life and sees the sterner side."

Meanwhile, Carrie's restless eldest son, C.W., was on the brink of finding a solution for his coffee-substitute problem. By mid-1894 C.W. had fired the Swiss chemist and was conducting the experiments himself. Already he suspected that he could imitate the taste of coffee with a combination of wheat, bran, and molasses. But the exact combination of those ingredients still eluded him.

Moreover, he had limited amounts of money to spend on the experiments. He also had a local audience of skeptics. C.W. once gave his fifteen-year-old assistant, Albert Henry, a five-dollar check and instructed him to go to the Reynolds and Ashley grocer for five gallons of molasses. When Henry placed his order, Reynolds regarded the check suspiciously. Then he rejected it. "Maybe," he drawled laconically, "Mr. Post had five dollars in the bank and maybe not."

Henry then drove C.W.'s one-horse wagon down to the Titus and Hicks mill to see if he could buy molasses and bran there. When Hicks asked Henry what C.W. wanted with all that bran, the youth told him about the project. "Another one for the padded cell," Hicks said with a snicker.

Later, when Henry told C.W. about Hicks's reaction, the inventor grinned broadly. Amusement, not anger, was the way to react to critics who did not have the facts. As Marjorie grew to adulthood and faced trials of her own, C.W. tried to impart this notion of magnanimity to her.

It was an attitude Marjorie clung to all her life. Because of her enormous wealth, people often asked her for money and occasionally took advantage of her. When her eldest daughter, Adelaide, brought such matters to Marjorie's attention, the heiress often swept the issue aside. "She would look at me and say, 'Adelaide, I don't want to know,' " recalled her daughter. If someone abused Marjorie's generosity, the heiress had no intention of attempting to seek retribution.

By late 1894 C.W. had finally perfected a formula for a tasty coffee substitute. The brew was composed of 22.5 percent wheat berries, 67 percent glutenous bran, and 10 percent New Orleans molasses. The last two ingredients were "mixed and browned in open pans" over a fire. The wheat, in contrast, was roasted separately, and its steamy vapors were expelled into a special container. The distillation was then retained and poured back into the berries. Then it was mixed with the bran and molasses and ground together. Ultimately it became "an article of food-drink of nourishing value." After some thought, C.W. named the drink Postum.

The inventor then tested his product upon Ella and Marjorie. He also gave it to the patients at La Vita Inn. Almost unanimously Postum was declared a success. In December 1894, convinced that he had finally created a commercial coffee substitute, C.W. invested $46.85 in kitchen equipment. Among his purchases were a secondhand two-burner stove, a secondhand peanut roaster, a coffee grinder, and several mixers. With an additional $21.91, C.W. purchased two bushels of wheat, two hundred pounds of bran, ten jugs of molasses, fifty packing cases, and two thousand cartons.

On January 1, 1895, C.W. and a helper named Charles "Shorty" Bristol fired up the two-burner stove and the peanut roaster in the white barn. Then they began mass production of the new coffee substitute. Thus was the Postum Cereal Company born.

To seven-year-old Marjorie, there was probably nothing extraordinary about C.W.'s new project. After all, her father had been experimenting with coffee substitutes for years. Moreover, she was quite accustomed to having strangers at the farm. Some were patients at La Vita Inn; others arrived in teams to work in the "Scientific Suspenders" room. The sight of Shorty Bristol roasting wheat over a heated ten-foot trough in the barn must have seemed merely another aspect of C.W.'s experiments. More than likely Marjorie had no inkling that the steaming vats of wheat, bran, and molasses would change the course of her life.

In early 1895, C.W. may not have even suspected it himself. Michigan winters are long, cold, and bleak, the kind that keep farmers and their wives indoors for weeks. What better time, C.W. believed, to market a hot breakfast drink? Soon C.W. was selling his product door to door. The response was less than enthusiastic. Occasionally, believing that the presence of a winsome child might soften hearts, he even let Marjorie try.

But C.W. was a man of large ambition. After several discouraging attempts in Battle Creek, he decided to try another approach. Local citizens, after all, already knew about Dr. Kellogg's Caramel Coffee. Why not try his luck in another town?

One day C.W. loaded his one-horse wagon with cartons of Postum and took off for nearby Grand Rapids. The biggest grocery store in town was owned by E. J. Herrick. With the sunny ease of an experienced salesman, C.W. approached the grocer. But Herrick was intractable; he was not about to store useless goods on his shelves. And coffee substitutes, he told C.W. plain and simple, were useless.

Sourly he beckoned C.W. to his back shelves. There, big bales of Kellogg's Caramel Coffee had been stored for eight years. "Some years I sell one package; and other years none," Herrick noted dryly. "You see, there is absolutely no demand and you better go home and get into something else there is some reason for."

But C.W. was not to be deterred. He persisted, praising the virtues of Postum; finally he begged. In the end he struck a bargain with the skeptical grocer. If Herrick would agree to take a few packages of Postum, C.W. would create a demand for them. Herrick would sell Postum only on consignment. If there were no sales, Herrick would not be out any money. Reluctantly, perhaps as much to get rid of C.W. as anything else, Herrick finally consented. C.W. then used the same approach with ten other Grand Rapids grocers.

Heartened by his success, C.W. headed for the *Grand Rapids Evening Press*. In a meeting with the editor, Willis H. Turner, C.W. talked about Postum. To Turner's astonishment, he set a small coffee urn on his desk, lit an oil lamp beneath it, and brewed the editor a cup of Postum. Turner took a few sips and was so favorably impressed that he called his staff over to taste it for themselves. By the time C.W. left Turner's office, he had persuaded the *Grand Rapids Evening Press* to provide free advertising for Postum.

C.W. was encouraged, but he knew he needed to create a sensation. The only way to do it was to show the public the benefits of Postum in an immediate way. Consequently, he hired a demonstrator to brew samples of Postum at Herrick's grocery store. In a matter of hours the store was jammed with customers. People began clamoring for Postum. Within a week Herrick was frantically begging C.W. to send more. The entrepreneur graciously complied.

C.W. knew he had hit upon a formula for success. Slyly he now decided to memorialize Herrick's initial snub. He would use the grocer's words as a slogan for Postum. "There's a reason" soon appeared in C.W.'s ad campaigns and became a catchphrase for the Postum Cereal Company.

Marjorie probably heard about C.W.'s triumph indirectly, either from her father himself or from conversations with her parents at the dinner table. At seven years of age she could not possibly have understood its financial implications. Henceforth Marjorie's destiny would be inextricably linked to C.W.'s eventual worldwide distribution of Postum.

3

A Battle Creek
Girlhood

*M*arjorie's life changed only gradually. For several years after C.W.'s initial success with Postum, Marjorie continued to live simply, her childhood still woven around the homespun patterns of school, family, and friends. These early experiences in Battle Creek ultimately gave Marjorie a common touch and an easy familiarity with people.

Decades later, while entertaining at her fanciful Palm Beach palace, Mar-A-Lago, or at her antiques-filled estate in Washington, D.C., a bejeweled Marjorie would astonish guests with those childhood memories: walking to school through snow, sewing clothes for her dolls, or catching lightning bugs in jars on summer nights. These were remnants from a middle-class childhood, not those of a girl from a life of privilege.

At Topridge, Marjorie's 207-acre Adirondacks camp, visitors often saw those same folksy qualities. She befriended the people who lived around Upper St. Regis Lake and invited them in for her twice-weekly movies. With her guests she thought nothing of hiking on muddy trails or, in her younger years, carrying a canoe on her back to the next lake for a picnic. In spite of her subsequent fabulous fortune, Marjorie Merriweather Post had deep roots in Middle America. She was midwestern—and egalitarian—to the core.

Marjorie had been trained to kindness from infancy. Part of it came from her parents' conversion to Christian Science. But gentleness was also in the genes. Charity, patience, and affection had warmed the original Post home in Springfield. Now in the late 1890s it wafted across the prairies and plains from Fort Worth to Battle Creek via the U.S. mail. The familial attitude was epitomized in a poem by her grandmother entitled "Affection." ". . . give me not 'jewels' / I not the boon, Their brilliance and luster / will fade all too soon. / Give me, O, give me / What dieth, ah, never! / Love, pure, fervent, free / and glowing forever!"

While she was geographically separated from the extended Post family, letters flew back and forth between Marjorie, her grandparents, uncles, and aunts. Within them were vivid descriptions of daily events, thank-you notes, drawings of gingersnaps, and even a pocketbook she had sewn as a token of affection for Aunt Mollie, or Auntie, as she was called. In the summer months there were visits from the elder Posts to Battle Creek; in other seasons Marjorie and her parents traveled to them in Fort Worth. During these visits there were lessons not only in needlework and embroidery from Grandma Carrie and Aunt Mollie but in acts of charity to the ill and the needy.

The virtues of hospitality and sociability were stressed on the farm as well. Because Marjorie was an only child living at a distance from downtown Battle Creek, her exposure to other youngsters was limited. To widen her social contacts, Ella and C.W. signed Marjorie up for dancing lessons.

One friend, Norma Eldred, who lived closer to downtown than the Posts did, first met Marjorie at Professor Frank Irwin's classes. Attendance at the dance master's school was a Battle Creek rite of passage. On Saturday afternoons reluctant groups of boys and girls dressed in their best would trudge up the stairs over Dudley's shoe salon to Centennial Hall. There Professor Irwin instructed girls and boys in the mysteries of the waltz, the two-step, and the quadrille as their parents watched. At first Marjorie was shy and balked at dancing with the boys. The usually reticent Ella was so distressed that she complained to Norma's mother. "What shall we do with 'daught'?" she lamented.

Eventually, however, Professor Irwin's early lessons in social graces made a permanent impression upon the young girl. By the time Marjorie reached late adolescence and bloomed into a beauty, she had become an expert ballroom dancer. Ella had no reason to worry about her daughter's social skills. In palaces, on yachts, and in her private railroad cars Marjorie later entertained ambassadors, diplomats, and royalty. She was internationally recognized as one of Washington's legendary hostesses. In Palm Beach she was universally acknowledged as its "queen." Had Ella lived to see her daughter's social prominence, she would have been gratified, but in the last decade of the nineteenth century there was no way to foretell Marjorie's future. To help Marjorie along, Ella and C.W. encouraged her to bring home friends. Girls like Norma, who lived too far away to visit after school, came on Saturdays and often stayed for the weekend.

For Norma and other youngsters, the farm was an intriguing place. One of its curiosities was the expansion of the Postum Cereal Company. In the early years of the company Marjorie and Norma used to sneak into the factory storage bins to bounce upon the raw wheat. Above it in the hayloft were other novelties, such as the boiling of odoriferous pots of glue that, when placed upon container edges and squeezed together with wood blocks, sealed the Postum packages. When Marjorie was a child, one of her favorite pastimes was to help C.W.'s one female assistant who worked in the hayloft with that "smelly old glue." "This," Marjorie recalled, "was playing for me." So distinctive was the glue and so earnest Marjorie's efforts to help that sixty years later she used to tell her friends, "I can still taste the labels I put on the packages of Postum."

In the late nineteenth century moleskin coats were considered the ultimate in luxury, and Marjorie had begged for such a coat for her dolls. C.W. thought Marjorie's request was extravagant. His daughter, he believed, should understand the practicalities of life. If Marjorie wanted a tiny moleskin coat, he thought she should learn to make it herself. So C.W. showed Marjorie how to set traps for the moles and to skin and tan them. Later, when the pelts were cured, she sewed them into garments.

School occupied most of Marjorie's waking hours. She was a bright student who quickly learned to read, write, and cipher in the first grade. As she progressed to higher levels, her teacher insisted that she keep a composition book. Within it, written in a clear, deliberate hand, accumulated Marjorie's essays on Pocahontas, the Eskimos, Benjamin Franklin, and George Washington as well as a meticulously drawn map of the state of Michigan.

Despite her careful compositions, Marjorie was not always a model citizen. Like Ella, Marjorie had a keen, satirical eye and a gift for mimicry. In the second or third grade Marjorie wrote to "Auntie" in Fort Worth about a teacher she disliked. "Teacher is cross as a bear. I must stop because it's time to go to bed. Please don't look at this letter because it was written in five minutes and I didn't have any lines. Your loving Marjorie Post." Beneath it Marjorie had penciled in a drawing of a Miss Wagner with a caption reading "Great heavens, truth. my fellow give me that." The teacher's feet, Marjorie noted, were very large and "took up the whole school room."

As she matured, Marjorie became an even more astute observer of human nature. Her conclusions were not always favorable, but she rarely aired her negative opinions about others even to her closest friends. "She was really a delight, and I think it was because she never took time to criticize people," said Henry Dudley, her last attorney. "If she couldn't say something nice about them, I found she just didn't talk. But she was cagey. At all times you felt that you were playing the game with her because you knew what she had in mind."

In childhood Marjorie's high spirits sometimes made her forget her manners. When that happened, Ella and C.W. reprimanded her in a stern, straightforward manner. In the fourth grade Marjorie once behaved badly to a teacher named Miss Mott. After a public scolding the teacher gave Marjorie a note to take home to her parents. Marjorie appeared in the classroom the next morning with a penitent attitude. After the prayers she apologized to the teacher and her class. This was a new, respectful Marjorie. It was a lesson in protocol she never forgot.

As a child Marjorie learned the value of true friendship through a dramatic event. One of her closest chums was Myra Kane. The two girls often wandered beyond the farm and crossed the tracks of the Michigan Central and the Grand Trunk railroads. One day as the two friends crossed the rails, the heel of Marjorie's high-laced shoe got stuck. A loud whistle announced the imminent approach of a train. In a panic Marjorie called to Myra for help. The girl came running and gave Marjorie a shove that sent her flying away from the track, moments before the train sped by.

Marjorie never forgot the girl who had saved her life. During her years in Battle Creek she remained Myra's closest friend. Years after the heiress moved out of town, she sent Myra gifts. Among them were jewelry, exotic presents from abroad, and even shares of stock in General Foods. When Marjorie returned to Battle Creek she invited Myra for dinner. In later years, when her friend was ill and widowed, Marjorie paid Myra's expenses in a nursing home.

The bane of existence of any young girl growing up in turn-of-the-century Middle America was to be teased by the boys. To get to school, Marjorie had to walk through a lumberyard owned by the Nichols and Shepherd Company. Since teenage boys were known to loiter in such places, Marjorie usually walked to school with Myra. Despite that precaution, boy bullies occasionally appeared in the yard, teasing the girls and blocking their way. Exasperated with the difficulties plaguing his daughter's arrival at and departure from school, C.W. decided to teach Marjorie to box. A few days later, as Marjorie and Myra crossed the lumberyard, a jeering boy appeared. The youth—one of those "flip devils," as the heiress later referred to him—walked ominously in front of the girls and heckled them. Marjorie soon lost her patience. Without a word, she let loose an uppercut that knocked the bully to the ground. The stunned youth peered at Marjorie with new respect. Before long word got around town. Fifty years later Marjorie still relished telling that story to her friends. "I could walk anywhere after that and wasn't bothered the least bit," she said, chortling.

The winter months presented a new set of challenges. In January 1898, when Marjorie was not yet eleven, C.W. wrote an indignant letter to the school principal. The subject was snowball fights.

> My little girl was struck in the ear yesterday and her hearing suspended for quite a little time. Another stroke on the leg with a piece of ice was given by a boy of almost a man's stature. . . . I would be one of the last persons to take away from boys the delightful privilege of snowball battles, such as I can remember participating in, years ago, but I feel that the privilege should be awarded among the boys who . . . are willing to take as many blows as they give, but the rough horse play terrorizes some of the little ones, particularly the little girls.

At the time of C.W.'s 1898 letter, he had bold new dreams for young Marjorie. Privately he had already begun to educate her in a way of life that transcended public school instruction. His daughter, C.W. decided, would be trained for a new world of men and machines. He wanted her to be as comfortable in that world as other women were in the schoolroom, the boudoir, and the nursery. She would be a new type of woman—feminine, but familiar with the world of smokestack industrialism, in an era in which ingenuity was measured by output and profits.

By Marjorie's ninth birthday she was already occasionally staying out of school to accompany her father on business trips. But C.W. was strict about the privilege. Her grades had to be excellent or she could not leave school. His standards were unequivocal. As a result, Marjorie recalled that she "worked like a little dog to have the marks good."

The trips were a high point of Marjorie's childhood, a chance to leave the predictability of the farm and school for the excitement of the road. It was a habit that stuck. As an adult Marjorie became an inveterate, almost compulsive, traveler, seldom staying at any of her homes for more than two or three months at a time. Even during her last illnesses Marjorie traveled to Florida, the Adirondacks, California, Arkansas, Europe, and the Mediterranean.

In 1898 the fastest mode of travel was the train. At Battle Creek, father and daughter boarded the Michigan Central and the Grand Trunk railroads and sped along their tracks, east to Detroit, west to Chicago, and to dozens of places in between. Along the way they stopped at many factories. "I think I saw the manufacturing of every kind of product imaginable in those days and every kind of machinery and equipment was explained to me by Dad," Marjorie wrote to her father's biographer, Nettie Leitch Major, some years later. "Some were very interesting, others dull and boring, some establishments were very decent places of manufacturing, but others had far from pleasant working conditions for the laboring man. This always distressed my father who believed so strongly in excellent working conditions. But I loved every minute of the trips with Dad and I know now that he had a purpose for everything he did—and I am sure I did learn a great deal."

Life on the road, even for a worldly man like C.W. and his well-bred daughter, presented certain challenges. Although he could order meals, fasten Marjorie's buttons, and make sure that she was properly dressed, C.W. could not fix her hair. One morning, when Marjorie awoke, her long braids had come undone. "Dad, can you help me?" the eight-year-old child asked. "Oh, heavens no! I don't know how to braid," said C.W. In a flash of inspiration, Marjorie's father walked through the train until he reached a Pullman, where he asked a woman to assist his daughter.

Another time C.W. and Marjorie were in Chicago on the eve of an important prizefight. In that era women and girls were not allowed to attend boxing matches. Yet C.W. felt uncomfortable about leaving Marjorie in the hotel room. Finally he dressed Marjorie in a suit of boy's clothes, tucked her hair into a cap, and took her along.

In later newspaper and magazine stories about Marjorie's life, some journalists interpreted the incident to mean that C.W. wished Marjorie were a boy. The heiress thought that interpretation was absurd. She once said she felt that C.W. honestly did not want to take her along. Yet he was so eager to go to the prizefight himself that he thought he had

no alternative. Whatever the truth was, one fact seems clear: The boxing match typified a spirited, convention-be-damned collusion that
C.W. and Marjorie enjoyed in her childhood years.

Even if C.W. did not perceive Marjorie as his surrogate son, she was his
indisputable heir. He expected Marjorie as such to understand his business. Often, when she returned home from school, Marjorie would find
a scrawled note from C.W. with the words "Come to the office."

On those occasions Marjorie would open the office door to find her father and his staff in a meeting. C.W. expected his daughter, beckoned
in, to sit down and listen carefully. Afterward the industrialist grilled
Marjorie on what was discussed and how it had been settled. The point
was to ensure Marjorie's understanding of the operations of the Postum
Cereal Company.

Why was it so important to him? Marjorie was, after all, his only
child. Women did not yet have the vote, but suffrage was clearly in the
wind. And as the Battle Creek bullies had graphically illustrated,
females were still regarded as the softer sex. When they grew to adulthood, they were likely to be preyed upon in a different way, by lascivi-
ous men, fortune-hunters, and opportunists.

C.W. would not tolerate naïveté in his daughter. Like Mark Twain,
his favorite author, he believed that "training is everything." He intended to teach Marjorie to "box" mentally, like a man, with wits and a
cool head. He would train her to understand every aspect of the business so she would never be manipulated by employees. If Marjorie
could not run a business herself—such a thing was still highly unconventional for any women except madams and frontier widows—he
would give her the next best thing: a clear comprehension of the inner
workings of the Postum Cereal Company. Later, as Postum's major
stockholder, Marjorie remained a voice of reason after C.W.'s death.

By 1898 C.W. had good reason to feel protective of the Postum Cereal Company. Since his initial success in Grand Rapids in 1895, the
company had grown dramatically. Customers in Grand Rapids, C.W.
observed some years later, "were paying us a profit of $500 a month
notwithstanding the pessimistic prophecy of good Brother Herrick and
the other Grocers." In May 1896 the Postum Cereal Company showed
a profit on its books of $16,452. Five months later C.W.'s assets were
$37,000; by September 30, 1897, they had grown to $68,544.13. In
October of that year the Postum Cereal Company held the first meeting

of its board of directors and issued its first dividend of 4 percent. C.W. was well on his way to acquiring a small fortune.

The company's meteoric rise had been carefully calculated. C.W.'s drive—and his belief in the importance of advertising—were largely responsible. Soon after his breakthrough in Grand Rapids, C.W. brought Postum to other Michigan towns. He repeated the same techniques—a consignment agreement with grocers, advertisements in the local papers, and free demonstrations of the coffee substitute in grocery stores—with similar success.

One of those towns was Detroit. As C.W. pitched Postum to the public, he made the acquaintance of an inventor named Henry Ford. Marjorie's father was not impressed. Later a skeptical C.W. told Ella that Ford claimed he had invented a horseless carriage. A few months later he saw it running for himself. On his third trip to Detroit he met Ford again. This time the inventor invited him to invest in the horseless buggy business. C.W. laughed him off. "Why, I wouldn't touch it with a ten-foot pole. I run my own show." Years later Marjorie sighed at her father's cynicism. "If he had put fifty cents in, it might have been very, very useful."

Like Ford, C.W. possessed voracious ambitions, ones that even the statewide sales of Postum could not satiate. There had to be more public announcements, more inducements, and more demonstrators—in short, more ways to give housewives a "reason" to buy Postum. Without it, Postum's current popularity might fade away, just as had happened with C.W.'s earlier enterprises.

Ultimately Marjorie's father decided to launch a national advertising campaign in magazines and newspapers. The idea was revolutionary. In 1895 advertising was still in its infancy. What existed was primarily announcements ordering people to buy gadgets, medicines, and household goods. Only a few food products were promoted. In the late nineteenth century the average housewife looked to her grocer—not to ads in newspapers and magazines—for her provisions.

C.W. had a new vision: He sensed that a provocatively worded ad about Postum placed in a well-known periodical might pique housewives' interest. If the ad was repeated enough times, matrons might buy C.W.'s coffee substitute out of curiosity. And after trying one twenty-five-cent package, he was sure they would buy Postum again.

With such a strategy, C.W. was able to persuade Chicago's C. H. Fuller Advertising Agency to take on the Postum account. In a show of good faith, the agency agreed to extend ten thousand dollars' worth of advertising credit to C.W. But the entrepreneur would have to do most of the work himself. If C.W. wrote the copy and designed the ads, the Fuller Agency would place them in prominent newspapers and magazines.

Soon after the Fuller campaign was launched, orders for Postum rolled in. They came in bunches, then bushels, so many that neither C.W. nor his assistant Shorty Bristol could fill them. More workers were hired. The equipment was expanded. But C.W. doggedly poured most of the profits back into advertising. The costs were daunting. "My bills for advertising are enough to intimidate a man," C.W. wrote his brother Aurrie in January 1896. "Last month one bill was $981.78, but I am convinced it will re-pay me two-fold."

Time proved him right. Intuitively C.W. had made a brilliant decision. Advertising was to become the most powerful way to promote a new product in turn-of-the-century America. A century later it still is. Advertising, C.W. surmised as early as 1892, was the wave of the future for American businesses.

From his travels C.W. could see that the era of hometown America and its agricultural society was coming to an end. In 1896, a year after establishing the Postum Cereal Company, C.W. wrote to a London merchant:

> On this side [of the Atlantic] all manufacturers who are succeeding . . . have been forced to observe a gradual change in the method of doing business. Formerly, we depended somewhat upon the ability of the merchant to whom we sold to favorably represent our goods . . . but at this time, if we rely upon the old method, the business will fail. . . . We are compelled to address advertising to and place it before the consumer, who by his demand, compels the patronage of the dealer. . . . Take the trade of *Pear's Soap*. . . . Whenever they reduce the amount of their advertising to any appreciable extent, it is quickly shown in the pulse of the trade.

C.W. had no tolerance for slow pulses. With new sales orders arriving daily, he stepped up the pace of Postum production. He bought even more equipment. He constructed a new building. By May 1896 he had enlarged his staff to twenty-seven men and women. Shrewdly he also applied for a patent on Postum. Within each package of Postum was a tiny booklet about health entitled *The Road to Wellville*, a synopsis of his earlier treatise *I Am Well*. By that time he had developed a logo for his product: a small drop of red ink with the words "It makes red blood."

C.W. had no proof for this statement. He simply believed that Postum was healthier than coffee. By that reasoning, it could only improve blood and hence make it redder. In 1895 medicine was not yet sophisticated enough to challenge the slogan's validity. Moreover, such claims were standard business practice for the era.

Soon C.W.'s long years of sales experience began to manifest themselves in a series of graphic displays incorporated into the text of his newspaper and magazine ads. Above all, the words had to be memorable, hypnotic, unforgettable. "There's a reason" became a refrain to inspire those who could not digest coffee into instantly recalling the Postum alternative. C.W. also appealed to the masses by avoiding fancy words in his advertisements. He was sometimes deliberately hokey. His eye-catching slogans were so ungrammatical that they even incited the wrath of educators. C.W. merely shrugged. He had no intention of changing them. He knew the public liked the way he imitated the popular vernacular in print.

> CAN YOU CUT OUT THE "YELLOW STREAK?" [read one turn-of-the-century advertisement for Postum]. All got one, you know. Some small, some large. The more "yellow" in your make-up, the less yellow gold in your character and pocket-book.
>
> Is your yellow streak the coffee habit? does it reduce your working force, kill your energy, push you in the big crowd of mongrels, deaden what thoroughbred blood you may have, and neutralize all your efforts to make money and fame? . . .
>
> Try leaving off coffee for 10 days. Build back to a clean, clear-cut mind and healthy body by *Postum Coffee*. That's the true route to health, and with bounding exuberant health you acquire "Energy plus."
>
> Then, to "do" things is easy. *There's a Reason. Have a try.*

One approach was not enough. C.W. also peppered his ads with catchy phrases that advocated Postum as a cure for "coffee nerves," "coffee heart," "brain fag," or "jangled nerves." To give credence to his conviction that Postum was a healthy substitute for coffee, he used professional testimonials.

One of these, from Dr. Bennett F. Davenport, a Boston medical and chemical expert, succinctly summarized the rationale for drinking Postum. It read, "The daily introduction of the drug [coffee] simply nullifies the best efforts of the physician. It is easy to command dismissal of coffee, but difficult to secure obedience, unless the patient is put upon Postum Cereal Food Coffee, for that furnishes the morning beverage without the drug."

Suddenly newspapers and magazines were filled with Postum ads that used folksy speeches, hard sells, testimonials, medical authorities, and persuasive arguments. For these contributions and his introduction of the aggressive ad campaign, C. W. Post has been called the grandfather of advertising. It is little wonder that by the end of 1897 Postum sales figures were over $250,000.

Inevitably C.W.'s success with Postum brought a rash of imitators, eager to cash in on the coffee substitute rage. By 1897 the nation's grocery shelves were stocked with more than a half dozen new brands of coffee substitutes. Two years after C.W.'s phenomenal success, speculators had jumped into the market with a series of new products purported to be better than Postum.

To break into the market, the imitators were selling their products at considerably lower prices than Postum. They did so, C.W. later told the National Association of Manufacturers, by giving grocers a higher percentage of the profits. Consequently, when customers came in and asked for Postum, the grocers offered the imitations.

Worst of all, C.W. observed, the imitators were deceiving the public. Instead of laboriously devising their own formulas, as had C.W., they deliberately duped the public by mixing small amounts of real coffee into their product. "Naturally, my business soon felt the effect and felt it seriously," said C.W. "I paid out that year something over $100,000 for newspaper announcements regarding imitations and kept explaining the real value of *Postum*."

The fight dragged on for nearly a year. Finally C.W. began to wage a war of his own. To do so, he organized a new company and produced a new carton stamped with the name Monk's Brew. The cartons were then filled with Postum but sold for a nickel, considerably lower than either Postum or its imitators. The grocers, believing it to be another, even lower-cost coffee substitute, willingly stocked the product. Predictably Monk's Brew sold well. The product was cheaper and better than the imitations and eventually drove the competitors off the market. "It was," said C.W., "one of the most complete commercial massacres ever seen." Ironically, the public soon became so suspicious of all new coffee substitutes, including Monk's Brew, that they switched back to the familiar Postum.

Another problem was the cyclical nature of Postum production. In the winter demand for the product peaked. In the summer C.W. was often left with extra supplies of wheat that turned moldy in storage. Moreover, the uneven nature of the production schedule created problems with staff, machinery, and distribution.

For years C.W. had contemplated the idea of a ready-made breakfast cereal. Few existed, except for the tasteless cereals patients ate at Dr. Kellogg's sanitarium. More often than not the average housewife rose at dawn and spent half an hour or so making eggs and flapjacks or stirring oatmeal over a stove. If she had heard about it, she might have tried the one fledgling breakfast cereal already on the market: Shredded Wheat.

Still, sales indicated that the American housewife was already familiar with Postum. The public knew the name. Why not produce a healthy, ready-to-eat breakfast cereal to go with it? Soon after establishing Postum, C.W. began a series of new experiments. This time he mixed whole wheat and malted barley flour with yeast and baked it slowly in loaves. The product was then sliced and rebaked for another twenty-four hours. Finally, it was processed through a coffee grinder so that it had a cereal consistency. Throughout the baking process, C.W. believed, the starches were reduced to dextrose, or grape sugar. The cereal also had a slightly nutty taste. Those two features convinced Post to name the new product Grape-Nuts.

C.W. had developed the new cereal in 1897, but it was another full year before he introduced the cereal with a major advertising campaign. In addition, C.W. issued a penny coupon for the cereal. Grape-Nuts, the ads proclaimed, was a "scientific" food that enabled people to be healthy. Like Postum, it made red blood. Grape-Nuts had other virtues as well: It could steady the nerves and aid digestion.

The cereal was, C.W. argued, so nutritious that children should eat it with ease. To prove his point, he put the picture of the most beautiful child he knew in an 1898 Grape-Nuts advertisement. It was a photograph of Marjorie in a tall bonnet taken many years earlier. Beneath it, Grape-Nuts was touted as "Marjorie's Baby Food."

By 1899 sales for the new cereal had skyrocketed. A decade later Grape-Nuts was selling twice as fast as Postum.

4

"A Little Like Playing House with Dolls"

*T*he transition from childhood to womanhood can be a perilous moment for a young girl in any era, but for Marjorie Post in turn-of-the-century Michigan, that magical bewilderment called puberty was compounded by twin family forces: C.W.'s rapid acquisition of a fortune and his unhappy marriage to Ella. Simultaneously magnetic and chilling, those forces pulled Marjorie in contradictory directions, toward a public world of material splendor and a private one of emotional longing.

With Postum firmly established as the nation's premier coffee substitute and Grape-Nuts its most popular breakfast cereal, Marjorie's father had become an overnight success. Yet he was still not content. His days were passed in a feverish pitch of activity; his nights were preoccupied with plans for new products.

By 1898 C.W. had added a new warehouse to the Postum Cereal Company. He also refused an offer from the American Cereal Company to buy out his business. The following year, frustrated with the high cost of ready-made containers, C.W. established the Battle Creek Paper Company. He went on a building spree, adding so many other structures—grain storage towers, production plants, railroad sidings—that his property began to look more like a factory than a farm. In 1900 C.W. even added a power station. In five short years the Postum Cereal Company had become an independent goods-producing industry that enhanced Battle Creek, its workers, and the lives of thousands of consumers across the nation.

Despite his prosperity, C.W. considered those achievements merely the superficial trappings of a successful life. Temperamentally he was an inveterate reformer, determined to correct as many of the world's ills as possible. Human existence, he believed, was a series of spiritual gradations through which man evolved to a higher state by virtue of his deeds. In the midst of the Postum company's phenomenal growth, C.W. wrote *The Second Man,* a summary of his theory on the triumph of mind over matter. Then, to solve the problem of sending money through the mail, C.W. drafted plans for a federally supported postal check, applied for a patent, and made trips to Washington to bring his idea before Congress.

The juxtaposition of C.W.'s philosophy and his pragmatic efforts to improve the world had a profound effect upon Marjorie. "That training meant that I want to keep it [money] working, producing one thing after another, helping people who are worthy and who need it, helping with education, helping with creating beauty," said Marjorie in explanation of her life some sixty years later.

The frenetic quality of C.W.'s activities may also have contributed to the emptiness of his and Ella's marriage. C.W.'s preoccupation with work gave him and Ella a built-in excuse to lead separate lives. Even when there was slack time at the factory, Marjorie's father worked long hours. When he was not on-site, C.W. was on the road—to Chicago, Detroit, New York, Boston, Philadelphia, and Europe.

As before, it was Marjorie, not Ella, who accompanied C.W. on those trips. One of their longest journeys began in April 1899 and included stops in New Orleans, Memphis, and Galveston. Along the way C.W. and Marjorie visited Fort Worth to see the Post family. But the trip was more than a family reunion. C.W. still had business holdings in Fort Worth that needed tending. He was also sorely overcommitted in Battle Creek and needed a second pair of capable hands. During the 1899 visit C.W. probably first entertained the notion of having his brother Carroll join him at the Postum company.

A year later, when Carroll visited Battle Creek, that decision would be confirmed. Carroll was to be made head of the Battle Creek Paper Company and sales manager of the Postum Cereal Company. Best of all, from Marjorie's perspective, Carroll's kindly wife, Mollie—Auntie—would move to Battle Creek with him.

On another trip in 1898 or 1899 Marjorie and C.W. visited the wild, semi-tropical west coast of Florida. The twisted vines, bright birds, and sprawling vegetation captured Marjorie's imagination. The twelve-year-old never forgot Florida's opulent fertility. Years later Marjorie traveled to Florida to vacation again. There, on Florida's east coast, she established her famous home, Mar-A-Lago, in what was still a dense patch of jungle growth bordering the Atlantic.

Usually, however, Marjorie traveled with her father for only a few days at a time because of her school obligations. Yet even when separated from her, C.W. constantly thought of Marjorie. By 1898 she was growing rapidly, already beginning to fill out with curves. Before his eyes the unmistakable blush of young womanhood was transforming her childish facial features into a mature radiance. No longer did Marjorie address him by her old baby name for him, Dada. Now that pet term was saved only for special letters. In contrast, C.W. retained his old nickname for Marjorie—Budge. And years later in his most solicitous letters, it was still Budgie. Marjorie was no longer C.W.'s little girl; she had become his little woman. Their relationship continued to be close.

If Marjorie was to be C.W.'s little woman, she must look the part. From Chicago and New York he ordered her fashionable dresses. These, he specified to shopkeepers, should be full-size, for his daughter was shooting up rapidly. Marjorie was not petite like Ella. She favored the Post side of the family and was going to be tall like Grandpa Rollin—and C.W. At twelve Marjorie was already larger than many of her classmates. When fully grown, Marjorie stood five feet seven inches in her stocking feet, a tall woman for her era.

Marjorie outstripped her peers in other ways as well. By about 1898 the Posts had moved off the farm to an elegant rented home on Maple Street. The house (which was probably on the site of the current First Presbyterian Church) was owned by Edward C. Hinman, president of the American Steam Pipe Company. According to the custom of the day, Ella, C.W., and Marjorie took up private residence in the mansion's well-appointed rooms while Mr. Hinman dwelled in another section with his two grown daughters and their stepmother, Isadore. As befitted their comfortable life station, the two families were tended by a staff of servants. This arrangement was the equivalent of a fine hotel. For Ella the move was a particular relief, for it meant she no longer had to care for a home or supervise a kitchen.

The move coincided with Marjorie's advancement to junior high school. She was already a gregarious child with a natural vigor that im-

mediately attracted other children. Like C.W., she radiated an excitement about life that others rarely forgot. Marjorie already had at least
one old friend in school, Norma Eldred, whom she knew from Professor
Irwin's dancing school classes, and before long she befriended other
youngsters. A half century later Marjorie's spirited personality continued to draw admiring friends. "She was the kind of person who had
a zest for life and for friends. Nothing got her down," said Anne Frailey
Braverman, who met Marjorie when she was well into her sixties. "She
had an unusual vitality, and she loved it in others."

The Posts' 1899 move to the Hinman house had other, unforeseen,
advantages. The owner's daughters, Gertrude and Belle Hinman, were
recent graduates of a fashionable finishing school in Washington, D.C.,
the Mount Vernon Seminary. The girls were cultured and refined, with
a worldly veneer that distinguished them from their homegrown Battle
Creek peers. Marjorie's parents were duly impressed and now began to
consider a similar progress for their own daughter. Would not the
Mount Vernon Seminary be a fine school for Marjorie when she
reached the proper age?

In the interim, C.W. continued to ensure gracious living for his family. To escape the fiery heat of Michigan summers, he moved Ella and
Marjorie to a rented cottage on Gull Lake. Although the setting was
rustic, Gull Lake was only fifteen miles from Battle Creek and accessible
by train. To Marjorie's delight, the cottage had a private boat dock with
rowboats of its own. It was there, Norma Eldred recalled, that she, Marjorie, and a third friend, Helen Davis, spent lazy days paddling in the
shallow water at the edge of the lake. A highlight of those visits was
C.W.'s efforts to teach the girls to swim.

Eventually Marjorie became a good swimmer, if not an enthusiastic
one, largely because C.W. promised her ten dollars if she learned. For
years the heiress refused to have a pool built at Mar-A-Lago in Palm
Beach. She swam only occasionally at the adjacent Bath and Tennis
Club. Primarily she objected to the sun. Even in an era when sunbathing and a healthy tan were considered essentials for feminine beauty,
Marjorie adhered to the nineteenth-century notion that sun permanently injured a woman's complexion. Long before other people began
to worry about sun-induced wrinkles and skin cancer, Marjorie took
elaborate pains to protect herself from ultraviolet light. "Stay out of the
sun," she once told her blond friend Gladys Heurtematte Johnston Bendetsen. "People who go in it look like alligators later in life."

To others, including Marjorie's own daughters, her efforts to protect herself from the sun sometimes bordered on the ludicrous. "Mom had these real long-sleeve bathing suits she had concocted for herself with bare midriffs and a little skirt. Then she'd wear her gloves and hat and her bathing cap and dark glasses," recalled her daughter Nedenia, who is perhaps better known as the actress Dina Merrill. "When I used to tease her about it, she'd say, 'Now just lay off. Go do your own thing.' "

Later in life Marjorie's precautions paid off. Well into her old age, people used to marvel at her fresh complexion. As one of Marjorie's guests was fond of saying, "She comes into a room and everyone else looks exhausted." Outsiders also used to wonder if she ever had a face-lift. In 1967, one week shy of her eightieth birthday, Marjorie assured a female admirer, "I have never had any plastic surgery done . . . the two skin specialists I have gone to from time to time are Dr. Ernst Laszlo of the Laszlo Beauty Institute and Dr. Howard Behrman, who is a medical doctor.

"You might be interested to know that I do not drink and I do not smoke. I try to keep regular hours and get plenty of fresh air, exercise, and rest."

It was inevitable that by 1899 or 1900 Marjorie's friends would become aware of her increasingly privileged existence. On the farm, for instance, Norma noticed that Marjorie had her own horse, not a pony, and a rubber-tire runabout with which to exercise him. And then there were the journeys—not just the serious business trips with C.W. but glamorous vacations with both parents to the 1900 Paris Exposition, to England, and to fashionable American resorts like Newport and Saratoga. On her return from those travels a starry-eyed Marjorie would talk about the lives of celebrities whose names her friends only vaguely knew: Lillian Russell; the actress Maxine Elliott and her frequent costar (and husband) Nat Goodwin; and the playwright Charles Hale Hoyt.

What was most surprising was that Marjorie was not spoiled. According to Norma, she was disciplined as fairly and consistently as was Norma by her own parents. Nevertheless, Ella and C.W. did treat Marjorie to amenities that were unthinkable to her Battle Creek peers: a sapphire ring surrounded by diamonds, trips to the hairdresser, and even lessons from a manicurist about her nails and hands.

Privately, however, Marjorie was struggling with personal disappointments that money could not resolve. Her mother was often away from home. By middle age Ella had begun to suffer a series of ailments.

Exactly what they were is not known, but by 1899 they were so serious that she was traveling to St. Louis for medical treatments.

In retrospect, Marjorie attributed Ella's declining health to the long strain she had endured during C.W.'s protracted illnesses. The unhappiness of their marriage had not helped. While Ella and C.W. rarely fought, they were no longer in love—and had not been for many years. Marjorie's parents consequently lived in an uneasy state of truce, quietly, perhaps even bravely, but without any real affection or hope.

Some years later C.W. told his staff that the marriage had been unhappy almost from the start. About a year after their wedding he and Ella had realized that "we both lacked mature judgment in the selection of a life partner.... [W]e each had high esteem and regard for the qualities of the other, but the home-making element was not there."

Try as they might, that "home-making element" never arrived. Nor, despite Ella's best efforts, did devotion to Christian Science seem to improve her health. Her trips to St. Louis became even more frequent. In response, Marjorie became even closer to her father. Ella's absences, said Marjorie, "left Dad and myself pretty much alone in the afternoons and evenings [at the Hinman house] and he finally decided that we had better entirely keep house and would get the kind of meals and various kinds of things we wanted."

With his usual efficiency, C.W. rented a house on Chestnut Street and hired a housekeeper-cook to perform the essential domestic chores. Marjorie was thrilled by this first foray into domesticity. At thirteen she had become the junior mistress of a home of her own, with C.W. enshrined as her man. Decades later, with three estates and a staff of two hundred, Marjorie would say that the Chestnut Street experience had been "a little like playing house with dolls." Nevertheless, the memory of a private domestic life with her ebullient, adoring father was indelible. Repeatedly Marjorie's friends observed that long after C.W.'s death, she spoke of her father in awed and loving tones. "She was obviously very much taken with her father. She was enormously influenced by him and sought to do what he envisioned," said Dr. Gordon Hoxie, a friend of Marjorie's and the first president of C. W. Post College in Brookville, Long Island. "She admired him so much, in fact, that I don't think any man could ever measure up to him."

Their time alone together was destined to be short-lived. A few months later Ella returned to Battle Creek with her health greatly improved. Once again Marjorie was reduced to childhood status, caught between concern for her quiet, unhappy mother and a passionate attachment to C.W. In the spring of 1901 the tension-filled family moved back to the farm.

By the dawn of the new century the profits from the Postum Cereal Company were already approaching a million dollars a year, and in 1903 they topped that figure. To maintain sales, C.W. purchased fifteen hundred bushels of wheat a day. With characteristic shrewdness, he had cornered the local wheat market by offering farmers five cents extra per bushel. As a result, farmers routinely lined up outside the Postum plant on their wagons to sell their crops.

Expansion of plant facilities had become an ongoing process. So had the creation of new machines devised by C.W.—among them conveyor belts, elaborate gluing machines, grinders, and heaters. By 1900 C.W.'s cereals were already acquiring an international reputation. Through missionaries, Tz'u Hsi, the dowager empress of China, had discovered Postum products and was importing them regularly. In 1900 C.W. also began exporting Postum and Grape-Nuts to Great Britain.

The heavy volume of Postum company sales now necessitated a twenty-four-hour production schedule. From the top of a factory building, a steam whistle sounded every twelve hours to remind workers of the next shift. Gradually C.W.'s staff had swollen to more than four hundred employees and now included factory workers, millwrights, machinists, and secretaries. Strangers, hearing about C.W.'s high pay—the "best wages in Michigan for like services"—stood in line for jobs.

But housing was scarce for Battle Creek factory workers and, with a steady influx of new employees, becoming more difficult to find every day. C.W. was determined to do something about it. For years he had known every employee by name and, as he once told his workers in a New Year's Eve speech, also "knew something of his hopes, trials and pleasures." Now he was beginning to fret about the growing size—and resulting impersonality—of his workforce. ". . . it comes over me with a feeling of disappointment that the numbers have grown so great and my cares, responsibilities and frequent absence, has taken from me the opportunity of being as close to our people as I used. . . ." C.W.'s paternalistic warmth was enhanced by his shrewd realization that the more contented his employees, the more efficiently they would perform their jobs. Moreover, he was already worrying about the early labor union movement and its likely effect upon his own workers. Thus it was that

Marjorie's father decided to provide his workers with homes of their own.

In 1900, C.W. purchased an eighty-acre tract of land adjacent to the plant. Once this so-called "Post Addition" was divided into lots, C.W. built 579 houses in the stylish Queen Anne or Colonial Revival mode. Between the plots were streets, laid out in grid fashion, many named after members of C.W.'s family—Marjorie, Lathrop, Rollin, and others—which still exist. While the houses were built at C.W.'s expense, they would not be a gift. Like Vice President Teddy Roosevelt, with whom Marjorie's father was already corresponding, C.W. subscribed to the philosophy that "the first requisite of a good citizen . . . is that he shall be able and willing to pull his weight." Each buyer was thus to be responsible for his own mortgage and monthly payments. Houses were offered to workers for eight hundred to three thousand dollars. Down payments were minimal—as low as four dollars—with monthly mortgage payments of eight to thirty dollars.

Like Andrew Carnegie, Marjorie's father also believed that "all surplus revenues [are] . . . trust funds, which he is called upon to administer to produce the most beneficial results for the community." C.W.'s personal motto was "Mix altruism with your business and business with your altruism. In both cases, let it be an altruism that breeds self-reliance in man and makes for individualism." Not surprisingly, the houses in "Postumville" sold quickly. For C.W. this was only a beginning, the first in a series of progressive worker-benefit programs he would gradually implement for Postum employees.

But the grinding work of building an industrial empire had taken a toll on C.W. Physically he was badly in need of a rest, but as in earlier days, he was restless and itching to create a new American industrial order. As his brother Carroll, who joined him in August 1900 in Battle Creek, observed, the load "was getting heavy. [C.W.] wanted freedom to travel around the country and abroad in order to keep abreast of the times and the needs of the public."

At the same time that C.W. longed for the freedom of the open road, other Americans were working feverishly to follow in his tracks. As had happened with Postum in 1897, C.W.'s seemingly overnight triumph with Grape-Nuts now bred a new generation of competitors. By 1900 a get-rich-quick mentality had inflamed the citizens of Battle Creek, many of whom were determined to cash in on the ready-made-cereal boom. In basements, kitchens, and rented buildings, the imitators established factories to manufacture cereals of their own. Other would-be entrepreneurs from out of town established residence so as to imprint the name Battle Creek on their labels.

Among the new companies were names like Malta Vita, Malta-Zwieback, Norka Oats, Tryabita, CaerFeuto, Malt-Ho, Trachews, and Oatsina. By 1910 there were more than eighty cereal companies in Battle Creek, and by World War I, more than a hundred such enterprises. In the twentieth century Battle Creek had developed a new identity. In addition to its old appellation as America's "Health City," Battle Creek was now becoming known as "Cereal City, U.S.A."

Ironically, the most famous cereal company of them all, the W. K. Kellogg Company, had not yet been established. During the years when C.W. was creating Postum in the white barn, the Kellogg brothers were conducting their own food experiments. The "little doctor" now wanted to produce a digestible substitute for bread. Allegedly the idea had come to him after an elderly female patient at the San had sued Dr. Kellogg when she broke her tooth on a piece of zwieback. Shortly after that incident the doctor heard about a new product that seemed to offer a solution, a pillow-shaped biscuit called Shredded Wheat that had been invented by an attorney named Henry D. Perkey.

In 1894 Dr. Kellogg visited Perkey in Denver and eventually made him a business offer. Somehow, though—and here the story gets garbled—the agreement fell through. Bitterly disappointed, Dr. Kellogg then publicly announced that "we would invent a better food."

Typically, when Dr. Kellogg said "we," he meant "he"—in the person of his younger brother, W.K. For months thereafter W.K. spent long evenings dutifully conducting experiments with wheat. The process was time-consuming and monotonous, for it involved boiling the wheat at various temperatures, running it through a dough roller, scraping off the batter, and finally baking it. Once, just before the Adventist Sabbath, W.K. thoughtlessly left a batch of boiled wheat standing on a counter. That Saturday night he and Dr. Kellogg decided to run the now slightly moldy batch through the rollers anyway. To their surprise, the dough came out in flakes. Inadvertently the Kelloggs had discovered the "tempering" process, whereby moisture is uniformly equalized in a batter.

Dr. Kellogg now demanded that W.K. break the flakes into pieces. But the younger brother refused. They should, W.K. insisted, be left in flaked form. Afterward, when the flakes were baked and served to San guests, they were hailed as a new kind of cereal. These first wheat flakes were called Granose. On May 31, 1894, Dr. Kellogg applied for a patent on "flaked cereals" with the right to make them out of various ingredients, including corn, barley, and oats. Although 113,400 pounds of Granose flakes were sold by year's end, Dr. Kellogg refused to market the flakes commercially. To W.K.'s mounting frustration, the new cereal could be sold only through *Good Health* magazine and other Adventist publications.

By 1898 W.K. could no longer contain himself. Having already witnessed the meteoric rise of C.W.'s cereal empire, he knew that flaked cereals had a commercial future. "Orders were coming in so rapidly with so little effort on the part of anyone that it seemed to me there was a great future for the food business if it could be conducted as a company and separately from the sanitarium." Finally, after pleading with several church board members, W.K. won; the board approved the creation of a new food company independent of the San. The Sanitas Food Company was finally opened in a two-story building on Aldrich Street in 1898. But W.K. had achieved only a Pyrrhic victory. The new flaked cereals were sold primarily to other sanitariums—and only by mail order.

Nevertheless, W.K. persistently maintained that flaked cereals were commercially viable and had, in fact, more money-making potential than the San itself. If it were given the opportunity, the Sanitas Food Company, W.K. predicted, "would develop in such a manner that the sanitarium would be only a side show. . . . I confess at the time I little realized the extent to which the food business might develop in Battle Creek." A series of bitter arguments, a fire at the sanitarium, and sibling rivalry forced W.K. to wait eight years to test his theory.

Meanwhile, the breakfast food business had grown into a national mania under W. K. Kellogg's thickly bespectacled eyes. The confluence of three then-fashionable ideas had contributed to its popularity: the concept of "home economics," that is to say the professionalization of home management preached to housewives by turn-of-the-century feminists and magazine writers; the "gospel of efficiency" epitomized by the writings of Frederick Taylor; and a burgeoning interest in nature and "natural" living evidenced in the work of John Burroughs and Teddy Roosevelt. These, combined with C.W.'s persuasive advertisements in publications like the *Woman's Home Companion*, *Saturday Evening Post*, and *Ladies' Home Journal*, had convinced many American housewives to give up making time-consuming breakfasts like eggs, sausages, potatoes, and pancakes for "efficient"—and presumably more healthy—ready-made breakfast cereals. Millions of Americans from Boston to San Francisco now consumed boxes of precooked grains daily. Every week thousands of tons of raw wheat, oats, corn, and bran arrived in Battle Creek and, after being processed and packaged, were shipped off on boxcars to grocery stores coast to coast. And the indisputable and charismatic leader of America's breakfast food craze was none other than C. W. Post.

By 1901 Marjorie's father was building a series of monuments in Battle Creek that would bear testimony to his empire. That year he completed the deluxe hotel known as the Post Tavern. C.W.'s hotel would feature conveniences unheard of outside large cities—among them electric lights, private telephones, private baths, an English-style pub, and an enormous ballroom. Although anyone who visited Battle Creek—and could afford high rates—could stay at the Post Tavern, C.W. initially promoted it as a kind of upscale La Vita Inn. Essentially the Post Tavern was very much like a contemporary health spa, where affluent and exhausted adults could "rest and be fed back to strength and comfort by expert food makers, who know how to select the right kind of food to rebuild worn out nerve centers."

The tavern also featured a luxurious apartment for C.W. and his family. For fourteen-year-old Marjorie, it was a chance to decorate her own room. She and Ella were taken by carriage to the furniture city of Grand Rapids to find suitable furnishings for their home. Marjorie's room had a handsomely carved wooden bed, a rocking chair, and stylish lace curtains. The rest of the apartment was opulently furnished with Oriental rugs, beaded lampshades, mahogany furniture, and oil paintings in the heavy late-Victorian style. Not long after the family was finally settled, Ella's health failed again. Before long she had returned to St. Louis.

Two women had already stepped in to fill the void left by Ella's frequent absences. The first was Aunt Mollie, who had arrived with her husband, Carroll Post, in Battle Creek in 1900. By then Mollie—Mary Staley Post—was a large, maternal woman in her mid-forties. From the time they were young brides together in the elder Posts' homestead in Springfield, Mollie and Ella had been close friends. Temperamentally they could not have been more dissimilar. Where Ella tended toward sternness and reticence, Mollie was vivacious and sentimental; while Ella enjoyed books and art, Mollie filled her house with people and entertainment. Unable to have children of her own, Mollie nevertheless radiated a maternal warmth that extended to Marjorie and into the community, where she devoted herself to helping others. So remarkable were Mollie's good deeds that at the time of her death local newspapers reported that she had endeared herself to Battle Creek as a "fairy godmother." She was, as Marjorie later put it, "beloved by every age of people that you can think of. She was a woman who loved to entertain. She had most of her pleasure, it seemed to me, in what she could do for other people."

Mollie's congeniality kindled a similar impulse in young Marjorie. Within a year Carroll and Mollie had settled into an exquisite forty-two-room mansion at 238 Maple Street (today called Capital, N.E.) not far from the Hinman house. There, beneath majestic Corinthian columns, delicate plasterwork ceiling friezes, and leaded glass windows, fourteen-year-old Marjorie often watched Mollie set an exquisite table with matching candles, flowers, and linens for friends and for her charitable events. When Mollie's guests gasped with delight at the fine food and exquisite settings, Marjorie vowed that she would someday inspire a similar response.

In an effort to train Marjorie in the rudiments of home management, Mollie gave her niece cooking lessons, but the girl apparently had no talent for it. When asked years later, Marjorie confessed that she could put together only the most rudimentary of dishes. Aunt Mollie had more success teaching her niece other domestic tasks—the concepts of keeping a house neat and orderly, knitting, embroidery, and other "refinements," such as wrapping presents. "Oh, there were so many little things like that. She taught me a great deal about running a house," Marjorie later recalled. "I speak of her so much because my mother, unfortunately, from the time I was quite young, early teens, was very ill . . . and it left me looking to the aunt more or less as another mother."

Despite his devotion to Marjorie, C.W.'s obligations kept him away from home at all hours of the day and night. In 1901 he completed a second downtown office building, called the Marjorie Block. The following year he erected a third structure, the Post Theatre. By then the fifteen wood-frame buildings of the Postum Cereal Company and its adjacent Post Addition were nationally publicized as "White City." A picture of the plant was circulated on cereal labels, postcards, and the company stationery. Not only was the external appearance of the brightly painted buildings, surrounded by green lawns and flower beds, unique in an era of industrial gloom, but it reflected C.W.'s enlightened ideas about the health and dignity of his workers and his insistence that they labor under safe and sanitary conditions.

In May 1902, 140,000 employees of the United Mine Workers went out on strike. To C.W. it was a portent of the coming struggle. Less than a year later C.W. wrote letters to national industry leaders advising them to "handle your employees one by one and gradually get them under the contract system . . . [and] you will discover that instead of belonging to a union and constituting a smoldering hotbed of hatred and opposition to you, they have become your friends and co-workers." This was the first of many positions C.W. took that drew him into the vortex of the national labor movement controversy.

That controversy, compounded by C.W.'s long hours and Ella's absences, meant that Marjorie arrived home from school at noon and in late afternoon with no one, except servants, to look after her. To provide his daughter with adult companionship, C.W. hired a young woman named Leila Young. Leila, the pretty brown-eyed daughter of Edna and Edward Young, had gone to work at Postum several years earlier. In 1899 or 1900, C.W. asked the elder Youngs if they would allow the twenty-two-year-old Leila to attend Marjorie when she arrived home from school and stay through her dinner. Simultaneously C.W. made Leila his private secretary.

This arrangement, according to Marjorie's father, brought a new sense of dependability and warmth to his home. In contrast with the tension-filled atmosphere of unspoken "friction, irritation and worry" when Ella was in residence, C.W.'s house was now "soft and balmy with peace." Marjorie's initial reaction to her new governess has not been recorded. If one trusts C.W.'s report, Marjorie must have found Leila a comforting presence. From subsequent events, however, it is clear that the girl never warmed to her new governess. At best, Marjorie found Leila a neutral figure who was unable to help her dispel the shadows of a baffling and lonely era.

5

"Twenty-seven Boils"

Washington, D.C., was an unfinished city in the autumn of 1901. Streets leading to the suburbs of Georgetown and the swamps of the Potomac were still unpaved. At Chevy Chase Circle, half a mile from Connecticut Avenue, red-coated hunters and their hounds followed the foxes. Downtown, the Library of Congress building was only four years old. A chain of trolleys swept down Pennsylvania Avenue. Massachusetts Avenue was abuzz with masons building granite palaces for a new breed of millionaires. Despite such signs of civic optimism, the city's flags flew at half-mast. On September 14 President William McKinley had died of gunshot wounds he had received in Buffalo, and his forty-two-year-old vice president, Theodore Roosevelt, had just been sworn in as the new head of state.

These events were the backdrop for Marjorie's new life as a student at the Mount Vernon Seminary. By mid-1901 two factors had convinced C.W. to enroll his fourteen-year-old daughter at the school: the increasing frequency of his trips to Washington and his disillusionment with the provincial life of Battle Creek. Marjorie, he had long ago decided, was to be educated in the East, close to the centers of power and privilege, and near to the country's old families. It was impractical to send his daughter to a venerable boarding school in a city like Boston or Philadelphia, where C.W. was only an occasional visitor. With its Washington location, the Mount Vernon Seminary was ideal. Besides himself, then, there would be professional teachers and chaperones to look after Marjorie and instruct her in the finer things in life.

Whatever trepidation Marjorie felt about C.W.'s decision soon disappeared. Her classmates were the daughters of prominent men—senators, representatives, and industrialists. Like Marjorie, they were astute, playful, and sophisticated, accustomed to traveling for pleasure, staying in fine hotels, and dining in fashionable restaurants. Years later Marjorie looked back upon her years at the Mount Vernon Seminary euphorically, as a sunny contrast with her last, lonely days at Battle Creek. "I . . . adored it," she recalled, "because I had so many girls of my own age to be with and it was all a new experience. . . ."

Although the Mount Vernon Seminary was located in a respectable and handsome section of the District, student behavior was still carefully monitored. Proper behavior was deemed so important that Marjorie kept a copy of school rules in her class scrapbook. Among them were admonitions against sitting or standing near windows "so as to be seen by persons outside." Students were expected to make their own beds in the morning, turn the gas low when not in their rooms, and put their trash in refuse bins. Lights went off at 10:00 P.M. sharp. Visitors had to be introduced to the school principal on Friday and Saturday afternoons. Permission to attend amusements, concerts, shopping, and dressmaking appointments had to be similarly cleared with school authorities.

Mount Vernon's aristocratic gray-haired headmistress, Elizabeth Jane Eddy Somers, tolerated no compromise. Miscreants were severely punished; girls who disobeyed were scrutinized with extra care, for they were considered potential rebels who might never settle into conventional patterns of female domesticity. The concept of what constituted an appropriate education for seminary students had grown out of Mrs. Somers's own ruminations about nineteenth-century feminism.

In 1855 the young Elizabeth Jane Eddy, daughter of a prominent Methodist minister, had graduated from the Ohio Wesleyan Female College. Thereafter she taught at the Northwestern Female College in Evanston, Illinois, where she befriended the feminist temperance leader Frances Willard.

During the Civil War and in the immediate postbellum era feminists were sharply divided about the education of women. If they wished to pursue a college education and a career, feminists like Susan B. Anthony and Elizabeth Blackwell believed, then they should not marry. If they did, they should not have children. Other feminists, like Anthony's friend Elizabeth Cady Stanton, had struggled with this concept in their personal lives; so, too, would Lucy Stone, Antoinette Brown, and Charlotte Perkins Gilman.

In part the anti-marriage stance was given credence by the practical difficulties nineteenth-century women had in combining marriage and children with a career; in part, it was helped along by theories about neurasthenia that suggested the pursuit of intellectual endeavors "weakened" a woman's procreative powers.

Some educators like Elizabeth Jane Eddy Somers believed that women could enjoy both higher education and a normal domestic life, but only if the former was modified. Thus in 1875 Mrs. Somers founded the Mount Vernon Seminary to offer young women the chance to study a college preparatory curriculum. Those interested in pursuing higher education could elect to study at the seminary for another two years; then, if still motivated, students could go on to complete their baccalaureates at established women's colleges. As Mrs. Somers once explained, the seminary was designed to accommodate "those young ladies who wish to avoid the stress and strain of the four year college and yet feel the inadequacies of the high school curriculum to prepare them for . . . life. . . ." To add dimension to that curriculum, Mrs. Somers invited authors, poets, and musicians to meet with the girls. By graduation Mount Vernon students were properly "finished"—that is, educated enough about art, literature, and history to make good companions to worldly men.

The seminary was famous for the quality of its alumnae. Among its graduates were women like Elsie Bell Grosvenor, wife of the editor of the *National Geographic* and daughter of Alexander Graham Bell, and Ada Louise Comstock, daughter of a Minnesota state senator and the future president of Radcliffe College. Such role models, C.W. concluded during his trips to Washington, were suitable inspirations that would transform Marjorie into an educated woman who would select a suitable husband under whose aegis the Postum Cereal Company would continue to grow.

There were other compelling reasons why C.W. had enrolled Marjorie at the Mount Vernon Seminary. By the end of 1901 C.W.'s political struggles necessitated such long stays in Washington that he decided to establish a residence there. By late 1901 or early 1902 he had acquired offices and a home on Vermont Avenue. C.W. seemed constitutionally unable to stay in one place for very long; moreover, his duties at the Postum Cereal Company and his far-flung national and international interests often meant he had to travel.

Despite the excellent supervision offered Marjorie at the Mount Vernon Seminary, C.W. worried about his daughter's being left alone in the District without the presence of a family member. Consequently Ella established herself "very comfortably" in an apartment in Washington not far from the school. It was then, in the first flush of young womanhood, that Marjorie began to grow closer to her mother. To her surprise, she discovered that Ella was "a very charming and lovely person, with nothing for me to be disgruntled over the way I was as a child."

At the time that Marjorie entered the school, the Mount Vernon Seminary had more than sixty students, who lived in four brownstones on M Street. A fifth building had been set aside for faculty and club rooms. The following year a sixth town house was acquired as a senior residence. Marjorie's dormitory was a handsome three-story building that looked out on tree-lined M Street. Within it were a sweeping staircase, double bedrooms, adjoining baths, sitting rooms, and formal parlors with Oriental rugs, crystal chandeliers, and marble fireplaces— accoutrements that befitted the privileged status of the student body.

According to the 1904–05 yearbook, the Mount Vernon faculty taught students a rigorous high school curriculum. Undergraduates like Marjorie attended classes in English language, literature, and composition; modern languages; European and American history; art history; and music. In addition, every student was drilled in Bible history. Although Marjorie's final school record has not been preserved, the one extant report card in her scrapbook, from December 1903, indicates that she was a good student who worked diligently and obeyed school rules.

The teachers praised Marjorie for her neatness and sense of order—a trait that would astound her friends and business associates throughout her life. "She had total recall," said her financial secretary Betty Cannella. "She was well organized and believed in the importance of keeping detailed records, [so much so] . . . that she'd assist me in searching through a year of files. It was tremendous."

Early in 1902 Marjorie joined Mount Vernon's "modern drama" group, known as the B.T.S. Her interest in the theater was already long-standing; as a child visiting London, Saratoga, and Newport, Marjorie had admired stars such as Lillian Russell, Mrs. Charles Hoyt, and Maxine Elliott and Nat Goodwin. On March 13, 1902, at the opening night of the Post Theatre in Battle Creek, Marjorie had even carried roses on-stage for Elliott and Goodwin, who, at C.W.'s invitation, had just given a performance of *When We Were Twenty-one.*

Mount Vernon's B.T.S. club was Marjorie's first chance to work in the theater herself. What seemed to fascinate her the most was its pageantry, an element she later integrated into her personal life. As Marjorie aged, that dramatic bent—the impulse to astonish and please her guests, to create a fairyland setting—evolved into more subtle forms. "There was this wonderful theatrical side of Mother that loved to give these enormous dinners with beautiful flowers and porcelains," said Marjorie's daughter Dina Merrill. "Every dinner was different. And lunch was different. And the flowers were different. She went to great effort to coordinate all of this . . . and make it interesting and beautiful and different for us every day. She was very aesthetic."

At Mount Vernon, Marjorie's first theatrical job was modest. In February 1903 she served as assistant stage manager in a play entitled *Russian Honeymoon.* The following year, perhaps because of her height, she played an old soldier in a play entitled *A Court Mask.* In a presentation by the Shakespeare Club, Marjorie was cast in the role of Romeo. An autograph in her scrapbook from a classmate reads "To my 'Maude Adams.' " According to the collection of preserved programs, Marjorie does not seem to have played starring roles, but membership in the school thespian society was clearly central to the young heiress's identity.

Inevitably school clubs were secondary to an even more challenging activity: attendance at college dances and games. A month after her fifteenth birthday Marjorie was asked on her first date by an older boy. The name of this admirer has been lost, but on April 19, 1902, Marjorie attended the "Winter Hops" at the U.S. Naval Academy in Annapolis with him—and carefully preserved the program in her scrapbook. Later there were other invitations: to Annapolis dances, Harvard-Yale football games, Yale Promenade concerts, Yale Glee, Banjo, and Mandolin club concerts, and U.S. Military Academy–U.S. Naval Academy football games.

Marjorie was flattered by this flurry of male attention and quickly learned to take it in stride. The flow of invitations that arrived for dances and football games was, after all, considered de rigueur among Marjorie's friends. It was an age when well-to-do girls were expected to marry early and well. Indeed, that was precisely why wealthy citizens sent their daughters to Mount Vernon: to meet eligible young men from America's elite colleges and military academies. By the spring of their senior year—or, alternately, after two years of postgraduate study— seminary students were often engaged to be wed.

Young men of the era were appropriately accommodating. The turn of the century was still a romantic era in whose glow young bachelors gallantly pursued the course of true love. Innocence was considered a desirable quality, even a cherished national trait. By 1902 the nation's favorite female paragon was the Gibson Girl, the ubiquitous creation of magazine illustrator Charles Dana Gibson. Miss Gibson, with her up- swept hair, finely chiseled nose, hourglass figure, and intelligent ex- pression, was pictured in hundreds of advertisements as the epitome of womanly virtue.

In photographs of that time, Marjorie's delicate features, full figure, and pompadour hairdo approached that ideal. Almost unanimously her classmates acknowledged that Marjorie was a beguiling beauty, and she was widely admired for her elegant, fashionable clothes.

By the time of Marjorie's early romances, her parents had given up on theirs. Ella and C.W. no longer shared the same residence. Neverthe- less, for the sake of propriety they continued to appear together in pub- lic as husband and wife, particularly on important occasions such as a January 1902 White House reception with President and Mrs. Roose- velt. The elder Posts' living arrangement was a mixed blessing for young Marjorie. One obvious advantage was that she was spared the tension of her parents' formerly unhappy cohabitation. By late 1902 relations between Ella and C.W. had seriously deteriorated. Around that time Ella began to travel to spas for her health and to foreign lands to fill her lonely days. As a result, Marjorie became a reluctant go- between for her alienated parents.

An October 13 letter of that year from C.W. reflects the bitterness of that separation. "Your Mother's whereabouts are unknown to me and I cannot forward mail to her," he complained; "for that reason you may hand her the enclosed letter or mail it to her as you please. I think she had better lodge with me her address so that mail can be sent to her." No doubt letters like these presented Marjorie with a difficult di- lemma, for she loved her mother too much to be the bearer of bad news.

Disturbing as her parents' separation was, it paled when compared with the rage C.W. sometimes expressed over Marjorie's admirers. In that same letter C.W. confronted his fifteen-year-old daughter with the fact that a certain "Captain" who had been C.W.'s guest "was talking love to you in New London and even had the audacity to kiss you. This was done in direct opposition to my request. . . . I supposed you felt I would be rough with him if you told me, but you should have made the matter plain to me and trust to my common sense to help you through the little difficulty. . . . I don't even want him to call on you down in Washington and if he dares do such a thing you telegraph me at once. . . ."

C.W.'s angry, authoritative tone revealed the strong currents of affection that still flowed between him and Marjorie. Although unhappily married, C.W. was an incurable romantic, a man true to his era who still believed that women—particularly his lovely daughter—needed coddling. Separation from his wife would not mean alienation from his daughter. Instead it offered him an opportunity to draw her even closer.

To calm his anguish—and perhaps to renew his fond days with Marjorie in the Chestnut Street cottage—C.W. now planned to build a new home. This was not to be another cottage but a majestic domicile for an illustrious father and his adult daughter. The site was to be Greenwich, a posh Connecticut suburb an hour by train from Manhattan. After much rumination C.W. had settled upon that Connecticut community because of its proximity to the nation's largest business hub and its reputation as an up-and-coming community for the eastern elite. Two of the Rockefeller brothers had already built estates in Greenwich; so had other multimillionaires like the railroad financier J. Kennedy Tod and the stockbroker Elias Cornelius Benedict.

The house was to be built in Greenwich's Rock Ridge section on a generous stretch of wooded land through which ran a roaring brook. Because it was designed for father and daughter, the new house was constructed in two wings—one for Marjorie and her future family; the other for C.W. But The Boulders, as the house was subsequently called, would not be completed until 1905. "It was a house that my father and I had planned for a long time," Marjorie told C.W.'s biographer some years later. "Dad and I had great fun with that house because he and I furnished the whole thing."

In 1902, C.W. became embroiled in a series of public controversies. From a late-twentieth-century perspective, one might say that C.W. was wrestling with a midlife crisis. C.W.'s twenty-eight-year-old marriage was on the brink of divorce. His daughter was growing into a woman and dating "dangerous" men. Professionally he was locking

horns with senators, representatives, and industrialists in a series of
fiery national debates. Among them was a congressional fight for the
creation of a small-bill postal check.

The battle had arisen out of C.W.'s observation that consumers who
wanted to purchase goods through mail order had trouble sending
small amounts of money through the U.S. Postal Service. Cash—in the
form of dollar bills and coins—was awkward to mail and liable to theft.
The alternatives—postage stamps, out-of-town bank checks, or express
company money orders—were either impractical or difficult to cash.
With typical ingenuity, C.W. had devised a solution: special currencies
printed by the Treasury Department in one-, two-, and five-dollar de-
nominations that could be either cashed at face value or, if signed over
to the recipient, sent through the mail like bank checks.

After an intensive lobbying campaign, C.W.'s "Post-check currency"
was introduced into Congress as the 1902 MacMillan-Gardner Post-
Check Bill. Influential groups like the National Association of Newspapers, the National Association of Manufacturers, and the Association of
American Advertisers initially hailed the plan as a boon to mail-order
businesses. The bill met heady opposition from other quarters, including the National Retail Grocers, some banks, and express companies.
Spearheading the resistance was New York senator Thomas Platt, who,
as head of the powerful U.S. Express Company, managed to stall the bill
in committee for months. For three years C.W. protested the stalemate
through lobbying, formal complaints to the Senate, and a public press
campaign. Eventually the frustrated industrialist even conducted an in-
vestigation of corrupt political practices on the Hill.

In the spring of 1902 that fight was just beginning to heat up. C.W.,
weary of the complexities of modern life, escaped into a wave of nostalgia. He longed for a return to simplicity, to the innocent trappings of a
bygone era. In that escapist mood C.W. and Marjorie sailed that summer to England, where they joined relatives on a stagecoach trip
through southern England. As usual, C.W. spared no expense. The old-
fashioned stagecoach had a driver, four horses, and a liveried footman
who took the party to Wells Cathedral and Stonehenge.

Marjorie never forgot the magic of that journey. "Well, there never
in the world was a trip that was more fun," she recalled. "We'd make
about twenty-five miles a day . . . and as we would approach a village or
town . . . the boys with the horns would announce our coming so that
the traffic would give way. . . ." Invariably, small groups of boys appeared in the streets to stare at the stagecoach and its passengers, who

merrily threw them coins. On that same trip—almost as an after-thought—C.W. and Marjorie attended the coronation of Edward VII.

By fall it was business as usual in Washington. C.W. continued his battle with Congress over the Post-check currency. The following spring, as a member of the resolutions committee of the National Association of Manufacturers, he launched an attack against the American Federation of Labor. In theory C.W. claimed that he supported the union concept. As he liked to remind others, he was not only a card-carrying member of the National Association of Stationary Engineers but also a founder of the National Trades and Workers Associations. What repulsed him were the coercive tactics of early organized labor. Above all, C.W. feared that union leaders might corrupt his workers at Postum, who, thus far, were well paid, well fed, and content in his "open shop."

In a 1903 speech before the National Association of Manufacturers, C.W. explained his objections. He was, he said in a challenge to Samuel Gompers, "decidedly in favor of the union . . . that will help the people keep in work and secure the highest wages in the land the business will stand. There is not one right-thinking man, whether union or non-union, . . . but will agree . . . that miserable and contemptible abuses have crept into both *capital* and *labor*, and these abuses must be corrected before fair treatment can be secured all around."

Years later Marjorie proudly noted that the Postum Cereal Company continued to maintain an open shop throughout C.W.'s life. "It was many, many years after he died that they finally unionized us," she said; ". . . he had very forward ideas about how to take care of your workers. . . . He used to look after his people beautifully."

In 1902 the fifteen-year-old Marjorie was focused on a far more personal battle: the war between the sexes. A steady stream of eligible bachelors now stepped forward to offer Marjorie invitations to college dances and games. But by mid-1903 a tall, handsome young man from Greenwich, Connecticut, had already caught Marjorie's eye.

He was Edward Bennett Close, the son of one of Greenwich's founding families, and a student at the Columbia Law School. It seemed to be love at first sight. In the summer of 1903 the twenty-one-year-old Ed Close met Marjorie at a dance at a Greenwich inn and became dazzled by her beauty. Four days later he proposed. That fall, back at the Mount Vernon Seminary, the sixteen-year-old Marjorie began to scratch Ed Close's name over and over again in her school scrapbook. He was clearly her favorite beau, one whom she seriously considered marrying.

But Marjorie was too young to think of such things, too young, as C.W. had recently reminded her, to think of anything practical. From his perspective Marjorie had reached that moment in human development when even the most sensible girl forgets her elders' wishes and becomes lost in romantic vapors.

On Marjorie's sixteenth birthday C.W. noted that while she was a "dear, sweet girl whom everyone seems to like," she had an "offhand, rather cold way of showing [her] affection." To correct it, C.W. counseled his daughter, she should try to cultivate "a medium character that will leave you happy and yet express your sympathy without being in the least hysterical."

"Hysterical." That word had unfortunate ramifications. To C.W. and probably to Marjorie, that word was the ultimate insult, a term that implied the excesses of womanhood, an extreme emotionality and an impracticality—the very qualities the entrepreneur had tried to drum out of Marjorie in childhood through his business training sessions. Despite his best efforts, those tendencies, or so C.W. implied, were in danger of surfacing in the teenage Marjorie.

By 1903 Marjorie was in the full flush of adolescence. She was young, she was beautiful, and like most teenagers, she felt invulnerable. Equally worrisome to C.W. was her extravagant taste in clothes—and her wanton use of her entire allowance upon them. "I wonder," he drolly conjectured in a letter to Marjorie on her sixteenth birthday, "if you are going to save enough out of your allowance to buy a few rags for your Summer wear. Of course, I would hate to have to take you around half dressed, and we don't know many people up in New England who would give you any clothes, so you had better look out for your money."

Discretion about money was the principle C.W. was trying to instill in Marjorie. The young woman was already fabulously wealthy in her own right. By the time she was fifteen, Marjorie's share of Postum stock had grown in value to nearly two million dollars. In honor of her sixteenth birthday, C.W. had added another million dollars to her estate, which he still cautiously held in trust for her.

Two years later Marjorie's fondness for finery still showed no signs of restraint. By C.W.'s standards, she had become even more excessive in her taste for clothes. Although she had graduated from the Mount Vernon Seminary in May 1904, C.W. still considered Marjorie immature and kept her on a strict allowance.

In a letter of January 27, 1905, C.W. explained why he had prohibited a servant from sending her more furs from storage. He objected:

> Not on the ground that you shouldn't have anything you want, but candidly you are daffy & will certainly bring ridicule upon yourself if you don't quickly check your gait of elaborate & variegated display. You have more than double the clothes shoes & stuff that *any girl* no matter how rich should have at 17. Now make some of the furs you have do & don't order any more dresses or clothes before you return. . . . [y]ou must have a breath of fresh air like this to waken you & show you how extreme you have become. Call in your level head & balance up. Dad wants you *sensible,* so go slow.

Ultimately C.W.'s admonitions fell on closed ears. Throughout her life Marjorie continued to dress lavishly and in a dizzying array of outfits. Her closets held hundreds of dresses, some made by Parisian designers, others sewn at her instructions by private dressmakers, but all expertly tailored and coordinated with matching hats, shoes, gloves, and furs. To enhance her statuesque beauty, Marjorie bedecked herself in gems from Cartier, Tiffany, Harry Winston, and the royal courts of Europe. In 1971, at the age of eighty-four, C.W.'s daughter was still considered one of the best and most expensively dressed women of the world, and her expenditures for clothing and accessories were in excess of $250,000 a year.

C.W. was equally disapproving of Marjorie's romantic attachments. For at least a year Marjorie had confided in her father about her preference for Ed Close. Secretly, or so Marjorie said years later, she had even become engaged to him. C.W. thought the idea ridiculous and made Marjorie promise to wait two years. In the interim, perhaps to rattle C.W., Marjorie entertained other suitors, among them a thirty-five-year-old man named Billy Lindley. C.W. objected to this beau even more strenuously than to the others because of his arrogance. With a characteristic mixture of love and sternness, C.W. lectured his daughter in a May 3, 1905, letter that she should not "let anybody dare to crowd you or hurry you a minute."

"You are," he reminded Marjorie in a paternal rage, "too valuable a prize for *anyone* to run in and hurry off with in a hurry, much less a young man we saw for 3 weeks and who presses hard without the courtesy of seeing Dad. . . . The waters should be approached in a more dignified way. He has shown no evidence. Why you should even consider him a suitor at all. If he is worthy, he will keep without ice."

Ultimately Marjorie bent to her father's wishes about Lindley, but she was already eighteen and had strong ideas of her own. Moreover, by the spring of 1905 she was nursing a deep psychic wound. On October 28, 1904, C.W. and Ella had divorced. Money had not been at issue. Quite willingly, as C.W. later told his employees, he had given Ella a generous number of bonds that allowed her to live and travel in luxury. The sum, C.W. publicly observed, was large enough "to keep a dozen families and sufficient to permit her to indulge her desire for travel to any limit."

One evening before the divorce, C.W. called on Marjorie at the Mount Vernon Seminary and took her to dinner. At the restaurant he made a solemn announcement. "Marjorie, I'm going to be married very shortly," he said. Marjorie stared at her father in disbelief. "Yes," C.W. persisted, "Leila and I are going to be married." Marjorie was horrified. "Oh, for God's sake, what'd you pick her out for? Why didn't you pick Maxine [another sweetheart]?" she protested, or his "beautiful widow" friend from St. Louis? But C.W. would not be moved. He would reply only that there were reasons for his choice, and that despite Marjorie's disapproval he had every intention of going through with the marriage.

On November 16, 1904, Marjorie's fifty-year-old father and the twenty-seven-year-old Leila Young were married by the Reverend W. S. Potter in Battle Creek. At the time of the marriage the *Kalamazoo Gazette* reported that the new Mrs. Post expected to continue her duties as C.W.'s private secretary. Her husband, said the bride before she and C.W. left on a honeymoon in New York, intended to remain president of the Postum Cereal Company and fulfill his other obligations because he became unhappy "if forced to be idle."

The marriage had a searing effect upon Marjorie. For the rest of her life she was convinced that Leila, "this creature who was only ten years older than I was," had become her governess with the sole intent of seducing C.W.

Sixty years later Marjorie still grimaced when she discussed her father's remarriage. "Did I have a mess on my hands after that. I was furious . . . the hair turned white . . . I had twenty-seven boils that year. I was wild."

THE MATRON

6

The Bride

*O*n July 1905 Marjorie made a startling announcement of her own: She had agreed to become the bride of Edward Bennett Close. Lovesick and living in Greenwich near her beau, Marjorie no longer saw any reason to wait. Ed Close had just graduated from the Columbia Law School. A full year had passed since Marjorie had completed her education at the Mount Vernon Seminary. On C.W.'s instructions, she was living at Greenwich's Edgewood Inn to supervise the completion of The Boulders. What, then, was to stop her and Ed from proclaiming their affection in a formal engagement?

The announcement came only eight months after C.W.'s wedding to Leila. It was a gauntlet thrown at C.W.'s feet, the challenge of a bereaved daughter determined to fasten her affection upon another man. C.W., after all, had married Leila with no consideration for Marjorie's feelings. Did not Marjorie have the right to choose her own mate as well?

At eighteen Marjorie could not openly confront her father with such thoughts. Despite her anguish over C.W.'s marriage, despite the boils and streak of white hair that appeared the year he married Leila, Marjorie still loved her father. She coveted his approval and feared his wrath. In the end Marjorie wrote her father a dutiful letter asking his advice.

C.W. understood that this was mere window dressing. The tone of Marjorie's letter suggested that her decision was already made. If he spoke ill of Ed Close, Marjorie would stiffen her spine against his disap-

proval. On July 6 C.W. wrote his daughter a loving but carefully
worded letter. "You ask what I think, my! I shall have to have a 'stenog'
to tell you one half," he began. "Be very sure that your heart tells you
that Eddie is the one. He is lovely and we like him very, very much, but
he must be *all* to you."

In an allusion to his own difficulties, C.W. reminded Marjorie about
the dangers of a loveless marriage. "You must be very, very sure he is
necessary to your happiness, for . . . if you did not love him just as you
should you might meet some one who you would love in the way you
should have cared for Ed and it would simply wreck your life."

Having warned Marjorie, C.W. placed the gauntlet back in her
hands. "If you decide that Ed is the one and you want to be married this
winter, I shall be just as happy for you as I possibly can be. Your happiness is first . . . to [me]. . . . As you know you have fulfilled the aching
void in my heart for a girl of my own. And I am with you in any thing
that means your happiness."

To Marjorie, C.W.'s letter signified approval. From her adolescent
perspective, Ed Close was the perfect husband. He was intelligent, attractive, and sociable. He came from an old eastern family, the kind
that C.W. had always wanted his daughter to marry into. He had a patrician sense of propriety that young Marjorie, even the sophisticated
Marjorie of the Mount Vernon Seminary, found fascinating. Moreover,
Eddie, as Marjorie called him, was straightforward and kindly and, if
not overtly charismatic, at least the type of man who was not likely to
stray. He was, as Hunter Marston, an old Connecticut friend and the
son of a New York banker, once said, "a very nice fellow but the type of
man who, unless you met him several times, you wouldn't remember
him at all. Everybody liked him, there was nothing about him to be controversial, nor to dislike. He was not a dynamic man but a very kindly
man." In his solidity Ed Close was a dramatic contrast with C.W. To the
young Marjorie he was a safe harbor, the halcyon heir of a clan inured
to wealth, leadership, and civic prominence.

On August 31, 1905, Ed Close purchased an engagement ring at Tiffany's. The diamond was large, of fine quality, and valued at sixty-five
hundred dollars. Young Close could afford such a gift. While not nearly
as wealthy as the Posts, Marjorie's beau was a member of the Brevoort
family, descendants of the old Knickerbocker line that had owned farm-
land in prerevolutionary Manhattan. A century earlier the Close
branch of Ed's family had been the first settlers of Greenwich.

The Close family's reaction to Ed's engagement has not been preserved. For all her beauty and wealth, Marjorie was considered by many an arriviste, a midwestern schoolgirl with a newly minted millionaire father, who—by the old-money standards of eastern society—was brash and flamboyant. At first the euphoric Marjorie did not sense this contempt or, if she did, paid little attention to it.

Moreover, Marjorie was immediately made welcome by Ed's friends—the Tilts, the McAlpins, and the Chesters—as well as by her fiancé's younger brother, Harry. Tall and lanky, with the slightly aquiline nose of the Closes, Harry had warmed to Marjorie at once. The truth was that he became infatuated with her, to the point that he grew despondent when Ed's engagement was announced. Family legend has it that Harry was so dismayed that immediately after the wedding he left town. "Harry took it so hard he went away to Alaska for two years," said Adelaide Close Riggs, Marjorie and Ed's eldest daughter. "Years later Harry's wife used to joke that whenever Marjorie called, he would drop everything and go running for her."

In early September, when C.W. arrived in Greenwich, Ed formally asked him for Marjorie's hand. Whatever doubts C.W. had about his future son-in-law were muted. True to his promise to foster Marjorie's happiness, C.W. threw an engagement party in her honor for twenty-four guests. That evening was one of the most exhilarating in the young woman's life.

Marjorie and Ed decided to have a small wedding. The awkward circumstances of C.W.'s divorce and remarriage to Leila had something to do with it. So did the fact that Ed's widowed mother, Emma, was an invalid, who had suffered a severe stroke. In compensation, C.W. told Marjorie that she could have anything she wanted for a trousseau and instructed her to "make it as lovely as possible."

Marjorie began shopping at once. She purchased dozens of dresses from New York's finest stores as well as nine ball gowns, eleven pairs of boots, and six sets of lingerie. And that is just a partial list. "The rest of the trousseau was really quite amazing," said Marjorie. The previous summer Ella had brought Marjorie exquisite sets of lacy bridal lingerie from Paris. Her dresses were made in "miles and miles of handwork, either in embroidery [or] ruffles." To complement them was a collection of hats, trimmed in matching velvets, lace, and ostrich feathers.

The wedding was to take place on December 5 in the chapel of Manhattan's Grace Church, on a stately section of Broadway between

Tenth and Eleventh streets. The site was a sentimental choice. A century earlier the land had been owned by the Brevoorts, until Ed's great-great-grandfather had donated it for the church.

As the wedding date drew near, invitations were engraved by Tiffany with the names of the bride, the bridegroom, and Marjorie's parents. The formal display of unity was only superficial. In reality, there was little harmony between Ella and C.W.; Marjorie's parents had been wrangling about the wedding for months, particularly about who should attend. Deeply embittered over C.W.'s remarriage, Ella had refused to attend the ceremony if Leila was present. With equal vehemence, C.W. had threatened to boycott the wedding unless his new wife was included. As earlier in her youth, Marjorie found herself in the middle. Finally her parents conceded. Everyone, including Leila, agreed to attend the wedding and behave politely. There was to be no reception, merely the appearance of Marjorie, Ed, and Ella at the photographer's studio after the ceremony.

Other tensions helped shatter Marjorie's nuptial radiance. The night before the ceremony something happened that profoundly changed her life. During the wedding rehearsal, as Marjorie walked down the aisle, two women from the Close side sat gossiping in one of the pews. "Well, she's a cute little thing considering who she is and where she's from," one of the women declared in a loud, haughty voice. The words sliced through Marjorie like a razor. Emotions ripped through her in rapid succession: hurt, rage, and a determination to get even. "I'll show those SOB's if it takes me sixty years," she vowed. Someday the Four Hundred would know who Marjorie Merriweather Post was, and that her lifestyle and lineage were a force to be reckoned with.

(Decades later, over lunch in the orchid-lined sunroom of her Washington estate, Marjorie recounted the story to her son-in-law the actor-writer Cliff Robertson. As she did, she took an uncharacteristic sip of wine and placed the glass emphatically on the table. "And you know, Cliff"—she smiled with undisguised satisfaction—"it has taken me sixty years.")

The next day, December 5, 1905, at noon, "while the subdued harmonies of 'The Voice That Breathed O'er Eden' floated softly through the perfume laden atmosphere of Grace Church," C.W. gave Marjorie away. The ceremony, which was officiated by the Reverend W. P. Huntington, had only two attendants: Helen Hibbs, Marjorie's best friend from the Mount Vernon Seminary, and Harry Close, who served as Ed's best man. Among the guests were C.W., Ella, Aunt Mollie, Uncle

Cal, and Leila. The last of these, Marjorie noted years later, was be-decked in a hideous blue gown and was deliberately seated in the church "stuck off to one side."

Several gifts from C.W. arrived on the train for the honeymoon. The first was a letter dated December 2, 1905, notifying Marjorie that a hundred thousand dollars in bonds had been given her as a wedding present. The second was the keys to the newly completed Boulders, which was to become Marjorie and Ed's new home.

The third was a letter from C.W. that Marjorie kept with her private papers for the rest of her life.

Dear Little Sweetheart.
Well the small toddler that['s] been over the road so long with Daddy is now a grown woman and a small toddler no more. It natu-rally brings a tinge of sadness to realize that the little girl of the past with whom I had so many good times has faded into the past, but I am more than comforted with the splendid young woman grown from my small pal of years ago. Daddy feels well repaid for every effort he has made for you my sweet daughter and now I feel very sure you are going to be happily married and I find myself liking Ed as I would a boy of my own. Always remember that Daddy is somewhere around in call and that he loves you always very sweet daughter.
Yours Daddy.

C.W. had also given Ed a separate wedding check from "wife and I." Accompanying it was a terse note, with the plea for Ed to "Be tender and kind to my little girl. She is the only one I have. I have full confi-dence you will. With all best wishes, Yours Truly, C. W. Post."

The wedding photographs show Marjorie to have been a beautiful, if somewhat timid-looking, bride. Her satin wedding gown was laced with point d'angleterre and trailing orange blossoms and trimmed with a waist knot of rhinestones and pearls. Two wedding presents—diamond earrings from C.W. and a diamond sunburst necklace from Ed worn over a strand of pearls—framed Marjorie's face. Under the dress, just below her left knee, Marjorie wore a traditional blue garter. Above it, her lace-covered corset was trimmed in gold.

The day after the ceremony, newspapers across the country—among them, *The Washington Times, The Detroit News, The Chicago Chronicle, The New York Telegraph,* the *New York Sun,* and the *San Francisco Exam-iner*—hailed the wedding as one of the most important matches of the year. One New York newspaper predicted that after their honeymoon the Edward Closes "will occupy a prominent position in the younger married set for the bride is twice a millionaire in her own right and the bridegroom is a descendant of one of the oldest families in the metropolis." On December 6 *The New Yorker* magazine noted that "the bride, who has already attained a wide reputation for exquisite charm, is probably the richest young woman in the United States in her own right, and in addition to her dower of beauty, is worth $2,000,000. . . . She is as well known in London society as she is here. . . ."

By then the young couple were honeymooning at the fashionable Homestead Hotel in Hot Springs, Virginia. Four days after the ceremony the newlyweds had their first spat. With no warning, Ed suddenly announced that he wanted his bride to give up Christian Science and join him in worship at the Episcopalian church. Marjorie was astounded. During their courtship Ed had occasionally attended Christian Science services with Marjorie and Ella. He was thus well apprised of his bride's commitment to that denomination. "Well, I am very sorry, but I do not intend to do that," Marjorie retorted. "I will go to the Episcopal Church with you, if you wish . . . but you knew before you married me what my religion was and should not attempt to upset it."

Nevertheless, Ed continued to badger Marjorie about her faith. Her first husband, Marjorie said years later, was clearly discomforted by the unconventionality of Christian Science and believed that "traditional things"—and traditional religions—should be their way of life. Ed's plea for conformity was to become a resounding theme in the marriage, one against which Marjorie increasingly rebelled. In 1905 youthful love and sexual passion muted those tensions. Only gradually did Marjorie come to realize one of the paradoxes of romantic love: The very qualities that draw one to a mate—in this case Ed's stability and sense of propriety—often assume such overwhelming significance over time that they can become abhorrent to a lover.

Still, when Marjorie and Ed visited Aunt Mollie and Uncle Cal that Christmas in Battle Creek, they seemed like any other dewy-eyed newlywed couple. By late January the young Closes were on the road again—this time to Fort Worth with Leila and C.W. to visit Grandma and Grandpa Post. The journey had its own unique set of tensions, for it was Marjorie's first visit with Leila since her marriage to C.W. Discretion and good manners had been impressed—or, as Marjorie would put it, "drilled"—into her from an early age. Despite her resentments, despite the thousand-and-one annoyances of traveling with a detested companion, Marjorie managed to remain civil. And so, apparently, did Leila.

Years later Leila's nephew Kenneth Montgomery commented on the uneasiness of that relationship. "I'm sure both Leila and Marjorie were aware of that gulf between them. I never heard Leila talk unkindly of Marjorie or Marjorie speak unkindly of Leila, but I felt that both of them had no respect or good feeling for each other." Nevertheless, the 1906 Texas trip came off without incident.

As usual, the journey had been one of C.W.'s brainstorms, the first of many that were to keep him in a frenzy of activity that year. C.W. was still fascinated by Texas. For years he had contemplated creating a model community there, a kind of Postumville without the customs and constraints of a well-established city like Battle Creek. With Marjorie's marriage and a new son-in-law, C.W. now saw the potential to make that dream a reality. Although Ed was still untested, C.W. hoped to train his new son-in-law to relieve him of some of his responsibilities. Eventually, if the young man proved capable, he could even become heir to C.W.'s sprawling industrial empire.

By early 1906 C.W. had engaged a local expert to survey land sites in the Texas Panhandle. To secure the requisite acreage meant that he and Ed had to inspect lands in the backcountry as well. For C.W. a foray onto the prairies on a springboard wagon with mule teams and outriders was a nostalgic return to his youth. But not so for Ed Close. He was a city slicker, a tenderfoot. Even worse, he was so intrinsically civilized that he was almost an embarrassment. On an early leg of the journey, C.W. and Ed stayed in a crude cowboy shelter. That night Ed started to don a pair of pink silk pajamas but at the last moment, scrutinizing his grizzled companions, thought better of it. Another time he was seen dashing out of a privy after he met up with a rattlesnake.

One morning, on a side trip that included Marjorie and Leila, Ed spotted the chuck wagon. With enthusiasm he told his companions about a good place to sit and eat their meal. Before they had a chance to protest, Ed settled himself in the spot—and just as quickly rose with a howl. To the amusement of his companions, Marjorie's husband had seated himself upon a cushion cactus. "We were days pulling those needles out of him, he was in agony," Marjorie later recalled with a giggle. On that same trip Ed also suffered intestinal discomfort from drinking large quantities of gypsum water. One memorable night, a helpless Marjorie watched Ed sit doubled over in pain, moaning, "My God, this place will never be like New York. Why did I ever come out here?"

Soon even worse troubles befell the travelers. On that same side journey Ed, Marjorie, C.W., and Leila got caught in a blue norther and sought shelter in a two-room shack. That night, as the foursome huddled together for warmth in a large pile of cottonseed, their horses escaped. Sleepless and worried, they heard coyotes howling around them, and in the wee hours of the morning mice scuttled through the cabin, eating the last of their provisions.

To Ed's humiliation, when C.W.'s land agent, Tom Stevens, reported the storm to the *Fort Worth Star*, he said, "I never saw two gamer ladies in my life than Mrs. Post and Mrs. Close. They never once grumbled nor expressed a wish that they were at home." Significantly he said nothing about the presence—or attitude—of C.W.'s son-in-law, Ed Close.

Despite the personal mishaps, C.W. declared the trip a success. He had purchased 213,000 acres of land in Garza, Hockley, and Lynn counties, 250 miles west of Fort Worth. In Garza, Marjorie's father set aside a large tract of land for grazing cattle and named it the Double U Ranch. He instructed his western agents to map out a model town nearby that would have electricity, power, and a waterworks system. At the center of each 640-acre plot of land he placed four farmhouses that shared a common well. Pioneers were encouraged to buy their farms on the installment plan. Within a year C.W. would pay for the Santa Fe Railroad to run a right-of-way through the town. Fittingly, the entrepreneur named his model community Post.

From the start C.W. knew that any newcomer—especially one forced to ride several hundred miles into the backcountry—was likely to have difficulty on the frontier. Consequently, C.W. had been patient; at times he, like Marjorie, had even felt pity for his hapless son-in-law. Still, the trip had given him a sobering new perspective. Ed was a reasonably good athlete, he was a fine hunter and rider, but he had no flair for frontier life. In all likelihood he would not be heavily involved in the supervision of Post. Yet Ed's bright mind, fine legal background, and willingness to please led C.W. to hope that his son-in-law was still a strong candidate for the presidency of the Postum Cereal Company.

C.W. had comparably high, if dramatically different, expectations for Marjorie. After the Texas trip she and Ed had settled at The Boulders in

Greenwich. For any eighteen-year-old girl the management of a two-wing eleven-bedroom mansion would have been daunting, but for Marjorie, who had not lived in one place for more than a few months at a time since childhood, the responsibility was awesome. "It was an enormous house that rather scared me," Marjorie later admitted. C.W. knew this. He nevertheless insisted that it was time for Marjorie to assume responsibility. Now that she was a married woman, it was her duty to manage her household in an astute and economical fashion. The young matron, like Ed Close, needed training.

Accordingly, C.W. hired an experienced housekeeper to instruct Marjorie in the rudiments of home management. The housekeeper was to stay for only six months, during which time she was to teach Marjorie about the laundry, shopping, kitchen supervision, and management of a large staff. To run The Boulders, C.W. had already hired a cook, maids, butlers, a laundress, a coachman, and garden workers. Because the new house needed landscaping, C.W. also engaged fifty garden workers to plant flowers, vegetables, and trees and to create a nine-hole golf course.

The heiress was overwhelmed by her duties, particularly the prospect of paying her employees. To her, it seemed that C.W. had "just dumped that in my lap and said, 'Here, Marjorie, you tend to that. These workmen had to be paid every week, and I want an account and it's got to be balanced at the end of summer.' " The responsibility was almost more than Marjorie could stand. The usually levelheaded young woman became nervous and frazzled. Between lessons in the kitchen, the laundry, the parlor, and the garden, she lost twenty-five pounds.

C.W. demanded that Marjorie divide her allowance in thirds. One portion was to go for the operation and maintenance of The Boulders; another third was for clothes, presents, and personal items; the last third was to be invested. To comply with her father's plan, Marjorie was to keep strict records in a ledger.

In September 1906, Marjorie anxiously handed over her account book to C.W. There was good reason for her anxiety: Try as she might, the accounts were off by four cents. After a quick perusal, C.W. refused to accept it: The account ledger had to be perfect, or it was not satisfactory. If it was off by four cents one year, could it not be off by four dollars or forty dollars—or four thousand dollars—another year? With gritted teeth, Marjorie returned to the books. Finally, she found the error. Thereafter her bookkeeping was painstaking, a quality the heiress

demanded from her own financial experts when she became independent.

At the time of its completion The Boulders was already considered one
of Greenwich's most beautiful and romantic houses. At one side of the
entranceway was a large medieval-looking stone tower. As guests
passed it, they rode down a long gravel driveway and then over a small
bridge to the front of the house. A giant veranda wrapped the fieldstone
mansion. Green-and-white-striped awnings framed its windows. Inside
were many rooms: seven bedrooms on the second floor, four on the
third, and separate suites for Marjorie and Ed and for C.W. Downstairs
was a spacious living room with a cathedral ceiling, a large fireplace,
and a double stairway; adjoining it was a dining room with blue velvet
walls and highback armchairs. The entire house had a dark Victorian
elegance reminiscent of the Post Tavern.

C.W.'s wing had a special flavor of its own, containing stylish Mission furniture made from dark oak and rich Spanish leather trimmed
with bronze-head nails.

In contrast, Marjorie's quarters were light and airy and painted in
pastels. To fit her feminine style, the heiress's bedroom had Louis XVI
furniture made from pinewood and mahogany inlaid with mother-of-
pearl. Above Marjorie's bed the ceiling was painted as pink and blue sky
and trimmed in flowered garlands. Throughout her life, no matter how
ponderous or formal the parlors and dining rooms were in her various
estates, Marjorie's private quarters were decorated in soft pastels, with
embellished woodwork and French furniture.

Despite the grandeur of The Boulders, Marjorie soon discovered that
there was nothing more lonely than a large empty house. After the
Texas journey Ed decided to set up a law practice in Manhattan with his
friend Henry Spaulding. The resulting commute by train and long
hours at work left Marjorie alone from dawn to dusk. At nights, especially on the weekends, the newlyweds filled their house with company,
but during the days Marjorie grew restless. To improve herself, Marjorie
studied art and architecture courses at a nearby private school called
Rosemary Hall.

The young Mrs. Close also looked up an old cousin named Julia Van
Tassel. The widow, formerly a teacher at a Hudson Valley private
school, agreed to tutor the heiress in two disciplines: art history and
mnemonics. Over the years Mrs. Van Tassel had devised an elaborate
memory association system using sounds, ideas, and the concepts of

opposites and similarities. Marjorie studied this system conscientiously. "That course stood by me in the most wonderful way," the heiress said when in her late seventies. "I have a filing system up in [my head]."

Those who knew Marjorie as an adult were often awed by her memory. "She knew everything she had in the house," said Jim Griffin, Jr., the superintendent of the 115-room Mar-A-Lago. "I don't know how, but she did, and if something wasn't put back in the right place, she would notice it."

Marjorie also had an uncanny ability to remember things that were important to people—not only their names but their interests. Once when the duke and duchess of Windsor were attending a party at Mar-A-Lago, Marjorie took aside her South American friend Gladys Heurtematte. "Gladys, please speak Spanish to the duke, and dance the paso doble with him. He loves it," she said. Dutifully Gladys followed Marjorie's instructions and led the duke out on the dancing floor. By the end of the hour the duke was beaming.

Another time, when Admiral Ray Hunter appeared at Hillwood for a formal dinner and stopped to admire the orchids in the foyer, Marjorie promised to introduce him to her gardener. Then she whisked him into the drawing room to meet her guests. A few days later Marjorie called the admiral and informed him that her gardener was at his disposal for lessons on orchid growing.

By the fall of 1907 Ed Close had become lukewarm about practicing law. C.W., sensing his son-in-law's ambivalence, now convinced him to come to Battle Creek to learn the cereal business. As an incentive, C.W. made Ed assistant treasurer of the Postum Cereal Company. At first Marjorie and Ed rented the old Hinman house in Battle Creek before buying a house of their own at 285 Maple Avenue. The new home, just a few doors away from Aunt Mollie and Uncle Cal, was a gracious three-story mansion with a forty-foot living room, decorative plasterwork ceilings, and a third-floor ballroom. While not as imposing as The Boulders, where Marjorie and Ed still spent the summer months, the Maple Street house was one of the most elegant in Battle Creek.

No sooner had the young couple settled than Marjorie invited the Postum Cereal Company treasurer, Marshall K. Howe, and his wife for dinner. For days before the dinner Marjorie's inexperience and desire to impress Ed's boss favorably made her edgy. Finally, on the designated day, the heiress's Irish maid, Margaret, assured her that everything was in order. The first course was well received. But just as Margaret appeared with the turkey, she dropped it with a terrible crash. Marjorie barely looked up from her plate. "I could have gone through the floor," she recalled.

After cleaning up the mess, Margaret reappeared and briskly announced, "Madam, I am serving the other turkey." It took all of Marjorie's self-control to nod her approval. "Of course, I knew damn well there was only one turkey"—Marjorie laughed years later—"so she brush[ed] it off and served it."

In reality, C.W.'s daughter was already becoming an accomplished hostess. Within a few months of her arrival in Battle Creek, Marjorie had begun to entertain her old Battle Creek friends with the artistry and aplomb that became her social signature. On Valentine's Day 1907 the heiress hosted a luncheon for twelve friends in a room that had been festooned in ribbons and red roses and made to resemble a candy box. The next day she held a second luncheon for another twenty guests. "Mrs. Close," a local newspaper duly noted, "is a popular lady among her circle [since] having taken up a residence here."

By 1908 it was obvious that Ed Close was not likely to follow in his father-in-law's footsteps as head of the Postum Cereal Company empire. There is no doubt that C.W. was an exacting employer. For any young man, he would have been a tough act to follow. Temperamentally Ed lacked a certain dynamic spark that C.W. felt should be essential in his successor, a consuming flame that, by 1908, was becoming increasingly indispensable to the ovens of the Postum Cereal Company. By 1908 there were dozens of breakfast food companies in Battle Creek. A new competitive threat had also arrived in the person of W. K. Kellogg, who, two years earlier, having finally broken away from his brother, was now successfully marketing his flaked grains under the auspices of the new Battle Creek Toasted Corn Flake Company.

In 1907 and 1908, C.W. and several of his Postum products also became the subject of a number of national controversies. The trouble began with C.W.'s new cornflake product, Elijah's Manna. To illustrate the trade name, C.W. had placed on the carton a picture of the prophet Elijah. A raven, perched upon his shoulder, dropped cornflakes into the prophet's hand. In pulpits across the country, the clergy denounced C.W.'s packaging, condemning the cereal as a "sacrilege" and an exploitation of the Bible. In Britain a law was even passed banning the import of Elijah's Manna. As usual, C.W. tried to defend himself in print. "Perhaps no one should eat Angel cake, empty Adams' Ale, live in St.

Paul, nor work for Bethlehem Steel," he railed. But the industrialist's words were ignored. Somehow, Elijah's Manna had become a symbol of sacrilege, a contemptuous parody of the sacred wafer and of all things holy. By 1908 a chastised C.W. was forced to recall his flaked cereal.

Soon thereafter he reintroduced the product as Post Toasties. This time there was no chance his cereal could offend. On the cover of Post Toasties was the demure picture of Cinderella, sitting by a fireplace with a black cat, a teakettle, a cream pitcher, and a few scattered cereal flakes. The new merchandising paid off even better than C.W. had anticipated. By September 1909 Post Toasties was producing over $2 million in profits a year, compared with $1.7 million for Grape-Nuts and $1.4 million for Postum.

C.W.'s difficulties with Elijah's Manna coincided with other, even more nettlesome publicity, this time an accusation from *Collier's* magazine that several cereal companies—especially Postum—had advertised in an unethical manner. For years, *Collier's* wrote, Grape-Nuts ads had claimed that the cereal cured many stomach and intestinal ailments, including appendicitis. A July 27, 1907, *Collier's* editorial entitled "Futility" noted that such ads were "lying and potentially deadly lying. . . . Similarly Postum continually makes reference to the endorsements of a 'distinguished physician' or a 'prominent health official,' persons as mythical, doubtless, as they are mysterious."

In defense, C.W. placed ads in other periodicals accusing *Collier's* of coercion. Those allegations, he countered, were revenge for his failure to advertise in *Collier's*. "When a journal wilfully prostitutes its columns to try and harm a reputable manufacturer to force him to advertise, it is time the public knew the facts." In response, *Collier's* sued C.W. for $750,000 for libel. Marjorie's father responded with his own libel countersuit. The controversy dragged on for years. Finally, in 1912, the case was heard in the appellate division of the Supreme Court of New York, after which a new trial was ordered. In 1913 the case was decided in C.W.'s favor. But the damage to his family could not be repaired.

The turbulent storm that broke over the Postum Cereal Company coincided with Ed and Marjorie's trial residence in Battle Creek and fairly washed them out. The outburst over Elijah's Manna, C.W.'s battles against organized labor, and the *Collier's* accusations were too much heavy water for a conservative like Ed Close to contemplate swimming against as a permanent career. By late 1907 the young attorney had lost all interest in becoming heir to the Postum Cereal Company presidency.

In early 1908 Marjorie and Ed made a momentous decision. Within a few weeks they would pull up roots in Battle Creek and return to live at The Boulders, independent of C.W. and the personal agenda he had hoped to set for their lives.

7

"It Wasn't Done
That Way"

*M*arjorie returned to The Boulders as an accomplished matron. In Battle Creek she had learned to entertain with style. She had become a strict manager of household finances. She had supervised a staff of servants with confidence. And in July 1908 she was to become a mother.

The event was eagerly awaited by everyone in Marjorie's family—Ed, C.W., Ella, Aunt Mollie, Uncle Cal, and the Post grandparents. Although Ella's own health was none too vigorous, she immediately rushed to Marjorie's side to be with her through the pregnancy.

There could not have been a more picturesque setting to await a first birth than The Boulders. By the time Marjorie and Ed returned to Greenwich, the mansion had been fully landscaped. A nine-hole golf course stretched over a hilly expanse of lawn. There were magnificent flower gardens. In the summer months a striped canvas tent was pitched on the grounds and filled with wicker furniture, and there Marjorie and Ed relaxed. Best of all for the pregnant Marjorie was the roaring brook that ran through the property and culminated beneath her window in a "marvelous waterfall" that kept her bedroom cool and airy.

On July 26, 1908, Marjorie went into labor. A few days earlier C.W. had arrived—without Leila—at The Boulders to await the birth of his first grandchild. In the first stages of labor Ella and a doctor were with the mother-to-be, but at the last moment a panting Marjorie called for her father. Trembling, C.W. consented to sit by his daughter's bed as Marjorie delivered a perfectly formed baby girl. During labor she squeezed C.W.'s hand so hard and exerted so much pressure upon his ring that his fingers began to bleed. The industrialist barely noticed. C.W. was so overcome watching the birth that he declared no one should ever have to bring forth human life. Though a confirmed teetotaler, the shaken C.W. then walked into the library and downed a shot of whiskey.

The new baby was named Adelaide Brevoort Close after one of Ed's cousins. From the beginning Marjorie was a proud and attentive mother, who routinely brought guests into the nursery to peek at the sleeping infant. She was so starry-eyed about having a girl, so filled with fantasies of mother-daughter ruffles and bows, that before Adelaide was two months old she hired an expensive New York photographer to take pictures of the two of them. To Marjorie's dismay, the pictures came out poorly. From his new home in Santa Barbara, California, C.W. advised her that next time she "had better patronize a moderate priced local photographer and don't attempt anything elaborate."

Despite her attachment to little Adelaide, Marjorie was not by disposition an "intimate" mother, the kind who enjoyed tending an infant's every need at all hours of the day and night. She had, in fact, little inclination in that direction with any of her children and was better at mothering them when they were past the diapers-and-bedtime-story stage. "Mom was wonderful when you got to be thirteen. But no good with little kids," said her youngest daughter, Dina Merrill. "I mean, I don't ever remember her reading me a bedtime story or anything like that. . . . But she would take me on a tour of the museum or the art gallery and teach me things."

In the pre–World War I era, there was nothing unusual about that attitude. At the time of Adelaide's birth, there was, particularly among the wealthy, plenty of support for that distanced approach. Youngsters were supposed to be seen and not heard; if they got noisy or disruptive, they were whisked away by nannies and governesses.

The diapering and feeding were done by a professional baby nurse. Just before her delivery Marjorie had hired a slightly stout, kindly-faced southern woman named Virginia Penn Pearson—or Pearcie, as she was fondly called. From the start Pearcie was a warm and comforting presence, the kind of nurse who reassured the anxious young mother and insisted that she get some sleep so that she could quickly regain her strength.

After the initial postpartum period Marjorie considered the idea of giving Pearcie up and having Adelaide raised by other members of her staff. To retain Pearcie meant still another salary to be supported out of the monthly household budget. But Marjorie had already become inordinately fond of Pearcie; the woman was smart, efficient, and loving. Moreover, she was from an educated and well-to-do southern family. When Pearcie was a young woman, her fiancé had died, leaving her with a strong, unfulfilled maternal streak. In the end the heiress decided Pearcie would stay on and become a permanent member of the Close family.

On September 6, 1908, C.W. wrote Marjorie applauding her decision. "I [am] glad you have decided to keep Miss Pearson. I think the money well invested. It would be wise to do this even if you felt that you had to cut off something else." Within a few months Marjorie was glad she had kept Pearcie. Little Adelaide was thriving, and Marjorie was once again pregnant.

When Adelaide was a year old, Marjorie hosted a birthday party in her daughter's honor. Being a celebration for a baby, it was a luncheon for young women and their children. By July 1909 Greenwich had become a bucolic haven for millionaires and their families. Many of them had fled New York for a cleaner, more comfortable existence in Connecticut, where they built country estates modeled on the grand palaces of Europe. With them, with their chauffeurs, maids, and automobiles, with their packing trunks to Saratoga, Newport, and the Continent, had come a patrician fondness for entertainment. In good weather there was tennis, golf, and hunting; for the cultured, there were exhibitions of music, dance, and art. At every season there were rounds of luncheons, parties, and balls to be attended in formal dress that were duly reported in Greenwich social columns.

Five months later Marjorie gave birth to another daughter, whom she and Ed named Eleanor Post Close. Initially the infant seemed healthy and vibrant, but within ten days she fell ill with pneumonia. Marjorie grew frantic, especially when, on the night that the baby passed through the crisis of the fever, Ed was out with friends. By Christmas little Eleanor had recovered and was beginning to grow. From Battle Creek C.W. wrote a relieved Marjorie a solicitous letter.

. . . It beats H——— a mile that the little cub should have pneumonia with all the care for warmth, food, attention, and everything else.

One thing you want to remember always and that is, so long as you do the best you can . . . you can sit back and . . . and let the big power do the rest of the work. I am very glad . . . that the baby is better and getting along. I hope this start off in the world will give her a right to a long life of comfort.

You know it's a little like playing a game of cards. Sometimes those who don't win very fast in the start come on the big winners at the end.

The same might have been said of Marjorie's first foray into Greenwich society. During her first years at The Boulders, Marjorie felt decidedly out of place. Although she was naturally outgoing, she had only a few good friends in the community. In contrast, Ed knew many people from the childhood summers he had spent in Greenwich with whom he still hunted or played tennis and golf. Marjorie did not approve. In fact, she did not like most of them. To her way of thinking, Ed's friends were a fast, sporty crowd with whom she had nothing in common. Her chief complaint was that they drank too much. At dinners Marjorie was often appalled at the amount of liquor they consumed and their tipsy behavior.

Above all, she railed against Ed's own drinking habits, which despite his vehement protests to the contrary, she believed excessive. At first Ed's friends disparaged Marjorie's attitude. "Come on," they'd coax her at dinners and balls, "oh, don't be a pussyfoot." Although Marjorie still practiced Christian Science, she was not an orthodox worshiper, and for the sake of being polite, she sipped liquor at parties. When Ed's friends pressured Marjorie to drink, the results were disastrous; invariably she became dizzy or sick to her stomach.

"Well, that kind of thing disgusted me," she told an interviewer years later. In retrospect, Marjorie observed that in spite of her far-flung travels with C.W. to some of the most sophisticated resorts in the world, she had been sheltered from seeing the effects of alcohol upon respectable men and women. That protection was probably deliberate. While C.W. was no longer a strict follower of Christian Science, he continued to believe in Mary Baker Eddy's assertion in *Science and Health* that "Drugs, Cataplasmas, and whiskey are stupid substitutes for the dignity and potency of divine Mind and its efficacy to heal."

The result, as Marjorie later observed, was that she had "never seen a man under the influence of liquor except a tramp at a circus until I saw my husband drunk. . . ." When that happened in the early years of her marriage, Marjorie became hysterical. "I was so mad—I was for leaving—I was going to walk straight out."

Coincidentally Helen Hibbs, Marjorie's friend from the Mount Vernon Seminary, was visiting at the time. Because her own father had been a heavy drinker, Helen felt herself in a position to give Marjorie some advice. Patience, Helen urged Marjorie, was the only solution. She simply had to take a more philosophical attitude toward Ed's drinking. "You've just got to adjust yourself," Helen insisted. But Marjorie was inconsolable. "I'll never do it," she snapped at her friend.

Half a century later Adelaide and Eleanor refuted the idea that their father ever abused alcohol. Their feeling was that their mother had been inappropriately priggish. "It made an exaggerated impression on her for the very simple reason that she had been brought up by a father who never drank and by very pious grandparents," said Eleanor. "She did not have the circle of friends that one would have in Long Island or Greenwich."

Nevertheless, Marjorie upheld the vow she once made to Helen Hibbs. Throughout her long and well-traveled life, throughout the years spent hobnobbing with industrialists, military men, diplomats, and royalty, Marjorie adamantly refused to tolerate the heavy consumption of liquor. Although she was not a teetotaler like C.W., she remained skeptical about the virtues of alcohol. At the most Marjorie sipped a glass of whiskey at parties—for "medicinal purposes," she often said—but never more than one drink.

Nor did the heiress tolerate guests who became drunk at her parties. Should someone become inebriated, Marjorie coolly instructed her butler to show that person the door. If the drunk lacked a chauffeur of his own, the hostess made sure that he was driven home by hers. "Mrs. Post was not overly fond of liquor and people who drank to excess," observed Dick Pearson, a National Geographic Society executive and a frequent guest at Marjorie's home. One of the hallmarks of a Post party was a "very limited cocktail period of approximately half an hour before dinner. Of course, wine was served with dinner, but the glasses were not constantly filled." Those who were veteran guests at a Marjorie Merriweather Post party and wanted to imbibe learned to save their heavy drinking for after hours. At eleven o'clock, when Mrs. Post's parties ended, they drove into Palm Beach or downtown Washington, D.C., to visit a local cocktail lounge or bar.

· · ·

Gradually other tensions strained the marriage. Among them was Ed's disapproval of Marjorie's tendencies to give opulent parties, to dress in certain high-style clothes, and to accept—or decline—invitations to certain affairs. The particular issues varied, but Ed's response was always the same. "It wasn't done that way," he repeatedly—and eventually wearily—explained to his eager, fun-loving wife. This argument, which began with Ed's objection to Marjorie's devotion to Christian Science, gradually became a sore point in the marriage.

Initially the fact that Marjorie and Ed came from two different worlds had been part of their attraction. But now that Marjorie was firmly transplanted onto Greenwich soil, old-family principles and the brash glitter of new money created a clash of values.

Privately Marjorie also grumbled that Ed did not pay enough attention to young Adelaide and Eleanor. Long after their marriage had ended, Marjorie claimed that she was not even sure that Ed had ever really wanted children. Her husband was almost obsessively social and so tied to his friends that he spent many evenings away from The Boulders. Even when he was at home, he seldom played with Adelaide and Eleanor. "I would be flabbergasted at the way he would come home from business at night and walk right by their playrooms, come to see me and never pay any attention to them," said Marjorie. In contrast, she watched their uncle Harry—who had long since returned from Alaska and lived nearby—play with her daughters for hours on end.

Despite growing resentments, Ed was passionately in love with Marjorie. Long after their parents divorced, the Close daughters believed their father remained enamored of Marjorie. "He was madly in love with Mother even when he married [again]," said Adelaide. "When Mother divorced E.F. [Hutton], my sister had one heck of a time stopping him from hopping a boat and coming home."

Somehow the marriage hobbled along, helped by the inevitable distractions of running a large house, caring for small children, and socializing in Greenwich. To their neighbors the Closes seemed the epitome of glamour. Ed, who had returned to law practice in Manhattan, was widely regarded as a model of patrician propriety. He was, as Greenwich native Bruce Finch observed, "a very good mixer and very proud of his Greenwich ancestry." And for all her midwestern origins, Marjorie was admired as an exquisitely beautiful, stylish young matron who lived in a glamorous house on "the ridge."

In keeping with their position, the Closes joined the elite clubs that appeared simultaneously with the development of Greenwich's newest properties in the Rock Ridge and Belle Haven sections. By 1910 Ed had become a member of the civic group known as the Edgewood Association. That same year, when the Field Club opened a clubhouse on Lake Avenue for tennis, Ed and Marjorie signed up. A year later the Closes joined the Greenwich Country Club shortly after it had raised its own new building.

During that same era Marjorie first became involved in community charities. By 1911 she was head of the advertisement committee for the First Charity Ball held at the Armory for the United Workers of Greenwich. This was the first record of many similar committees upon which Marjorie served to benefit the aged, the infirm, and the poor. Two years later Marjorie became treasurer of a "Kirmess Historic Pageant," another fund-raiser organized to support the preservation of Greenwich's historic Putnam Cottage.

Like C.W., Marjorie had always believed that the best charity was one that enabled the needy to help themselves. Although she continued to subscribe to that notion, the Greenwich years broadened Marjorie's attitude. She began to realize from her work on the First Charity Ball, which had raised four thousand dollars for the destitute, that sometimes people were too disabled to help themselves. In such cases, direct contributions—rather than subsidies or "hidden" aid—were necessary. Nevertheless, in that rosy prewar period, Marjorie's philanthropic acts remained conventionally group-oriented; there was nothing to suggest that her future munificence would become so unique that newspapers like *The New York Times* and *The Washington Post* as well as the *Congressional Record* would characterize her as a "philanthropist," a "lady bountiful," a "truly noble aristocrat," or a "truly grand and gentle lady."

Another paradox was Marjorie's photographs from the era, which showed little hint of the fame she later attained as one of the world's most glamorous women. To her casual companions, she was an admittedly lovely but nevertheless conventional-looking Greenwich matron in lacy frocks and stiff ball gowns who often posed with her little girls in look-alike dresses. In the prewar years it would have been hard to imagine that the young Marjorie was destined for anything other than a cozy domesticity and a bland maturity in the outposts of metropolitan New York.

Only a few who knew Marjorie well realized that beneath her well-manicured veneer was a woman of unusual vigor. Hunter Marston recalled that he met the Closes through Adelaide McAlpin, who was Ed's second cousin. From Hunter's perspective, Ed and Marjorie were a decidedly mismatched couple. "He [Ed] was a very good-natured person. A gracious fellow, but no originality," said Hunter. "[L]ike a good many fellows married to extremely intelligent women, Ed . . . let Marjorie carry on the full responsibility of everything. . . . She had the ability and the drive to go forward. . . . Ed was just as pleased to let it be that way because he then wouldn't have to bother to make up his mind about anything."

But in The Boulders years that ability was often stalled. There was nowhere for Marjorie to go and use her extraordinary energy except within Greenwich. Occasionally there were glimpses of another existence, another life that beckoned to Marjorie with the excitement and verve she craved, in cities she visited like Palm Beach and Manhattan. Typically her visits to those towns were brief and limited to Ed's social circle. The situation only fed, rather than relieved, Marjorie's sense of stasis.

In 1909 Marjorie made her first trip to Palm Beach. That year and for the next five or six winters, Ed, Marjorie, the Marstons, and other friends rented a seaside cottage together. In that era Palm Beach, the barrier island on Florida's eastern coast, was, like Greenwich, just beginning to acquire a reputation as a playground for the wealthy.

Seventeen years earlier railroad king Henry Flagler had chopped trees and cleared lands for a railroad that ran from Jacksonville to Miami. Then he built a giant luxury hotel in Palm Beach called the Royal Poinciana, a mammoth white-framed building with 1,081 guest rooms that were decorated in white and green. For the hefty sum of one hundred dollars a day, wealthy guests like the Vanderbilts, the Astors, and the Goulds enjoyed sumptuous food, drink, and service in a balmy, semitropical setting. So enthusiastic was the response to the Royal Poinciana that Flagler was soon building other luxury hotels, the most famous of which was a U-shaped five-story structure known as The Breakers.

By the turn of the century other developers were erecting elite homes and cottages in Palm Beach as well. When Marjorie and Ed first arrived in Palm Beach in 1909, they found a small beach colony that stretched lazily across the shoreline near the Flagler hotels. Whatever roads existed on the barrier island were unpaved and dusty; the shops were modest and the restaurants few. In keeping with Flagler's original plan,

Palm Beach was a discreet luxury resort. The vast majority of the commercial activity, and the houses of the black population that served the resort, were to be restricted to the other side of Lake Worth in what was called West Palm Beach.

In contrast with bustling contemporary Palm Beach, the resort was still very much an island in 1909, connected by a single railroad bridge. The only way tourists and workers could gain access was by boat across Lake Worth or by train over the bridge. In 1909 there were no cars, horses, or carriages on the island. To travel locally, guests were transported by wheelchairs, or "Afro-mobiles," which were pushed by black valets. "One got about the Beach area on his two feet, the wheelchairs, or the bicycles," recalled Marjorie.

The first trips with the Marstons were filled with more urbane pleasures: sunbathing, fishing, and visiting friends in the houseboats that were docked along the beach. Occasionally, after dinner there would be memorable midnight excursions by wheelchair through the jungle trails where the mosquitoes were so large they "would practically carry us off alive." The wildness of Palm Beach, its insect-infested climate, and the lack of a nearby hospital made it impractical for Marjorie and Ed to bring their daughters with them, and their visits lasted only a few weeks.

Even so, the silvery days spent at Palm Beach made a permanent impression upon Marjorie. Here was a breathtaking stretch of the ocean, as raw and open as the society of the old West, that was already attracting a population of new-breed millionaires. An idea began to take shape in Marjorie's mind. Would this not be an ideal place to establish a winter home far from the tyranny of the old East? A place where Marjorie could put her unique mark on a mansion? Would it not be a community where the young heiress could do as she pleased, dress with the panache she longed for, or entertain as splendidly as her imagination demanded? Since Palm Beach traditions were not yet set in stone, the words "It wasn't done that way" were irrelevant.

Between 1912 and 1914 two events forced Marjorie to tuck away her role as the coddled daughter of millionaire parents. On October 22, 1912. she received a telegram from Washington, D.C., that her mother had died in her sleep.

The night before her death the sixty-two-year-old Ella Post had attended the theater with her friend Mrs. Joseph Brechens. The next morning, when Mrs. Brechens had gone into Ella's bedroom to announce breakfast, she found her friend dead. Although Ella had died of natural causes, Marjorie always blamed C.W. for her mother's untimely death. "She always said it was from a broken heart," recalled Marjorie's daughter Eleanor.

A numb Marjorie rushed to Washington to make arrangements for Ella's funeral and subsequent burial in Springfield, Illinois. From Chicago, Aunt Mollie wired Marjorie: "Shocked. Hear your mother[']s going away. Do you want me." The words were not a euphemism, but rather a reflection of the Christian Science belief in the immortality of the soul.

Ella's death, as a somber C.W. later wrote Marjorie in a letter, was a reminder "that we are and in part of a great and kind Power, of which our knowledge is but little."

Nineteen months later, on May 9, 1914, Marjorie received another shattering telegram. That morning at ten in Santa Barbara, California, C.W. had died without warning. At twenty-seven years of age, Marjorie was to inherit the Postum Cereal Company.

8

The Postum Cereal
Company Heiress

*T*he truth was that C.W. had not died of natural causes. On Saturday morning, May 9, 1914, the sixty-year-old entrepreneur had penned a letter to Marjorie and Leila at his Santa Barbara home. Then C.W. had dressed in his best clothes, lain upon his bed, put a rifle in his mouth, and pulled the trigger.

The newspapers offered various theories for the suicide. *The Los Angeles Herald*, recalling that C.W. had spoken of those who killed themselves as "cowards," thought he was temporarily deranged. Others noted that he had recently become jittery over his health. *The Battle Creek Journal* reported that C.W.'s private-duty nurse said he had been recently suffering from "extreme nervousness" and a "suicidal mania."

Whatever finally pushed C.W. over the edge seems to have been related to the return of his old stomach troubles. To those not intimately acquainted with the industrialist, C.W. seemed a healthy man. He had, after all, created a cereal empire on the principles of eating sensibly to maintain good health. Moreover, his flamboyant public appearances in Congress and in the press had made him a celebrated symbol of vibrancy, a feisty champion of national causes, living proof that Post products kept people on the "Road to Wellville."

In reality, C.W. had never fully conquered his digestive difficulties, which had continued to wax and wane throughout the years. By December 1913 C.W.'s stomach problems had grown so severe that he was forced to cancel a speech he was to make in Philadelphia against

Woodrow Wilson and the new income-tax amendment. The attack was a humbling defeat for C.W. Despite his brilliant efforts to create foods to aid the digestive system, his body had betrayed him. And so, ultimately, would his spirit.

That winter the mercurial millionaire's health, and his moods, began to fluctuate as wildly as they had some twenty-three years earlier, when he first arrived in Battle Creek. With characteristic resolve, C.W. refused invasive medical treatments. His objections, Marjorie later recalled, had less to do with his erstwhile devotion to Christian Science than with a morbid fear of surgery. "He'd have one attack after another and he was scared to death of an operation because he studied medicine for two years so he was petrified of what they'd do to him," explained Marjorie.

By March 1, 1914, C.W.'s doctors were convinced that he was suffering from appendicitis. Since he refused to be operated upon by anyone but the Mayo brothers, C.W. was rushed across country with Leila by private Pullman to the famous clinic. The frantic rail trip of March 2–5 broke speed records from Santa Barbara to Rochester, Minnesota, and attracted so much attention that the newspapers churned out stories about C.W.'s trip as "a race against death."

By March 10 the Mayo brothers had successfully operated on the millionaire for "chronic stomach trouble" and appendicitis. At C.W.'s request, Marjorie, who had hurried north from Palm Beach, was present at the operation. A half century later she recalled how the Mayo brothers had shown her C.W.'s appendix: sixteen inches long and "the worst looking thing you've ever seen."

With the successful conclusion of that surgery, C.W.'s anxieties abated. By mid-April he had returned to Santa Barbara with Leila to recuperate. From there he had cheerfully written Dr. Charles Mayo that he was "in the best of spirits" and apparently considered himself on the road to complete recovery. But within a matter of days C.W. was again uneasy about his health. His emotional condition was eerily reminiscent of the "nervousness" he had suffered two decades earlier. As Dr. Charles Mayo noted in a subsequent United Press International account of C.W.'s suicide, the industrialist seemed to him to be a man of "sudden impulses."

According to family legend, C.W. became morbidly depressed because he was convinced that he had the one disease he had worked all his life to prevent: inoperable stomach cancer. If so, it was predictable that C.W. would not wait passively for his own end. In death, as in life, the industrialist insisted upon shaping his own destiny.

Just before his death C.W. left Marjorie and Leila a letter with an oblique explanation for his suicide.

> Forgive me dear Leila and Marjorie if any sentiment I have expressed is not in harmony with your own convictions.
> I had to give vent to pent up feelings—
> So I *talked* with our dear son—he seemed so near, and perhaps suggested or helped me.
> Oh! happy soul!
> So free from earth's
> Grandeur and suffering.

The news of C.W.'s death pierced Marjorie to the very marrow of her bones. Woodenly the twenty-seven-year-old heiress went through the rituals of the funeral. For the second time in two months Marjorie boarded a train north, this time with her husband, to Battle Creek. Simultaneously, in Santa Barbara, C.W.'s corpse was laid in a private railroad car called the *Lecompton* and began the journey east with Leila and other mourners. This time there was no need for a rapid passage. At Albuquerque, C.W.'s brother Carroll and a key employee named Henry C. Hawk met the funeral train and accompanied it to Battle Creek.

In preparation for the funeral, the city had been draped in black. By the afternoon of May 11, 1914, all traffic had ceased as pallbearers carried C.W.'s coffin into the Battle Creek Independent Congregational Church. Since dawn many citizens, some of them still weeping, had waited outside the church in hopes of attending C.W.'s funeral. The newspapers later reported that about twelve hundred people attended the service. Among them were manufacturers and business representatives from various parts of the country who had known C.W. through his political leadership, advertising campaigns, and national lobbying efforts. In addition, one thousand Postum employees served as the honor guard for C.W.'s funeral.

One of the attendees was C.W.'s first Postum employee, the aged Shorty Bristol, who, poignantly, wanted so desperately to attend that he had been transported by carriage from a sickbed to the church. Other admirers remembered C.W. in death with the same flamboyance that had characterized his life. Hundreds of telegrams and letters arrived expressing sympathy; there were also dozens of floral arrangements—several of monumental size—sent from around the country. Some of the arrangements stood eight feet long, including one that was a casket cover containing five hundred American Beauty roses.

The funeral was conducted by the Reverend George E. Barnes, and a eulogy given by a distant cousin of C.W.'s, the Reverend Rosewell O. Post. Afterward throngs of mourners walked from the church to Battle Creek's Oak Hill Cemetery, where C.W. was laid to rest in a temporary mausoleum until his final resting place—a massive gray granite monument that still dominates Oak Hill—could be prepared.

Newspaper accounts reflect the profound sense of sorrow over C.W.'s death that affected the residents of Battle Creek. Marjorie's father was one of the city's most beloved citizens, a dreamer who had left a unique mark upon Battle Creek, an inventor whose genius spawned a new national industry that brought the city unbounded prosperity at the dawn of the twentieth century. It was little wonder that his death kindled communal mourning. As one reporter wrote, "In the portentous hush of a Mayday noon hour, under skies that beamed brightness, but reflected not the broken spirit of a grief-stricken population, into the midst of a waiting throng of thousands with saddened faces and tear-dimmed eyes, Charles W. Post, Battle Creek's foremost citizen and the man who for years had been such a tremendous factor in the commercial importance and upbuilding of the community, returned home today."

Other accounts portrayed depths of sorrow that sound akin to what many Americans felt fifty years later after the assassination of President John F. Kennedy. "That Mr. Post was the 'Father of Battle Creek' and a man loved and admired by his business competitors, honored and respected by his political enemies was made strikingly evident by the demonstrations of the audience," observed another local newspaper. "The community took leave of its benefactor. The country took leave of a great industrial figure. And many sad hearts took leave of their friend—and theirs was the loss hardest to bear. . . . In all the romance of American business achievement, there will be no more romantic story than his," lamented the *Enquirer*.

C.W.'s death was a loss to which Marjorie was never fully reconciled. Throughout her life she recalled C.W. lovingly, as a uniquely brilliant and charismatic being to whom she owed her wisdom, organizational skills, and perspective. When she was well into her eighties, friends would recall, the heiress's eyes invariably brightened when she spoke about C.W. "Mrs. Post was enamored of her father, so much that I believe no man could ever live up to him," said a frequent Washington guest, Dick Pearson.

"She used to tell me that she learned so very much from her father," observed her attorney, Henry Dudley. One day Marjorie asked him why he thought she could not find a satisfactory husband. The lawyer hesitated for a moment before giving his reply. "I think the reason is that you try to make them all Mr. Post," he told her gingerly.

With C.W.'s death, Marjorie not only lost an adored male figure but found herself becoming the subject of front-page news. Then, as throughout her life, publicity was something she attempted to avoid. But in 1914 there was no way for Marjorie to escape the spotlight. Less than a month after C.W. died, his will was published in the newspapers. What seemed to fascinate the public most was that the entrepreneur had left half of his $22 million estate to Marjorie and the other half to his second wife, Leila.

Specifically C.W. had divided his Texas properties between his daughter and his wife. To Leila, he left all his Santa Barbara property and all his holdings in Battle Creek. The only exception was the Marjorie Block in Battle Creek and the *Enquirer*, which, along with The Boulders in Greenwich, were willed to Marjorie.

The biggest source of public speculation was the distribution of the Postum Cereal Company common stock. According to C.W.'s will, half the shares were to go to Marjorie, and the other half to Leila. To outsiders there was nothing untoward about this arrangement. In fact, when these shares were added to the preferred stock Marjorie already owned in her inheritance from Ella, she was the single most powerful force in the Postum company.

Nevertheless, Marjorie was incensed. That C.W. had left her only 50 percent of the common stock struck the heiress as not only unfair but illegal. From childhood—or perhaps from Ella's instructions to her daughter before her own death—Marjorie had been told that the common stock of the Postum Cereal Company belonged to her solely, per C.W. and Ella's 1895 agreement at the establishment of the company.

Within a few weeks there were rumblings of litigation. Family lore has it that Ed Close now came to Marjorie's rescue. In a paper chase that lasted several months, Marjorie's husband leafed through old documents at Postum headquarters in Battle Creek. Finally he found the original document drawn between Ella and C.W. promising that the overwhelming majority of Postum shares would belong to Marjorie upon her father's death. With satisfaction Ed presented the document to his wife.

How many threats of litigation, how many angry phone calls went between Marjorie and Leila's representatives, can only be imagined. Finally, in December 1915, Leila conceded to the terms of the original arrangement and tried to hush up the rumors that she and Marjorie had quarreled. As the headlines in one local newspaper put it, NO LITIGATION IN SIGHT, HUSBAND'S MEMORY TOO DEAR FOR MRS. POST TO OPPOSE HIS DAUGHTER.

Ultimately Leila surrendered all her interests in the Postum Cereal Company. In exchange she received a cash settlement of six million dollars. Allegedly the precedent for the arrangement had been established by Marjorie's possession of the preferred shares of Postum stock. "There is no trouble between Mrs. Close and myself," Leila assured a local newspaper reporter. "A peaceful settlement has been made and there will be no litigation whatever."

One of the stipulations for the settlement was that henceforth the two women would rarely meet for business, and then only for their mutually shared Texas properties. "Mother hated Leila!" Marjorie's daughter Eleanor once said. "We were all brought up to think that she was terrible, but probably Leila wasn't that bad." The only remaining link between the two women was their respective memories of the brilliant and bombastic man who had been an adored father and husband. During C.W.'s lifetime the two women had been forcibly bound in polarities of love and hate; after his death Marjorie and Leila contemplated each other from a permanently chilly distance.

With the 1915 settlement Marjorie became the sole inheritor of the Postum Cereal Company, but her voice would be heard only indirectly. Almost immediately after C.W.'s death, Marjorie and Ed established a residence in Battle Creek so that Ed could represent Marjorie on the board of directors. Despite C.W.'s early training, Marjorie did not expect to serve on the board herself. Such liberties were simply not taken by "respectable" heiresses in 1914. In that era women were still fighting for suffrage. Marjorie could not serve on the Postum Cereal Company board even if she was its major stockholder. That duty was to be assumed by her husband.

Even so, for all of Ed's conscientiousness in finding the key document that established Marjorie as rightful heir to the Postum company, he had no talent for the business. Nine years earlier that fact had been unequivocally established when Ed expressed his desire to leave the company. C.W. had put others in place to ensure strong leadership for the company, and by the time of the industrialist's death a "cabinet" of capable men was running Postum. At its head was C.W.'s brother Carroll Post, who, in 1914, was still vice-chairman of the Postum board of directors. Ed Close's old boss, Marshall K. Howe, was still Postum's treasurer. Other key executives were Henry C. Hawk, secretary of the board, and Harry E. Burt, the business superintendent. With characteristic foresight, C.W. had made this cabinet the executors of his will, thereby ensuring, as the *Journal of Commerce* put it, "the continuance of the great management." Subsequently, Ed Close's appointment to the Postum Cereal board and Uncle Cal's election as its new chairman gave Marjorie instant access to what was going on in the company as well as a chance to comment upon every major corporate decision. In that proper, if distanced, Edwardian manner Marjorie thus exercised some "control" over her father's business. The heiress did not question her position. In the pre–World War I period, observed Marjorie's daughter Eleanor, "Mother was much too feminine to consider herself a feminist. It was only gradually that she grew to believe that women could do things."

Soon after C.W.'s death Marjorie and Ed also rented an apartment at 375 Park Avenue in Manhattan. Officially they acquired it to facilitate management of the Postum Cereal Company from the East Coast. "Things became very active for me. I had to take over the many irons he [C.W.] had in the fire," Marjorie explained. Although Ed was the "official" board member, the heiress assumed responsibility for most of the major decisions. "She had to do all the thinking and make all decisions," recalled Marjorie's Connecticut friend Hunter Marston. Ed "simply was not willing to assume grave responsibilities of the business."

The new apartment was more than just a place from which to run the business. It was also a toehold in New York, a glamorous aerie from which Marjorie could indulge her pent-up desire to dally in the social life of Manhattan. By day there was a myriad of affairs to attend to, loose ends from the C.W. era that needed attention and management decisions. Occasionally there was time for lunch at restaurants like Delmonico's, a tour through local art and antiques galleries, or a stroll past the glamorous Heckscher Building on Fifth Avenue at Fifty-seventh Street or the newly completed Woolworth Building, Manhattan's first "cathedral of commerce."

But at night, ah, at night! In 1915 more than fifty legitimate theaters lit up the Great White Way. There were concerts at Carnegie Hall, operas at the Metropolitan Opera House, dinners and balls at the Ritz-Carlton, the Waldorf-Astoria, and the Savoy. Each of these required fashionable clothes and presented the implicit obligation of returning the invitation. It was, Ed railed at Marjorie, too glittering, too ostentatious a lifestyle. Although he had grown up in New York himself as a member of the Four Hundred, Marjorie's husband preferred a quieter, more discreet existence spent at the Greenwich homestead or at the local clubs with his less showy, if no less sober, Connecticut friends to the glamorous mix of old and new society types from Broadway and Wall Street that Marjorie seemed to enjoy.

The heiress listened to her husband's complaints respectfully. After a while she stopped listening completely. With C.W.'s death Marjorie was suddenly no one's little girl or little woman. Slowly she was beginning to test her independence. And increasingly she favored New York over Greenwich, despite Ed's preferences to the contrary.

Simultaneously, the new responsibilities of the Postum company began to weigh heavily upon Marjorie. She began to worry about the competence of those C.W. had left behind to run the company. To make matters worse, she did not feel confident that Ed was fully representing her views at Postum board meetings.

The Park Avenue apartment was another problem, for while it was a convenience for Marjorie and Ed, it was too tiny to accommodate Adelaide and Eleanor. Moreover, the commute back to Greenwich after a nighttime concert or a dinner party was too long to be practical on a daily basis. The Closes began to feel torn—and guilty. "It seemed to me that we were in New York so much that it was wrong to leave the children in the big house in the country . . . we were commuting weekends," recalled Marjorie.

Finally, in 1915, Marjorie and Ed decided to rent a town house at 2 East Ninety-second Street in the section of New York's Upper East Side known as Carnegie Hill. For a quarter century the distance that stretched up Fifth Avenue from Fifty-ninth Street to 110th Street had been known as Millionaire's Row, and featured, as *Valentine's City of New York* of that time noted, "the homes of New York leaders in society, finance and commerce." By 1915 Carnegie Hill, especially the streets between Ninetieth and Ninety-sixth, had become prime residential property because it was beyond the route of the noisy double-decker buses that lumbered down Fifth Avenue.

Carnegie Hill had been named for its proximity to Andrew Carnegie's mansion on Fifth Avenue between Ninetieth and Ninety-first streets. Nearby lived other tycoons and members of the New York *Social Register*, among them the industrialist Otto Kahn, Payne Whitney, Vincent Astor, Aimee Guggenheim, and the Frank Woolworths.

The Closes' new home was still owned by the Burden family, who had enjoyed its wood-paneled dining room, glassed-in breakfast rooms, and spacious high ceilings for several generations. There was plenty of room for Adelaide, Eleanor, Pearcie, and the family pets. Moreover, Marjorie soon discovered that the town house next door at 4 East Ninety-second Street was vacant. With their niece's encouragement, Aunt Mollie and Uncle Cal bought the building and made it their permanent New York residence.

For a year Marjorie and Ed lived with the Burden family furniture until they were allowed to buy the house. By then it was late 1916 and the United States was being reluctantly drawn into the great European conflict. A few months later, on April 6, 1917, the United States entered the war being waged by France, Great Britain, Italy, and their allies against Germany, Austria-Hungary, and the Ottoman Empire.

From the beginning the war made a heavy impact on the Postum Cereal Company. With the declaration of war, the U.S. government immediately commandeered the nation's raw foodstuffs in order to feed the troops, including prime supplies of corn and wheat normally used in products like Postum, Instant Postum, Grape-Nuts, and Post Toasties.

To Marjorie, who was still feeling her way with Ed on the Postum board of directors, the timing could not have been worse. "I was catapulted into this thing, with our government taking our raw supplies away from us, practically trying to put us out of business, we felt," she recalled. Gradually Marjorie and the board of directors adjusted. In lieu of traditional cereal products, Postum dietitians began experimenting with kafir corn and mila maize in their recipes. While those grains were traditionally reserved for animal consumption in times of peace, they were, according to Marjorie, "perfectly good cereals [that] roasted well and . . . were nutritive" and could thus be used as substitutes.

To maintain the company's prewar levels of raw supplies, the Postum company (which formerly purchased many ingredients preground) was now forced to build its own corn and wheat mills. To the astonishment of the board of directors, the corn mill was inordinately profitable and eventually spawned several new businesses. "[I]t had so many by-products after we got our kernel . . . we found ourselves in the chicken-feeding business, food for cattle, oils, everything you can think of," Marjorie reminisced.

Several months into the war Marjorie and Ed faced another trauma. By then they had worked out an uneasy compromise between Greenwich and New York. On weekends, holidays, and in the summer they spent as much time as possible in Greenwich. So it was that on Tuesday, May 29, 1917, the Closes had gone directly from Manhattan to a dance at the Greenwich Country Club. Soon after their arrival an attendant interrupted them with a phone call. A distressed voice on the other end advised them to return to The Boulders at once. A fire had broken out in the house. Young Adelaide and Eleanor were safe and had already been taken to their neighbors, the Chesters, to rest. But the conflagration was raging through the upper stories of the mansion. C.W.'s wing had already exploded.

Later, Greenwich officials concluded that the fire was caused by faulty electrical wiring in Marjorie's bedroom. Eleanor, who was eight years old at the time, later recalled that she and Adelaide had been rushed out of the house with their dog, Woofie, just before the gas explosion in C.W.'s wing. In 1904 and 1905, when The Boulders was being built, C.W. had insisted upon having gas installed in his wing for heat. "My grandfather, like Mother, always liked to have the latest innovations," explained Eleanor.

The sight of The Boulders in flames horrified Marjorie. By the time she arrived, firemen were throwing treasures out of the mansion windows. European paintings, furniture, linens, china, and even lead crystal were strewn across the lawn. Powerful sprays of water from the firemen's hoses added to the confusion. The spectacle of the burning mansion had also attracted a crowd of sympathetic onlookers. "It was horrible, a mess as you can imagine, all the lovely paintings . . . were all spread out on the lawn and firemen were running everywhere," recalled Marjorie. In the panic, firemen had pitched old storage trunks out of the attic. Some of them contained precious collections of lead crystal and china purchased by C.W. on the occasion of Marjorie's marriage. Others held clothes and household items. One trunk in particular caused Marjorie some embarrassment, for it contained love letters, still tied with pink and blue ribbons, from old beaux. "The trunk broke open and Mrs. [Elsie Stillman] Rockefeller, who came to see the excitement of the fire, picked up a great many of them and got them all together for me," recalled Marjorie.

The fire at The Boulders transformed Marjorie's life. At first the spectacle of the mansion in charred ruins—especially the explosion in the C.W. wing—was nearly more than she could stand. "My room was a mess from water and smoke and the room above which Adelaide . . . used when she was a baby . . . was almost completely destroyed . . . [as was] my father's end of the house, I tell you there the explosion made a mess," Marjorie recollected.

In the end the fire had shattered far more than the eaves of Marjorie's house; it forced the heiress to examine the basic framework of her existence. In her heart Marjorie already knew that the tranquil teas of a Greenwich afternoon were too pallid to last a lifetime. The Postum Cereal Company demanded her rapt attention, as did Manhattan, that enchanting city of culture, entertainment, and endless possibilities. After careful consideration Marjorie gave up on The Boulders. It was, as she later said, "silly to put it back in order . . . because within a short time of the fire we decided not to go on living there." Eventually the heiress sold the damaged Boulders to a private school. Today, after several subsequent ownerships, The Boulders is known as the Eagle Hill School of Greenwich.

The Closes moved their children and household staff into Manhattan. Improvements were already under way at 2 East Ninety-second Street. The garden was expanded at the back of the town house. A bridge was erected between the mansion and Mollie and Cal's house next door so that Adelaide and Eleanor could wander freely between the two homes. Fine French furniture had already begun to replace the Burdens' old shabby-genteel chairs and couches.

Marjorie's taste was becoming more sophisticated. By then she had begun taking art courses at the nearby Metropolitan Museum of Art. Free for the first time to decorate a home completely of her own, Marjorie began to experiment. Under the tutelage of British art dealer Joseph Duveen (later Lord Duveen), with whom she studied at the Metropolitan, Marjorie began amassing valuable objects. A set of Beauvais tapestries after designs by Boucher and other antiques purchased in Manhattan's finest art galleries appeared in the town house. So did Sèvres porcelains, Aubusson rugs, antique lace, Louis XVI furniture, Rubens's *Adoration of the Magi*, and paintings by Gainsborough—often despite Ed's disapproval of Marjorie's "ostentation."

By and large Marjorie ignored her husband's objections. No longer was she an intimidated midwestern youngster. She was, after all, a matron of nearly thirty years of age. She was also sole heir to the Postum Cereal Company. Other people—neighboring millionaires, members of New York society, celebrities, financiers, and theater people—seemed charmed by her enthusiasms. In their eyes Marjorie had intelligence, glamour, and verve. Increasingly she began looking toward them and away from her disapproving husband for the standards of a new lifestyle.

In that same era—and probably not coincidentally—Marjorie became convinced that women should have the vote. As a young girl, and especially as a lovesick young woman at the Mount Vernon Seminary, there was nothing Marjorie could do about women's suffrage. By 1917 the heiress was experimenting with a new sense of her own power, trying on different roles to see which one fitted best. That year on October 25, in the only documented politically feminist act of Marjorie's life, she met with Woodrow Wilson in Washington as a committee member of the New York State Woman Suffrage party.

Within a few months, however, the suffrage cause was overshadowed by America's entrance into World War I. Marjorie became as passionate about the war effort as she was about women's rights. She began sewing and knitting for the boys "over there." She also rolled bandages at local Red Cross stations in Manhattan and in Greenwich. In Marjorie's widening perspective, these were paltry and commonplace efforts. Though unable to fight herself, she vowed to contribute her own brand of ammunition to the Allied cause. As the European conflict grew more bitter, as more and more young Americans, including her own husband, were drafted, Marjorie began to brood about wartime casualties. She believed it was incumbent upon her to do something extraordinary, something that would make a significant difference to the course of the war—or at least to the welfare of the soldiers who were injured in the Allied cause.

As an extension of her work for the Red Cross, Marjorie decided to fund an Army hospital in France. According to the Red Cross, which ran hospitals for the military, the cost of such a unit was around seventy-five thousand dollars. On July 30, 1917, through an arrangement with the U.S. military, Ed Close, his brother, Harry, and several other Greenwich area soldiers sailed on the SS *Saratoga*, which was bringing Marjorie's medical supplies to France. Adelaide Close, who was only nine at the time, remembered watching with her mother the camouflaged ship set sail from New York Harbor. No sooner had the vessel started on its journey than it was inadvertently rammed by the SS *Pan-*

ama. Before long it began to sink. While the crew—which included Ed, his brother, friends, doctors, nurses, and soldiers—was rescued in lifeboats, all the supplies on the *Saratoga* were lost.

Marjorie was not to be deterred. Eight days later she funded a second round of supplies, which was transported on the SS *Finland.* This time the vessel, which was part of a convoy of troopships, sailed across the Atlantic virtually without incident. As the *Finland* approached the French coast, it was attacked by German submarines, but Allied destroyers came to the ship's rescue. The medical staff and supplies reached Savenay, where they established the Number 8 Base Hospital. In time that hospital grew to some three thousand beds and became the largest such Red Cross institution in wartime Europe.

A half century later Marjorie was formally honored with a Red Cross Certificate of Appreciation for the base hospital and other contributions to the American Red Cross. On April 7, 1957, the French government honored Marjorie with that country's highest civilian award, the French Legion of Honor. To guests who attended those ceremonies, the establishment of Number 8 Base Hospital in Savenay, France, was simply one in a long chain of charitable acts that had characterized Marjorie's life. In essence, it was Marjorie's fledgling foray into independent philanthropy, her first attempt to make a significant difference to human history.

The establishment of the Army hospital also reflected Marjorie's rapidly evolving personal philosophy: that women, particularly wealthy ones, could exercise power by using their money for politically redeeming purposes. While still barred from becoming a member of the board of directors of the Postum Cereal Company, the thirty-year-old Marjorie had at least become the mistress of her own philanthropies. And she had done so with a special focus. As she once proudly told Dorothy McCardle of *The Washington Post,* "I am not the richest woman in the world. There are others better off than I am. The only difference is that I do more with mine. I put it to work."

The words might have been spoken by a philanthropist of the lean 1990s rather than an heiress of the early twentieth century. By virtue of her wealth and brains, Marjorie was always ahead of her generation. To those who knew her well, that position would be both a blessing and a curse.

9

Daring Propositions

The war years intensified Marjorie's sense of personal power. With Ed stationed overseas, Marjorie was a woman alone, forced to carve out a matriarchal existence. For female companionship there was Aunt Mollie. In Connecticut there were also her good friends the Hunter Marstons and the Colby Chesters, but Marjorie was not content to spend her days idly socializing. At 2 East Ninety-second Street, a series of important duties beckoned: work with the Postum company, volunteer service to the Red Cross, art lessons at the Metropolitan Museum of Art—and the raising of Adelaide and Eleanor. Although the particulars varied with the passing years, these three interests—business, charity, and family—became, and would remain, Marjorie's abiding concerns throughout her life.

From infancy Marjorie's daughters had distinctly different personalities. Adelaide, who was eighteen months older than Eleanor, was a thin, serious child who, to Marjorie's ongoing frustration, was almost painfully shy. In contrast, Eleanor was bubbly and extroverted, at times so filled with high spirits that she seemed giddy. Despite their contrasting temperaments, the girls were close and often operated as a team, hatching devilish pranks that frequently drove Marjorie and their nurse, Pearcie, to distraction. "My sister was forever in trouble, and she used to look at me to bail her out," Adelaide recalled. "I was full of mischief," Eleanor agreed. "In fact, we had a Mischievous Club at The Boulders, and I was its president."

One of Adelaide's and Eleanor's favorite pranks was to turn on the bidets in the bathrooms in The Boulders and get themselves soaked. Once, when Marjorie found Eleanor at the controls, she reminded her that she and Adelaide had been warned repeatedly that the bidets were not to be used as toys. The heiress did not believe in spanking, except when the situation was extreme. This time, in her opinion, it was. She placed Eleanor on her knee, and as she raised her hand, Marjorie "was promptly attacked by the older sister. So, I had to spank her too . . . it was a melee," the heiress reminisced many years later.

Early on Marjorie knew that her daughters had spirited dispositions. How to shape the girls, how to discipline them without breaking their spirits or losing her own composure, perplexed her. Characteristically, whenever Marjorie was faced with a serious problem, she sought advice from the experts. Her attitude toward parenting was no different. As a young mother she thus attended a series of lectures on the latest techniques in child raising.

The lectures Marjorie attended stressed the importance of using psychologically oriented forms of punishment. One strategy was to make the disobedient child sit in a chair with his feet flat on the ground, his hands folded, and his eyes shut for three minutes without moving. "I had to use it . . . many times on poor Eleanor, she was always into devilment," Marjorie recalled.

Since Marjorie was a passionate animal lover, her daughters were always surrounded by pets. At The Boulders, Adelaide and Eleanor had not only cats, dogs, and ducks but a pet lamb that Marjorie had brought them from a trip to Saratoga. When it was little, the girls nursed it with a bottle, and as it grew it followed them around like a dog. Another time, in one of the many food fads of Marjorie's life, she became impressed with the virtues of goat milk. Before long she had a small herd of goats at The Boulders.

Ultimately this early association with animals made such an impact upon Adelaide that as an adult she became not only a fine equestrian but a judge and master breeder of prize horses and dogs. In fact, in 1993 Adelaide's colt Woods of Windsor competed in one of the three most important horse races in the United States, the Preakness Race held at Pimlico racetrack in Baltimore.

Whatever else the girls gained from genteel country life in their Connecticut childhood was counterbalanced by their subsequent cultural education in Manhattan. From 2 East Ninety-second, an urbane world of art, dance, theater, and music, a world that Marjorie already enthusiastically embraced, was open to them. As preteens Adelaide and Eleanor routinely visited art galleries, the American Museum of Natural History, and the Metropolitan Museum of Art. They also attended the Metropolitan Opera, concerts, and Broadway shows. As Marjorie hoped, Adelaide and Eleanor gradually developed an appreciation for culture that made them sophisticated and worldly. Eleanor, especially, seemed to "take" to the cultural life of New York and became keenly interested in music and art. As a young woman she was to study in Paris and become an expert on French antiques.

The girls, like children everywhere, presented Marjorie with unusual challenges. Once, for instance, Adelaide refused to kiss Marjorie goodbye when she was off to a luncheon. "I don't want to say good-bye," the child said, pouting.

"Don't you love your mother?" the heiress asked.

"No, and I won't come and kiss you good-bye," Adelaide reiterated emphatically.

Distressed, Marjorie instructed the butler to call the hostess and make excuses for her delay. Simultaneously she took off her hat, gloves, and coat and talked tenderly to the child. "Adelaide, do you realize that you were carried next to my heart for almost a year before you were born, so I knew you very intimately before anybody ever saw you? Of course my devotion to you would be very heartfelt, and I have always been so proud of you because you are a beautiful child . . . a healthy child . . . an intelligent child, and I can't believe that you don't love your mother." At those words Adelaide began to sob and told Marjorie how much she loved her. The argument was thus settled. As Marjorie put it, "I never had to meet that situation again, ever."

Years later, after she was a grandmother herself, Adelaide described Marjorie as a strict, authoritarian parent who was nonetheless very loving. "My mother was one of those people who'd give and give. She was very reasonable with us," said Adelaide. Despite the deep tides of affection that flowed between Marjorie and her daughters, she demanded absolute obedience. "She was very definite . . . [so] when Mother spoke, we moved," said Adelaide.

Among the girls' closest friends were Mary and Genie Chester, daughters of Jessie and Colby Chester, Sr., of Greenwich. The elder of the Chester girls was Mary, who, being a year older than Adelaide, fascinated her with her long dresses and grown-up privileges. While bright and fun-loving, Genie had been stricken with polio at an early age and was hence an invalid. Despite that disability, the Chesters took Genie everywhere.

The Post and Chester girls were present at the review of General Pershing's troops following the 1918 World War I armistice. In anticipation of the general's victory march down Fifth Avenue, Marjorie had invited the Chesters to travel from Greenwich to watch the parade from her Manhattan town house. As usual, Marjorie decided to make the occasion festive. Eleanor recalls that her mother had a special grandstand built at the garden wall where they could have a good view of the soldiers.

That day, New York went wild. According to one published account, the crowds stood for hours on Fifth Avenue from 110th Street to the Washington Square arch to watch the spectacle of General Pershing, seated upon a magnificent bay and followed by thirty thousand men "with all their gear, from airplane to trench mortar . . . from fat breeched howitzer . . . to the gargantuan caterpillars which drew the guns."

Shortly afterward Ed Close returned home a hero, decorated by the French government with a Medal of Honor. Nevertheless, his homecoming was less than happy. In his absence Marjorie had grown increasingly independent. Although at first Ed may have thought the change in his marriage had to do with his readjustment to civilian life, Marjorie seemed almost indifferent, and certainly far less affectionate than she had been. After a few months their relationship was no better, though there was little open rancor. Whatever magic once existed between Marjorie and Ed had long since dissipated. The reality was that the couple had grown apart, had indeed been growing apart for years.

The war, and Marjorie's time alone in New York without Ed, had enabled her to consider the possibilities of another existence. To Ed's consternation, his wife finally asked for a divorce. Years later Eleanor sighed as she contemplated her father's reaction. "It must have been a terrible shock for him when he got back from the war to find that Mother wanted a divorce."

Rumor has it that at the time Marjorie gave Ed a large settlement, but the man was too much in love with her to be consoled by money. Marjorie's former husband made a hasty retreat to Greenwich. Within a few months he met a feisty and attractive southern girl named Elizabeth Taliaferro. By late 1919 she had become Ed Close's second wife.

Within a few years she produced twin sons, one of whom later fathered the actress Glenn Close.

Marjorie, meanwhile, had plans of her own. In 1917 at a Long Island house party, she had been introduced to a handsome, blond, blue-eyed stockbroker named E. F. Hutton, who was then married to Blanche Horton. Marjorie, who had known E.F.'s brother, Franklyn Hutton, and Franklyn's late wife, Edna Woolworth, from New York's Upper East Side, struck up a polite conversation. Two years later, in the winter of 1919, Marjorie bumped into the broker again, this time at a Palm Beach houseboat party. To her astonishment, E.F. had become a widower. A year or so earlier Blanche had died in the postwar influenza epidemic, leaving E.F. with a teenage son.

If it was not love at first sight in 1917, the second meeting between Marjorie and E. F. Hutton in 1919 was at least infatuation. At thirty-two the heiress was a dazzlingly beautiful woman whose familiarity with the rudiments of American business and the cultural life of New York made her an extraordinary companion. By 1919 Edward Francis Hutton—E.F., as he was commonly known—was already a Wall Street legend. While not a tall man, he was movie-star handsome, a dashing dresser, and a gifted raconteur. He was, as his now-elderly cousin W. E. Hutton, Jr., remembers him, "very gregarious, charming. The gals all loved him. . . . I can see when he [first] met Marjorie . . . that she was fascinated with him."

E.F. had a humble background. Though he was born in New York City on September 7, 1875, his roots were in Ohio. His father died when E.F. was ten, leaving E.F.'s mother a widow in poverty with two sons to raise. Family finances were so tenuous that at fifteen E.F. was forced to leave school and take a job for five dollars a week as a mail boy in a securities firm. Two years later he got a better job with an investment trust company, which he held until that firm went bankrupt.

E.F. was hardworking and determined. At night and on weekends he studied finance at the Trinity Chapel School and at Packer's Business College in New York. By twenty he had become a partner in his uncle W. E. Hutton's Cincinnati brokerage firm of Harris, Hutton & Company. Eventually W. E. Hutton decided to establish his own firm. By 1901 E.F. had persuaded his uncle to open a branch office of W. E. Hutton & Company in Manhattan, with himself as its resident partner.

The young broker had a special genius for business and soon began turning a handsome profit. Within a few years E.F. was itching for new markets and new ways to test his ideas. After a business trip to San Francisco E.F. became convinced that there was a fortune to be made on the West Coast. To do so, it was necessary to establish a San Francisco office equipped with a private telegraph wire. E.F. was convinced that with such technology clients would be privy to valuable information transmitted across the country long before the rest of the Wall Street brokerage houses heard about it.

E.F.'s uncle was skeptical. The West Coast, W. E. Hutton contended, was simply too far from Wall Street to conduct business efficiently. He dismissed the idea. Before long E. F. Hutton opened his own San Francisco firm with a partner named George Ellis and his younger brother, Franklyn Hutton. To provide clients with quality service, the new E. F. Hutton Company had a telegraph line to New York.

On April 18, 1906, the unthinkable happened. At 5:13 A.M. the ground beneath the city of San Francisco began to tremble violently. According to some accounts, E. F. Hutton immediately wired his East Coast contacts about the earthquake and liquidated his clients' interests in all San Francisco companies. Customer accounts were thus protected from the disaster, long before news of it had spread to other brokerage houses.

W. E. Hutton's son, W. E. Hutton, Jr.—who is still in the brokerage business—believes this story to be apocryphal. "The earthquake and the fire of San Francisco caused another national panic, and the E.F. company went busted," he insists. According to W. E. Hutton, Jr., it was E.F.'s brother, Franklyn, who bailed the company out. By then Franklyn was already married to Edna Woolworth. His father-in-law, F. W. Woolworth, "listened to his tale of woe and . . . staked him again. So they [E.F. and Franklyn] went back into business and learned their lesson about failure and did remarkably well after that."

Whoever ultimately financed the recovery, the upshot was that the E. F. Hutton Company became not only the leading California brokerage firm but one of the most prestigious on Wall Street.

Such was E.F.'s rise to national prominence. To Marjorie, the story of the broker's life was spellbinding, a unique mixture of intelligence, ruthlessness, and daring she had not glimpsed in any man since her father. The forty-five-year-old broker was the closest thing Marjorie had known to C.W., for he radiated the same charisma and unpredictability. Despite herself, despite any misgivings that she might have about a second marriage, Marjorie could not stop daydreaming about E.F. In short, the heiress fell madly and irretrievably in love. E.F. was equally smitten. On July 7, 1920, they were quietly wed at 2 East Ninety-second Street.

Neither Adelaide nor Eleanor was pleased with the marriage. That both their parents had divorced and found new partners within a matter of months had been difficult. Nevertheless, soon after her new marriage, Marjorie began to hint that E.F. was willing to adopt the girls; in fact, they were already being introduced in public and in the newspapers as Adelaide and Eleanor Hutton.

To their surprise, there were some unanticipated advantages to their mother's marriage. By virtue of Marjorie's union with E. F. Hutton, the girls had a new stepbrother, Halcourt Hutton, who, at eighteen years of age, was about to enter Yale University. Privately eleven-year-old Adelaide and ten-year-old Eleanor giggled about Halcourt. He was, they whispered to each other, very handsome. Halcourt accepted Adelaide's and Eleanor's crush with good-natured humor. During the short time they had already spent together, Halcourt had begun to refer to them teasingly as "the peskies" because they seemed to shadow him everywhere.

That first summer, Marjorie was deliriously happy with E.F. Although the heiress wed twice more after her marriage to Hutton, her closest friends and family members believe that E.F.—or Ned, as Marjorie used to call him to distinguish him from Ed Close—was the grand passion of her life. "The impression I had was that the only man she really loved was Hutton. There is no doubt about it," said Marjorie's last beau, Fred Korth. In retrospect, even Marjorie's second daughter acknowledged the intensity of her passion for E.F. "She was madly in love with him," said Eleanor.

In the summer of 1920 the Huttons frequently visited E.F.'s hunting lodge in Bay Shore, Long Island. One September morning Halcourt mounted his horse for a ride. Adelaide, who was playing in a nearby field, recalls that she saw at a distance her stepbrother with his groom. At eighteen Halcourt was a confident and skilled equestrian. But as his horse began to trot, the saddle came loose, twisted around Halcourt's legs, threw the youth forward and finally upside down. Despite Halcourt's frantic shouts, the frightened animal began to gallop, knocking his master's head against the cobblestone pavement. A day or two later Halcourt died. E.F. was mute with grief. Marjorie was bowled over with shock. Young Adelaide and Eleanor wept bitterly.

After the funeral Marjorie made a private vow. She would try to have a child for Ned, a son to replace the one he had loved and just lost.

. . .

The war years not only stiffened Marjorie's resolve to change her personal circumstances but also convinced her to forge a new type of management for the Postum Cereal Company. By 1919, as *Fortune* magazine noted, "Marjorie Post Close suddenly became an active volcano" who bubbled over with new business ambitions. For more than two decades Marjorie's uncle Cal, now sixty years of age, had borne the burden of running the Postum Cereal Company. It was, the heiress believed, now time for younger, more forward-looking individuals to take on that responsibility, men who could transform the old company into an exciting new entity. Years earlier C.W. had talked to Marjorie about that possibility, about enlarging the company or joining with others to create a new organization.

Before she could make such a dramatic leap, it was necessary to ensure the stability of the company management. During the war years Marjorie had carefully considered her options. With Ed Close no longer her proxy, Marjorie wanted a new advocate on the Postum board, a man she knew and could trust. Finally, after much consideration, she approached her old Connecticut friend Colby Chester, who had just returned home from the war. For years Marjorie had admired Colby's intelligence and business acumen. In 1919 the heiress thus made a tempting proposition. Would Colby—Clare, as he was commonly known—be willing to give up his law practice and join the Postum Cereal Company to serve in an executive capacity?

Marjorie's motives for enlisting Chester, according to his son Colby junior, were clear. The heiress had become increasingly dissatisfied with the way her uncles were running the company. What Marjorie proposed was to hire Clare Chester as Postum's assistant treasurer. In that capacity he would learn how Marjorie's uncles managed the company. Once familiar with the situation, Clare was expected to point out flaws and offer suggestions so that the Postum company could turn a larger profit.

Initially Clare was surprised by the offer, but his wife, Jessie, was not. A few months earlier, when the Chesters were vacationing in Atlantic City, a fortune-teller had predicted that Clare would receive an offer that would "change his life." At the time the cynical lawyer had scoffed. Now, when Marjorie made her offer, Clare accepted it almost immediately.

After a few months at Postum the new assistant treasurer confirmed Marjorie's suspicions that the company was being mismanaged. Gradually, as the elder Posts were gracefully "retired," Clare Chester rose through the ranks. By 1923 he had become president of the Postum Cereal Company.

Marjorie had even grander managerial plans for E. F. Hutton. As her husband, the broker was obliged to become involved in the Postum Cereal Company; he was simply too brilliant, and too much in love with Marjorie, to do otherwise. The nature of E.F.'s initial contributions and his financial arrangements with Marjorie have not been preserved. Yet by the early 1920s the impact of E.F.'s business acumen was already being felt. In 1922 E. F. Hutton transformed the Postum Cereal Company from a private company into a public one that was listed on the New York Stock Exchange. Marjorie still retained a majority interest in her father's old company and received ten million dollars from Postum's bankers, Goldman, Sachs, for her release of the remaining shares. By 1923 E. F. Hutton had become chairman of the Postum Cereal Company. A decision had been made to move company headquarters to Manhattan. In preparation for that corporate reorganization, Marjorie's husband relinquished his position as chairman of the E. F. Hutton Company on Wall Street.

The corporate "wedding" of E. F. Hutton to the Postum Cereal Company had personal analogies in his marriage. Socially, news of the wedding of the beautiful heiress to the brilliant broker had created a sensation. To many New Yorkers at the dawn of the Roaring Twenties, Marjorie and E.F. were a fairy-tale couple, the epitome of romanticism in a world weary of war and death. The Huttons had emerged from the depths of personal despair—from divorce and widowerhood—to be "saved" in a happy new marriage.

The Huttons had married at the dawn of the Jazz Age, as F. Scott Fitzgerald dubbed that era, a time when "a new generation [had] grown up to find all Gods dead, all wars fought, all faiths in man shaken." To the cynical youths who smoked cigarettes, drank bootleg whiskey, became flappers, bought on margin, and lived on credit, Marjorie and E.F. were heroes. While divorce was still considered scandalous to New York's Four Hundred, it was accepted, and even winked at, by a new, more glamorous group of people loosely known as New York's younger "social set"—a glittering cadre of celebrities, show people, new tycoons, football players, opera singers, and youthful renegades from High Society—whose names and lives were increasingly visible on Millionaire's Row and in tabloid "society" columns.

The Great War had largely been responsible for the social shakeout—of behavior, privilege, and pleasures—among young men and women then coming of age. Society youth had donned gas masks along with farm boys from Kentucky, and together they had crawled through the thick trench mud of France. Poor women had rolled bandages in the same Red Cross stations as wealthy ones and observed the same "meatless" and "wheatless" menus in accordance with wartime food rationing. Educated women had worked in munitions factories with women who had never graduated from high school.

In postwar America a new sense of well-being—and anything it took to get it—was thus becoming a national imperative. Being "smart" and "sassy" replaced being "proper" and "respectful" to elders who had sacrificed less than their children to win the war. If life was short and unpredictable, if God had died in a bombed-out church in northern France or been gassed in Belgium, what, then, was the fuss over a bunch of rigid rules from an obsolete and stuffy age?

The fairy-tale quality of the Huttons' romance eerily approximated that of the protagonists of Fitzgerald's most acclaimed novel, *The Great Gatsby*, which was not published until 1925. Like its hero, Gatsby, E.F. was a self-made man with humble roots. Like Fitzgerald's heroine, Daisy Buchanan, Marjorie was beautiful and petted, with a voice that sounded "full of money." If the Huttons were not Fitzgerald's "careless" people, they were at least carefree, at liberty to come and go as they chose, free to do as they pleased without social or financial restrictions.

That, at least, was the Huttons' public image. Privately they were considered parvenus by the inner sanctum of old-line New York society, nouveau riche with ostentatious appetites and a lifestyle to match. While E.F. had long been a member of several New York clubs—among them the Metropolitan Club and the Union League—he had never been invited to join the most prestigious ones signifying "old money" and "ultimate power," like the Union Club or the Downtown Association. The snobbish attitude expressed at Marjorie's first wedding was still in force. And now added to the burden of her midwestern roots was her divorce from Ed Close, the son of one of Manhattan's most revered old families.

Whatever hurt Marjorie and E.F. suffered from this snobbery was minimal, because Old Society as a dominant social force was already breaking down. By the twenties, High Society, as Allen Churchill has noted in *The Upper Crust*, "was losing its unique identity." With the youth revolution of the Roaring Twenties, the old social lines were increasingly blurred by an influx of celebrities, entertainment and sports figures, many of whom bought costly apartments and estates, frequented resorts, and attended charity balls that had once been the sole domain of New York's Four Hundred. Marjorie and E.F. were part of this new society, moving easily from friendships with old-line New Yorkers to more glamorous celebrity types. Among their friends in this period were celebrities like Flo Ziegfeld, Billie Burke, Douglas Fairbanks, and Mary Pickford, businessmen like IBM's Thomas J. Watson, international heroes like Lord Louis Mountbatten, and politicians like Grover Whalen.

Moreover, the newlywed Huttons soon set about building a new life for themselves in several choice communities: on Long Island, where they planned a new estate on the North Shore; in South Carolina, where E.F. had a shooting lodge; and in Palm Beach—especially in Palm Beach, the elite Florida playground that, in 1920, welcomed wealthy newcomers regardless of their births or past histories into the inner sanctum of its brief social season.

No one had illustrated that open-door policy more dramatically than the lovely gray-haired Eva T. Stotesbury of Philadelphia, who was known to Palm Beachers as the "grande dame of the winter set." Although her own social credentials were impeccable and her second husband, Edward, was a senior banking partner of J. P. Morgan's Drexel and Company, the Stotesburys had never fully been accepted by old-line Philadelphia society.

Undaunted, Mrs. Stotesbury had resolutely established herself in the years before the war as Palm Beach's most prominent hostess. Her proper, if slightly iconoclastic, style is perhaps best described by an anecdote: On one midday occasion, when Mrs. Stotesbury wore a gingham dress and a string of exquisite pearls, a guest coyly sniped, "Pearls, in the daytime?" Mrs. Stotesbury was too skilled socially—and too confident of her position—to show offense. "Yes, my dear. I used to feel that way too. But that was before I had the pearls," she deftly replied.

By the end of World War I, other movers and shakers were carving Palm Beach into new social duchies. Paris Singer, heir to the sewing machine fortune, had already asked New York society architect Addison Mizner to build a convalescent home for wounded veterans on the site of a humble Palm Beach attraction once known as Joe's Alligator Pit. The result was a handsome Spanish-style building called the

Touchstone Convalescents' Club, situated on Worth Avenue at the shore of Lake Worth. When the veterans failed to materialize—probably because of Florida's isolation and their desire to return home at war's end—the disappointed Singer rethought his venture. By then he was determined to make Palm Beach the American Riviera and had the building converted into an exclusive club with private rooms, dining halls, and, eventually, tennis courts and a golf course.

On January 25, 1919, Singer opened the doors of the new Everglades Club with twenty-five charter members. In contrast with the older Royal Poinciana and Breakers hotels, the Everglades Club had an informal daytime style reminiscent of the Riviera that instantly appealed to the chic, younger crowd. At night, however, formality was still the rule, and guests routinely appeared in jewels, gowns, and tuxedos. Every week the Everglades Club sponsored member dinners; a daily tea dance was also held in its orange court. That first winter a gala costume ball was so successful that it became the talk of the social season. Clearly the stuffy old atmosphere of the Flagler hotels was losing ground to a younger, more abandoned style that would increasingly attract wealthy and stylish clients.

That same year Eva Stotesbury, sensing the arrival of a new order in Palm Beach, ensured her preeminence by constructing an enormous beaux arts–style mansion. The new estate, which was sited on acreage that stretched from Lake Worth to the ocean, was also built by Addison Mizner. Ultimately it would be in this marble-halled and columned palace called El Mirasol, or The Sunflower, that Mrs. Stotesbury entertained hundreds of guests and where, in confirmation of her role as social doyenne of Palm Beach, she was revered by a younger generation of resorters as the very "soul of graciousness."

Among those guests were Marjorie and E. F. Hutton, who had rented a maisonette at the new Everglades Club in the winter of 1920–21. To Marjorie, Mrs. Stotesbury was a woman to be emulated, one who had bested Old Society by establishing a new order with brilliance and panache. Eventually, as Marjorie later told the *Palm Beach Daily News*, Eva Stotesbury became "an aunt to me and a dear friend" who gave out advice and groomed the heiress to become her social successor.

This relationship developed gradually and only after Marjorie was better established in Palm Beach. It was true that E. F. Hutton had opened a brokerage house at The Breakers to serve the resort's affluent population. It was also true that the Huttons socialized with other scions, among whom were the Rodman Wanamakers, Gurnee and Charlie Munn, Madeleine Force Astor, the Horace Dodges, the Barclay Warburtons, the Pillsburys, the Biddles, and the Phippses.

Marjorie and E.F., like their friends, also frequented Bradley's Beach Club, known for its fine food and elite gambling casino, and Alibi's, a fashionable restaurant on Worth Avenue. Yet, in the early twenties, despite their appearance in the "right" Palm Beach social circles, the Huttons were still attempting to establish a style of their own.

Even their living quarters were unsettled. A few weeks after Marjorie and E.F. moved into the Everglades Club apartment, they discovered that they did not like it. Their apartment, according to Marjorie, was "so horribly noisy on both sides of it that we just couldn't cope." Finally, "in desperation" the Huttons decided to buy a place of their own. In that same winter of 1920–21 they purchased a triangular piece of land just east of the Everglades Club golf course, somewhere "between the first and third hole." Before long they had engaged a soft-spoken, Paris-educated New York architect named Marion Wyeth, who constructed for them an attractive Spanish-style house with iron grillwork and a three-story tower on Golfview Road. The Huttons named it Hogarcito, the Spanish word for a country cottage. Today the house is still standing, a handsome pink stucco residence with tiled floors and beamed ceilings built around a courtyard with an enormous rubber tree.

In comparison with the palatial El Mirasol, the Huttons' Hogarcito was a modest affair, hardly the type of residence that presaged Marjorie's future as the widely acknowledged "queen of Palm Beach." In 1921 Hogarcito was nevertheless a beginning, a starting point from which the heiress would plot her social evolution to establish herself and E.F. as Palm Beach's premier young couple.

Coexisting with these ambitions was Marjorie's genuine desire to help improve the community. In the immediate post–World War I years, Palm Beach was still a relatively underdeveloped, almost somnolent resort that lacked many amenities of everyday life. A series of lackluster wooden cottages, most of them owned by The Breakers, still lined the shore. Shops were almost nonexistent, and the purchase of household goods usually required a trip to West Palm Beach. Architects like Addison Mizner, Marion Wyeth, and Mario Fatio, who would transform the nondescript wood-frame buildings of Palm Beach into stately marble palaces, were just beginning to appear. Most distressing of all was the lack of a nearby full-service hospital.

In the winter of 1920–21, Marjorie, E.F., and their friends decided to establish a benefit to raise money for a hospital to be established in West Palm Beach. Until then—perhaps because of the brevity of the winter "social season"—when a Palm Beacher fell ill, he received little more than the most rudimentary medical care in a makeshift clinic. In a real emergency an ailing resorter had to be driven several hours south to the city of Miami.

The Huttons and their friends believed the situation should be corrected at once. "We decided that we young marrieds would raise money for the start of a hospital and that we would put on [a] play and each of us would be performers," Marjorie recalled. At that time the Huttons' good friend Flo Ziegfeld was at the pinnacle of his career as a theatrical impresario with his annual *Follies*. The Huttons prevailed upon Ziegfeld to lend some of his Broadway costumes and stage sets for a performance of what would be called "Ziegfeld's Palm Beach Nights." For this show the actors and actresses were Palm Beach resorters, combined with professionals Ziegfeld brought from New York.

Since the costumes were borrowed from the *Follies* and had to be returned immediately after the benefit, they could not be altered. Consequently, as Marjorie recalled, "the only way we were selected for the parts was by the fact that we fit the costume." To her delight, she was one of the lucky women who managed to squeeze into a *Follies* dress. For the benefit, Marjorie appeared in a glittering costume as one of the girls in a Palm Beach wheelchair.

Marjorie had not, however, inherited her mother's singing voice. Years later the heiress joked about how fortunate it was that she "was not asked to sing and more fortunate for the audience." Instead Broadway crooner Harry Fender played Marjorie's lover and sang "Florida, the Moon and You" to her. When Harry finished, Marjorie got out of the chair and danced with him. "That didn't bother me. Dancing was my complete joy," she recalled. Had Ella Merriweather Post still been alive, she would have burst with pride. The dancing lessons at Professor Irwin's school in Battle Creek had paid off. Young, shy Marjorie had become a glamorous, confident woman at home in one of the most sophisticated resorts in the world.

That first benefit was so popular that Marjorie and her friends raised $110,000 toward the establishment of what became the Good Samaritan Hospital of West Palm Beach. Thereafter the Hospital Ball became an important annual Palm Beach institution, a sparkling social event that has endured to the present day.

Social power, as Marjorie was learning from her first days in Palm Beach as E. F. Hutton's wife, was best achieved if it came gradually and from a groundswell of respect and approval. And power was what Marjorie unconsciously craved: not the kind that exploits, but rather the kind that is meant to nourish others. Above all, Marjorie longed for approval, an acknowledgment of her vision and style that transcended the old rules of eastern society and led to a higher human order.

In time Marjorie became so successful as a benevolent Palm Beach force that her reputation outlived the glow that once surrounded Mrs. Stotesbury.

PALM BEACH
DAYS—AND
NIGHTS

10

It Was "Quite a Place"

$\mathcal{F}$rom the moment of her marriage to E. F. Hutton, Marjorie began to think of herself differently. No longer was she compelled to don dowdy dresses and act the part of a mature matron. Nor did she have to stifle her desire to wear lavish jewelry or clothes. With her new husband, the thirty-three-year-old Marjorie had license to taste life wholly, to place less emphasis on her age, and to give vent to her most fanciful appetites.

It was not that Marjorie became wild in the twenties but that she was liberated from old constraints. The newlywed Marjorie's dresses became more stylish, with shorter skirts, jeweled embellishments, or dramatic trains. Her gems from this period became increasingly elaborate and included pieces like a Cartier emerald necklace and matching brooch in the fashionable East Indian style. No longer did Marjorie let her hair remain prematurely white. Instead she began to color it, leaving only one white streak for a dramatic accent.

Despite such outward signs of worldly sophistication, Marjorie remained a conservative wife and mother. As a philanthropist she donated money thoughtfully; as a businesswoman she was steady and hard-driving. Personally she was free to indulge her instincts for world travel, for the entertainment of large flocks of adoring guests—in short, for an expansive existence she had never tasted under the aegis of her father, C.W., or her first husband, Ed Close.

Doubtless E. F. Hutton's temperament influenced Marjorie's new outlook. Where Ed Close had been conservative, E.F. was iconoclastic; where Ed had stood in awe of old conventions, E.F. simply ignored them. There was nothing in the brilliant broker's experience to suggest otherwise; his daring on Wall Street had, after all, been the very key to his success. Inevitably that dynamism was translated into a personal philosophy that Marjorie's friend Hunter Marston later characterized as E.F.'s "joy of living." As a result, said Hunter, "He and Marjorie were always traveling in high gear, whereas the first marriage was always in the low gear."

There were other factors contributing to E.F.'s outlook. He was still recovering from the untimely deaths of his first wife and son, the sort of events that tend to make people live in the present. Moreover, the broker was forty-five and already confronting a sense of the passing years. The flamboyant mood of the twenties was also an influence—especially among those young or wealthy enough to throw the corseted old conventions of prewar society to the wind.

Another, perhaps more subtle influence was Christian Science, which encouraged its advocates to live positively and to embrace life wholeheartedly. While little is known about Marjorie's spiritual life during her first marriage, after the divorce she was free to study Christian Science openly. In those years Marjorie not only embraced her faith more freely but befriended a Manhattan practitioner named Katherine Ross from whom she frequently sought advice.

In time the resolution to live life optimistically became imprinted upon Marjorie's personality. Decades later Marjorie's first granddaughter, Marjorie Durant Dye, called Marwee, who often lived with her, observed that although life did not unfold as the heiress wished, Marjorie was not one to sit around and mope. "My grandmother lived life to the fullest. She made sure to enjoy herself despite the problems she had," said Marwee.

Anything, in Marjorie's view, was possible, if one thought positively enough: the conquest of illness, sorrow, a broken love affair, and even advancing age. The accumulation of the passing years was, in fact, something that Marjorie disparaged throughout her life. A half century later, when Marjorie's friend Gladys Heurtematte Johnston (later Bendetsen) mentioned that she felt old, Marjorie snapped at her. "Old? Don't mention that word. If you feel old, you'll be old," the heiress chided.

The new houses the Huttons built in the twenties reflected Marjorie's instinct for grandeur. Soon after their wedding, the heiress and her husband planned a country estate on 176 acres in Brookville, Long Island. The mansion, which was called Hillwood because of its wooded, hilly terrain, was designed by New York architect Charles M. Hart in the half-timbered style of an English manor house.

The majestic sweep of rolling lawn leading to the mansion caused Hillwood to bear a strong resemblance to the country seats of British peers. Marjorie's preference for a noble Anglican style was predictable. Ever since her childhood trips abroad with C.W., she had been fascinated by royalty and particularly that of the British Empire. "Mom had a bit of a fixation on titles and royalty, and to her, the English royal family was 'it,' " said her daughter Dina Merrill, who spent much of her childhood at Hillwood.

At the mansion's entranceway guests passed through a low-ceilinged room and made their way toward the Great Hall, a dramatic wood-paneled living room with a double staircase that resembled a medieval hunting lodge. Wood-beamed ceilings, mullioned and leaded windows, artful nooks and crannies, all contributed to the medieval atmosphere. A series of gardens designed by Marian C. Coffin heightened the European mood; among them were a formal cutting garden, a rose garden, and a topiary garden. In a concession to the latest sports rage, Hillwood had its own tennis court. Here, too, as at all of Marjorie's subsequent estates, was a place for her to practice golf, a circular putting green.

Adjoining the main house were several wings, separated by courtyards, which housed the children's quarters, guest rooms, and servants' dormitories. These additions made the house appear, as Liisa and Donald Sclare, authors of *Beaux-Arts Estates*, subsequently noted, more like "a small English country village . . . than a single building."

It was no accident that Marjorie and E.F. had chosen Long Island as the site for their new estate. The broker had owned a country house on the South Shore in Bay Shore for years, and Marjorie had no desire to return to Greenwich. What she craved was a great stretch of countryside that was accessible to Manhattan and one that was near "excellent duck (and snipe) shooting" for Ned. The property could not, however, be just any isolated stretch of land; it had to offer tranquillity, recreational activities, and proximity to people Marjorie and Ned would enjoy.

Long Island offered all those features. Among those who spent their summers upon what was already being called the Gold Coast of Long Island—an area including the North Shore of Nassau County and fifteen miles of western Suffolk County—were Charles Payson, F. W. Woolworth, Payne Whitney, John E. Aldred, Louis Comfort Tiffany, Condé Nast, Ralph Pulitzer, and William Randolph Hearst.

The term *Gold Coast* was aptly applied. Some of the area's estates resembled baronial castles; others looked like French châteaux; still others were marble Mediterranean palaces of icy splendor or models of Georgian resplendence. Whatever they were, they were girded by dozens, hundreds, or sometimes even thousands of acres, protected from the hoi polloi by private roads and boat docks, high walls, private police, and watchdogs.

Within these bastions of privilege, life was conducted with the effervescent immediacy of a newly opened champagne bottle. Guest lists for parties often numbered in the hundreds for gatherings held beneath gilded ceilings and Baccarat chandeliers, by goldfish- and orchid-filled swimming pools, or aboard private oceangoing yachts with white-coated crews that ferried party members around Long Island Sound in the moonlight.

Despite war rationing and Prohibition, the finest French wines and champagnes flowed freely. Rum-running became an unofficial sport of the idle rich—or at least of their staffs. Originally, long tunnels had been built from the great estates to the shore so that barges could deliver coal. Now rumrunners used them as storage bins; many stills were also sequestered in the basements of Gold Coast mansions.

Money was spent with a reckless abandon never again seen in the twentieth century. Rare furs, exotic feathers, couturier gowns, and diamond, sapphire, and emerald jewelry fairly dripped from partygoers and party givers. Precious stones were considered so commonplace that they were often given away as party favors. Lavish costume balls were the order of the day. So were exotic orchestras, among them a calypso band imported from Jamaica for a night. Adding to the excitement were frequent appearances of stage and screen actors like Ed Wynn, Basil Rathbone, Errol Flynn, and Leslie Howard. At other parties, *Ziegfeld Follies* stars, opera singers, and other celebrities appeared as friends of the hosts.

To amuse their guests, many hosts had their stables filled with exotic African animals and their gardens with peacocks and other unusual birds. The giddiness of the era was epitomized in the female penchant for kicking off one's lingerie at a host's gates on the way home. Money itself seemed so meaningless that at some parties cigarettes were wrapped in hundred-dollar bills. At Otto Kahn's Easter egg hunts, guests who scampered through his estate gardens on Easter Sunday were rewarded with eggs stuffed with thousand-dollar bills.

In their zest for an opulent lifestyle Marjorie and E.F. were in good company. With the construction of Hillwood, the Huttons' vision of a fashionable country house with access to golf links, sporting fields, and like-minded friends was thus fulfilled. It was hardly coincidental that after an enthusiastic 1924 visit to the International Polo Matches held at Westbury and a subsequent refusal to travel anywhere else in the United States but Long Island, young Edward, Prince of Wales—who, years later, with his new American wife, Wallis Simpson, became Marjorie's friend—pronounced America "a country in which nothing was impossible." Had anyone asked Marjorie for her opinion in the palmy twenties, the beautiful heiress would likely have agreed.

Even so, the sybaritic society surrounding Hillwood did not wholly satisfy Marjorie's appetites. Another, more sensible urge tugged at the heiress: for simplicity, for a return to basic pleasures like sun, water, and the pristine beauty of nature. For years Marjorie and Ed Close had rented camps in the Adirondacks with their Connecticut friends and cousins the McAlpins. Now that she was remarried, Marjorie insisted that it was time for her and E.F. to buy a camp of their own.

Already the usually strong-minded broker was learning to yield to Marjorie on the subject of the purchase of their homes. "Although E. F. Hutton made money, she was the boss all the way down the line, 'cause she had the do-re-mi," observed Marjorie's private chauffeur Vincent "Jimmy" Sottile. In 1921 the Huttons thus purchased a 207-acre camp in the Adirondacks at the far end of Upper St. Regis Lake, about ten miles from Saranac Lake.

Hutridge, as the camp was called, sat on a hogback of forested land behind which were twin bodies of water called the Spectacle Lakes. Because the ridge rose higher on the St. Regis side, Hutridge sat eighty feet above the water on that shore. With lakes on all sides and no road, Hutridge was a water-locked camp. Everything—including guests, food, and supplies—was transported by staff motorboat.

Marjorie, at least, delighted in this isolation because it guaranteed her privacy and a retreat from civilization. "This has been our refuge for the whole family for years and years," she once explained. "The medium is quiet and peaceful and the only people we really see much are the various campers around the three lakes."

Marjorie's explanation was a characteristic understatement. Despite the woodsy environs, the Adirondacks—particularly around St. Regis

Lake—were a haven for the wealthy. The first influx of summertime visitors had occurred in the late nineteenth century. To city people, the Adirondacks region of upstate New York, with its craggy mountains, deep lakes, and dense forests, was a hunting and fishing paradise. By the turn of the century there were more than two hundred Adirondacks hotels for sportsmen and their wives, offering dinners of fresh venison and fish and a nearby taxidermist's office.

The benefits of fresh air and health attributed to outdoor living by citizens of the Gilded Age also attracted flocks of invalids suffering from tuberculosis, which Marjorie, coming to the north woods some twenty years later, must have found reminiscent of her father's preoccupation with health.

The Adirondacks, geographically speaking, were only a few miles north of the famous spa Saratoga Springs. Socially and philosophically, however, the two were worlds apart, the former populated by well-to-do men and their wives who sought authentic "natural" experiences in the north woods. By the 1880s, however, a social "Saratoga mentality" had already begun to seep through. At the beginning of that decade sugar-refining heir Frederick C. Durant had erected an elite six-story hotel deep in the woods, thirty miles from the nearest railroad. That three-hundred-room resort, known as Prospect House, bore a strong resemblance to Saratoga's Grand and United States hotels. Like them, it began to feature masquerades, balls, concerts, and parties. Before long Prospect House was known as "the most luxurious hotel in the woods." Among its guests were inhabitants of the New York *Social Register*, like the Astors, the Stuyvesants, and the Biddles.

The "folks around the lake," as Marjorie referred to her neighbors, were not middle-class year-rounders, as her phrase implies, but some of the wealthiest families in America, who came to "camp" in summer to escape the stifling heat of urban town houses and suburban estates. Among the "folks" were people like Mildred Phelps Stokes Hooker of the New York banking family, the Whitelaw Reids of the *New York Tribune*, the Robert Huntingtons, the George Vanderbilts, and the Herbert Pratts.

The "camps" were as upscale as the "folks" who inhabited them. While built in the unpretentious "Adirondacks style" as large one-story cabins with corner-notched logs, deliberate displays of unpeeled bark and tree roots, and raised stonework chimneys, these rustic hideaways for the wealthy were actually elaborate compounds. Within them were deluxe comforts like hot and cold running water, electricity, dressing rooms, private baths, sitting rooms, fireplaces—and, inevitably, staffs of servants to take care of them.

Visits between the residents of Upper St. Regis Lake were no less stylized than their camps. When Marjorie first summered in the Adirondacks with the McAlpins, they were expected to visit the Whitelaw Reids and the Robert Huntingtons. "They were always at home at tea time and one must go—it was a very formal performance, too, you left your card and God knows what," said Marjorie. "It all seemed so funny up there in the woods back to nature."

Ironically, Marjorie maintained her own brand of formality in the woods until the last summers of her life. Each cabin on her property had its own maid and butler. Every meal was announced with a bell, and guests were expected to be on time. While guests could swim, fish, canoe, or engage in other activities of their choice during the day, they were expected to appear for dinner every night in gowns and tuxedos.

Hutridge had originally been owned by the Lothrops, cofounders of the famous Washington, D.C., Woodward & Lothrop department store. When that family first built the camp in the 1880s, they had erected guest cottages and a main lodge reinforced with huge logs and two massive stone fireplaces. Marjorie later insisted that these had to be remodeled and other guest cottages and staff quarters added.

To do so, she commissioned a Manhattan architect to draft plans, which she subsequently presented to a local contractor named Ben Muncil. After perusing the blueprints, Muncil bluntly told Marjorie that he not only had trouble reading the plans but thought them "inappropriate" for an Adirondacks camp. The comment took the heiress by surprise. Humbled, Marjorie asked Muncil to draw up his own plans. Within a week the contractor had done so, and after several revisions by Marjorie's friend the architect Theodore Blake, Muncil supervised the construction. After an expenditure of half a million dollars, Hutridge emerged as a handsome complex of sixty-eight rustic buildings that included a newly renovated main lodge and eighteen guest cottages that were later "noted for [their] beauty of design and [their] perfect harmony with the Adirondack setting and surroundings."

In season—mid-July to Labor Day—the camp was staffed by eighty-five men and women, who cooked, maintained the property, and served as guides, boatmen, and naturalists for the Hutton guests. To Marjorie the brevity of the season was worrisome. How, she wondered, would her staff get work in the long winter months? To ensure their well-being, she employed many local staff members throughout the year.

"She used to come up here before she left and call Ed Russell [the general manager] and assign certain things she wanted done in the winter . . . that would keep these fellows working until the springtime," explained her chauffeur Jimmy Sottile.

Early on, Marjorie also purchased a fleet of canoes, rowboats, and motorboats, the last of which were used to ferry guests and supplies from Hutridge to the "town" side of Upper St. Regis Lake. As guests approached Hutridge on one of Marjorie's boats, they were inevitably charmed by the quaintness of the boathouse, an Adirondacks classic, with support beams of curved and polished branches, twigs, and tree roots that were whimsically incorporated into the building design.

Another feature was an open-air funicular that, according to family lore, Marjorie built so that the now-elderly Aunt Mollie would not have to climb eighty feet above the St. Regis Lake boat dock to enter the camp. For years Marjorie's aunt had lavished praise upon her niece for her generosity and bright spirit. As Aunt Mollie wrote in a 1918 letter, ". . . *you*, my dear, are the dearest thing in my life—sometimes the notes of a happy song will bring me a thought of you, sometimes a flower as I pass along, or a sky that is azure blue."

Now Aunt Mollie decided to reward Marjorie's latest kindness at Hutridge with another. To enhance the rustic Adirondacks atmosphere, she gave Marjorie a collection of authentic American Indian baskets and blankets. Over the years the heiress carefully added to this collection. By the end of Marjorie's life the collection included priceless objects like a Ute feather headdress, a deck of rare Apache playing cards, Native American baskets, and a famous tapestry by the Navajo curer and weaver Hosteen Klah. An Eskimo kayak hung suspended from the rafters. Below it, on tables, chairs, pianos, and shelves, were stuffed owls, foxes, opossums; animal pelts covered some of the couches and chairs. Beneath them were wolf, pony, and bearskin rugs.

To guests who entered the main lodge in subsequent years, this collection—some would call it a hodgepodge—of native artifacts, stuffed animals, birchwood "wallpaper," Adirondacks-style antelope-horn chandeliers, and other "things made of things" was a visual feast. It was, said Liz Carpenter, Washington journalist and onetime White House press secretary to Lady Bird Johnson, like gazing at "the lobby of a great hotel with lots of things to see, including playing cards, made with the skins, scalps, I guess . . . it had an Indian touch to it . . . somehow it was pixie." As in the heiress's other homes, the Native American artifacts epitomized Marjorie's love of the unusual and her insistence upon collections of first quality.

Today many pieces from this collection are on display at Marjorie's Washington estate, the second Hillwood. At this writing the main lodge at the heiress's old Adirondacks camp (now privately owned) still contains a dazzling array of Native American blankets, tomahawks, bows and arrows, beadwork, and lamps made from animal skins.

Ultimately, Hutridge (Topridge it was later called) was one of the few real estate properties that Marjorie retained to the end of her life. Over the years virtually everyone important to the heiress—among them, ambassadors, four-star generals, statesmen, and diplomats—visited the Adirondacks for one of the heiress's legendary weekends. It was here that Madame Nehru, the Greek ambassador and Mrs. Aleco Matsas, the Clifford Folgers, World War II hero General Anthony "Nuts" McAuliffe, Dr. and Mrs. Leonard Carmichael, Admiral Ray Hunter, Clement Conger, Baroness Scheyven (wife of the Belgian ambassador Louis Scheyven), Princess Cito di Bitetto, Lady Braebourne, and other notables spent memorable four-day weekends. It was here, too, that Hedda Hopper presented Marjorie one of her famous hats, that journalist Liz Carpenter and society columnist Betty Beale trampled across overgrown trails for group picnics known as "carries." To visit Marjorie's Adirondacks camp, as Beale wrote in a 1964 *Washington Star* column, "is to get a glimpse into the life of a queen and a unique example of a bygone era."

That same year Marjorie had other reasons to be filled with hope. A new life was stirring in her womb. Fervently she prayed that it would be a boy; to give Ned a son would have been the sweetest accomplishment of all. But it was not to be. Despite Marjorie's care during the pregnancy, she miscarried in the third month. Had the child lived, it would have been a boy.

Several years later Marjorie became pregnant again, and this time, to her and Ned's delight, the heiress delivered a healthy girl. Officially the Huttons named their little daughter Nedenia, but by everyone who knew her, the baby was called Deenie. From the start, the child was unusually beautiful, with blond hair, blue eyes, and fine features that seemed a dazzling combination of Marjorie's and E.F.'s good looks.

Later, when she was grown up enough to understand, Marjorie told Dina about the miscarriage of the little brother who had preceded her and the great sorrow of that event. "I was named for my father," the actress recalled, "He was called Ned, and so I was supposed to have been the Ned. Nedenia. My parents did the best they could under the circumstances."

By 1924 Marjorie had decided to sell her town house at 2 East Ninety-second Street. She did so for several reasons. To start with, the congestion of the city was creeping northward—and with it, the noisy street traffic. Moreover, a developer named George A. Fuller had approached E.F. with an offer to buy the Burden mansion and put an apartment house on the site. Yet neither Marjorie nor E.F. had any intention of giving up their Manhattan address. In the end the Huttons agreed to sell the old Burden mansion to Fuller with the proviso that he build them a triplex apartment on the top of his apartment house, a dozen stories above the noise from the street. In addition, Marjorie insisted that Fuller build an adjoining apartment for Aunt Mollie and Uncle Cal that would open into their own living quarters.

The idea of abandoning a town house for apartment living was already de rigueur among New York society. By the 1920s the movement was fast becoming a trend, hastened by the high cost of maintaining a single-family dwelling in Manhattan and fears about the growing incidence of crime. As early as the post–Civil War period, the wealthy had begun moving into swank Manhattan apartment houses like The Stuyvesant, but it was not until 1908, when William Randolph Hearst took the top three floors of the Clarendon at Riverside Drive and Eighty-sixth Street, that wealthy people began to consider apartment living a viable option.

Marjorie's highly ordered mind was never more obvious than when she designed her homes. Before the apartment house was erected, the heiress had insisted upon incorporating into the plans every luxurious feature of town-house living she had enjoyed in the Burden mansion. A private entrance was so important that Marjorie insisted that her address be retained as 2 East Ninety-second Street. The other residents entered on the Fifth Avenue side of the building at number 1107. Similarly, Marjorie insisted upon keeping her rights to a private parking garage within the building. She later reminisced, "We had a perfectly lovely porte cochere where we drove the cars in under the building and there with a beautiful entrance hall a fireplace at one end, a fountain at the other." There was also a private elevator "with no stops til it got up to our main floor."

Marjorie put similar thought into the living space itself. The new apartment, like the other homes she built in that period, was not only a residence but an entertainment pavilion. It was the urban equivalent of a royal palace. Marjorie had not forgotten the old crack at the Close wedding about her midwestern roots and would see to it that 2 East Ninety-second Street would go a long way toward countering that snub. At its completion Marjorie's fifty-four-room triplex apartment was widely acknowledged as "the largest and very possibly the most luxurious apartment ever created anywhere."

From the private elevator, guests walked through a set of large French doors into an enormous hall, which could be converted into a ballroom. To the left and right of the entrance were cloakrooms for men and women. The ballroom floor was trimmed in marble and inlaid with fine woods that contained a sunbird pattern and the Hutton-Post monogram. When the apartment was not being used for a party, the hall was covered with thick Oriental rugs, antique tables, and chairs.

Adjacent to that expanse was a drawing room with an enormous Palladian-style picture window on the Fifth Avenue side of the building overlooking the Central Park reservoir. On the other side of the elevator was a wood-paneled dining room capable of seating as many as 125 people. Scattered throughout these formal rooms were paintings by Gainsborough and Rubens, sculptures by Houdon, tapestries by Boucher and Aubusson, and antique Oriental rugs. Behind the formal rooms were a butler's pantry, a wine room, kitchens, and eighteen staff rooms. "The apartment really offered a most wonderful place to entertain and . . . enjoy people," Marjorie once said with typical understatement.

The east side of the apartment was equally luxurious, but far more intimate, containing a library and a glass-paneled breakfast room. Being quite fond of the library paneling in the old Burden mansion, Marjorie had had it saved when the town house was torn down; later it was reinstalled in her new Manhattan triplex. With equal care, she preserved the Burden mansion's dining room mantel. Years later the "thrifty" heiress recycled favorite features of this Manhattan apartment in her other new homes.

The second and third floors of Marjorie's Manhattan apartment were reserved for private living. Half of the second floor was reserved for

Aunt Mollie and Uncle Cal's apartment; the other half included a guest room, a gown closet, dressing rooms, a secretarial office, adjoining bedrooms for Marjorie and E.F., and, in those days before air-conditioning, a sleeping porch.

Above these, on the top floor of the building, were the children's bedrooms and playrooms, a laundry room, and sleeping quarters for the housekeeper and secretary. An added luxury was a private terrace on the roof that had a carefully manicured garden and a place for the girls to play.

All in all, as even the heiress admitted, the new 2 East Ninety-second Street was "quite a place." The triplex was, in fact, so satisfying that Marjorie retained it for another two decades, until personal circumstances drew her away from the magnetic center of her old Manhattan dream.

11

Voracious Appetites

*T*he completion of the Huttons' new homes enabled Marjorie and E.F. to enjoy a peripatetic lifestyle, flitting from location to location as season, whim, or personal need demanded. In summer the couple visited Hutridge in the Adirondacks. In spring and fall they commuted between Manhattan and their Long Island estate. In the winter Marjorie and E.F. dallied in Palm Beach. In between there were hunting expeditions to E.F.'s shooting lodge in South Carolina, trips on the broker's yacht, and sojourns in spas like Saratoga and Hot Springs, Virginia.

Yet Marjorie and E.F.'s life was not as carefree as it superficially seemed. In the first years of their marriage the rhythms of their days were punctuated by the ticking of a distant but relentless clock: the industrial timepiece that hung over the production buildings of the Postum Cereal Company in Battle Creek. Beneath their glittering arrivals and departures, beneath their dinners, parties, and balls, E.F. and Marjorie had another agenda that alternately united and separated them: the growth and development of the Postum Cereal Company.

In 1923 E.F. became chairman of the Postum Cereal Company board. Although the job was demanding, Marjorie's husband collected no salary; instead he was given a large block of stock. While E.F. was a millionaire in his own right, retirement from the management of his own brokerage house, the E. F. Hutton Company, was still a sacrifice. At the very least it signaled E.F.'s confidence in the stability of his mar-

riage, a sentiment that Marjorie shared in their first years together.
Decades later the heiress told an interviewer that she had attempted to
compensate E.F. by allowing him to dip into her private funds.

In his capacity as chairman of the Postum board, E.F.'s financial wiz-
ardry produced almost immediate results. At the end of 1922 the
Postum Cereal Company had issued an annual report announcing sales
of $11.5 million and a profit of $1.4 million. A year later, with E.F. as
chairman, those sales had climbed to nearly $13 million, with a profit
of $1.8 million.

Even those sums, E.F. and the new Postum president, Clare Chester,
privately believed, were only a beginning. A larger vision tantalized the
two businessmen: that of a corporate dynamo with a thrust so powerful
that it would transform C.W.'s old cereal company into a giant food
conglomerate.

The first step in this master plan was the relocation of Postum corpo-
rate offices. So it was that in late 1923 E.F. and Clare Chester moved
Postum headquarters to offices at 342 Madison Avenue in Manhattan.
This was only a way station. What E.F. and Clare envisioned was an of-
fice building of their own that would proclaim the significance of
Postum to Wall Street and corporate America.

In the boom years of the 1920s such ambitions were hardly unusual.
By mid-decade other Manhattan-based companies were already beginning to erect steel-frame monuments to their industrial magnificence.
Among them was the dramatic American Radiator Company building,
completed in 1924 in black brick and terra-cotta. Its dramatic nighttime lighting made the building appear like a warm glow heating the
Manhattan skyline. For more than a year New Yorkers had been gazing
at the steel-frame foundation of a skyscraper that was to rise seventy-
seven floors above the street and be known as the Chrysler Building.
Later in the decade these were followed by other "cathedrals of commerce," among them the New York Central Building, the Fred F.
French skyscraper, the RCA Building, and the Chanin Building.

By the time the Battle Creek moving vans rolled into midtown Manhattan, E.F. and Clare had fulfilled at least part of their goal. While
Postum was not yet ready to build a skyscraper of its own, plans were
under way to renovate a building at 250 Park Avenue, conveniently
near Grand Central Station. Marjorie's "men" were as sensitive to publicity as they were to stock fluctuations. The move to the Postum Building, as the new location would be known, was scheduled for January
1925, the thirtieth anniversary of the Postum Cereal Company.

When the move was first announced, a hue and cry arose from employees at Battle Creek. But E.F. and Clare were prepared for the protest. This was no time, they gently reminded Postum employees, for hometown sentiment. The Postum Cereal Company was big business, and in the boom years of the mid-1920s there was every reason to believe it would continue to expand.

The United States had emerged from World War I as a great international power. An era of optimism was sweeping the country. Industrial output had reached new peaks of national growth. America's citizens were hardworking and inventive, its businesses among the most productive and prosperous in the world. In 1925 even Herbert Hoover, then the popular secretary of commerce, had praised the nation's economic strength and linked it to the ambitious American character. As he said in 1925, "The high standards of living enjoyed by the American people are the result of steadily mounting per capita productivity." To maximize that productivity, to keep abreast of the latest trends and a bullish stock market, it was necessary for Postum to be headquartered in New York, close to the center of the nation's financial heart.

Whatever qualms Marjorie had about moving the company to Manhattan were negligible. To start with, the changes would not affect the lives of most Postum workers in Battle Creek. C.W.'s old plant and production facilities would continue to run around the clock as they had for nearly three decades. Although certain executives and other key personnel were relocated to New York, the Postum company had assured workers that no one would lose his job. With such a policy, C.W.'s paternalistic "spirit" toward his workers would be honored, and with it, Marjorie's conscience cleared.

In reality, Marjorie supported the move for deeply personal reasons. The truth was that the relocation to New York would relieve the heiress of a painful emotional burden: the necessity of making annual trips to Battle Creek. It was not that Marjorie disliked or disdained her hometown; she still had fond friends there like Myra Kane, Norma Eldred, and Henry Hawks's daughter Lucy. In the years following C.W.'s death, however, Leila had become a highly visible force in the city. This became especially apparent after her 1916 marriage to the handsome Post Tavern manager Lawrence Montgomery. In 1922 Marjorie's stepmother had donated seventy acres of land on the outskirts of Battle Creek to be used as a public arboretum. The following year, in an effort to honor her aging mother, Leila bought an old mansion, which she converted into the Emily Andrus Home for elderly women. In 1925 she laid the groundwork for an even larger civic institution. That year Leila P. Montgomery donated five hundred thousand dollars for the creation of a new Battle Creek hospital that eventually carried her name.

Although the citizens of Battle Creek now regarded Leila as a revered civic benefactress, Marjorie's feelings toward her remained negative. In the decade since C.W.'s death nothing had changed between the heiress and her stepmother. Privately Marjorie still smoldered over the memory of the lawsuit about the Postum stock. Moreover, Leila had kept all of C.W.'s personal memorabilia for herself, a slight the heiress never forgot. It was not until after Leila's death in 1940 that her nephew and executor, Kenneth Montgomery, finally had C.W.'s personal belongings sent to Marjorie.

These bitternesses, combined with Leila's recent gifts to the city of Battle Creek, led Marjorie to retreat from the town as a civic patron. In late 1924, when Postum workers invited Marjorie to the dedication of the employee clubhouse, which was on the site of C.W.'s old office building, the heiress politely declined. As Doris Lambeer (whose husband, George, was president of the Post Division of General Foods) recalled years later, Marjorie made virtually no contributions to Battle Creek during her stepmother's lifetime. When natives approached Marjorie for civic donations, her characteristic response was " 'Let Leila do it!' You just couldn't approach her on the subject."

In 1941, a year after Leila's death, Marjorie explained her cool attitude to a Battle Creek friend: "In all the many years past I have purposely not gone to Battle Creek for the reason that it was Leila's home, and after the lawsuit . . . I always felt that it was just better not to inject another personality into that location."

In 1924 E.F., Clare Chester, and the Postum board of directors unveiled a new plan for the Postum Cereal Company: They were going to expand beyond cereals into other types of ready-made foods. In spite of strong sales, other breakfast food companies were eating into their market. Chief among these was the W. K. Kellogg Company of Battle Creek, which was now run solely by Dr. John Harvey Kellogg's younger brother, Will.

In 1906, after years of bitter litigation, W.K. had wrested control of the old Toasted Corn Flake Company from Dr. Kellogg. Finally, in 1920, after still another round of court battles, a triumphant W.K. won the exclusive right to use the Kellogg name for his cereal company. So obsessed was W.K. with his hard-won autonomy that he now created a slogan in fiery red ink that he placed upon cereal cartons: "The Genuine Bears This Signature—W. K. Kellogg." For years W.K. had been applying modern sales techniques to his product. Now aggressive Kellogg advertisements began to appear in national women's magazines, newspapers, and radio ads. By the mid-twenties Kellogg's Corn Flakes had become a well-known household product that was rivaling better-established cereals like Postum's Grape-Nuts and Post Toasties.

Competition—and relations—between the two Battle Creek companies grew increasingly tense. In 1923 in-house market researchers assured Postum company executives that their company still made higher profits than Kellogg's: 13 percent compared with an alleged 9 percent margin for their rival. Even so, E.F. and Clare thought the gap was too close for comfort. Diversification into other products, rather than an intensified struggle with up-and-coming competitors, was their solution. Specifically what E.F. and Clare envisioned was expansion into a variety of products that included not only ready-made cereals but other types of prepackaged foods.

By the early 1920s the American consumer was ready for such products. Prepared, or prepackaged, foods were just beginning to capture the public imagination. An important part of their appeal was their timesaving benefit, something the hurried young women of the postwar years craved. In their emphasis on convenience, ready-made foods were emblematic of the Jazz Age itself, an era when everything seemed to get done faster. Moreover, such foods could be rapidly purchased in another modern convenience, the new supermarkets that were springing up across the land from Maine to California.

Although E.F. and Clare ultimately were given the credit for the decision to diversify the Postum Cereal Company, Marjorie played an important behind-the-scenes role. In her unequivocally feminine but all-powerful voice as Postum's major stockholder, she reminded her husband and Clare that she wanted to fulfill her father's long-term plans for the business. In the last years of his life C.W. had repeatedly confided in Marjorie that he hoped to join ranks with other companies. "So with the war being over, we decided that we might look around and see whether it might be a good idea to broaden our base," Marjorie once told an interviewer. Like E.F. and Clare, the heiress had come to believe that the key to broadening that base was the acquisition of ready-made foods.

Although Marjorie herself did not cook, she was sympathetic to the drudgery shouldered by the average housewife who was unable to afford hired help. In part, she had learned that perspective from C.W., whose invention of Grape-Nuts had relieved women from cooking oatmeal for breakfast over coal stoves. For years her father had preached to Marjorie what is known today as consumer awareness. It was a basic principle of good business—and a charge that the heiress eventually accepted as her personal mission.

On December 31, 1925, the Postum company board of directors made a startling announcement. That day C.W.'s company exchanged 570 shares of common stock for all the capital stock of the Jell-O Company, Inc., of Le Roy, New York. With the addition of Orator Francis Woodward's famous dessert company, a new corporate era had begun.

Jell-O was only an appetizer, an hors d'oeuvre on a Postum menu that soon began to look like an elaborate banquet. In early 1926 the Postum company purchased Iglehart Brothers, Inc., of Evansville, Indiana, producers of Swans Down cake flour. By October 31 Postum had swallowed the Minute Tapioca Company, Inc., of Orange, Massachusetts. Little by little the Postum Cereal Company was growing; by the end of 1926 sales had swelled to an impressive $20 million, with profits of $11.8 million.

In October 1926 a company report, "The Handwriting on the Wall," explained Postum's acquisition strategy as an effort to capitalize on economies of scale. "It is our opinion," says the report, "that American industry stands on the threshold of the most prosperous era in its history. Yet . . . we foresee a trade competition that will be even more revolutionary . . . than the advent of machinery and mass production. Manufacturers . . . are already feeling the pressure of this competition. The war for supremacy is on. . . . We propose to group under one head a number of nationally advertised, non-competitive food specialties, for the purposes of mutual economy and greater service."

Six months later, in March 1927, C.W.'s old corporation assumed a new name. No longer was it to be known as the Postum Cereal Company. Now it was simply the Postum Company. In testimony to the company's profitability, E.F and Clare went on another food binge; this time they purchased Walter Baker & Company, the Log Cabin Products Company, Richard Hellman, Inc., and the Sanka Coffee Corporation. The last company's product—a noncaffeinated coffee substitute that continues to be popular to the present day—must have given Marjorie pause as she recalled a vision of her sweating father bent over a pan of roasting wheat, bran, and molasses in the white barn. But money talks louder than childhood memories, and by the end of 1927 it fairly shouted Marjorie's reminiscences down. That year sales for the Postum Company built to a deafening $37 million, with profits of $13.6 million.

By 1928 the Postum Company was percolating at even higher levels. That year, it acquired Calumet baking powder, La France laundry products, and a $45 million product that C.W. had railed against for years, a coffee that was already famous because of its association with former president Theodore Roosevelt. According to legend, Roosevelt had visited President Andrew Jackson's home in Nashville, Tennessee, where he was served a cup of coffee from the nearby Maxwell House Inn. When asked if he wanted a second cup, he had replied, "Will I have another? Delighted. It's good to the last drop."

To Marjorie, the addition of Maxwell House coffee to the Postum Company bordered on sacrilege. "That nearly finished me off," she recalled. "I had been raised with the idea that coffee was just like taking dope." Nevertheless, profits from Maxwell House were so strong that even Marjorie was forced to concede. At year's end the Postum Company had sales of $56.5 million and a net profit of $17.5 million.

For years, in a preemptive parody of George Bernard Shaw's apocryphal response to Marlene Dietrich's proposal, E.F. had been fond of saying that with his luck and Clare's brains the company should go far. Already it seemed that the prophecy had come true. Ten months before Wall Street's Black Tuesday crash of October 29, 1929, the Postum Company had become one of the largest prepared-food corporations in the world.

Coincidentally, the heady winds of travel that became a signature of the Hutton lifestyle thrust Marjorie and E.F. into another business venture—this time one that would give the couple a rocky course.

For years E.F. had been an avid yachtsman and fisherman. Long before his marriage to Marjorie, the broker had owned several yachts and been a member of the prestigious New York Yacht Club. Soon after their wedding he had introduced Marjorie to the sport, and she had taken to it avidly.

Much as Marjorie liked sailing, she was insistent about creature comforts, including spacious living quarters, an elegant decor, and privacy. To accommodate his wife, E.F. in 1923 purchased a new yacht, the fourth one he would name *Hussar*. The *Hussar IV* was a handsome three-masted schooner that was over three hundred feet in length and powered by a six-hundred-horsepower diesel engine. Within it were five handsomely appointed staterooms with private bathrooms, a dining room, a kitchen, and a living room large enough to contain an Oriental rug and a grand piano. The yacht, as *Town and Country* magazine observed in September 1923, "will be used for extended cruises and the living quarters are consequently unusually spacious and comfortable."

In the first summers with the *Hussar IV*, the Huttons often sailed up the East Coast. On one occasion Marjorie and E.F. moored in a rocky cove of Gloucester, Massachusetts. As it happened, Marjorie knew a local resident, John Hays Hammond, who often spent his winters in Palm Beach. That elderly gentleman, who had been a geologist with Cecil B. Rhodes in South Africa, had several sons, one of whom, Harris, had befriended Marjorie and E.F. Shortly after a visit with the Hammonds, Marjorie and E.F. were served goose aboard the *Hussar*. The dish was surprisingly tasty. When Marjorie asked where the cook had purchased it, he explained that he had bought it frozen in Gloucester.

The heiress was fascinated. Keeping enough fresh food on a yacht to last several days at sea was a perpetual problem, even with the latest shipboard refrigerators. Unwittingly Marjorie's cook had stumbled upon a solution: poultry that could be frozen and stored almost indefinitely.

Exactly what happened next is unclear. According to one version of the story, Marjorie ordered the yacht back to Gloucester Harbor to find out who had frozen the goose. In another version the Huttons continued their trip up the coast toward Maine, and on their return E.F. went ashore to search out the inventor. What is certain is that ultimately the Huttons discovered that a man named Clarence "Bob" or "Bugs" Birdseye—a friend of Harris Hammond's—had been freezing foods for years. In fact, Birdseye had a small factory in Gloucester Harbor known as the General Seafoods Corporation.

The more Marjorie learned about Birdseye's company, the more fascinated she was. Frozen poultry was only a small part of Birdseye's business. The entrepreneur's main endeavor was freezing fish by a new method that kept the product nearly as fresh as when it was first caught. For years Birdseye had also experimented with the freezing of vegetables and fruits.

The fact that Birdseye was producing "frosted" vegetables and fruits as well as fish and meat struck Marjorie as a remarkable innovation, one that had profound ramifications for the food industry. Like most nineteenth-century youth, Marjorie had grown up watching her mother can fruits and vegetables every fall. Even in the industrialized twenties, most American women still spent several days or weeks each fall canning the harvest for their families' winter dinner tables.

Now it occurred to Marjorie that if the Birdseye process was as good as it sounded, the average housewife could eliminate the tedious canning process by shopping for frozen foods year-round. Nature—and the perennial food shortages caused by weather fluctuations—would have been tamed. In winter housewives would be able to serve strawberries and fresh peas; orange juice could be consumed year-round; even difficult foods like oysters—traditionally eaten only in the *r* months—could be served at whim. The seasons would no longer have relevance to what was sold in grocery stores.

The idea was revolutionary. "Frosted foods," Marjorie began to believe, were a wave of the future, something the time-pressed housewife would rush to buy as soon as those foods were widely advertised. With the addition of Birdseye's "frosted foods," the Postum Company would have a distinct advantage over competitors.

The only stumbling block was that in the twenties, frozen foods had a bad reputation. In the public view, the term *frozen* was, in fact, almost synonymous with spoiled or off-flavor food. As early as the Civil War people had experimented with frozen foods, but they were rarely served with pride. Thrifty American housewives also froze foods that were beginning to spoil; later, when defrosted, they never tasted particularly good. Even foods that were frozen fresh often lost their flavor when thawed.

This happened, as Birdseye later understood, because the conventional slow-freeze method, which relied upon ice to chill food down, tended to separate the water from the solid protoplasmic materials of the cells. As it froze, that water formed large, sharp ice crystals, which, in turn, destroyed the cell walls. Consequently, when those products were thawed or cooked, the moisture poured out of the cells and rendered the food tasteless or spoiled.

As a young man the scientifically bent Birdseye had traveled to Labrador and studied the problem. Ultimately he invented a quick-freeze method that enabled fish, meat, and poultry to be as fresh when defrosted as when market-fresh. In his zeal and salesmanship the inventor bore a striking resemblance to Marjorie's father, C. W. And like him, Birdseye had arrived at his discovery through a combination of hard work, a disappointing life experience, a knack for business, and a determination to create a new industry.

The resemblance between Birdseye and C.W. was so uncanny that eventually Marjorie asked Postum vice-president Clarence "Clare" Francis—who had been a classmate of Bugs Birdseye's at Amherst College—about his stability. "Bugs? Why, sure," the executive assured her. "He's completely crazy, but completely reliable."

Birdseye first conducted experiments in instant freezing at the Clothel Refrigerating Company of Bayonne, New Jersey, where he discovered that when food was frozen rapidly, there was no time for large ice crystals to form. In their place were small ice crystals that kept the cells intact. Hence the food was perfectly preserved.

To standardize his rapid-freeze process, Birdseye devised an iron container with steel plates. Within them he placed packages of fresh fish in a low-temperature brine refrigerant. Knowing that the public would be wary, Birdseye named the contraption a froster rather than a freezer. Soon afterward the inventor applied for patents on his process, set up shop in Manhattan and began selling Birdseye's Frosted Foods to the railroads.

In spite of this early success, Birdseye was an inherently modest man. "There was nothing very remarkable about what I had done. I did not discover quick-freezing," the inventor insisted to the *American* magazine years later. "The Eskimos had used it for centuries and scientists in Europe had made experiments along the same lines."

In 1924, after a silent partner had pulled out of the business, Birdseye reorganized his company and moved it to Gloucester, Massachusetts. He had chosen the New England location for a specific reason. Then, as today, Gloucester was one of the largest fishing towns on the East Coast, and it provided Birdseye with ready access to the day's catch. Before long the inventor was packaging, freezing, and selling haddock to the public through his new enterprise, the General Seafoods Company.

To speed production, Birdseye introduced an assembly-line version of his original quick freezer called the belt froster. This machine consisted of an industrial track surrounded by a set of metal plates, one of which was sprayed with a brine of calcium chloride chilled at minus 40°F. As whole or prepackaged fish passed down the track, it made contact with the unsprayed metal plate, which, having absorbed the cold from its treated twin, instantly froze the fish.

About that time, Birdseye changed the name of his business to the General Foods Company. The alteration was about more than semantics. Despite the establishment of a viable retail operation, the scientifically inclined Birdseye wanted to head a research company that would develop many types of frozen foods and license them to other food companies.

When Marjorie learned about Birdseye's goals, she became even more interested. To her, the inventor's "frosted foods" and his long-term plans made the company a potential Postum acquisition. Marjorie now began to promote the idea aggressively to E.F. "You've got to buy Birdseye, Ned," she urged her husband. "I'm speaking for the housewife here. Frozen foods will reduce her work considerably. It's an opportunity we can't afford to miss."

E.F. was not impressed. From his perspective, Birdseye's products were still highly experimental. Moreover, he believed the public would never buy them. That Birdseye called his foods frosted rather than frozen was immaterial. There were other practical considerations. Even if Postum decided to invest in the Birdseye company, what was to guarantee that wholesalers and grocers would be willing to buy the new, expensive freezers to store them? "Marjorie, listen to reason," E.F. argued. "Every grocer in the land would have to buy big appliances for their stores. What would make them willing to make that investment? And what makes you think the housewife would be willing to do the same?"

As it happened, E.F. was right. By the end of 1928 Birdseye had a worrisome 1.6 million pounds of frozen fish piled up in his warehouse. Ironically, the inventor's problem was not demand for the fish—there was clearly a market for it—but how to distribute the frosted foods. Even in the boom years of the 1920s there were simply not enough refrigerator trucks and railroad cars to transport Birdseye's frosted foods to other cities. Nor were there adequate freezer warehouses or supermarket freezers to store them when they arrived.

Still, Marjorie could not be talked out of her convictions. As a woman with concrete ideas about what the average housewife wanted, as an heiress to the business tutored upon C.W.'s knee, she believed that such obstacles could be overcome. Any investment made by the Postum Company to solve the distribution problem, Marjorie countered, would ultimately be worth it. "Believe me, Ned, they'll buy the appliances. They'll do it," she insisted. "At least find out how much Birdseye wants for the company." Reluctantly E.F. agreed. Legend has it that Birdseye's initial asking price was somewhere between $10 million and $12 million. For a year or two the Postum Company backed off from the negotiations.

Marjorie, meanwhile, kept hammering away at her husband. The couple argued about the Birdseye company so often that their exchanges became almost ritualistic. "Ned, you've just got to buy Birdseye," Marjorie would insist. "Aw, forget it," the broker would reply. The idea, he told his wife, was just plain "impractical." Finally, in 1928 or early 1929, E.F. had a change of heart. What seems to have convinced him was that after years of heavy investment in research and equipment, the Birdseye company was finally beginning to turn a profit.

In April 1929, Sidney Weinberg, an agent for Postum's bankers, Goldman, Sachs & Company, approached Birdseye representative Isaac L. Rice. "Tell me about Birdseye. . . . We'd like to buy it. Name me a price. A million dollars one way or another means nothing to us!" said Weinberg. Rice was stunned. After a series of discussions with Birdseye, Rice named what he considered a ridiculously high figure: $12 million for three quarters of the stock.

If Weinberg was surprised, he did not show it. A few days later he called Birdseye's representative back. "We don't want three quarters of anything. Name a price for your last quarter. We expect to pay more."

Once again Rice consulted with Birdseye. Ultimately it was decided that if Postum was going to buy out Birdseye so that the inventor and his top executives would have no future stake in the profits, the price tag would be even higher. In June 1929 the negotiations were finished. Postum had agreed to buy the rest of the Birdseye stock for an additional $10 million, bringing the total sale of the company to $22 million.

Marjorie was pleased, but the sale left the heiress and her husband uneasy. Had E.F. purchased Birdseye's company before 1929, had he listened to Marjorie's earlier pleas, Postum could have obtained Birdseye's frozen foods industry at a considerably lower price.

The words *I told you so* were not part of Marjorie's vocabulary. She was too tactful a woman, and too much in love with the dynamic stockbroker, to rub her business acumen in E.F.'s face. Moreover, such a discussion was unnecessary. E.F. was an intelligent man and could not help contemplating the many times that Marjorie had nagged him to buy Birdseye in the past. What was also left unsaid was that the heiress was relatively untutored in modern business techniques—especially when compared with E.F.'s strong track record. Yet her hunch about Birdseye had been more astute than his perception.

A sense of humiliation seeped through E.F. as insidiously as an encroaching tide upon a sleeping sunbather. Just as silently that flood of mixed emotions ebbed away into a groundwater of hidden resentments. On the surface, nothing seemed to change in their marriage or in the management of the business. After all, E.F.—and Clare Chester—were indisputably responsible for the phenomenal growth of the Postum Company. What did it matter that Marjorie had spotted Birdseye first?

For years the heiress had praised E.F.'s financial management of her father's old company. As she wrote Hutton's friend Max Sindt in 1927, "I am sure it has been gratifying to you to know the marvelous things he [E.F.] has done with the Postum Co. He has more than tripled what my holdings were when we were married and it takes a smart man to do that."

Nevertheless, the memory of Marjorie's earlier advice nibbled at E. F. Hutton. For all his brilliance, his wife was more powerful than he could ever be. Now, in addition to her inherited fortune, Marjorie had topped him again with advice he had chosen to ignore—until he had been forced to pay a higher price.

It was true that the acquisition of the Birdseye company was not expected to result in immediate profits. Everyone, from E.F. and Clare Chester down, knew that it would take several years for Postum to market and distribute Birds Eye products to grocery stores, supermarkets, and consumers before there would be a profit. Still, the purchase of Birdseye's frozen foods industry signified the completion of a dream, the final notch in a five-year expansion plan that elevated the company to another corporate level: that of a megabusiness that would coordinate separate commercial entities.

As a result, the name *the Postum Company* no longer seemed adequate. For years E.F. and Clare had tossed around the idea of changing the corporate name. In July 1928 Clare had even explained the rationale for doing so to members of the board of directors. In an official letter he had written:

> The main reason prompting this suggestion is that our present name is restrictive. *Postum* is one product out of our total of sixteen and from a sales standpoint its volume is and will continue to be below the average of the others. . . . The chief value of our corporate name (since each product is manufactured, advertised and sold under its own brand name) is in its relation to our capital stock and its purchase and sale on the Exchange. It is quite possible that a po-

tential stockholder will be deterred from an investment in Postum because the name "Postum Company" does not put him on inquiry as
to the extent and diversification of our business. . . .

With the June 1929 acquisition of Birds Eye products, diversification—not only into other types of prepared foods but into other aspects
of the food industry—had become a reality. On July 24, 1929, C.W.'s
old company ceased to exist. Thenceforth the group of food companies
collected under the aegis of the original Postum Cereal Company would
be known on the New York Stock Exchange as the General Foods Corporation.

Ironically, the final catalyst for that change had been the acquisition
of Birdseye's General Foods Company, the brainchild of E. F. Hutton's
untutored wife, Marjorie.

12

"Such Scrambling
as We Did!"

"To understand the gala and extravagant behavior in Palm Beach in the '20's one must realize that World War I was over, the world was 'safe for democracy,' and prosperity was rampant in the days of low taxes," said Marjorie of her Jazz Age experiences in southeastern Florida. As the twenties spun faster, the heiress and E.F. became celebrated figures in Palm Beach, leaders of a vibrant young set that created fresh standards of style and behavior for future generations of resorters. That the Huttons were good-looking and glamorous was indisputable. That they dressed with panache was a given. That they traveled between New York, the Adirondacks, Long Island, and South Carolina in a heady mix of business and pleasure added to their aura. But what lent Marjorie and E.F. their special charm was their sense of fun and penchant for exotic and exciting people.

Despite the brevity of the Palm Beach season—in those days, from early January to February 22—Marjorie and E.F. fashioned a magnetic lifestyle that drew others to their side and amended social rituals to include innovations like cabana beach clubs, costume balls, and theatrical extravaganzas. Among their friends were the Palm Beach doyen Paris Singer; the former duchess of Marlborough, Consuelo Vanderbilt Balsam; the urbane brothers Gurnee and Charlie Munn (the latter's patented "mechanized rabbit" and "totalizator" had revolutionized racetrack betting); Philadelphia publisher Barclay Warburton; the amiable J. Anthony "Tony" Drexel Biddle, Jr., and his wife, Mary; Mr. and

Mrs. John Pillsbury, of the flour family; and Amy Phipps, of the Carnegie steel fortune (and the wife of the courtly British parliamentarian the Right Honorable Frederick E. Guest, cousin of Winston Churchill). And, of course, Marjorie's protectress, Palm Beach grande dame Eva T. Stotesbury.

Added to these was a glamorous mix of artists and European aristocrats who provided an exotic, theatrical aura to the rarefied social life of Palm Beach in the twenties. These included names like the White Russian prince Serge Obolensky, who wed Alice Astor in 1924; the duke and duchess of Sutherland; Lord Thurston; the duchess de Gaument; Countess Salm; Adolph Zukor, head of Paramount Pictures; novelist Arthur Somers Roche; writer Anita Loos; dancer Irene Castle; and Billie Burke and her husband, Flo Ziegfeld. The last two, in particular, were close friends of Marjorie and E.F.'s, and it was not long before the Ziegfelds' diamond-studded warmth swept the Huttons into a dazzling group of Broadway stars and silver-screen idols.

The mingling of society and show-business celebrities soon made the already posh Palm Beach legendary. Stuffy silver-trayed parties attended by matrons in stiff ball gowns, heavy jewels, and upswept hair, accompanied by men with pince-nez and top hats, were replaced by spotlit galas where heiresses, movie idols, and millionaires mingled in short, sequined dresses or jauntily tailored tuxedos or danced at costume balls to the tango and Charleston.

The latter affairs, in particular, served to whet Marjorie's naturally dramatic appetites. From Billie Burke, the heiress first learned to put on lipstick and other makeup and to style her hair more fashionably. With the Ziegfelds' encouragement, Marjorie began to experiment with costumes and even indulged in ones that, ten years earlier, she would have considered risqué.

At one 1927 Palm Beach party, set designer Joseph Urban transformed the newly built Bath and Tennis Club into a Persian palace. To the music of *Scheherazade*, a dramatically robed "prime minister" escorted Marjorie down a golden stairway. As the *New York Journal* reported that March, "Mrs. E. F. Hutton . . . was exquisitely beautiful in a stunning scarlet and black costume." The affair created such a sensation that the following November Marjorie repeated it for her New York friends at Manhattan's Ritz-Carlton Hotel.

The opulence of the heiress's costumes was merely one ingredient in Marjorie's widely admired beauty. At another Palm Beach dinner dance hosted by Joseph Urban, Marjorie won first prize in a "foot and ankle" contest. To hide the identity of the women from the judges, the contestants appeared onstage behind a partially raised curtain.

Theatricality and the high jinks that often accompanied it were not confined to the ballroom. In the spring Marjorie and E.F. customarily took fishing trips on the *Hussar IV* to the Florida Keys. Among the Huttons' favorite guests were Billie Burke and Flo Ziegfeld. The latter was not only one of E.F.'s closest friends but one he considered "a most agreeable fisherman" because he brought his own equipment and took the sport seriously. Flo was also a gourmet cook whose meals were eagerly anticipated by his shipmates. One afternoon, the tall, balding impresario created a sensation by serving a luncheon dressed in a woman's one-piece bathing suit. The outfit, he solemnly assured his howling guests, was purely accidental. "For some unknown reason, Flo had forgotten to bring his bathing suit . . . and how he got into it [friend Tess Gibbon's bathing costume] will never be known," Marjorie later recalled.

On another occasion Billie Burke made elaborate preparations for a dinner party she gave each February in Palm Beach. One year she amassed a particularly impressive guest list that included the Gurnee Munns, the Stotesburys, Leonard Replogle, the John Hays Hammonds, and Jerome and Eva Kern. For days the actress had labored over a lavish menu, which was to consist of cucumber soup, stone crab, baby trout, roast beef, chocolate mousse, and an angel-food cake with coconut icing prepared by a renowned Palm Beach pastry chef.

On the morning of the party, when Billie left for the hairdresser, as her daughter Patricia Ziegfeld Stephenson recalls in *The Ziegfelds' Girl,* Flo rushed into the kitchen and ordered the cook to halt her activities. Then the grinning impresario opened the back door to the kitchen, where a truck was just arriving. Before long men were marching in, carrying large pots of corned beef, cabbage, turnips, and potatoes.

That night young Patricia anxiously peered through the banister of the stairway as the butler and footmen carried the covered food on silver dishes into the dining room to the gowned and bejeweled guests. When one of the footmen placed a large server of mashed turnips before Mrs. Stotesbury, the grande dame "half rose from her chair, her hand pressed to her bosom, and then sank back. Uncle Leonard, looking bewildered, took off his pince-nez, which had become fogged with cabbage steam, and polished them with his napkin. Mother took one look at the fifty pounds of Irish potatoes and gave a little shriek.

"The pantry door swung open. Every head turned to watch Sidney [the butler] march solemnly into the room carrying an enormous silver tray loaded with dozens of bottles of ice-cold dark Pilsener beer.

"And then, suddenly, all those elegant dinner guests burst into shouts of laughter and began to clap their hands and slap each other on the back and carry on in general as though they were in a back booth in Joe's Diner instead of at a formal Palm Beach dinner."

Other aspects of Flo Ziegfeld's flippant attitude toward life were considerably more disconcerting. The Ziegfelds lived extravagantly and, at times, even more flamboyantly than the Huttons. But for all their fame and international glory, neither Flo nor his talented wife seemed able to keep money in the bank. Despite two large incomes, the Ziegfelds spent money even more quickly than they earned it.

Flo's finances routinely fluctuated from millionaire status to near bankruptcy, but the impresario continued to spend money with abandon. Sometimes the taciturn creator of the *Ziegfeld Follies* rewarded his stars with diamond necklaces; at other times he rented mansions, bought luxury automobiles, and floated new shows on the sheer credit of his name. Like most Palm Beach resorters, Flo also frequented Bradley's, an elite gambling casino with fine food and a genteel atmosphere known for its high-stakes roulette wheel, faro, and French hazard tables.

Flo regarded Bradley's Beach Club as if it were a stage set where nothing—including colored gambling chips that represented thousands of dollars apiece in hard cash—was real. The impressario was among a cadre of high-stakes gamblers—among them Leonard Replogle of the Replogle Steel Company, the Wall Street wizard Jesse Livermore, and the Oklahoma oil magnate Joshua Cosden—who, as Marjorie later said, "would lose a hundred thousand an evening and not turn a hair." To the heiress, who often visited the casino for meals with her friends but maintained a conservative cutoff point at the gaming tables, there was an irony to the gambling fever of self-made tycoons. "It seems a strange thing," she once mused, "that men who had been successful in business would be willing to throw money around the way those men did."

While she knew that her broker husband, E.F., was "naturally quite a gambler at heart" and occasionally gambled "all out of bounds," Marjorie took comfort in the fact that intrinsically "he was nothing like these men." One night, when the broker's luck was running sour, E.F. purchased a large stack of green chips worth twenty-five dollars each.

A disapproving but silent Marjorie watched from the sidelines as E.F. placed bet after bet on the green baize table in what was obviously a relentless losing streak.

On the way home Marjorie finally asked the broker how much money he had gambled. A heavy silence ensued. Twice the heiress repeated the question before E.F. admitted he had lost fifty thousand dollars. "I almost fell out of the car, I thought it was perfectly terrible. I could only think how much good that $50,000 could do if properly placed where it was needed," Marjorie recalled.

The next day she had a "serious" talk with Ned, expressing her concern about the previous night as well as the high stakes he often played on the golf links. With a severity that must have sounded like C.W. and his pious midwestern parents, Marjorie reminded her husband that she knew serious gambling also occurred in the private railroad cars that brought the wealthy, including the Huttons, to Palm Beach. Once wives and children abandoned them for hotel rooms and private estates, those same cars quietly served as male "smokers" for private card parties that continued throughout the "season." In his defense, E.F. retorted that gambling was a way of life in the fashionable Florida resort, something that was hard to avoid if one was to be social. C.W.'s self-righteous daughter was not satisfied with E.F.'s glib explanation. The issue was not gambling per se, but the unnecessarily high stakes E.F. played on the game. "If I ever hear again that you have lost this amount willingly at Bradley's, I am going out and spend double of whatever amount you lose, and Ed Bradley will tell me what you lost," the heiress threatened. "You wouldn't do a thing like that," E.F. scoffed. A determined Marjorie assured him she would.

A few nights later E.F. returned to Bradley's gambling tables. Again the broker hit a streak of bad luck, and once again he refused to give up. Later that night Marjorie cornered Colonel Bradley in the back office and learned that her husband had lost another $50,000. On the way home the smoldering heiress confronted E.F. with the sum and announced that she was going to carry out her threat.

The next morning Marjorie left with her chauffeur and "negotiated for an extremely lovely strand of pearls and sent him [E. F. Hutton] the bill." The price tag came to a little more than $100,000. "He went straight in the air like a geyser . . . he paid the bill, but I had something permanent to show for my expense. I never found that he was gambling as heavily again," said Marjorie.

.   .   .

Despite the luxurious appointments of Palm Beach, it seemed to Marjorie that many practical amenities were still missing for vacationers who had traveled south for a few weeks in the sun. At the old Breakers Hotel, for instance, there were only thirty-nine cabanas available to protect hundreds of guests from the gusty winds and strong sun of the Florida winters. Moreover, nothing was served to cabana guests at the noon hour but cold food. To provide a better cuisine, the community-minded Marjorie used to send her chef Ernest down to The Breakers' beach to build a fire in the sand and make pancakes for the guests.

It was quickly becoming apparent to old-guard Palm Beachers that the Huttons were movers and shakers who were bringing new ideas and new institutions to the resort. On another occasion E.F. and Hunter Marston were playing golf at the newly established Gulf Stream Golf Club fifteen miles south of Palm Beach. Ahead of them was the slower, aging millionaire carpet manufacturer John Sanford and his valet. When Hunter asked if he and E.F. could play through, the older man snapped at him: "Hunter, you young snips make me mad. We old men put up all the money for this club, and you young snips want us to stay on the side lines while you race through. No, stay behind up in turn."

The younger men exchanged glances. Shortly afterward, E.F., Hunter Marston, Tony Biddle, and other members of the "young set" purchased a large tract of land on the north side of Palm Beach and established the Seminole Golf Club.

But the Huttons were far more than just young brash people with lots of money and friends. Palm Beachers, who were already impressed with Marjorie and E.F.'s commitment to civic life, became positively awed by their behavior during a fire at The Breakers. The conflagration began in the early afternoon of March 18, 1925, and quickly spread through the south wing of Flagler's famous wood-frame building. Although the Huttons were not guests at the hotel, E.F. had long maintained a branch of his brokerage house in an office off the hotel porch.

Coincidentally, at the moment that the fire broke out, Marjorie had just stepped into the lobby to meet a friend. Alarm bells suddenly began to sound, the lights went off, and the pungent odor of smoke began to snake through the halls. In the confusion hotel guests, some in bathing suits, others in light clothes, were soon scurrying through the lobby, screaming, and scrambling up the stairs to retrieve valuables from their rooms. Simultaneously, others ran down the steps, hauling golf clubs, jewelry, and ball gowns. Outside a brisk southeastern wind was fanning the flames and carrying sparks to other parts of the building so rapidly that it later seemed to Marjorie that the entire hotel "was down to the ground in less than half an hour."

With the first warning bells Marjorie had rushed outside to tell E.F., who was waiting in a nearby car. Together the couple rushed into the E. F. Hutton Company brokerage office. "Such scrambling as we did to rescue his valuable papers and documents!" Marjorie recalled. Once the company papers were safely secured in the Huttons' automobile, Marjorie and E.F. returned to the hotel, where they "helped the other guests remove their belongings, staying in the burning edifice until the last of the occupants left." Before long their heroism had captured the attention of the press, which praised the Huttons in subsequent newspaper accounts for their "clear-headedness" in the face of the panic.

The ability to remain calm and charitable to others less fortunate than themselves was to win Marjorie and E.F. a permanent place in Palm Beach history.

13

Mar-A-Lago

*B*y the mid-1920s Marjorie and E. F. Hutton were acknowledged young pacesetters in Palm Beach. But to maintain that position, to preside with dignity and style over the younger set of Jazz Age resorters, required a grander setting than Hogarcito. No sooner was it finished than Marjorie realized the inadequacy of the Spanish-style mansion she and E.F. had just built on Golfview Road. Despite its charm, Hogarcito was more a honeymoon cottage than a winter homestead for a growing family and its guests.

By 1923 Adelaide and Eleanor were teenagers who often brought friends with them to Florida. To accommodate them, Marjorie and E.F. gave the girls their bedroom suite and created a separate wing for themselves beyond the patio. Soon even that expansion proved inadequate. While there was now ample room for the girls, the house was built on too small a scale to satisfy Marjorie's ambitions as a hostess. What she wanted, Marjorie told E.F., was a "larger cottage" where they could entertain in a grander style, like the others in her social circle who were building houses in Palm Beach's postwar "Palacios Era."

The broker, who was already used to granting Marjorie freedom in the design of their homes, accordingly acquiesced. By late 1922 the heiress had plans for a stately mansion that would not only rival the splendor of Mrs. Stotesbury's El Mirasol but fascinate Palm Beach with its unique architecture.

To do so, it was first necessary to locate a property with a dazzling view of the ocean, like the fashionable estates built by architect Addison Mizner. Among the most admired of Mizner's Mediterranean Revival palaces were Playa Riente, built by Oklahama oilman Joshua Cosden and described in *Vogue* magazine as "the finest private residence in America in the early 1920's," and John S. Phipps's Casa Bendita, which *Time* magazine dubbed "a castle by any standard."

Marjorie envisioned something majestic overlooking the Atlantic. The property also had to be safe, and by the heiress's standards, that meant it had to be built upon solid terrain that would survive the hurricanes that struck southern Florida with frightening regularity. As Marjorie recalled, she was "determined to find a coral reef that was the right distance from the ocean [so that] the house could be anchored to it by steel...."

To do so required vigorous fieldwork and the acquisition of a geological survey to pinpoint the location of the most solid part of the coral reef forming the barrier island of Palm Beach. With that survey in hand, Marjorie began inspecting large tracts of undeveloped jungle land that lay between the Atlantic Ocean and Lake Worth. So resolute was Marjorie's search that she even crawled through the undergrowth herself. For weeks on end she, her real estate agent Lytle Hull, and a carpenter named James Griffin became "quite used to the idea of following the animals' paths on our hands and knees."

In early 1924 Marjorie finally settled upon seventeen acres of property south of The Breakers in a patch of jungle between Lake Worth and the Atlantic. With the exception of Cielito Lindo, the $2 million estate belonging to E.F.'s relatives James and Jessie Woolworth Donahue, there were no other houses nearby. The estate Marjorie envisioned was to be erected in the middle of the seventeen-acre lot, which, when cleared of jungle growth, would be surrounded by great stretches of rolling lawn with views of Lake Worth and the Atlantic.

For an architect Marjorie and E.F. chose Marion Wyeth, who had designed Hogarcito. This time the heiress had a different concept, one more inspired by her Adirondacks experience than by the gleaming crop of Mediterranean Revival–style palaces then appearing in Palm Beach. Her thought was that "a Florida house could be constructed with the background idea of [a] camp, namely a main building and the different guest rooms and family rooms [that] would be connected by the patio." Through the winter of 1924 Marjorie worked closely with

Wyeth, and by spring they had developed a floor plan of a house that connected a large group of rooms to one another through a large central patio.

The question of its exterior continued to baffle Marjorie. "When we finally came to the idea of what type of outside I was a little vague about exactly what I wanted," she recalled. What was clear was that she did not like any of Wyeth's conservative designs. Nor did she have any desire to hire Mizner, despite the fact that his Mediterranean-style villas were already considered status symbols. Nor was Marjorie pleased with the suggestion that the exterior of the house be modeled upon the façades of old European buildings. All too often, she told Wyeth, those had an "ecclesiastical aspect" she found dreary. What she craved was an imaginative and romantic abode that defied architectural kinship to any other house then being built in Palm Beach.

By the spring of 1925 Marjorie was still floundering for an exterior design and an architect to create it. The solution came from an unanticipated source. While on a fishing trip to the Florida Keys, Flo Ziegfeld suggested that Marjorie hire Joseph Urban, the brilliant Viennese architect and set designer who had created the Ziegfeld Theatre, backdrops for the *Follies*, and designs for the Metropolitan Opera. Prior to his arrival in the United States, Urban had served as architect for Emperor Franz Josef, Hungary's Count Carl Esterházy, and the khedive of Egypt. So taken was Marjorie with Urban's credentials that she cabled him at once. Within ten days the personable 250-pound Austrian arrived in Florida and, after several meetings with Marjorie, created a model for the new estate. Like the renowned pastries of his native city, Urban's architectural confection simultaneously thrilled Marjorie and threatened to ruin her million-dollar budget.

Urban was irrepressible. In his thick Viennese accent, he carefully explained his model to Marjorie: a crescent-shaped Hispano-Mooresque structure topped by a solitary tower. Below it, at the center of the estate, would be a large circular patio that was to serve as the centerpiece for the 115-room estate.

Inspired by its views of both the Atlantic and Lake Worth, Marjorie planned to call her home Mar-A-Lago, from the Latin meaning "from sea to lake." Even so, the planned mansion's proximity to South Ocean Boulevard worried her because of its visibility to passersby. Marjorie consequently told Urban to make sure that the house did not appear too large from the road, the same Route A1A that skirts the Palm Beach shoreline today.

In response, Urban designed the main body of the house to face Lake Worth. Not only would that side of the house be less accessible to strangers, but it was to be landscaped with thick vegetation, fruit groves, a cutting garden, and a nine-hole pitch-and-putt golf course. The crescent-shaped patio was to face the lake, girded by a curved cloister facing that shore. From the patio guests could descend to the lawn or enter the cloister, which would have staircases leading to second-story bedrooms.

Within the main house itself would be another staircase circling Mar-A-Lago's central "keep"—a deep thirty-four-foot-high drawing room at whose center would be a massive plate-glass window looking out over the front lawn toward the Atlantic. Above the building would loom a dramatic bell tower seventy-five feet high, with spectacular views of Palm Beach, which guests would approach by climbing a spiral stairway from the second floor.

At first Marjorie was so enchanted with Urban's idea that money was no object. She gave permission for gold fixtures to be installed in the women's powder room in the entrance hall. "Gold is so much easier to clean," she was fond of explaining to her guests. Nevertheless, Urban's vision proved so extravagant that it soon exceeded even Marjorie's concept of luxury. More artist than architect, the Viennese designer was an impulsive man whose sudden creative inspirations made planning a building difficult. At nearly every juncture Urban burst forth with ideas that added new dimensions—and extra dollars—to the construction of Mar-A-Lago.

At first Marjorie greeted these ideas with enthusiasm. But eventually, as the bills began to pile up, she grew skeptical. "How much is that going to cost, Joseph?" she was soon coolly inquiring. Another sixty or seventy thousand was his usual response. When Marjorie protested, Urban would clasp his hands together and lament, "But, Mrs. Hutton . . . eet iss so beootiful."

Finally, in exasperation, Marjorie asked E.F. to call on their original architect, Marion Wyeth. "You've got to come back on this job because Joe Urban may be an artist but he's not a practical man. He doesn't know much about plumbing or heating or electricity or any of the basic things that go into a house," E.F. explained. In the end Wyeth agreed to assume closer responsibility for the internal workings of the estate and keep Urban's wild flights of fancy under control. The Viennese architect was directed to concentrate upon the things that were his specialty, the decorative features that gave the mansion its unique flair and style.

. . .

Urban's theatrical vision, epitomized by dramatic decorative carvings, friezes, grillwork, and arches resulted in the extraordinary building known as Mar-A-Lago. Wyeth was less than pleased with the results. In the end he hotly denied responsibility for the look of the house.

Years later, when explaining how Mar-A-Lago was built, Wyeth maintained that his own style was far more classical. Although he had worked with Urban on the project, the result was "not very fruitful." The clash was more than just a matter of contrasting temperaments. "I had been trained at the Beaux Arts in Paris along very classical and traditional lines, and Joe was a product of Jugendstil [art nouveau]." As a result, Wyeth observed, he "could not influence the design or the cost, which was to have been my function." While Mar-A-Lago was later categorized as an example of Hispano-Mooresque architecture because of its stucco exterior, antique-tile embellishments, rambling outbuildings, and red-tiled roof, the estate was actually a carefully crafted amalgam of architectural styles blended together to display the most admirable features of several European countries.

As a result, Mar-A-Lago was impossible to place in one singular architectural category. From South Ocean Boulevard guests entered Mar-A-Lago through a large arched gate past a palm-lined driveway into a porte cochere. The main house's pink stucco exterior was fortified with rich brown and rust-colored Doric stone that had been brought in three boatloads from Genoa. Directly beyond the driveway were the kitchen's iron grille windows with stone carvings reminiscent of medieval shop signs—among them a wine merchant, a poultry man, a fishmonger, and a vegetable peddler. At the center of the building gleamed an enormous plate-glass window, edged with stone pelicans and lacy iron grillwork. At the roof and on the drainpipes were fanciful carvings of monkeys, parrots, and ram's heads. These, created in stone and wood by the Swiss craftsman Franz Barwig, lent an enigmatic, mythic quality to the estate that hinted at great treasures from the ancient world inside.

Added to this was Wyeth's acquisition of a rare collection of antique Moorish and Spanish tiles from the nineteenth-century estate of New York socialite Mrs. Horace Havemeyer. Many of the tiles of the collection were of the so-called plus-ultra variety dating back to the fifteenth century. At the time of their purchase, appraisers believed there were about twenty thousand antique tiles in the collection, but when the shipment arrived, there were, in Marjorie's words, many "more than you really bargained for"—some thirty-six thousand all told. With such an abundance the tiles were used to decorate doors, arches, and walls throughout the house. So valuable were these relics that when Mar-A-Lago was finally opened to the public, an awed local architect maintained that there were "more antique Hispano-Mooresque tiles in Mar-A-Lago than in any other building in the world, excepting the Álcazar in Spain."

Inside, at the mansion's center, a thirty-four-foot-high living room had been designed around a series of tall silk needlework tapestries which once hung in a Venetian palace. To sustain this Italian theme, the ceiling was hand-gilded in a sunburst design modified from the "thousand-winged ceiling" motif of the Accadèmia in Venice. Marjorie disliked ecclesiastical themes, so gold sunburst patterns were substituted for the angel faces of the original Accadèmia ceiling. Similarly, the seven arches surrounding the living room were decorated in a millefleur background with armorial insignia of Venetian doges in lieu of those of monks of the Accadèmia. Beneath this design hung rare gilded Spanish lanterns.

At the back of the living room, which was carpeted with a sixteenth-century Spanish rug, was a hooded Italian Gothic fireplace. Just beyond it one arch led to a small room called the "monkey loggia," which contained whimsical stone carvings of those creatures. Through a triple arch at the front of the living room was another small room, entered by way of four marble steps flanked by northern Italian Romanesque columns mounted upon stone lions. Within this tiny chamber were frescoes copied from the Riccardo Medici palazzo in Florence. Beyond it was the immense plate-glass front window, said to be the largest ever made in North America, with its view of the Atlantic.

Other rooms in the estate were furnished to heighten Mar-A-Lago's Mediterranean mood. The dining room, paneled in old English walnut, was copied from one in Rome's rarely seen Chigi Palace and included frescoed copies of the palace's original paintings. (At the time Mar-A-Lago was being built, the original dining room in Rome was being used as Mussolini's office.) Beneath Mar-A-Lago's frescoes was a dramatic black-and-white marble floor that had been imported from an old Cuban palace and covered with a huge Oriental rug. A final breathtaking touch was an enormous four-thousand-pound ballroom-length multicolored marble table inlaid with semiprecious stones, designed by Joseph Urban after models in Florence's Uffizi and Pitti galleries.

To reach the outdoors and Mar-A-Lago's circular patio, guests could exit from nearly every first-floor room except the dining room. Even the detail work of the round terrace illustrated Marjorie's flair for the unusual. One day, while walking through Ned's hunting preserve at Islip, Long Island, Marjorie found by the seashore a unique, smoothly polished sausage-shaped stone. Upon closer scrutiny, she noticed dozens of other similarly shaped stones in black, white, yellow, and multicolored hues. These, she realized, filling her pockets with them, would make an interesting addition to Mar-A-Lago's patio. Within a few days she had a crew of men picking the stones off the beach and had them sent by train to Florida.

Some months later, when Marjorie discovered that the two tons of stone delivered to the Florida construction site decorated a mere ten feet of the patio, she ordered more stones from Long Island. Try as she might, Marjorie could not seem to order enough stones to finish the patio. Week after week she sent north for more stones until finally, she recalled, the contractor was "perfectly exhausted with us and said there weren't another stone on the beach." To Marjorie's relief, the weary employee finally found another beach with enough stones to complete Mar-A-Lago's patio.

From the patio, guests could either descend one of the stairways flanking the patio to a goldfish and water lily pool decorated by stone parrots or enter the curved cloister and climb stairs leading to Mar-A-Lago's second floor. There guests could enter one of the five bedroom suites designed to represent furniture styles from different historical eras and countries. Among these were the Adams suite, a Venetian room, a Portuguese room, a Dutch room, and a Spanish room. Beyond them, through another staircase, were two more bedroom suites, furnished in a stark "modernistic" style for the younger set, that led to a metal spiral staircase ascending to the bell tower.

Off the patio in a separate wing were Marjorie and E.F.'s private quarters, which contained adjoining bedrooms, private baths, and sitting rooms. Nearby, Urban built another ground-floor apartment that eventually became Deenie Hutton's nursery. Since the suite was intended for an infant, Urban decorated it fancifully. After passing through an anteroom, one arrived in an oval bedroom at the far end of which was a plasterwork beehive fireplace. From the beehive dome above the fireplace, pink plaster rosebushes radiated across the ceiling and over the windows, culminating in two branches opening toward the bed. Upon them, in plasterwork, sat cheerful yellow canaries.

When Deenie grew to little-girlhood, Urban designed a canopied bed with a Sleeping Beauty theme painted in silver, topped by four squirrels perched upon the bedposts. On the floor was a large, brightly colored rug with that same Sleeping Beauty motif, containing a castle with moat and drawbridge, ladies-in-waiting, and knights. The bathroom wall was similarly decorated with two full-color rows of fairy tales. "That was the most wonderful thing for a kid," Dina Merrill reminisced. "I used to sit in that bathtub learning to read and practicing reading . . . the little rhymes and looking at the pictures and memorizing."

Outside, beyond the main house of the estate, was a tidy series of buildings decorated in pink stucco and red-tiled roofs containing staff quarters, service buildings, and greenhouses. Taken as a whole, the house was a stunning amalgam of architectural details and furniture styles that seemed simultaneously inviting, mysterious, and theatrical.

Despite the praise or criticism leveled at Mar-A-Lago, the approval from local workers was unanimous. For more than three years, an army of six hundred skilled men—artisans, carpenters, joiners, masons, electricians, and plumbers—was employed in the construction of the estate. While Marjorie could easily have employed fewer men, she deliberately retained the entire staff of original workers. The heiress had done so in the spirit of what she considered her philanthropic duty, just when southern Florida was suffering its first land bust.

In 1925 Waldorf restaurant tycoon Harry Seymour Kelsey had sold his interests in a model city north of West Palm Beach named after him to the Royal Palm Beach Company for $30 million. With Kelsey City as a model, the West Palm Beach Chamber of Commerce had joined local businessmen to lure tourists to buy land in Florida. Newspapers like the newly established *Palm Beach Post* and *Palm Beach Times* had jumped on the bandwagon by reporting the opening of new land developments and boasting about the profits that would accrue to their purchasers.

One of the most highly publicized of those new model cities was Boca Raton, backed by architect Addison Mizner, whose vision had grown beyond the mere creation of individual estates into that of entire communities. Among Mizner's grandiose plans had been the April 1925 announcement of a new luxury sixteen-thousand-acre community whose centerpiece would be a $6 million shorefront hotel called Castillo del Rey. The backing for the project had come from a syndicate of blue-chip tycoons, among them William K. Vanderbilt, Paris Singer, Rodman Wanamaker, T. Coleman du Pont, and Elizabeth Arden.

Some months later, when the Ritz-Carlton organization took over the Castillo del Rey operation, Mizner announced the construction of still other projects: a hundred-room hotel on Lake Boca Raton, a casino, an air terminal, a Spanish village, and an Irving Berlin cabaret. Simultaneously developers, eager to cash in on the Florida land boom of the mid-1920s, snatched up large tracts of land as far south as Fort Lauderdale and began promoting them in brochures and northern newspapers.

Mizner, meanwhile, had overextended himself. Since prospective buyers put down only 20 to 25 percent of the investment in cash at the time of their commitments, the architect was obliged to continue selling large tracts of land to pay his obligations. By August 1925 northerners had begun to attack Florida land developers for fraudulent claims of profit investment. One of the catalysts was a railroad embargo on construction materials that soon spread statewide.

In October, T. Coleman du Pont, chairman of the board of the Boca Raton and Mizner Development corporations, and several other syndicate members resigned on the grounds that their names had been falsely used in land development advertisements.

The Florida land boom thus ended with a resounding thud. By 1926 small and large investors had lost their confidence in Florida. Speculators, who had planned to turn over their lots for higher profits within a year, began to default on their payments. Despairing municipalities that had floated bonds to provide new water treatment plants, seawalls, paved streets, and bathing facilities in anticipation of the boom watched future tax revenues shrivel up and disappear. Ancillary services such as construction companies, architectural services, building supply houses, and real estate firms failed. And so did many Florida banks, among them the Commercial Bank and Trust Company, whose largest investor, at $700,000, was the city of West Palm Beach.

While the scions of finance and industry living in Palm Beach were largely immune to the effects of the 1926 bust, the bankruptcies and massive unemployment that afflicted local workers worried Marjorie. Costs for the completion of the exotic Mar-A-Lago had already soared above budget, running at nearly twice the original $1 million planned for the estate. E.F. was furious, and Marjorie knew it. There was thus every reason for her to cut costs by dismissing some of her men in favor of mechanized labor.

Marjorie was ever mindful of C.W.'s philosophy that money was to be used to help others—especially in the face of a crisis. "We refused to stop construction after nearly everyone advised us to stop. Had we stopped and discharged workmen, this would have added more unemployed. Hence we went ahead," Marjorie reasoned.

In January 1927 Mar-A-Lago was complete. For months Marjorie had been fighting off requests from publishers like Condé Nast and society magazines like *Vogue* and *Town and Country* to visit the house and take photographs. Local newspaper coverage was more difficult to avoid. The Palm Beach press went wild, hailing the mansion as "original" and "unique." So remarkable was Mar-A-Lago that the Hutton style was soon considered synonymous with uniqueness itself. When the press discovered that Marjorie had ordered a tunnel built from the front of the estate under South Ocean Boulevard to the beachfront, it was hailed as being "quite in keeping with the Hutton idea of originality . . . [it] runs from their picturesque domicile to the Bath and Tennis Club."

The cost of Mar-A-Lago was an estimated $2.5 million. Marjorie wrote to her cousin Dolly Morrow that April:

> The house here is about finished. It is very large and very beautiful, but like all building operations, it has cost far more than we had any even wild idea of. Apparently, building estimates are not worth the paper they are written on and as a result, they have sunk our finances beyond anything we had imagined, so I have been having trouble with Ned about it. . . . I have been having a d—— hard time of it and it has almost taken the pleasure out of the house itself. . . . [I]t means we have got to sell some of our pet Postum stock and you can imagine how unwillingly we part with it.

Remarkable as Mar-A-Lago was, the estate had created strains in Marjorie's marriage, which, coupled with her pleas to buy the Birdseye company, were leading E.F. to disapprove of his wife's spending habits. When acquaintances expressed their fascination with his new Palm Beach home, the stockbroker often shrugged cynically. "You know Marjorie said she was going to build a little cottage by the sea. Look what we got!"

DEPRESSIONS

14

"Despite the Forty Added Summers"

*A*brupt changes swept over Marjorie's personal life in the late twenties like a shattering Florida hurricane, events that forced her to reassess her status as a young wife, mother, and hostess. Foremost among these was the fact that Marjorie was no longer young. In March 1927 the heiress had turned forty, an age that, in the first half of the twentieth century at least, was widely acknowledged as the end of youth and the beginning of matronly maturity.

Two years earlier the sobriety of that position had been foreshadowed by the death of Aunt Mollie. With the demise of her adoring mother surrogate, Marjorie became a senior member of the family, one who no longer had a loving parent figure to inquire after her well-being.

For decades Marjorie had benefited from her aunt's approval. Their warm personal relationship made Marjorie feel that she was cherished for her special qualities. Over the years the heiress showered her aunt with gifts: jewelry, clothes, and even fine lingerie. A month before her death an ailing Mollie had written Marjorie from her home in Pasadena, California: "You have been my inspiration from the day you opened your eyes." With such consistent and unqualified love, what woman could not help believing in herself?

A few weeks after this letter Mollie's health took a turn for the worse. Marjorie rushed from Palm Beach to Pasadena to be at her aunt's side. The end came on May 26, 1925, when Marjorie's beloved aunt Mary

Staley Post, suffering from "tumors and complications of bladder trouble," died and left the heiress in a colder, less reassuring world.

Although the heiress was already a confirmed altruist whose contributions to the Palm Beach community were becoming legendary, Mollie's death served to underscore that commitment. To raise money for a new Bethesda-by-the-Sea Church, Marjorie sponsored a benefit with Metropolitan Opera singers Doris Doe and Rafaelo Diaz. In a 1928 gesture of appreciation, Marjorie hosted a party for some eleven hundred members of her own staff and those serving other Palm Beach estates. In March 1929, immediately after hosting three performances of the Ringling Bros. and Barnum & Bailey Circus for her friends, she opened Mar-A-Lago to children from the county home and the Girl Scouts to see another professional circus performance.

Aunt Mollie had imparted other lessons to Marjorie as well, especially the importance of private, unrewarded acts of charity. Shortly after her marriage to E. F. Hutton, Marjorie's old "memory teacher," her distant cousin Julia Van Tassel, had died. Just before the widow was to have a life-threatening operation, she asked Marjorie for a favor. The crowning glory of her life had been her son, Ernest, a brilliant and ambitious Yale graduate, who had been stricken with a crippling disease. Would Marjorie be willing to help young Ernest if Julia did not survive the operation? She was, after all, the older woman reminded Marjorie, Ernest's closest living relative.

Marjorie readily assented. True to her promise, she "stepped into the gap" after Julia's death. Actually she did much more than that. At Ernest's request, she sent him to Hawaii, then a distant and exotic island chain still owned as a territory by the United States government. Shortly after he was settled in Honolulu with a nurse, Marjorie received a letter. Although a semi-invalid, Ernest was "exploding with restlessness to get into something where he could be active." In his search he had become intrigued with an unusual kind of nut called the macadamia, which had originally been cultivated in Australia. Since Hawaii's main industry was then pineapple, also originally imported from Australia, Ernest felt sure that macadamia nuts could be similarly successful in Hawaii.

Letters went back and forth from Hawaii for months. Would Marjorie be willing to lend Ernest the money to buy macadamia seedlings? Admittedly the scheme was experimental; among its obstacles was the necessity of waiting seven years for the seedlings to mature into nut-bearing trees. There was also the problem of how to crack the hard-shelled nuts without breaking the kernels. Marjorie, nevertheless, agreed to support Ernest's idea. She took practical steps to help her cousin start his business, among which were using her personal contacts in the agricultural industry and making a special arrangement with General Electric to create a macadamia shell-cracking machine.

In time the company was known as Van's Macadamias and became the leading U.S. producer of the product. When Van Tassel's organization was finally in the black, Ernest offered to repay Marjorie the money. The "great-grandmother of the macadamia nut industry," as Marjorie teasingly dubbed herself, refused. "I didn't loan it to you. I gave it to you," she told her cousin with a sweetness that he never forgot.

According to her daughter Dina, Marjorie typically gave money to many people who were down on their luck. "Mother looked after a lot of people that nobody really knew about," said Dina. "If somebody got ill and couldn't take care of themselves, she saw to it that they were looked after. She did many many kindnesses like that, very quietly; even we didn't know much about it."

Above all, Marjorie enjoyed helping people who had plans to build productive careers or businesses. "She was very much for anybody who was pulled together and trying to do well," said the Reverend Julia Sibley, whose theological training was later paid for by the heiress. Occasionally, however, Marjorie gave money to people who were unlikely to use it in a responsible fashion. When Marjorie's eldest daughter pointed out that her gift was likely being squandered, the heiress characteristically waved her away. "Adelaide, I don't care," she said. "I really don't want to know."

By the mid-twenties there were other unfortunates who sought comfort in one form or another from Marjorie. Among them was Marjorie's young niece Barbara Hutton, daughter of E.F.'s brother, Franklyn. In 1917, when Barbara was four years of age, her beautiful mother, Edna Woolworth Hutton, had died in her apartment at the Plaza Hotel. Although newspaper accounts initially attributed the heiress's death to an ear infection, more recent accounts say that Edna committed suicide and that little Barbara discovered the body. Allegedly Edna had poisoned herself when she discovered a letter her husband had written to a mistress.

Whatever the truth of the matter, Barbara, granddaughter of F. W. Woolworth, was already growing up as an unhappy, confused child by the time Marjorie married E.F. Although Frank Hutton had remarried, both he and his new wife, Irene, treated the child coldly. In fact, despite the $25 million fortune Barbara inherited from her grandfather, which Frank brilliantly parlayed into $50 million on Wall Street in the space of a few short years, Barbara was essentially a neglected child, the original "poor little rich girl" of the tabloids.

Barbara Hutton had more money than almost anyone else in America, yet she seems to have grown up with less love than the average pauper's child. After Barbara's eccentric grandfather's death in 1919— her grandmother was still alive in 1923 but already either senile or psychotic—the child was brought up by a coterie of nannies and governesses. Finally Frank Hutton sent Barbara at age twelve or thirteen off to Miss Porter's School in Farmington, Connecticut.

Unfortunately life at that elite institution did not prove any happier for Barbara. Within a few weeks her classmates, sensing Barbara's unhappiness and shaky self-image, began to snub her. Even at holiday time, when the other girls went home to their families, Barbara was seldom invited to spend time with Frank and Irene. "At one time Barbara told me that they had left her up at Farmington for Christmas vacation," recalled Dina.

The sensitive and now-adolescent Barbara looked for guidance increasingly from her uncle Ned's new wife, Marjorie Post Hutton. Marjorie, horrified by her niece's profound distress, perhaps even vicariously reliving her own adolescent discomfort with a despised stepmother, went out of her way to comfort Barbara. Often Aunt Marjorie and Uncle Ned invited Barbara with them on trips. Even after Marjorie and E.F. sold Hogarcito to "Uncle Frank," Barbara often preferred staying with them at Mar-A-Lago to living with her father and stepmother.

During those visits Marjorie tried to correct what she saw as alarming tendencies in her niece, among them her mood swings, temper tantrums, and spending sprees. Although she could not replace the love the girl had lacked as a child, Marjorie tried—much as had her own aunt Mollie—to provide Barbara with a good role model. Temperamentally Marjorie was not disposed to hugging and kissing. As her own granddaughter Ellen MacNeille Charles said years later, "Grandmother did not have a warm, cozy relationship with us, but she cared a great deal."

The caring with Barbara took more subtle forms. As an aunt, Marjorie went to great lengths to make Barbara feel loved by listening to her, inviting her to holiday and family celebrations, and remembering her birthday.

Barbara, in turn, warmed to Aunt Marjorie and confided her hopes and dreams to the older woman. From Barbara's adolescent and starry-eyed perspective, Marjorie was perfection itself—a woman at once beautiful, polished, and urbane, as much at home with European aristocrats as with American business tycoons, a figure as respected in Palm Beach for her philanthropies and kindnesses as for the millions she had in the bank. As a surrogate mother, Marjorie thus left an indelible imprint upon the adolescent girl.

Years later, long after Barbara was grown and rushing from one unhappy marriage to another, she continued to hunger after Marjorie's love and advice. At Christmas and Easter she sent her aunt lavish bouquets of roses, orchids, and other exotic blossoms. Often she telegrammed Marjorie in gratitude for a phone call, a visit, or a present, praising her as "the kindest and dearest person in all the world" or reassuring her that she was "taking her advice." In short, as Adelaide put it, Barbara was "devoted to Mother" in a unique lifelong bond.

Despite her counsel, Marjorie could not seem to teach Barbara certain basic emotional lessons: how to control her impulses, how to develop a good sense of judgment about people, and how to curb her spending sprees.

At the same time that Marjorie was attempting to soothe her niece Barbara and help curb her extravagant appetites for men, money, and materialism, she was waging quite a different battle with her own daughter Adelaide. By nature, her eldest daughter had been a shy and retiring child, one who preferred life at home with a few friends or loved ones to the glittering world of parties and theatrical galas that delighted Marjorie. Strong currents ran through Adelaide that disapproved of the perennial opulence of New York and Palm Beach night life. "I don't like big parties, and I never did. It used to drive Mother up the wall," said Adelaide.

Her naturally conservative bent made Adelaide seem more temperamentally similar to her father, Ed Close, than to the extroverted, flamboyant Post side of the family—characteristics that must have rankled Marjorie as an "echo" of her old struggle with the Closes.

At first those temperamental differences were merely annoying tendencies that Marjorie believed could be amended through proper child rearing. Only as the willowy and aristocratic Adelaide came of age did they surface as real differences between mother and child that led to a permanent disparity in their lifestyles. With maturity, Adelaide increasingly shunned the parties so favored by her mother in favor of a life in the country, where she bred prize dogs and horses.

The first inkling of Adelaide's resistance came when Marjorie placed her daughter at her old alma mater, the Mount Vernon Seminary. Soon after she arrived, Marjorie sent Adelaide's nurse, Pearcie, to see how the girl was. The girl hated the boarding school so much, slept so little, and cried so often that she had begun to look ill. "It took me about five minutes to say, 'Pearcie, terrible things are going to happen if you don't take me home,' " recalled Adelaide. With that the alarmed governess informed the headmistress that in her role as Marjorie's proxy she was removing Adelaide immediately from the school.

Once at home, Adelaide had to face her mother. Marjorie was steaming over the incident, but she listened patiently to the child and grasped the depth of her unhappiness. Perhaps, she mused, it was just a quirky incident, something about that particular setting, or that particular combination of classmates, that had set Adelaide on edge. "All right, you don't have to go back there," Marjorie finally relented. "But next year you're going to Farmington, and nobody is going to see you."

Adelaide was determined to get out of going to boarding school—any boarding school, regardless of its reputation. Before long the girl was scheming. Realizing that her slender frame always worried the health-conscious Marjorie, Adelaide decided to become even thinner. "I went on a strict diet and lost a lot of weight. And then I finally did get home permanently," she recalled with a triumphant grin. For her secondary-school years, Marjorie's eldest daughter lived at 2 East Ninety-second Street in Manhattan and attended the nearby Nightingale-Banford day school.

As Adelaide approached the age at which she was to make her debut, another power struggle ensued between her and her mother. As the daughter of a midwestern industrialist, Marjorie had never had a debut. The heiress was thus particularly eager for her own daughters to be presented to New York Society. Moreover, in that era between the two world wars, another even more prestigious honor was accorded the daughters of wellborn, wealthy Americans: a formal presentation to the king and queen of England at the Court of St. James's. With her long-standing reverence for British nobility and desire to have her daughters acknowledged in the best international social circles, Marjorie was intent upon having Adelaide "presented."

At seventeen the girl was already determined to extricate herself from Marjorie's ambitions. "I told Mother I didn't want to come out and I didn't want to be presented at court," said Adelaide. "And since I had to do one or the other, I came out."

In that era debutante balls were held during the holiday season from Thanksgiving to Christmas. In late fall 1926 Marjorie and E. F. Hutton hosted a debut for Adelaide at the old Ritz-Carlton Hotel. Traditionally these presentations in High Society East Coast cities like Boston, Philadelphia, Baltimore, Atlanta, and New York were held to announce the eligibility of the young daughters of the wealthy—usually at eighteen years of age—for marriage. In that sense, Adelaide's debut was unnecessary. In Palm Beach the young woman had already met a handsome Yale graduate from Connecticut, Thomas "Tim" Welles Durant, with whom she was deeply in love.

The day after her debut Adelaide announced her engagement to her twenty-eight-year-old beau. "Mother thought I was too young. Ha! Eighteen. She was eighteen, too," said Adelaide some sixty-three years later. "She was right, and I should have listened to her. I mean, she didn't disapprove [of the match], but she thought I should wait." At Adelaide's insistence the wedding was scheduled for January 19, 1927, in Manhattan—just a few days before the Huttons were to celebrate the long-awaited opening of Mar-A-Lago in Palm Beach.

At thirty-nine years of age, Marjorie was thus thrust into another "mature" role—that of mother-in-law to the winsome Tim Durant and his shy but quietly determined bride, Adelaide.

With characteristic zeal, Marjorie devoted herself to making her daughter's wedding one of the most memorable events of the decade. The ceremony took place on a bright, cold Wednesday, January 19, 1927, at St. Thomas Episcopal Church on Fifth Avenue in Manhattan. Three days before the event so many rumors proliferated about the splendor of the affair that the *Palm Beach Times* said it promised "to rival any in point of glamour and attendance." Nearly all of the five hundred guests, said another account, were "people who put the 'so' in society," and who "were there in force." In fact, the wedding was considered so important that many northerners who would ordinarily have traveled to Palm Beach after New Year's had delayed their trip until after the event.

If Adelaide refused to be presented to royalty, Marjorie would at least assure that she would be attired in its trappings. On her wedding day Adelaide was dressed in a magnificent satin gown with a four-foot-long court train edged with white silk net and decorated with orange blossoms. Most impressive of all was Adelaide's headdress, made from antique lace that had been worn by a Hapsburg bride a century earlier and that Marjorie had had fashioned into an exquisite veil.

As mother of the bride Marjorie was outfitted in dignified elegance. For the ceremony she wore an attractive velvet gown of embroidered gold and bronze, accented with sable furs and a brown velvet turban—a combination that enhanced her light hair and golden complexion.

The bridal attendants, like Adelaide, were dressed in white. Adelaide's sister Eleanor and friend Mary Todd were maids of honor and were followed down the aisle by six bridesmaids, all of whom wore white velvet dresses trimmed in white fox. Upon their heads were white velvet turbans, decorated with jade and pink onyx pins set with brilliants—wedding gifts from the bride. The young women were paired with Tim Durant's best man, Anthony Drexel Biddle, and ushers from some of New York's most prominent families.

"The grandeur of the beautiful and luxurious Hutton-Durant wedding solemnized yesterday afternoon in St. Thomas church will linger long in the memory of the 500 guests who crowded every nook & cranny of the great Fifth Avenue edifice," rhapsodized columnist Cholly Knickerbocker in the *New York American*. "Not since the era of lavish Vanderbilt weddings has metro society gazed upon such a picturesque scene as was furnished yesterday. . . . It is doubtful if any marital alliance solemnized in the socially popular St. Thomas' ever had such an exquisite setting."

Afterward the guests returned to the Huttons' triplex apartment at 2 East Ninety-second for a reception held under a lavish canopy of smilax and white roses. As was the prevailing custom of the day, hundreds of wedding gifts in sterling silver, gold, and leaded crystal were displayed in adjacent rooms for the admiring guests. These, apparently, were so costly that even the jaded Cholly Knickerbocker could not help exclaiming that Adelaide had virtually been showered with "a fortune in wedding gifts."

While Marjorie ultimately accepted the marriage, she sensed instinctively that Tim Durant was not the right choice. Privately she suspected that her new son-in-law had a slippery moral character. In a telegram to Eleanor just two months after the wedding, Marjorie confided that she was "quietly disturbed over that degenerate." Superficially Tim had all the right credentials. He was, after all, the son of a retired judge from a Connecticut family with roots dating back to the Revolution. The dark-gray-eyed bridegroom was also very handsome, with a wiry athletic body that once won him a baseball scholarship to Yale University. Tim also had a quick wit and a gift of gab that made him, as Cholly Knickerbocker observed, "one of the most popular younger men of New York Society." It was little wonder, then, that the twenty-eight-year-old Tim had swept young Adelaide off her feet.

To honor Adelaide and her bridegroom, E.F. promptly established Tim Durant in the brokerage business. Marjorie even bought him a seat on the New York Stock Exchange. She also had a separate cottage built for the young couple at Hillwood so that they could spend their springs and autumns on Long Island. Meanwhile, with Tim's new position on Wall Street, the newlyweds were expected to take an apartment in Manhattan.

From the beginning Marjorie watched the young couple with keen interest, hoping theirs would be a relationship like hers and Ned Hutton's. As she wrote in a letter to a cousin, "They [Adelaide and Tim] are back in town now and in a great state of excitement, having just leased an apartment for five years. I am anxious to see it and see how their judgement is."

After the excitement of a wedding that would have exhausted most women for weeks, Marjorie's social responsibilities for the winter of 1926–27 were just beginning. Throughout the fall architect Joseph Urban, general contractor Cooper C. Lightbrown, and teams of craftsmen had been working feverishly in Palm Beach to complete Mar-A-Lago by December 1926. Shortly after Thanksgiving, Marjorie and E.F. had already shuttled south to Florida in their private railroad car to inspect the final details of their estate. Immediately after Adelaide's wedding they traveled to Palm Beach again to begin the round of parties and social events that marked the 1927 "season." Although Mar-A-Lago was barely finished, they had scheduled several affairs for the new estate.

The first of these was on March 1, when Marjorie and E.F. held a large dinner party preceding the annual Everglades Costume Ball. The party was so exquisite that the *New York Evening Post* singled it out for description: "Their guests were seated at small tables on the patio which commanded a view of both ocean and lake. Amid the luxuriant tropical plants in the patio were growing orchids, while the tables were adorned with miniature orange kumquat trees and clusters of gladioli, fresias, and roses. From the Moorish tower a blue moon [a blue light] beamed upon the guests."

To enhance the Mediterranean flavor of Mar-A-Lago, antique Spanish lanterns illuminated lace-covered tables where guests were served food on Spanish pottery and Venetian glass. At intervals throughout the meal, two performers, accompanying themselves on accordions, sang Neapolitan folksongs and operatic selections.

In anticipation of the Everglades Costume Ball, Marjorie and E.F. appeared in clothes from one of the heiress's favorite periods in history, the reign of Louis XVI of France. Mrs. Hutton, said the *Palm Beach Times*, wore a "lovely ensemble of green taffeta fashioned with a loose fitting bodice and bouffant skirt." E.F. wore an eighteenth-century court outfit in matching green.

Despite Marjorie's regal appearance, she was struggling to maintain her composure. In her eagerness to showcase the new Palm Beach home, Marjorie had overcommitted herself as a hostess. In a March 9 telegram to her friend Mrs. Jorge Andre, she explained just how hectic that pace had become. "You have no idea what I have been up against. Three groups of people have arrived with children, some of them have been sick. . . . At the present . . . there is not an unoccupied bed in the house and in a few days Eleanor arrives with six kids in tow."

Four days later Marjorie and E.F. nevertheless managed to appear cool and collected before another two hundred guests they had invited to a second, even more unprecedented event. This one was a "soiree," as the New York *Evening Sun* termed it, in which the avant-garde modern dancers Ruth St. Denis and Ted Shawn and their company, the Denishawn dancers, were to perform a "ballet-in-time."

The event, said the *Palm Beach Times*, "promises to go down in the annals of this season's social highlights as one of the largest and most delightful affairs of the season." For the occasion Marjorie had a large platform built on the back lawn facing Lake Worth. In front of it was Mar-A-Lago's elegant fountain flanked by stone stairways that led to the mansion's semicircular patio. From that vista, surrounded by glowing lanterns that illuminated lush blossoms, the Huttons' guests gazed at the stark, graceful movements of the Denishawn dancers behind a curtain of spray in the deepening twilight.

The evening left nearly as indelible an impression upon the dancers as it did upon their audience. A day or so later Marjorie cabled her appreciation to Ruth St. Denis and Ted Shawn. On March 27, 1927, Shawn wrote Marjorie that her telegram was "just one more gesture which proclaimed you the rare and beautiful person we discovered you to be on that memorable Sunday."

Marjorie turned forty—quietly, and without a party or public celebration of any kind—on March 15, 1927. For the heiress it was a day for contemplation. Despite her beauty, vigor, and energy, Marjorie had reached the halfway point in her life. A great deal of history had passed before her eyes and had left her in happy circumstances. She had much to be thankful for: a loving husband, healthy daughters, wealth, friends, and the joy of knowing she had helped others. Still, the fact that she was now an "older" woman disquieted the heiress.

The next day Marjorie wired Eleanor from Palm Beach that she "had a very happy day despite the forty added summers." Later that month she penned a letter to Florence Howard of Pasadena, California, with a summary of the year's events: "My debutante child with her various parties, with her wedding, then this huge beautiful thing [Mar-A-Lago] here to equip and furnish, has kept the old lady well on the move."

It was one of the few times Marjorie ever referred to herself—even lightly—as "the old lady" in print. Thereafter the word *old* would be permanently banished from her vocabulary.

If Adelaide had proved a reluctant debutante, Marjorie's second daughter, Eleanor, was a willing one. From the start Eleanor had exhibited an exuberant disposition, which at its worst got her into mischief and at its best made her a charming and lively companion. As she matured, the blond-haired, blue-eyed Eleanor demonstrated a sly sense of humor that captivated—and occasionally exasperated—Marjorie.

In contrast with her older sister, Eleanor was a decidedly social creature who enjoyed the parties and balls favored by her mother. With characteristic vigor, she had thrown herself into the social life at Miss Porter's boarding school and made many friends. Nevertheless, Eleanor had firm ideas about the men she found attractive, and often they were different from the High Society European aristocrats whom Marjorie sought for her. To start with, a title meant far less to Eleanor than the essence of the man himself, and the essence had to be romantic. When beaux of her mother's choosing were foisted upon Eleanor, the girl's reaction was to discourage them—usually through some clever subterfuge or plot.

Once, at a formal dinner at the Plaza's Persian Room, Marjorie had insisted that Eleanor be seated next to an eligible Bulgarian prince whom her "friend," the conniving social climber Elsa Maxwell, had assured the heiress would be a "perfect" beau. Because she had no choice, Eleanor gracefully assented, but when she met her dinner partner—a pompous, cross-eyed suitor—she became incensed. Worst of all, the prince seemed infatuated with Eleanor. During the course of the evening Eleanor quietly bribed the waiter to spill soup on the prince. Although the waiter attempted to mop the mess off the prince's tailcoat and shirt, the aristocrat finally left the table in a huff. "And that"— Eleanor giggled nearly sixty years later as she retold the story—"took care of the prince's attentions once and for all."

Despite such capers, Eleanor was a dutiful debutante who came out with grace and style at Christmas 1927 at the old Ritz-Carlton Hotel. For the occasion Marjorie had festooned the Grand Ballroom with bowers of smilax, begonias, and pink roses. To add a youthful theatrical touch, Joseph Urban had created a series of modernistic designs out of silver gauze backlit with spotlights.

The glitter of the occasion was hardly the end of Eleanor's ceremonial appearances in society. The following spring, in May 1928, Marjorie's second daughter was presented at the Court of St. James's. To Marjorie, it was the dream of a lifetime fulfilled to have her daughter curtsy before King George V and Queen Mary. The social benefits of the presentation were incalculable: It not only added to Eleanor's luster but might well lead her to marriage with a British aristocrat.

In preparation for the event, Marjorie had designer Madame Frances create a turquoise blue gown for Eleanor. For months she savored the thought of watching her daughter carried in a limousine toward Buckingham Palace, where she would appear in the throne room to curtsy before the British monarchs, but E.F. was adamantly against Marjorie's making the trip. Already, he complained, Marjorie was away too much at spas and at her various homes while he was stuck in New York on business. There was no need for her to go; one of Marjorie's close friends could accompany Eleanor to England.

In the end Marjorie assented. Her good friend and family physician Dr. Samuel Brown and his teenage daughter accompanied Eleanor to

London, where they were joined by another of Marjorie's friends, Prince Pate Gino Patenziano, the mayor of Rome.

The following year Marjorie herself was presented at the Court of St. James's. For years the heiress had thought such an honor to be out of the question. She was, after all, a divorcée, a designation traditionally frowned upon by British aristocrats.

Yet Marjorie had enough connections in the British nobility—among them Lady Wavetree, Lady Lewis, and the duke and duchess of Sutherland—to be invited to Buckingham Palace. In June 1929 Marjorie Merriweather Post Close Hutton curtsied deeply to a smiling George V and Queen Mary.

For Marjorie it was a triumph over the scorn with which she had been greeted twenty-two years earlier on the eve of her wedding to Edward Close. "Mother had always wanted to be presented at the Court of St. James," recalled Eleanor. "From the time I was a little girl she had talked about it. In fact, when I was a child, we practiced how to curtsy in preparation for that event."

At home, all seemed well. That same month E. F. Hutton had purchased Clarence Birdseye's company. Within thirty days the Postum Company would be transformed into the General Foods Corporation. Daughter Adelaide and her husband, Tim Durant, had just produced a baby, a little girl they named Marjorie Merriweather Durant. Eleanor had bloomed into a gorgeous young debutante. Marjorie and E.F.'s little daughter, Nedenia, was already developing into an exquisite, sweet-tempered beauty.

But Marjorie's happiness, which seemed so complete that summer of 1929, was short-lived. On Tuesday, October 29, the stock market crashed, and the golden twenties faded as a dream. The specter of ruined millionaires plunging from skycrapers and the unemployed starving in the street stirred Marjorie in ways that profoundly changed the course of her life.

15

"Lady Bountiful"

*T*he Depression sent shock waves through Marjorie that permanently altered her thinking. No longer would she spend her time on ball gowns and costumes, on galas, or on theatrical extravaganzas. This was a new Marjorie, an heiress grown thoughtful about wealth and poverty, a socialite so moved by the personal tragedies around her that she promptly put her jewels away in a safety-deposit box. With the money saved from jewelry insurance, she financed the Marjorie Post Hutton Canteen.

At its inception Marjorie insisted that the canteen—which was first established at the Bethany Church at Tenth Avenue and Thirty-fifth Street—be created specifically to feed women and children. A tide of thankful diners benefited from the food station. Among them were newly impoverished college graduates, unemployed schoolteachers, secretaries, and mothers with seven or eight children who would have starved in the streets without Marjorie's help. Beyond the socialite's original intention, the canteen also provided nearly seven thousand meals to men who were either too old or too infirm to make the trip downtown to Seventeenth Street, where her husband established the Edward F. Hutton Food Station for Men.

The plight of innocent men and women hurt by the Depression so disquieted Marjorie that immediately after "Black Tuesday" of October 1929 she began fund-raising. By February 1930 she was head of the special gifts campaign committee of the Salvation Army's Women's

Emergency Aid Committee. Before year's end the heiress had raised more than $50,000 toward the Salvation Army's $500,000 goal.

At the time of the crash, Marjorie, like many of her friends, reached out to help the most desperate: men and women of her acquaintance who were impoverished overnight; workers dismissed from their jobs; investors whose portfolios had gone bust. She also answered appeals from major charitable organizations. As the horrors of the Depression deepened, as the spectacle of men jumping off buildings, of college graduates selling apples in the streets, of mothers giving up children they could no longer afford to feed, and of families living in city parks and "Hoovervilles" became common, it seemed to the heiress that the entire social fabric of America was dissolving. With this, Marjorie observed, had come an alarming deterioration of the traditional values of home and hearth that had once made the nation great.

Marjorie had a distinctly old-fashioned, protective, even courtly attitude toward women who were victimized by the Depression. There was no reason, she believed, for any woman or her children to stand in breadlines with rough or desperate men to wait for meals. In such a situation, women not only would be forced to endure the rain, heat, and cold while waiting to eat but would likely be subjected to crude speech or jokes.

In the Marjorie Post Hutton Canteen, as a *New York Herald and Tribune* reporter could not resist observing in a June 1930 story, were several refinements not usually seen in Depression soup kitchens. Among them was a "clean blue oilcloth covering the tables and splash of color added by bouquets of red . . . roses," which gave the diners a sense of dignity and comfort familiar to them in better days. What the article failed to mention was that the white-coated waiters—unemployed men eager for work—served the meals in a multicourse fashion reminiscent of the normal home life and restaurants of pre-Depression America.

From 1930 to 1935 the Marjorie Post Hutton Canteen was a hallowed Hell's Kitchen institution. Each year, on the anniversary of its establishment, Marjorie hosted a party. One year it was a pie-eating contest; another year saw a fashion show in which girls, dressed in new clothes Marjorie had provided, strutted across a stage modeling their finery. In appreciation the girls composed a song for their benefactor:

> To the needy and the hungry in our land
> It is you who give them all a helping hand.

Marjorie's close contact with those who benefited from her charities was typical of her largesse. Later in life, when asked about the Depression-era soup kitchen, Marjorie invariably played down her contribution. "I like to think that the young people fed nourishing meals during the Depression are healthier and strong men and women today because of that help," she would simply say.

Simultaneously Marjorie was involved in other charitable causes. Wealth, she explained whenever anyone broached the subject, was best used in a robust manner and for diverse purposes. "Keep it moving, make it work, make it create, make it do good, and make it help in many hundreds of ways," she often told friends and interviewers.

Thus it was that in January 1931—shortly after she established the Marjorie Post Hutton Canteen—she sponsored a recital with her favorite Metropolitan Opera singer, Rafaelo Diaz, to raise money for the Samaritan Home for the Aged. That spring Marjorie hosted a tea and cochaired a charity ball at Madison Square Garden for the Judson Health Center. Gradually, as the Depression deepened, as more than fifty-five hundred banks failed, as the unemployment rate climbed to a record 25 percent and left some sixteen million people out of work, Marjorie felt compelled to do even more.

A corollary to Marjorie's public-minded spirit was participation in an anticrime campaign for the United States Flag Association. She was patriotic to the core, and this was just the sort of contribution that appealed to her sense of keeping America strong against the rising threat of crime. On behalf of the Flag Association, the heiress subsequently headed a special women's "watchdog" committee to scrutinize the ethics of judges, lawyers, and public officials.

Staff members of the association were awed by Marjorie's businesslike approach. In fact, they soon came to the same conclusion about the heiress's efficiency as had her father several decades earlier: that "If Marjorie was cast ashore on a desert island, she'd organize the grains of sand." In late 1932 Marjorie received a call from the United States Flag Association. So impressive had been her contribution that on December 12 she was to be awarded the association's Cross of Honor by none other than the nation's incoming first lady, Eleanor Roosevelt. With the designation of "Lady of the Flag," Marjorie followed a distinguished list of previous honorees—among them Calvin Coolidge, Herbert Hoover, Charles Lindbergh, and Amelia Earhart.

Another cause Marjorie espoused in that era was the Gibson Unemployment Relief Committee, through whose ranks she rose to become vice-chair of the women's division. Among her duties was the traditional round of charity teas and balls that were designed to attract wealthy donors. By temperament Marjorie was an activist. As vice-chair of the committee she wanted to do more than serve merely as a charity cheerleader. What was needed, she believed—and told others on that committee—was a hands-on example of the hard work involved in collecting money in the streets for the needy.

One day, on which Marjorie had volunteered to station herself at rush hour at Manhattan's Park Avenue and Forty-sixth Street to solicit money from workers returning home, there was a violent downpour. Nevertheless, reported *The New Yorker*, "at precisely five she stepped from her car in a raincoat and rubbers. The debutantes, huddled miserably under awnings, had no idea that she would show up and still recall it as proof of her Spartan spirit."

Gradually the Depression had a dramatic impact upon Marjorie's own view of her wealth. If her fortune was to be maintained with any degree of respectability in the face of the personal tragedies being played out on city streets, in idled factories, and on foreclosed farms, Marjorie believed she had to use her money as a philanthropic instrument. Above all, wealth was no longer to be flaunted. While an ostentatious display of money might have been de rigueur in the Golden Twenties, it was decidedly out of fashion in the desperate days of the Destitute Thirties. The splashy parties the socialite once gave and attended in the twenties in New York and Palm Beach now dwindled to a trickle and were replaced with charity teas, luncheons, and fundraisers.

In contrast, and to Marjorie's profound dismay, her niece Barbara Hutton seemed determined to spend money as flamboyantly as possible. On the morning of Barbara's debut on December 21, 1930, New York newspapers blazed with headlines like RICHEST GIRL IN THE WORLD COMES OUT TONIGHT AT FABULOUS RITZ DINNER DANCE.

Angry Depression crowds increasingly menaced Barbara whenever she stepped from her huge Rolls-Royce to go to Cartier's or even to visit Ethel Merman backstage. Finally Barbara became so terrified of going out alone that her father hired two bodyguards to protect her. Hate mail, criticizing the dime-store heiress's lavish lifestyle, her opulent parties at the Central Park Casino, and her extravagant gift giving, arrived regularly from as far away as Kentucky, Montana, and Oregon.

In 1933 Barbara pursued the recently divorced Russian prince

Alexis Mdivani despite Marjorie's disapproval. "Barbara, you must forget this cheap Russian. All the Mdivani brothers are bad news. You don't want to be taken and made a fool of, do you?" Marjorie tried to reason with her twenty-two-year-old niece. Her pleas were ultimately ignored. Shortly after that conversation, in June 1933, Barbara Hutton wed Prince Mdivani in Paris.

A few months later, when the prince's brothers, David and Serge, were apprehended for embezzling their wives' fortunes, American newspapers began speculating about Barbara's own future.

The wealthy are always good copy for hungry newspaper reporters, and never is this more true than in times of economic upheaval. Years earlier, at the time of C.W.'s death and Marjorie's ensuing lawsuit with Leila, the heiress had witnessed the power of the press and realized how adverse publicity could damage her and her family. As a result, Marjorie was never eager to be written about in the newspapers.

Even at the opening of her beloved Mar-A-Lago, Marjorie had shooed away reporters from *Town and Country* and *Vogue* with the excuse that "I have refused every magazine and paper." Instead—and with the diplomacy that eventually made her one of the most popular and admired hostesses in Washington—the heiress suggested that they contact her in a year, at which point she would allow them to photograph her Palm Beach estate. A month later, when another magazine photographer asked to take Marjorie's picture, she had curtly replied, "I do not care to have any photographs of myself reproduced in magazines. We have entirely too much publicity, as it is."

Even later in life, when she befriended members of the Washington press corps like Roy Meacham, Liz Carpenter, and Betty Beale, Marjorie guarded her words and the details of her personal life carefully. "Once I became a reporter again, once I had become part of something she always instinctively shied away from called the media, our conversations were very pleasant but very distant," recalled Roy Meacham, who at various times in his career served as a staff reporter for *The Washington Post*, a public relations officer for the National Symphony, and a reporter for the Washington Post Broadcast Division.

Compounding Marjorie's natural instinct to eschew publicity was the Lindbergh kidnapping of 1932. Thereafter the heiress vowed that nothing like that would ever happen to her youngest daughter or her grandchildren. From the moment Nedenia was born, Marjorie had insisted the child be closely guarded. The Sleeping Beauty suite built for Dina at Mar-A-Lago had heavy bars upon the windows. A watchman stood guard at the entrance. And later, as Marjorie and E.F.'s daughter grew older, two Pinkerton guards followed her around.

Still later, when Dina was an adolescent and begged to be free of her protectors, Marjorie insisted upon retaining the bodyguards. Finally, when Dina was eighteen, the aspiring actress begged her mother to "call off the Pinks."

At the onset of the Depression sensational headlines were nevertheless hard to avoid—particularly when they involved members of Marjorie's family. Once, on a visit to Palm Beach, Eleanor suddenly announced that she intended to marry the Broadway playwright (and later Hollywood screenwriter and director) Preston Sturges. Marjorie immediately expressed her disapproval. Eleanor's beau was not only considerably older but had been married and divorced. Moreover, although Sturges was already a recognized writing talent whose play *Strictly Dishonorable* was a smash hit on Broadway, he had a reputation for frequenting dance halls and speakeasies. It was also said that he had a bad temper. And despite his recent Broadway success, Marjorie and E.F. feared Sturges was a fortune-hunter. All in all, Marjorie was so adamantly opposed to the match that she threatened to disinherit Eleanor.

The young woman was intractable. She boarded a train for Manhattan, where Adelaide, who had just received a frantic call from Marjorie, tried to talk her sister out of the marriage. Adelaide had no more luck than her mother.

Soon afterward, Sturges appeared before E. F. Hutton to ask for Eleanor's hand in marriage. In his autobiography, Sturges recalled that Hutton asked if the young man could support Eleanor in the high style to which she was accustomed. Preston replied by asserting that he was already a writer of proven talent: Two of his plays were then running on Broadway, and one of them brought in fifteen hundred dollars a week. "That's pin money to her," E. F. replied.

Thereafter, wrote Sturges, E.F. hired detectives to follow him around and "dig up a bad reputation for me." Although they were unable to locate one, the romance attracted wide press attention and an eager readership that followed with glee the young couple's determination to marry.

Occasionally Eleanor's sense of humor leavened the drama of her plight. One day, for instance, the beautiful debutante invited a friend to dinner and piled her into one of the family's chauffeur-driven Rolls-Royces. When the limousine rolled up at the doors to the Automat, Eleanor explained that her choice was deliberate. The Automat, she told her bemused guest, was all she could afford in view of the fact that she was going to be disowned. A few days later Eleanor carried out her intention: On April 12, 1930, she eloped with Preston Sturges to Woodstock, New York.

A few days after the marriage, the newspapers reported that Eleanor Hutton and Preston Sturges had been married with just seven dollars to their name, a sum that had been borrowed from the bridegroom's mother, Mary Desti. To quell rumors of Eleanor's disinheritance, E. F. Hutton played down the family's dismayed reaction to the marriage. When asked point-blank by a *New York Times* reporter if Eleanor was going to be disinherited, E.F. had replied: "Of course these things are always forgiven. We were taken by surprise by the news of Eleanor's marriage Saturday. We would have liked to have given them a nice church wedding. Her mother would have preferred to have put the ceremony off for six months or so, but what's done is done. He seems like a nice young fellow, so they have our blessing."

And initially, all seemed to go well for the newlyweds—despite the fact that Marjorie had indeed cut off Eleanor's allowance—but other pressures began to take their toll. Two of Sturges's new plays folded on Broadway, his beloved mother died, and Eleanor required an emergency appendectomy. Years later Sturges recalled that while neither he nor Eleanor was very happy in their first year of marriage, they were "still very much in love." By 1932, though, it was clear that their marriage had indeed gone sour.

On May 28, 1932, the *New York Post* announced that "their romance is to end. Sturges is said to have been served with papers preliminary to a suit for annulment of the marriage." Sixty years later Eleanor regarded the Sturges marriage as a youthful blunder. "Not that I was in love with him, but he was fascinating," recalled Eleanor. "He would say, 'It's such fun taking your mind out of baby ribbons.' "

However painful Eleanor's elopement had been and whatever flurry it had kicked up in the press, the scandal was overshadowed by Marjorie's public image as a hardworking and humane philanthropist. By December 1932 the heiress had been named as one of the "10 Women over 30 as Most Charming in the Nation" by Dagmar Perkins, president of the National Association for American Speech. The honorees, as Miss Perkins explained over WINS Radio, were chosen not only for their beauty but because they "had devoted themselves to public service."

. . .

Ironically, the crash had come just as Marjorie and E.F. were at the peak of their powers, at a time when Mar-A-Lago was newly completed and the Birdseye company had just been purchased. Moreover, the heiress and her husband were awaiting the arrival of a new yacht, one larger and more spectacular than J. P. Morgan's *Corsair*, Harold Vanderbilt's *Defender*, or Walter Gubelman's *The Seven Seas*, one that was hailed in newspapers—and, later, in the *Guinness Book of Records*—as the largest private sailing yacht in the world.

The *Hussar V*, as the Huttons' new auxiliary bark was called, was a diesel-powered four-masted windjammer. Measuring 316 feet from bow to stern and with a displacement value of over three thousand tons, the steel-hulled boat was heavy enough to be a battleship, but far more luxurious.

In yachtsmen's vernacular, the *Hussar* was a "four poster"—that is, a four-masted sailing ship with square rigs on three sides and a spanker (a fore or aft sail) on the fourth. With fifty-five thousand feet of sail and four diesel engines that provided an additional thirty-two hundred horsepower to two twin-screw electric-drive propulsion motors, Marjorie and E.F.'s new yacht had a cruising range of twenty thousand miles, large enough to travel the continents. The *Hussar* was reputed to have been built at a cost from $1.2 to $1.5 million in 1931, which, by today's standards, would put its worth into the tens of millions of dollars.

The yacht had been designed by the famous American naval architects Cox & Stevens. E.F. then had the blueprints sent to the Krupps' shipyards in Kiel, Germany, because of that company's reputation for superior workmanship and lower costs. By early 1931 the construction was finished, but it would be nearly a year before the boat would arrive in Bermuda. In the ensuing months the teakwood-encased *Hussar* was taken on a shakedown cruise before final adjustments were made for its journey across the Atlantic.

The yacht's storage facilities were enormous. To ensure that there could be enough provisions for long oceangoing trips, E.F. and Marjorie had installed forty tons of refrigeration equipment that accommodated thirty-five tons of frozen food as well as generous stores of fresh fruits, vegetables, and dairy products.

Seventy-two men staffed the *Hussar*, servicing such amenities as a barbershop, a bar, a smoking room, a laundry, and a movie theater.

There was even a medical unit on board where staff doctors could perform operations in case of an emergency.

Similar attention had gone into the *Hussar*'s safety provisions. The yacht had not only a ship-to-shore radio, but several lifeboats, a whaleboat, and even a twin-screw fishing boat. There was, in fact, so much attention paid to safety that one wag could not resist observing that "even Mrs. Hutton's lifeboats have lifeboats."

Legend has it that the *Hussar* was so beautiful that when sailors first saw it, they began to weep. Marjorie and E.F. were equally awed. In the heiress's first scrapbook on the *Hussar* she hastily scrawled, "Saw ship first time from deck of *Monica Bonita,* morning of November 30, 1931. She was lying in inner harbor and before we could see her we saw the great masts and yards. Great kick! She came up to all our expectations."

Before long Marjorie and E.F. climbed aboard for the christening. Nearly forty years later the heiress recalled her first moments on the *Hussar.* "I was so excited and pleased the moment I saw her. . . . I went aboard and visited each room, knowing beforehand where everything would be. I remember [E.F.] said, 'How do you know your way around so soon?' and I told him, 'This is my child. I know her.'"

Because E.F. was an expert yachtsman, Marjorie had left the exterior construction of the *Hussar* to him. Then, once she had the Cox & Stevens blueprints in hand, Marjorie set about creating a luxurious interior for the windjammer. To do so, she rented out a Brooklyn warehouse, where she had the plans for each of the *Hussar*'s three decks chalked out. For weeks she studied the dimensions of each deck so that she could furnish the rooms within them. Before long she plotted out not only the placement of stateroom beds, tables, lamps, and chairs but even where paintings should be hung.

The *Hussar*'s living room had a charcoal-burning fireplace framed by a marble mantelpiece. Above it was a painting entitled *The Constitution,* which was later hung at the U.S. Naval Academy Museum in Annapolis. Another wall contained a mahogany breakfront that displayed one of E.F.'s prized scrimshaw collections. A grand piano, comfortable library chairs, and couches had also been nailed into place to ensure that the *Hussar*'s main salon was elegant and comfortable.

Marjorie's stateroom was equally luxurious. Like the heiress's private quarters in her other homes, it was decorated in her favorite Louis XVI style. On the floor was an Aubusson rug. There was also a canopied bed and a charcoal-burning fireplace. Adjacent to the bedroom were a dressing room and a bathroom of pink marble with gold fixtures. Porcelain figurines decorated the bedside tables, and in a nearby hall stood a glass cabinet containing some of Marjorie's favorite china plates.

Years later *Washington Star* columnist Betty Beale, wondering how such delicate china was preserved from toppling over in rough seas, discovered that the plates were either nailed or glued down. Marjorie's private quarters, she concluded, was hardly reminiscent of a stateroom on an oceangoing vessel. More accurately, it resembled "an exquisite suite in a palatial French château."

Beale was not the only one who thought so. During the twenty-five years Marjorie owned the yacht, European monarchs, princes, presidents, cabinet members, world leaders, and celebrities like the duke and duchess of Windsor frequently visited the *Hussar*. The seven guest staterooms were decorated nearly as opulently as the one belonging to Marjorie. All were embellished with wooden paneling, gold leaf, and marble and furnished in styles that ranged from Early American to Queen Anne. In keeping with the *Hussar*'s elegant tone, each bedroom had its own private bath with gold fixtures and a working fireplace.

In 1933, when King Haakon and Queen Maud of Norway were invited aboard the *Hussar* for a luncheon, they were seated by white-coated footmen at a table laden with priceless china, silver, crystal, and lace tablecloths. The tiny queen (who was of British birth) turned with wonder to her hostess. "Why, Mrs. Hutton!" she exclaimed. "You live like a queen, don't you?"

Marjorie could not refute it. In the depths of the Depression such living was best done quietly—preferably at sea rather than on land, where it might attract more attention. Quite deliberately Marjorie, E.F., and young Dina spent at least six months each year from 1932 to 1934 aboard the *Hussar*, traveling the world.

On the 1932 maiden voyage the Huttons put more than sixteen thousand miles on the *Hussar*, sailing from Cuba to Panama and the Galápagos and back again with stops in Kingston, Jamaica; Martinique; and Curaçao. On one memorable trip to the Galápagos, Dina "adopted" a large sea turtle (the adoption has been preserved in family photographs). In December 1932 the Huttons sailed from Bermuda to France, arriving at the Loire River on Christmas Day. Over the years there were other trips as well to the Caribbean, the Continent, the South Pacific, and Alaska.

To Dina the *Hussar* soon became a second home, a place where adventures took place with surprising regularity. "Mother was an explorer. And so was my father. In different ways. With my father we'd go to the Galápagos, to Tahiti, all through the Caribbean, and we'd find a nice little sand atoll and go swimming and drop the hook anyplace we felt like it."

Because Dina was away from shore so often, Marjorie hired a tutor to help her keep pace with her peers on the mainland. "Life was fairly simple on the long cruises," Dina recalled. "I'd do my schoolwork early with Mrs. Tytler, my governess. Then I'd meet Daddy in the crew's galley, and we would have a huge breakfast. . . . Whenever we could, we'd swim in the open sea. . . . She [the *Hussar*] was so much a part of my life."

Although the Depression had put strains on General Foods, the corporation was still in the black. It was one of the few companies on Wall Street to withstand the crash and its aftershocks and maintain a solid financial record. While Birdseye was not yet profitable and would not become so until after World War II, the acquisition of the frosted foods company had not damaged General Foods' viability.

If anything, General Foods stock had become increasingly popular after its name change and 1929 acquisition of Birdseye. According to the company's annual report for that year, "The number of stockholders has increased so rapidly that many are not thoroughly familiar with the structure and operation of [General Foods]." After the crash, commodity prices had fallen; accordingly, General Foods had purchased its natural resources at reduced costs and in greater quantities than before, resulting in a lower ratio of "quick assets to liabilities."

Profits were still pouring in to the tune of over $19 million. Even as the nation's economy worsened between 1930 and 1932, General Foods continued to make money, albeit at a slower rate. In 1933, the most perilous year of the Depression, profits had decreased to $11 million—nearly half of what they had been in 1929. Still, the company was holding strong and paying its stockholders $2.10 per share of common stock.

In spite of General Foods' success and the good times aboard the *Hussar*, Marjorie and E.F. were beginning to drift apart. Years later the press blamed their disaffection upon the Depression—or, more precisely, on their disagreement about how great wealth should be utilized and how taxpayer dollars should be applied for the common good.

By 1932 Marjorie and E.F.'s politics had sharply diverged. It was true that several years earlier Marjorie had agreed to take advantage of the lower costs of building the *Hussar* in Germany at a time when, as *The New Yorker* sharply observed, "American shipyards were short of work." It was, that magazine also reminded its readers, "the last grand gesture in a phase of Mrs. Hutton's life which was passing."

By then Marjorie had become increasingly liberal in her politics. FDR and his New Deal concept of government intervention in free enterprise and his package of economic programs to help the unemployed, she believed, were the only way that America would climb out of the Depression. E.F. vehemently disagreed. In 1932 he had opposed the presidential election of New York governor Franklin Delano Roosevelt, whom in later years he dubbed a dangerous socialist demagogue. In particular E.F. objected to Roosevelt's fiscal policies, based as they were upon the concept of "redistribution of wealth."

A better solution for difficult economic times, E.F. believed, was for the wealthy to stimulate the economy with large expenditures. His friends, he believed, should follow his example with the *Hussar*. "If all big-boat owners would follow [my] suggestion," E.F. told his friend Ferdinand Lundberg, "the nation might yacht its way out of the depression." Arrogant as that may have sounded, there was nothing new in E.F.'s theory. Marjorie had implicitly subscribed to that same philosophy for years; in fact, she had argued as much when she insisted upon completing the building of Mar-A-Lago during the Florida land bust. But E.F.'s attitude was one that Marjorie could no longer support.

E.F. was convinced that his approach was sound. With cool assurance, the General Foods chairman of the board clung to conservative Republican principles that saw little need to extend government beyond its traditional scope, even in the bleakest days of the Depression. By January 1935 E.F. had even joined the American Liberty League, an organization dedicated to minimal government intervention in the marketplace and the private lives of citizens.

Exacerbating the couple's political differences was something even more disquieting, a personal suspicion that was to torture Marjorie for the rest of her life—an intimation that her once-beloved Ned was no longer faithful and was bedding other women practically before her eyes.

16

A Mere Clash of Wills

*T*he realization that E.F. was cheating on Marjorie came upon her only gradually. At first the heiress ignored her suspicion, believing it the paranoid by-product of her passionate attachment to her husband. Eventually the signs became too obvious to dismiss: E.F.'s sly wink to a guest; the abrupt departure of a chambermaid or staff secretary; the too-familiar embrace of an attractive female at a party. These, coupled with Marjorie and E.F.'s sharply divergent views on FDR and his New Deal policies, turned the marriage decidedly cooler.

To the public the Huttons had seemed an "idyllically married" couple, hailed in the press as the epitome of connubial bliss, whose union represented "one of the most socially and financial powerful marriages in this city." Occasionally stories of their devotion even found their way into the newspapers.

One of these occurred in January 1929, when E.F. decided to surprise Marjorie on the morning she had planned a trip south by decorating their private Pullman railroad car with orchids. But that night, when E.F. arrived home at 2 East Ninety-second Street, Marjorie was still there. She had, she explained, decided to postpone her trip for another day. Secretly Hutton telephoned the florist, asking him to remove the day-old orchids and festoon the car with new ones.

The next night, when E.F. returned home, "there was Mrs. Hutton and his slippers, both by the fireside!" A second time E.F. called the florist, who, given the high cost of the job, "was half delirious with joy."

Again E.F. instructed the florist to fill the railroad car with fresh orchids. The third morning Marjorie finally departed, thrilled with the bower of exotic blossoms that decorated her railroad car. Left behind in Manhattan was E.F. Hutton with a five-thousand-dollar flower bill.

Romantic demonstrations of affection like these—and, no doubt, others that would not find their way into the press—had made an indelible impression upon Marjorie. "She loved him deeply," said her friend Estelle Vesugar Needham. "And let's not forget that he had greatly increased her fortune."

Although the heiress had not been able to give E.F. a son, the birth of their daughter, Dina, seemed more than compensation. Ned, Marjorie joyfully observed, was a deeply devoted father who seemed to take special delight in raising their beautiful blond daughter.

As Marjorie once confided to one of E.F.'s West Coast business associates, "I am thankful every time I see [Dina] and her father together, that I had the courage, after so many years to undertake bringing her into the world. She seems to add very much to his pleasure and I hope the fact that having again, something that was part of him, has helped to ease the void left by Halcourt's going."

To Dina, E.F. was an ideal father. "Dad was a real huggy bear. He would come home from work and play with me," she recalled. "He liked to play cards . . . he would roughhouse with me and tell me stories about Nick and Dan, the fire horses . . . and he'd read books to me. . . . He was a real hands-on father."

E.F. had become far less tolerant of the values that Marjorie deemed important. Among his gripes was that his wife's lifestyle was too grandiose, too "proper" to suit his more casual style.

In Palm Beach and New York—and in a dozen places in between—there was ample opportunity for E.F. to meet attractive women. Not only was the graying chairman of General Foods still handsome and charming, but Marjorie was often out of town. Several times a year the health-conscious heiress religiously visited spas to take the "cure"—at Saratoga, at Hot Springs, Arkansas, and even occasionally overseas at Carlsbad or Vichy. On those occasions E.F. was left to his own devices.

Ostensibly there was nothing unusual in such an arrangement. Wealthy married couples of that era often traveled separately for business or pleasure. Many a dinner party—particularly in what Cleveland Amory calls the "fast marital pace" of Palm Beach—was attended by married men or women whose mates were temporarily out of town.

What was unusual was Marjorie's devotion to her husband, an affection she retained for the rest of her life. "She told me Ned Hutton was the only man she ever really loved," said her granddaughter Marwee. "He was such a free spirit, so bright, so handsome and dapper, so entertaining, and such a personality, with children and right on up to adults. Unfortunately with other women, too, be they maids or duchesses—and right under her nose."

The tragedy of their marriage, according to close observers like their employee Jim Griffin, was that E.F. was equally in love with Marjorie. Although he enjoyed other women, Marjorie was still his favorite. "There was no two ways about it," Griffin insisted thirty years later.

So powerful was the attraction between Marjorie and E.F. that the heiress initially ignored her suspicions. She would, she decided, do nothing drastic until she had definite proof of E.F.'s infidelity. "That Ned Hutton! I used to think, if only I could catch him!" she told friends later in life.

What made it all especially painful was the rumors about E.F.'s infidelity. For a while Marjorie waved them away; they were, she desperately wanted to believe, just idle gossip, the kind she never gave much credence to, the machinations of catty women with too much time on their hands. "Mother," as Adelaide put it, "did not want to have unpleasantness."

But the rumors—and Marjorie's own suspicions—increased. It was little comfort that for years her friend Billie Burke had bravely endured Flo Ziegfeld's infidelity, even when the newspapers were blazoned with reports of his affair with actress Marilyn Miller. "Mother always felt sorry for Billie," said Adelaide.

Marjorie, unlike her long-suffering friend, had no instinct for martyrdom. Her tendency was to express her disappointment, if not openly, then with a carefully directed barb. A photograph of Marjorie from that time given to E.F. exposes her attitude toward him. Upon it, beneath her pretty face and beautifully marcelled curls, she had sarcastically written, "To Ed, [from] your favorite wife at the moment."

Long-term bitterness was not Marjorie's style. In her tumultuous emotional state, the heiress turned to her Christian Science practitioner, Katherine Ross, and to readings from Mary Baker Eddy's *Science and Health*. In the chapter on marriage, Mrs. Eddy counseled her readers on the virtues of wedded life, even when love seemed one-sided. "Human affection," she wrote, "is not poured forth vainly, even though it meet no return. Love enriches the nature, enlarging, purifying, and elevating it."

While Mrs. Eddy (who was herself divorced and remarried) praised marriage as an institution that "should improve the human species," she admitted that this was not always the case. Yet she believed that "husbands and wives should never separate if there is no Christian demand for it. It is better to await the logic of events than for a wife precipitately to leave her husband or for a husband to leave his wife. If one is better than the other, as must always be the case, the other preeminently needs good company."

For a time Marjorie adhered to that philosophy, but eventually the thought that E.F. was cheating on her became unbearable. Marjorie's intolerance for infidelity had deep roots in her childhood. Adultery was the sin she was sure her father had committed with her former governess, Leila, the deed that had permanently alienated her from her stepmother. "Nobody fooled me. I heard them go up to the bedroom at night when they thought I was asleep," she used to tell her granddaughters Ellen and Melissa later in life.

Adultery—and the alienation of spirit that it signified—was the reason, Marjorie believed, that her mother had "died of a broken heart." On that basis alone, Marjorie vowed she would have no part of a philandering husband.

In her view, E.F., like her own simultaneously adored and resented father, had violated the "Christian" part of his wedding vow.

It was not until after Marjorie suspected that E.F. was consorting with her French maid that she vowed to catch him in the act, *flagrante delicto*. With such proof, the heiress intended not only to humiliate her husband with his infidelity but to obtain a divorce in the state of New York. At that time the only ground for divorce for New Yorkers was adultery. Without proof a divorce would be impossible, unless, of course, Marjorie was willing to travel to Nevada for a "quickie" dissolution of the marriage. To do so would require a residency in that state for six weeks or more—but no settlement in terms of property or child custody.

To obtain proof of adultery, Marjorie hatched a variety of schemes at her several homes and at E.F.'s hunting lodge in South Carolina. Among them was a plan whereby a series of barely visible silken threads were attached across the threshold of an adjoining door between E.F.'s bedroom and the entrance to her maid's quarters. Initially this scheme was unsuccessful—both in New York and in Palm Beach.

Later, when Marjorie realized that E.F. had other "mistresses," she grew even more inventive. This time she attached weights to the bed and a bell that would ring when the body weight in E.F.'s bed exceeded his alone. Once again the plan failed.

On another occasion the heiress again had silken threads positioned at the entrance to E.F.'s bedroom. This time Marjorie ordered her husband's valet to dust the floor of his bedroom with talcum powder and make up his bed with silk sheets. Legend has it—the court records being sealed—that the threads were found broken and two sets of footprints imprinted in the talcum powder on the floor by the bed (and, allegedly, in the bed as well). At last Marjorie had "proved" E.F.'s infidelity.

Originally Marjorie and E.F. had planned a trip to the Continent for the spring of 1935. As the date approached, the heiress announced that she intended to cross the Atlantic ahead of time, accompanied by friends and Dina. E.F., who planned to meet his wife in Europe later, accordingly went to the pier to say good-bye. It was then, just before the departure, that Marjorie confronted E.F. with her discovery and her decision to divorce him.

Adelaide, knowing nothing about her mother's plans, had also arrived to say good-bye. On her way onto the ocean liner she passed E.F. as he was leaving the ship. The usually cool and composed broker seemed noticeably distraught. "I took one look and said, 'Good grief, what have we?'" Adelaide recalled.

The way Marjorie broke the news to E.F. was typical of one of her worst characteristics: the awkward, cowardly behavior she often exhibited at times of personal crisis. "Grandmother was really terrified of confrontation . . . with someone she had been close to. She didn't have any trouble getting angry if the food wasn't right or there was a spot on the carpet, but with her husbands she had difficulty," said Marjorie's second granddaughter, Ellen MacNeille Charles. Until the moment of decision, the heiress's style was to keep her turmoil to herself or, at the most, confined to a few close friends and her Christian Science practitioner.

Marjorie's placid exterior at times of private turmoil might well explain why young Dina was shocked when she learned of her parents' forthcoming divorce. After dinner one night they called her down for a chat. Until that moment, Dina recalled, "I never saw any evidence that there was any problem with them. Then, suddenly, here were these two people I didn't even recognize. I mean, it was the strangest experience. . . . I walked in and looked at my mother and my father, and they were total strangers. Total strangers. I didn't know what was coming, but they weren't people I knew. Then they told me."

The preparations for the divorce took the better part of the summer of 1935. To minimize speculation about Marjorie and E.F.'s relationship, the heiress's Long Island attorney, Henry A. Uterhart, kept a tight clamp on the trial proceedings. At that moment the Hutton name was already being sensationalized, especially because on May 13 Barbara Hutton had divorced Prince Mdivani and, in a matter of hours, married the Danish count Kurt von Haugwitz-Reventlow. On August 16 Marjorie and E. F. Hutton's separation was announced in the newspapers. Thereafter Uterhart refused to give further information to the clamoring press.

In reality the divorce was proceeding apace. During the private trial proceedings E.F. hotly denied Marjorie's accusation of adultery. Testimony from the broker's personal valet and one of Marjorie's maids nevertheless satisfied court "referee" Percy E. Stoddart that the heiress's complaint was valid. Finally, on September 7, after a secret hearing in Patchogue, Long Island, that lasted several weeks, Marjorie obtained a divorce from E. F. Hutton on the ground of adultery.

Even after the final divorce decree on September 7, Uterhart stonewalled all speculation about the case. The next day he bluntly told *The New York Times* that "the papers in the suit were ordered sealed by the court and that he would not discuss evidence upon which the divorce was granted."

Even so, the "corespondent"—the unnamed woman, or "siren," as Marjorie had allegedly called E.F.'s partner—was described in the *New York Mirror* as "five feet one inch tall, blonde, and chic."

In February 1936 E.F. married a slender, dark-haired beauty who did not fit the description of the woman mentioned in the divorce proceedings. Hutton's new bride was the twenty-eight-year-old Dorothy Dear Metzger, who had just divorced her husband, Homer, the previous October. Ironically, she had first met E. F. Hutton through Marjorie's daughter Adelaide, who once extended an invitation to the Metzgers to spend a weekend with her and other friends at Hillwood.

The day after the Hutton divorce the *New York Sun* expressed surprise that the cause was adultery. "Until today's disclosure, society here thought that the discord in the Hutton 66 room triplex apartment at 2 East Ninety-second street had arisen from a mere clash of wills."

There were logical reasons for that assumption. Several months before the divorce, in his capacity as chairman of General Foods, E.F. began rallying big business to speak out against Roosevelt's New Deal legislation.

In an open letter to William Randolph Hearst that appeared on the editorial page of the Hearst-owned *New York American*, E.F. wrote: "In my opinion, Mr. Hearst, the responsibility of management is not a PLATFORM OF SILENCE. . . . Management must take more interest in its Government obligation. . . . If management had been interested in Government and had supported Congressmen and Senators in respect to proper legislation we would not be where we are today."

On June 30, 1935, E.F. excoriated Roosevelt's June 19 message to Congress, attacking the president in the pages of the *Detroit Free Press* for "adopting as his own the rabble-rousing battle cry of 'soak the rich and redistribute wealth' and for joining forces with Senator Huey Long, Father Coughlin, Dr. Townsend and Upton Sinclair in his program for 'bigger and better taxes.'

"What makes him think that he can increase the purchasing power of the American people and add to the National income by increasing their tax burden? . . ."

On August 21—the same time that the divorce hearings were gaining momentum—E.F. became even more outspoken. In an article for the *New York Evening Journal*, the General Foods chairman wrote: "Personally I would be glad to give the government every dollar of income which I may receive for the next five years and live on principal . . . if the Administration will undertake to fulfil the promises made in the Democratic platform in 1932."

The coup de grâce would not come until after the divorce was effected. In November 1935, E. F. Hutton, writing in *Public Utilities Fortnightly*, castigated the American business community for failing to unite against hostile government forces.

Should the current government of "radical socialists" prevail in its attempts at collectivism, he predicted, American industry would eventually cease to exist. In the "death struggle" to preserve the American way of life, it was incumbent upon the utilities to demand the support of big business and the financial community, just as those industries should expect help from the utilities.

> So I say, Let's gang up.
> The business men . . . owners of stocks and bonds . . . insurance

policies, and . . . depositors in banks must realize that the only way to prevent regimentation, collectivism, or any other ism, is for all groups to join together . . . [to] help any individual group when it is attacked.

To say that Marjorie was infuriated by E.F.'s public pronouncements is an understatement. Not only was it personally embarrassing to her that her ex-husband was blasting Roosevelt for his New Deal policies, but it was unconscionable that E.F. would do so in his capacity as chairman of her company, General Foods. Such speeches could do irreparable damage to the $67 million food corporation, to its public image, and to the perceptions of the middle-class consumer who had been the mainstay of General Foods and Postum sales from their inception.

Within twenty-four hours of the publication of the *Public Utilities Fortnightly* article, Colby "Clare" Chester publicly denied that E.F.'s statements had anything to do with the General Foods Corporation. According to Drew Pearson and Robert S. Allen's nationally syndicated newspaper column, "The Washington Merry-Go-Round," of November 27, 1935, "Chester informed the Commerce Department head that Hutton was talking only for himself, that he [Chester] and other officials of the firm were attending to business and not meddling in political affairs."

In a related statement on November 20 to the *New York American*, Chester insisted that "General Food Corp has no political attitude on any subject. We had no knowledge in advance of the published statement by Mr. Hutton and it must be considered as an expression of Mr. Hutton's personal views."

While admitting that he had used the phrase "Let's gang up" to motivate businessmen to unite to protect their legal rights, the term had been grievously misunderstood, E.F. insisted. It was, in fact, an innocent expression that E.F. had used since childhood. "All I had in mind to say was 'Let's get together.' Any wrong inference from the use of the word 'gang' is wholly unwarranted." Moreover, since E.F. had published that statement, he had experienced a change of heart about the Roosevelt administration because it had recently taken "steps in the right direction" to protect the rights of big business.

Above all, E.F. stressed that his statements were his alone, and should in no way be construed as the views of the General Foods Corporation "of whose board I happen to be chairman."

But the damage had already been done. Within a month E.F. was forced to resign as chairman of the board of the General Foods Corporation. According to Clare Chester, who was to succeed Hutton as chairman, the resignation had long been contemplated. In a December 11, 1935, *New York World-Telegram* story, Chester explained that "Mr. Hutton had intended to resign for some time, postponing it until he was satisfied that the depression neared its end. He is not in good health . . . and not active in business affairs."

The anguish that Marjorie suffered knowing that E.F. lusted after other women nearly broke the still-beautiful heiress. "She loved him so much. He must have hurt her so badly that she never got over it," said Dina.

In revenge, Marjorie vowed that she would keep young Dina away from her father, and in September her wish was mandated by the court into law. The outcome was predictable. At the time fathers were rarely granted child custody and generous visitation rights, especially in cases of proven adultery. Consequently, E.F. was allowed to see Dina only every other Christmas, every other spring vacation, and one month each summer.

As a result, the close father-daughter relationship E.F. and Dina once enjoyed was shattered. Thereafter, Dina recalled, "there was not the free give-and-take that I wanted certainly and that he did. . . . [My parents' divorce] was a low point in my life. In fact, I think it was one of the worst experiences I ever had. . . ." Eventually, when Dina was older, she was sent to Washington, to Marjorie's alma mater, the Mount Vernon Seminary. "For two years I was the youngest girl in the school. They had to start a special class for me. They didn't have one," the future actress recalled.

From time to time Dina called E.F. and begged him to visit or get her released from school. "I can't. And you know I can't," an anguished E.F. replied. "Oh, why do you do this to me?"

As the *New York Sun* noted at the time of the divorce, there was no alimony or financial settlement "as Mrs. Hutton is far wealthier than Hutton." What was not publicized was that Marjorie was to enjoy full ownership of Mar-A-Lago, of Hillwood, of 2 East Ninety-second Street, of Camp Hutridge, and of the *Hussar V*—properties that were either held in the heiress's name from the beginning or awarded at the time of the divorce.

By a private verbal agreement, E.F. also promised to leave Dina $4 million in his will, a sum that, according to Post family legend, Marjorie had lent E.F. at a time when General Foods funds were too depleted to pay stockholders a good dividend. Years later, in 1962, when E.F. died, Dina was stunned to learn her father had left her only $25,000. It was a far cry from the millions he had promised Marjorie on Dina's behalf.

The bulk of E.F. Hutton's estate went to his wife, Dorothy, and his stepdaughter, Joan Metzger Patterson.

According to E.F.'s cousin W. E. Hutton, the former chairman of General Foods ruminated about his will for months. "Ed told me any number of times that 'when Marjorie died, Deenie was going to have far more money than I ever had. Why [E.F. reasoned] should I provide for her and not leave it to my wife and my stepdaughter?' "

AMBASSADRESS
TO THE
SOVIET UNION

17

Mrs. Joseph Davies

$\mathcal{M}$arjorie's spirit was so shattered in the tension-filled months before the divorce that she turned increasingly to Christian Science. Simultaneously she tried to create a new existence independent of E. F. Hutton. Years earlier the heiress had assured her daughters Adelaide and Eleanor that divorce was not the worst thing in the world. She had, after all, ended her own marriage to their father, Ed Close, and found a more fulfilling life with Ned Hutton. Was not that proof that divorce was sometimes for the best?

By late 1934 or early 1935 Marjorie was repeating that same philosophy not only to herself but to Adelaide, who was on the brink of a divorce from Tim Durant. The marriage had been unhappy for years. Tim had not only placed some of Adelaide's inheritance under his own name but had also lost her fortune in the stock market—much of it in the "good" years before the crash. He was eventually asked to give up his seat on the New York Stock Exchange. Worse, he was cavorting with other women.

Eleanor had had similar disappointments. In 1933 she embarked upon a second marriage with a French polo player named Étienne Marie Robert Gautier. Shortly before the wedding a worried Marjorie talked to her future son-in-law. "Now look, Robert, you are marrying an American girl. They are very different from the French. We all know about the French attitude towards mistresses. Eleanor will not put up with that so you'd better treat her . . . as an American husband would treat his wife and be faithful to her or she will leave you."

Yet within a year, Eleanor had filed for divorce. By 1935 she was married to George Curtis Rand.

While Marjorie supported Adelaide and Eleanor, she remained depressed about her own future. The confirmation of E.F.'s infidelity had been a crushing blow to her self-esteem and sense of herself as a beautiful and desirable woman. In despair Marjorie became convinced that she would never find love again. She was, she believed, too old—and too disillusioned—to risk feeling anything for any man.

One night in February 1935, while Marjorie was in the midst of planning her divorce with lawyer Henry Uterhart, a chance encounter changed everything. Marjorie had been invited to a Palm Beach dinner party at the home of friends May and Jay Carlisle, where she was introduced to a handsome Washington attorney named Joseph E. Davies. At fifty-eight years of age, Davies was at the peak of his career in corporate and international law. He was also a friend of President Franklin Delano Roosevelt's. To Marjorie, Davies resonated charm and authority, and he had a magnetism that she could not easily forget.

As Marjorie subsequently wrote Adelaide and Eleanor, her new beau was "a man of mature years—of success and achievement . . . [and] he has fine high qualities." Most surprising of all, the attraction, "this wonderful thing . . . has come to me—strangely enough so late in life."

Joe, as the attorney was known to Washingtonians, fell in love with Marjorie at first sight. At forty-seven Marjorie was still an attractive woman whose keen interests in American business and commerce coincided with his own. From their first introduction, Joe later told newspaper reporters, he considered her "a grand and glamorous woman." There were, however, two monumental obstacles to the relationship: Marjorie had not yet filed for divorce from E. F. Hutton, and Joe Davies was still married. He had a wife, Emlen Knight Davies, beloved by Washington society, three grown daughters, and a handsome town house on Massachusetts Avenue.

Marjorie's first meeting with Joe Davies has become part of Washington legend. According to one version of the story, the attorney was so taken with Marjorie's beauty and brilliance that others at the dinner party noticed his attraction. Years later Davies's eldest daughter, Eleanor Tydings Ditzen, said it seemed to the family as if Joe had actually been struck by lightning. "The guests were having cocktails in the garden and Marjorie came in and down the stairs and that was it."

Another version suggests Marjorie and Joe were drawn together by mutual political sympathies. A decade later a story was still circulating in Washington that at that same Palm Beach dinner some of the Carlisles' businessmen guests complained about Roosevelt and his policies. An impassioned Joe Davies stood up, scrutinized the assembled party, and chastised them for their short memories. Were they not honestly better off in 1935 than they had been in the credit-bloated years of 1928 and 1929?

So struck was Marjorie by the eloquence of Joe's speech that she rose from the table herself. According to some, Marjorie then walked over to the attorney and kissed him, explaining, "That's what . . . [I've] been wanting to say to this crowd." Others claim that she made no direct reference to politics whatsoever but put her arms around Davies's shoulders and simply said, "You're the man I want to marry."

Given Marjorie's usually discreet style, the second story sounds unlikely. It does, however, illustrate a truism about the heiress that was repeated later in her life. Marjorie, like the movie star Mae West, seems never to have allowed herself to "get down to one man—or one dollar."

Although puritanical about extramarital romance when her marriages were good, Marjorie somehow managed to put those values aside as soon as they went bad. An introduction through mutual acquaintances—as had occurred with E. F. Hutton at the end of Marjorie's marriage to Ed Close—often led Marjorie to a new romance. "There was always," as Marjorie's son-in-law Cliff Robertson observed, "somebody to take the former husband's place."

An escort—preferably one who was handsome, charming, and in love with her—was a practical necessity in Marjorie's life. Without a husband, it was difficult for the socialite to entertain, to attend parties at the homes of her friends, even to travel. Privately, too, Marjorie believed that a woman alone could not have a fulfilling life. "She always wanted to get married; she loved to be married," said her granddaughter Melissa Cantacuzene.

Once, when Marjorie was eighty, she told her daughters that she was considering marriage for the fifth time. Horrified, Adelaide, Eleanor, and Dina, who were standing beneath their mother on the staircase of her Washington estate at the time, tried to dissuade her. The heiress glared icily at her offspring. "You're not the one sitting here alone at night," she retorted.

·   ·   ·

Within days of their introduction Joe was courting Marjorie by every means within his power: by phone, by letter, and in person whenever business trips to New York would allow. By early March 1935 the couple had acknowledged their mutual infatuation.

At fifty-eight Joe was still a dark, handsome man whose receding hairline was compensated for by piercing brown eyes and a dramatic, captivating manner. Of Welsh descent, the attorney sported a gold-tipped walking stick, wore an opera cape on formal occasions, and was fond of quoting poetry—particularly Shakespearean love sonnets—to Marjorie. Added to this was Joe's easy familiarity with congressmen, senators, and Franklin Delano Roosevelt. The attorney's office wall was replete with photographs of famous Washington personalities, among which was an autographed picture from the president that read "To old Joe, from his sidekick, Franklin Roosevelt."

"Mother was enchanted by him. She'd never run into anyone like that before," recalled Dina. "To my knowledge, she had never known many people in government or in the international world except for social figures, and this whole idea of getting involved in government was fascinating to her."

Joe Davies hailed from Watertown, Wisconsin. He was the son of an alcoholic Welshman named Edward and a woman named Rachael, a thrifty, soft-spoken ordained minister of the Welsh Congregational church. By the time Joe was ten his father had died, and the boy came under the influence of his prosperous paternal uncle John, who impressed him with the virtues of hard work and American industriousness. After graduation from the University of Wisconsin in 1898 and its law school in 1901, Joe became active in Democratic politics and embraced the progressive movement then sweeping the state. In 1912 he was western campaign manager for the Democratic National Committee in Chicago on behalf of Woodrow Wilson's nomination. The following year, at President Wilson's invitation, the attorney arrived in the capital, where he was offered several jobs—among them the ambassadorship to Russia and the governor-generalship of the Philippines.

The politically ambitious Davies turned these down and instead became the commissioner of corporations. By 1916 Davies had risen to become the first president of the new Federal Trade Commission, where he set policies on fair business practices. With that background, Davies served as Wilson's economic adviser at the Paris Peace Conference.

By 1918 Davies's lifelong political ambitions had reached the boiling point. For years he had longed to become a U.S. senator, and when, in the spring of 1918, Wisconsin's Democratic senator suddenly died, the opportunity presented itself. After the ballots were counted, Davies's ambitions were dashed; the Republican opponent had won by a slim five thousand votes.

Thereafter the attorney turned his attention to building a successful practice in international law. Over the next seventeen years his reputation as a legal adviser in international arbitration grew, bringing him many clients, personal friendships with senators, congressmen, and foreign leaders, and a substantial income. By virtue of his earlier position as the first chairman of the Federal Trade Commission, Davies was eminently skilled at keeping businessmen within the law and offering them advice about proposals for expansion. In Washington he was alternately regarded as brilliant, more clever than a good lawyer, and a formidable cross-examiner—in short, a successful and controversial figure who often served as a hired gun or legal lobbyist.

Despite Davies's cagey assessment of an opponent's strengths and weaknesses, he often tried to avoid trials. "A poor settlement," he was fond of telling his clients, "is better than a lawsuit." Another favorite adage was "Collect for the coffin while the tears are still flowing." Davies's most renowned suit was a domestic one, a tax case involving the Ford Motor Company, a 1927 triumph that won him a $2 million fee. As Davies described himself years later to *The Milwaukee Journal*, he was "one of those birds in the 1920s who put the big business combinations together . . . all strictly within the law . . . and made a fortune doing it."

Another, later coup was Davies's 1934 success in obtaining an extension on the Dominican Republic's debt to American bondholders. Despite criticism from the State Department that the republic's leader, Rafael Trujillo, was a "dictator in the making," Davies characterized his economic policies as "in the New Deal mold" and ultimately convinced the Council of Foreign Bondholders to reach a settlement.

Davies's triumph incited wrath from certain members of the State Department and political columnists Drew Pearson and Robert S. Allen. In a nationally syndicated November 1935 "Washington Merry-Go-Round" column, Pearson and Allen wrote that "Davies was a charming and opulent gentleman" with a "unique reputation among Washington legal-lobbyists. Many lobbyists work for or against legislation for Government contracts, against tax increases. But Joe has the distinction of keeping in power, single-handed, the president of a country. The president in question is Rafael Trujillo, dictator of the Dominican Republic."

The attorney paid little, if any, attention to the reproach. He had won a fee of $480,000, and although political pressure forced the White House to demand its reduction to $300,000, Davies was still on good personal terms with his old friend FDR. With his semipolitical career and successful Washington law practice, Joe Davies was widely regarded within the Democratic party as an advocate of New Deal politics. Moreover, Washington insiders considered the self-described "corporation lawyer with a liberal viewpoint" a man with a bright political future. When he met Marjorie, his name was already being mentioned in the newspapers as a potential candidate for an ambassadorship. He was, predicted Washington's *Evening Star*, "likely to go up the ladder before long."

Subconsciously—or perhaps deliberately—Marjorie had chosen a man diametrically opposed to everything that E. F. Hutton stood for—especially in politics.

By March 1935 Marjorie and Joe were exchanging love letters. At first the heiress had qualms about the relationship. She and Joe were still legally married to other partners. Although she was already preparing to divorce E. F. Hutton, the official proceedings had not yet begun. Moreover, written evidence that Marjorie was having a relationship with another man at a time when she was planning to sue Hutton for adultery was risky. By mid-March Marjorie had telegraphed Joe to stop writing altogether.

In response, the attorney wrote: "I was quite disconsolate when you suggested stopping my letters. —All sorts of fears come crowding into my mind when I realize you are away from me for so long a time and I want to banish them . . . by knowing that I can tell you all the times and again and again that I love you so much and so dearly. That takes away from some of the sense of futility that overcomes me when these fears come. You are so extraordinary and so wonderful that I cannot believe that your love for me is something that has come to stay."

By return mail Marjorie assured him of the sincerity of her love. Five days later Davies wrote Marjorie again:

Dearest, dearest, dearest,
What joy your Daily Dozen gave to me. . . . It happens that I re-

Charles William Post
(by permission of Hillwood Museum)

Ella Letitia Merriweather Post
(by permission of Hillwood Museum)

Charles Rollin and Carrie Lathrop Post *(courtesy of the Bentley Historical Library)*

C. W. Post and Marjorie
Merriweather Post
(*by permission of Hillwood Museum*)

Marjorie Merriweather Post
birthplace, Springfield, Illinois
(*courtesy of the Bentley Historical Society*)

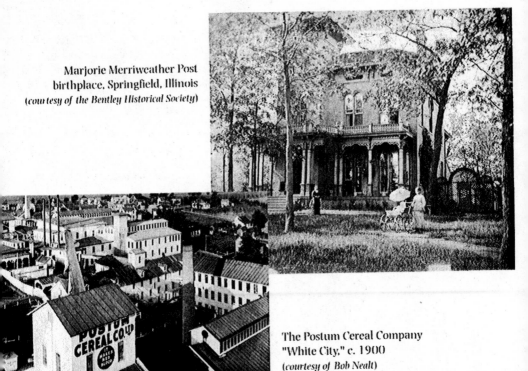

The Postum Cereal Company
"White City," c. 1900
(*courtesy of Bob Nealt*)

Marjorie Merriweather Post as a young
woman, c. 1903–1905
(by permission of Hillwood Museum)

Marjorie Merriweather Post and
Edward B. Close at the time of their
marriage, December 1905
*(by permission of the Historical Society
Palm Beach County Reproduction)*

Marjorie Merriweather Post Close
as a Greenwich matron, c. 1913,
with daughters Adelaide (left)
and Eleanor *(by permission of
Hillwood Museum)*

The Boulders
*(by permission of the
Bentley Historical
Society)*

Edward F. Hutton
(by permission of Hillwood Museum)

Marjorie Post Close Hutton, c. 1920 1925
(by permission of Hillwood Museum)

illwood, Brookville, New York (*by permission of illwood Museum*)

Marjorie Post Close Hutton, gowned for presentation to the Court of St. James's (*by permission of Hillwood Museum*)

Marjorie with baby Nedenia at Hillwood (*by permission of Hillwood Museum*)

The boathouse at the
Adirondacks camp Hutridge
(later renamed Topridge)
(courtesy of Henry Dudley)

Interior, Hutridge
main lodge
*(by permission of
Hillwood Museum)*

Hutridge guest cottage
*(courtesy of the Bentley
Historical Society)*

Living room on the *Hussar V*
(later renamed *Sea Cloud*)
(courtesy of the Bentley Historical Society)

The *Hussar V*
under full sail
(by permission of
Hillwood Museum)

F. Hutton aboard the *Hussar V* (from
the Spur)

Marjorie and Nedenia aboard
the *Hussar V* (by permission of
Hillwood Museum)

Mar-A-Lago
(by permission of the
Historical Society
Palm Beach County
Reproduction)

Drawing room,
Mar-A-Lago
(by permission of
Hillwood Museum)

The beehive fireplace in
Deenie's room, Mar-A-Lago
(courtesy of the Bentley Historical
Library)

Adelaide, Nedenia, Marjorie, and Eleanor
(by permission of Hillwood Museum)

Marjorie Post Hutton receiving the
Cross of Honor of the United States Flag
Society from Eleanor Roosevelt, 1932
(by permission of Hillwood Museum)

Marjorie at her wedding to Joseph
Davies, with her attendants,
granddaughter Marwee (left)
and daughter Nedenia
(by permission of Hillwood Museum)

Ambassador and Mrs. Joseph E.
Davies in front of Spaso House,
Moscow, 1937 (by permission of
AP/Wide World Photos)

Opening night at the opera:
Marjorie in the late thirties
(*by permission of Hillwood Museum*)

The duchess of Windsor (second from the
left), the duke of Windsor, Marjorie, and
Joseph Davies aboard the *Sea Cloud*; the
man at the extreme left is unidentified
(*courtesy of Nedenia Hutton Hartley*)

Marjorie, Eleanor, and
Marwee (*by permission of
Hillwood Museum*)

Hillwood, Washington. D.C. (*by permission of Hillwood Museum*)

The central staircase, Hillwood (*by permission of Hillwood Museum*)

Marjorie inspects the table before a formal dinner at Hillwood (*Alfred Eisenstaedt, Life magazine © Time Warner, Inc.*)

The central hall, Hillwood (*by permission of Hillwood Museum*)

in stole and jewels *(by permission of AP/Wide World Photos)*

Marjorie and her daughter Nedenia, the actress Dina Merrill *(courtesy of Nedenia Hutton Hartley)*

Marjorie and her granddaughter Marwee, poolside at The Homestead, Hot Springs, Virginia *(courtesy of Marjorie Durant Dye)*

Marjorie Merriweather Post at one of her legendary square dances (*Alfred Eisenstaedt, Life magazine © Time Warner, Inc.*)

The board of directors of the Washington Ballet Guild: Gladys Heurtematte Johnston, Katherine Dunlap, Gerson Nordlinger, Marjorie Merriweather Post (*courtesy of Gerson Nordlinger*)

Marjorie and Herb May at their wedding, June 18, 1958 (*by permission of* The Washington Post/*Jim McNamara*)

At the dedication of the C. W. Post football field, Battle Creek, Michigan: Battle Creek school superintendent Harry Davidson, Marjorie May, and George Lambeer, director of the Post Division of General Foods (*courtesy of Harry Davidson and* Battle Creek Enquirer)

Marjorie Merriweather Post and escort Fred Korth (*by permission of Hillwood Museum*)

Marjorie Merriweather Post at the 1967 International Red Cross Ball, wearing a diadem of diamonds and turquoise given by Napoleon I to his wife Marie Louise (*by permission of Richard Morgan, Jr., Bert & Richard Morgan Studio; courtesy of Historical Society Palm Beach County*)

Marjorie Merriweather Post in old age (*by permission of* Battle Creek Enquirer *and* AP/*Wide World Photos*)

ceived your note just as it arrived last night at the Club and how I did devour it. It was the sweetest note ever . . . that you have written to me. It was so dear, so joyous & so like my wonderful you. . . . I don't want any letters kicking around—It might start a conflagration!!!! . . . There are so many many things I want to talk to you about. There are so many wonderful expressions I again want to see in those beautiful eyes looking up into mine. There are so many little places in my heart . . . that cry out for you dearest girl. . . .

Marjorie replied to these letters passionately. On April 6 she wrote Joe:

> My dearest—
> And at what hours! Have been awake—off and on in the night— was always thinking of you—what you mean to me, what you have brought me—and the joy I find in it all. To have come to me just now when I need you so is too wonderful . . . how happy I am dearest deep inside. . . ."

A month later Marjorie was far more articulate about her reasons for loving Joe—and more philosophical about the unhappiness she had suffered in the last years of her marriage to E.F. On May 6 from Chicago she wrote: "I find it wonderful, dear, that we are permitted to experience this glorious thing. I am so deeply grateful always. It's a marvelous gift at any time to be in love, but the rare and tremendous thing is to have been chosen as the one to find *you*—mature, brilliant—idealistic intense. . . . Dearheart, I love you so deeply—so completely—and I am so proud & happy about it all—Perhaps it took all the *lack* & heartaches to make it so wonderful & so deeply appreciated."

By May, Marjorie and Joe had reached a decision: They would divorce their legal mates as soon as possible and get married. Coincidentally, Marjorie and Joe each intended to visit Europe that spring: The heiress had plans on the Continent; Joe was slated for Paris on business, after which he was to visit London, where he was to meet his wife, Emlen, for the presentation of their youngest daughter, also named Emlen and known as E.K., at the Court of St. James's.

The opportunity to travel together was too good to pass up. Marjorie and Joe booked passage on the same ocean liner. Officially the heiress and the attorney were traveling apart, each with friends or family members. Marjorie planned to sail with Dina and her friends the Hills. Joe was to travel with his eldest daughter, Eleanor, who was herself in the midst of a divorce. Aboard ship it was thus inevitable that all of them would meet.

To Dina, Joe Davies was merely another of her mother's business acquaintances, one whom she immediately disliked. "The first time I met him, I couldn't stand him," she recalled. "But he was on the boat, and we saw a lot of him."

In England, Joe's wife, Emlen, was equally oblivious of the truth. By early June the attorney had completed his business in Paris and arrived in London. It was then, in a fashionable London hotel, that Joe broke the news to his wife of thirty-three years. "Mother," as the Davieses' daughter Eleanor put it, "was devastated."

So was Eleanor Davies herself, who only reluctantly saw Marjorie again after all of them had returned to the States. "When I knew that my mother was being divorced, I quite frankly told her [Marjorie] if there was anything I could do to break up the romance, I would do it," she recalled. To the young woman's surprise, Marjorie received her future stepdaughter's threat with calm dignity.

"I would not have any use for you if you didn't feel that way about it," she told Joe's daughter. The comment thoroughly disarmed Eleanor. It was, she realized, a refreshingly candid acknowledgment of the difficulty of the situation. "I thought she was very honest, and I couldn't help but respect her," Eleanor recalled.

By late summer 1935 Eleanor and her mother had traveled to Reno for a double divorce—one for each of them. Joe breathed a sigh of relief and in a letter to Marjorie praised his former wife for giving him "freedom rather than live a life of lies and hypocrisy."

For weeks the press had been buzzing with reports of Marjorie's impending marriage to Joe. In late September 1935, soon after Emlen had returned from Reno with her divorce, Marjorie visited Washington and registered at the Shoreham Hotel, where Joe then lived. Reporters pestered Marjorie so relentlessly with questions about her alleged marriage to Davies that she grew disgusted. "Mr. Davies is handling a tax case for me and that's all. Can't I be single?" she snapped.

In reality the couple was already planning a wedding for December. In the intervening months Joe's daughter Eleanor had come to know Marjorie and even to admire her. Just a few days after her father's marriage to Marjorie, Eleanor was to be wed to Senator Millard Tydings of

Maryland. In anticipation of that event, Marjorie had given Eleanor a set of Parisian lace lingerie for her trousseau. "She was a remarkably generous woman, and of course, she was in love with my father, and so she showered his children with gifts," Eleanor recollected.

Even more important was the way Marjorie conducted herself as Eleanor's future stepmother. "We were absolutely honest with each other. I mean, there was never any subterfuge between us," Eleanor said. Just a few days before his wedding Joe Davies wrote Marjorie that his daughter Eleanor had praised her as "one of the finest and noblest women I have ever known."

On December 15, 1935, Marjorie and Joe Davies were married at 2 East Ninety-second Street in what was portrayed to the press as a "simple, quiet and dignified wedding."

The word *simple* was a bit of a misstatement; rarely did the heiress celebrate important life events in a plain manner. To do so, Marjorie believed, was to belittle the importance of the occasion. Above all, one's surroundings, meals, and celebrations had to be aesthetically pleasing. "Mother felt that if you were looking at beautiful things, it enhanced the experience," explained her daughter Dina.

On her wedding day Marjorie was dressed in a flowing pink velvet gown, whose colors were replicated in a 300-pound—or, by some accounts, 150-pound—wedding cake topped by a "temple of love" surrounded by spun sugar roses and doves. A thousand chrysanthemums dyed pink to match Marjorie's dress bedecked her Manhattan triplex. The ceremony, which was held on Saturday—a day earlier than that officially announced, in order to avoid newspaper reporters—was witnessed by seventy guests, among whom were Bernard Baruch; *New York Tribune* publisher Ogden Reid; Senator James J. Davis; Roosevelt's private secretary, Stephen Early; Attorney General Homer S. Cummings; U.S. Treasurer William Julian; and the now-widowed Billie Burke Ziegfeld.

At that moment, as Joe wrote in a rapturous poem to his bride shortly before the wedding, their union seemed blessed by man and God. "You are the Best / of Me / and Praise be / I am the best of you."

On the day of the ceremony members of the press who had learned about the event were refused entrance to Marjorie's Fifth Avenue apartment and forced to wait outside. In compensation, one of Marjorie's staff issued bulletins about the progress of the ceremony via telephone to a messenger in the apartment house lobby who, in turn, relayed them to the press.

Miffed at having been excluded from witnessing the wedding firsthand, reporters made the most of whatever scraps of information they could glean. The only one that seemed vaguely sensational was Marjorie and Joe's wedding cake. According to Helen Worden of the *New York World-Telegram*, the cake had cost three hundred dollars. After the wedding Worden had interviewed Marjorie's pastry chef, Moresi-Mazetti, who claimed that only forty people had attended the ceremony. According to Worden, that meant each slice of Marjorie and Joe's wedding cake cost seven dollars. Although the chef quickly justified the cost of the cake by explaining it was filled with fruit and could easily have been cut to serve five hundred people, the *World-Telegram* story read, "$7-a-Slice Cake Eaten as Mrs. Hutton Weds."

A day or two later the seven-dollar-a-slice wedding cake story was picked up in other newspaper reports. Among them was a United Press story that sniped at the alleged extravagance of the wedding. It read: "Mrs. Post Close Hutton Davies' luxurious 62-room apartment was deserted last night except for her twenty-five servants, the lingering perfume of $4,800 worth of flowers, and the remains of a $7-a-slice wedding cake. The thrice-married Postum and Post Toasties heiress, whose income is estimated by her neighbors at one million dollars a year, was speeding southward with her most recent bridegroom, Joseph E. Davies. . . ."

Immediately after the ceremony Marjorie and Joe slipped away for a few days themselves, before returning to New York for Christmas. Then they boarded the *Hussar V*—now renamed the *Sea Cloud*—for a honeymoon cruise to the West Indies. Accompanying them were Dina, the newlyweds Eleanor and Millard Tydings, and another couple. By March the honeymooners had returned to the North American continent, landing in Palm Beach, where Edward and Eva Stotesbury held two parties in Marjorie and Joe Davies's honor. With the blessings of the now-elderly "grande dame of the winter set" upon Marjorie's third marriage, the euphoric bride then moved into an apartment with Joe at Washington's fashionable Shoreham Hotel.

In spite of Marjorie's national prominence, some members of Washington society regarded her with frank disapproval. For months before the wedding, ugly rumors had plagued the couple. Marjorie, it was whispered, had stolen Joe Davies away from Emlen Knight Davies by dangling her checkbook before her. The General Foods heiress had essentially blackmailed Emlen Davies, offering the beleaguered woman two million dollars if she would give Joe a quick, scandal-free Nevada divorce.

The Davieses' daughter Eleanor Tydings Ditzen has long regarded those rumors as "completely untrue." As she has insisted, "My father didn't need to be bought. He just fell in love, that's all. He was one of Washington's wealthiest lawyers." Furthermore, both sides of Emlen's family were wealthy. The maternal side came from a Maryland family that was among the state's first white settlers. Emlen's father, Colonel John Henry Knight, had been a Delaware attorney and colonel in the Union Army. Her grandfather had been a prominent Wisconsin lumberman who owned several large hotels. "So there was no question of anybody buying my mother. It was an outrageous lie. She had a magnificent home on Massachusetts Avenue and her father's beautiful house in northern Wisconsin. She also received a handsome settlement from my father, which was paid by check from his law firm every month," said Eleanor.

At the time of the divorce Washington's old guard was up in arms. It was "a roaring scandal," as Joe's youngest daughter, E.K., put it. And "most everybody, certainly the old ladies, took my mother's side," recalled her sister Eleanor. "Some women never talked to my father again, among them Senator Borah's wife and Mrs. Woodrow Wilson." The "everybody" also included the District's "cave dwellers," the rarely seen but powerful descendants of the capital's early settlers who were seldom seen in official circles.

Nearly a decade later some of Washington's old families were still sniffing about Marjorie Davies. Among them was society columnist Betty Beale, who was just starting out in her profession. Beale, who was herself from an old Washington family that had known Joe, Emlen, and their three daughters, naturally had a preconceived—and unflattering—view of Marjorie. "I thought it was a terrible thing what he [Joe Davies] had done, to leave a wife of . . . thirty-three years . . . and just walk in and say, 'I want a divorce.' . . . And I thought it was terrible that she [Marjorie] had taken this man from his wife. . . ."

But eventually, as Betty Beale became better acquainted with Marjorie, whose new stepdaughters now accepted her warmly, the columnist had a change of heart. By the mid-1950s Betty Beale was not only a frequent guest at Marjorie's parties but one of the few reporters whom the

legendary Washington hostess trusted with news-breaking stories
about her personal life.

With each divorce and remarriage Marjorie grew increasingly autonomous. By late 1935 she was no longer content to be merely a successful
socialite and philanthropist. The heiress wanted to be at the center of
power herself or at least privy to its inner workings.

Months before her marriage to Joseph Davies, Marjorie had begun to
test her wings, to flex her fiscal muscles in ways that would have been
unthinkable a decade or two earlier while she was still married to Ned
Hutton or Ed Close. No longer was she willing to be a hidden navigator,
a "behind-the-scenes voice" at General Foods. Now, with 10 percent of
the stock still in her name, she wanted to have an impact upon corporate decisions herself. She wanted to become a director on the General
Foods board.

By 1935 such a position was not only thinkable but attainable—albeit for only a small, select group of American women. Roosevelt's secretary of labor, Frances Perkins, was the most public example of that
changing attitude. Behind her were millions of women who had
worked twelve-hour shifts in World War I factories, who had demanded suffrage in 1918, and who had flouted Victorian sexuality in
the Roaring Twenties in search of independent selfhood. For these
women, grinding poverty, stifling social mores, and the absence of male
breadwinners had been a grim reminder of the perils of dependency.

For Marjorie, the catalyst had been infidelity, the chill wind of be-
trayal that blew away all illusions of male protectiveness and trust for
the second time in her life. Monumental wealth, the bitterness of divorce from E.F., and disgust with the consequences of letting others assume responsibility for the management of her company enabled
Marjorie to begin the journey to personal autonomy a full half century
earlier than most other American women.

Intuitively Marjorie had been training for that responsibility for years.
From early adulthood she had monitored the quality of Postum and
General Foods products herself. Wherever she traveled, the heiress ordered for her meals boxes of Post Toasties, Grape-Nuts, and other company products. If she deemed a product less than satisfactory, the
heiress wired an angry telegram to Clare Chester at General Foods
headquarters in New York.

Even when on vacation, Marjorie was vigilant about potential new markets for General Foods. On December 1, 1933, while at the Arlington Hotel in Hot Springs National Park, Arkansas, Marjorie wrote Clare Chester: "I have been doing a little advertising job for you out here and would like some samples of the Frosted Foods sent . . . would suggest the following . . . porterhouse steak, chicken, turkey, oysters, liver, corn on cob; asparagus, strawberries (whole): loganberries, blueberries; scallops. . . . As this is an enormous hotel and they have the most stupendous menus, I suggested to the manager that he could make an enormous saving and have equally as good, if not better food. . . ."

By September 1935 Marjorie was no longer content to be merely a long-distance adviser. Three weeks after her divorce from E. F. Hutton, she asked Clare Chester to put her on the board of directors of General Foods.

A few days later Chester wrote his approval. "Since our talk of Tuesday, all the directors (not members of the management) have been sounded out on the general subjects which you outlined. I am expressing the unanimous opinion in writing you that any time you wish we will be delighted to elect you a member of the Board of Directors, and this would carry to anyone you might nominate in your place. I hope I made clear yesterday that any information about the company which you may want is available to you at any time. This is almost superfluous to say."

By April 9, 1936, the press had announced Marjorie's appointment, noting that she was "the first woman director in the company's history." The position, observed *Fortune*, was well deserved because Mrs. Davies was "altogether conversant with the corporation detail." *Literary Digest* reported that General Foods was expected to benefit from Mrs. Davies's appointment because it brings to the board "a person respected among her associates for her sound business sense." Marjorie nevertheless approached her new job with a certain amount of trepidation. Even after attending her first few General Foods meetings, she told a *New York Sun* reporter that "until I understand how things are being done, I just intend to sit in and learn."

By then, as other periodicals quickly reminded their readers, E. F. Hutton was no longer chairman of the General Foods board. He was, however, still a director who owned an estimated 1 to 2 percent of General Foods stock and in that capacity was still expected to make corporate decisions with Marjorie and fourteen other members of the board of directors.

The ugliness of the divorce—and the public debacle over the "gang

up" speech that led to E.F.'s resignation as General Foods chairman—
were still too fresh a wound. In early meetings Marjorie and E.F.
managed to avoid each other altogether. When Marjorie appeared at
the April 1936 board of directors meeting, E.F. was absent. At other
times the situation was reversed. By February 1937 E.F. had resigned
from the General Foods board.

With his disappearance Marjorie no longer had to contend with the
threat of intervention from a former husband. C.W.'s farsighted ambitions for his little daughter, Marjorie, had at last been fulfilled. Under a
newspaper clipping in her scrapbook announcing her election, Marjorie had triumphantly written, "Again back into my Daddy's business!"

Despite the significance of her new position, Marjorie never lost her
traditional sense of femininity. Years later her granddaughter Ellen recalled that Marjorie took special pains over her appearance before the
General Foods board meetings. "I always have to get dressed up for my
boys' meetings," she explained. "You know they like a woman to look
nice, even if they don't say anything about it." She often scoffed at career women who attempted to act like men in the business world. At
board meetings Marjorie appeared in businesslike, well-tailored suits
with feminine, but not frilly, blouses. "She wanted to show the world
that a woman could be a good businessperson and didn't have to pretend to be a man," said Don Handelman, her financial manager at the
Meyer Handelman Company. As former *Washington Post* reporter Roy
Meacham put it, "She kept that steel-trap mind behind a veil of femininity."

To Marjorie that veil was an all-important weapon, as compelling as
her holdings of General Foods stock. Not only had she captivated Davies
with that veil, but she would use it to fulfill another ambition: to
become the glamorous wife of an internationally acclaimed public figure. Marjorie, as *Fortune* observed in a 1936 portrait, not only was "socially ambitious" but "without question sought to translate all this into
power."

For years Joe Davies had burned with unfulfilled political ambitions
of rising to the Senate, even of attaining the presidency. By 1936
he had risen no farther than chairman of the executive committee of
the Democratic National Committee and a speaker for FDR's second
term as president. Now an impassioned Marjorie vowed to see her new
husband's dreams at least partly realized. To achieve this, she gave a
generous sum of money to Roosevelt's 1936 reelection campaign, considerably more than Joe contributed in his own name. Estimates in the

newspapers and from family reports range from $17,500 to $100,000. "But whatever it was," said Dina, "it was a lot of money for that time."

The contribution was well spent. It could not, of course, buy Joe a presidency; it was too late in the attorney's life and too late in his career for that. But it did buy Marjorie's husband a position in international politics.

On August 26, 1936, Joe received a call from Roosevelt's personal secretary, Stephen Early, at Marjorie's Adirondacks camp—now no longer called Hutridge but renamed Topridge. The attorney left immediately for Washington, where, at a desktop lunch, Roosevelt announced he was appointing Joe a U.S. ambassador. His assignment was to Soviet Russia, which was then under the iron rule of a short, crafty shoemaker's son named Joseph Stalin.

With his beautiful and gracious wife, the attorney was expected to make a positive impression upon the leaders of the Communist party in Moscow. Officially his duty was to find out if the Soviets were potential allies in what was widely regarded as the coming European struggle between the forces of fascism and democracy that threatened to explode into another world war.

18

First "Ambassadress"
to the Soviet Union

*A*t first Marjorie was horrified with the news that Joe was assigned to Soviet Russia. The country was remote, its climate harsh, and its politics hostile to Western democracy—hardly the glamorous European appointment she had envisioned for herself and her husband. The Moscow post, as *The New Yorker* put it, was "the bleakest and dullest one that rates an ambassadorship."

For months the press had speculated that FDR would assign Joe and Marjorie to France, Great Britain, or Germany. Instead the vacant post in France had gone to William C. Bullitt, former ambassador to the Soviet Union. Robert Bingham remained ambassador to Great Britain. In Germany political conditions were so volatile that FDR retained the ambassador, William E. Dodd. Still, as Davies recalled in his memoir, *Mission to Moscow*, the chief executive expected the Russian assignment to be temporary. The "ultimate plan," he said, was "that I was to go to Berlin as Ambassador within the year."

In private, State Department aides speculated that Davies had ruined his chances for the ambassadorship to France by assuming it was a fait accompli. Others thought Davies had been assigned to Moscow as a corrective, as a way of signaling that FDR could not be bullied into diplomatic appointments. Raymond Clapper, the United Press Washington bureau chief, believed it a "touch of Rooseveltian humor" that the president had assigned William Bullitt to a new post in France while relegating Davies to the USSR.

Society reporters also chortled over Davies's appointment. Joe's luxury-loving wife, Marjorie, they predicted, would make a poor adjustment to Soviet Russia. In fact, they speculated that she would not "put up" with the USSR "for more than a year." Mrs. Davies, noted *Newsweek*, was going to "the one country on the United States calling list where it is as difficult to be a millionaire as it is to be a pauper in the Post end of East 9 2nd Street."

In spite of the gossip, Marjorie radiated pride in Joe's assignment and presented herself in public with a "determined air of satisfaction." Behind closed doors the nearly fifty-year-old heiress was frightened, so profoundly that she considered forgoing the opportunity altogether. "I said to Mr. Davies at one point, 'well it's been awfully nice knowing you . . . have a good time in Russia. I can't go,' " Marjorie later recalled.

One of Marjorie's fears was the sub-zero temperatures of the Russian winter. "I had been living in the semi-tropics in the winters for at least thirty years and while I was raised in a country of heavy snows . . . it had been a long time since I had experienced anything like that," she said.

The spirit of the little girl who had once braved the Michigan snows in bare feet at C.W.'s instruction was not entirely forgotten. When Marjorie first expressed dismay over the assignment, Joe reacted patiently. Enamored as he was of his new wife—"almost embarrassingly so," as his youngest daughter, E.K., recalled—the attorney wanted his beloved "Blue Eyes" to share his excitement about the Russian assignment. To persuade Marjorie, he arranged a luncheon between her and William Bullitt, the former ambassador, to discuss life in Moscow. By the end of that afternoon Marjorie had a new attitude. "I began to feel that I was going to be extremely stupid if I didn't make the effort to go and . . . have this thrilling experience."

Whatever the Soviet appointment lacked in social cachet was more than compensated for by its exotic flavor. From that perspective, it was not a disappointment at all but an opportunity for adventure. Once committed to an idea, a cause, or a man—or all three, as was the case in 1936—Marjorie threw herself into it wholeheartedly. "She loved the idea of being a diplomatic wife, and she just dove into it headlong," said her daughter Dina.

The decision to go to the Soviet Union ultimately transformed Marjorie's life. No longer would she be considered merely another wealthy socialite—albeit the highly respected "Lady Bountiful of Hell's Kitchen"—even one who, as a 1936 *Fortune* magazine article observed, had "an edged energetic participation in things that has given her the staying power to carry on three separate . . . careers: business, philanthropy, social life." Now, as a diplomatic representative of the United States, Marjorie would rub shoulders with American statesmen, Soviet dignitaries, European ambassadors, and other political "movers and shakers" who were molding the course of world history.

What intrigued Marjorie most of all was FDR's instructions to Joe to "befriend" the Russians, a duty that, by extension, also fell to her. "Mother loved to entertain," said Dina, "and here this was part of her job. She thought she'd died and gone to heaven."

Another incentive was the distinction of serving as the first American "ambassadress" to the USSR. It was only three years since the United States had granted political recognition to the Soviet Union, and William Bullitt, America's first ambassador to the USSR, was divorced. The presence of a female representative of the United States—especially one as celebratory of the capitalistic way of life as Marjorie, one who, as social historian John Ney put it, "has no sense of guilt about the posses-sion of money"—was something the Russian leaders had never known.

Tensions between Washington and Moscow had existed since the Bol-shevik revolution of 1917. At issue was the Communists' vow to de-stroy democracy throughout the world and their insistence upon atheism. Nor had the Soviet Union made any effort to pay off old debts incurred at a cost upwards of $150 million during the revolution. A re-sentful and passionately isolationist United States had consequently been the last of the Western democracies to recognize the USSR as a le-gitimate nation.

That recognition did not come until late 1933, when FDR, urged by Secretary of State Cordell Hull and his assistant William Bullitt, agreed to normalize relations with the USSR in hopes of stabilizing the political balance in Europe and Asia. In September 1933 FDR declared that it was time to bring "this whole Russian question into our front parlor in-stead of back in the kitchen." On November 1, ignoring advice from State Department officials—those "fossilized bureaucrats," as FDR dubbed them—that he proceed slowly, the president rushed through diplomatic recognition before agreement about the debt could be ham-mered out. FDR had done this out of anxiety; if war broke out in Europe, he wanted to ensure that the Soviets were on the Allies' side.

Since recognition the American-Soviet relationship had flagged. In spite of Ambassador Bullitt's efforts to pin Foreign Commissar Maxim

Litvinov to a debt repayment schedule, a plan had never been established. Davies's assignment was to erase the resultant bitterness by befriending the Russians. To do so, he was instructed to ignore the propaganda issue and take no initiative on the Soviet debt.

Initially the November 20, 1936, announcement of Joe's appointment was hailed in the press as an optimistic sign for American-Soviet détente. The appointment, said *The New York Times*, "served to emphasize the importance which the President attaches to Russian relations." According to Washington's *Evening Star*, "It is felt certain in official quarters that Davies, because of his wide experience and capability, will make many friends for America in Moscow." The attorney's foreign business background, observed another *Evening Star* commentator, made him "peculiarly well fitted to take up the vital question of trade in the Soviet. . . ."

Still, the Washington press corps was not universally pleased. While conceding that Davies had qualifications "which go far to compensate for his lack of direct experience," *The Washington Post* complained that "President Roosevelt has not seen fit . . . to appoint as Ambassador to Russia a man professionally qualified for that important and arduous post by long years of training and experience in the American Foreign Service."

State Department aides echoed this complaint with the assertion that Davies was little more than a political appointee, one who neither spoke Russian nor had previous diplomatic experience but had received the post as a "payback" for his faithful support for FDR. Nevertheless, the chief executive had named Davies to Soviet Russia precisely because of his successful track record with foreign governments.

The attorney was flattered and appreciative. Davies repeatedly expressed his gratitude. On November 22, when he was sworn in as ambassador, he telegraphed FDR: "Am deeply moved by the great privilege of being afforded the opportunity of serving you and our country as a part of your administration which is destined to be in my opinion one of the greatest in our history. . . . I cannot let the day go by without thanking you warmly again."

FDR had several expectations for Davies as ambassador. Among them was his hope that his new appointee would encourage a new trade agreement that would allow the Soviets to buy American domestic goods. This agreement, which would guarantee the sale of at least forty million dollars' worth of American goods, interested FDR for its potential to boost the still-ailing American economy. As *Fortune* reminded its readers nearly a year after Davies's appointment, "He . . . went to the USSR as, more than anything else, a *business* Ambassador."

Davies's final tasks were the most critical of all: an assessment of the industrial strength of the USSR and its commitment to the preservation of European peace. By 1936 the signs of the coming international struggle could no longer be ignored. By March 1936 Hitler had defied the Versailles peace treaty by rearming Germany and sending troops into the demilitarized Rhineland. A year earlier Mussolini had invaded Ethiopia, and in 1936 he and Hitler helped overthrow the democratic government of Spain. In the Far East, Japan, dissatisfied with its 1931 invasion of Manchuria, eyed the rest of China hungrily.

One of the few strategic "wild cards" in the tense international configuration was the USSR. Were the Soviets inclined to join with the major Allied powers—America, Britain, and France—against German fascism in the interests of protecting themselves from Japanese imperialism? Or would they bid against those democracies in favor of the Nazis? Davies's assignment was to tease the answers out the Soviets' hand.

As ambassadress, Marjorie's obligation was to represent the United States in as flattering a light as possible. That meant showing the Russians that capitalism was a good way of life, one that enabled people to live comfortably and in charitable consort with others.

To live well in the glaring spotlight of the diplomatic community of Soviet Moscow would require adjustments. Like Bullitt, the Davieses were expected to live by the privileged standards of international diplomacy but not as opulently as they had in the United States. Marjorie left behind most of her jewelry. "She learned not to wear so many jewels in front of the Communists. She was probably more simply dressed there than at any other time in her life and, for that reason, probably more beautiful," said E.K., who accompanied her ambassador father and Marjorie to the USSR.

Despite Marjorie's efforts to dress more conservatively, her beauty, enhanced by ball gowns and dresses that were "more appropriate to the court of Versailles in 1750 than the Moscow embassy in 1937," inevitably inspired admiration from the diplomatic community. The American ambassadress, declared the wife of an embassy aide who met Marjorie in Moscow in 1937, was "the most stunning woman outside of *Harper's Bazaar*." The Russians were equally captivated. "They were absolutely goggle-eyed," said Dina. "They'd never seen anything like that before. They looked at Mother with her clothes and jewels and [wondered] if the tsars had come back."

In that era professional diplomats—even those with "political appointments" like Joe Davies—were expected to use their personal possessions to enhance entertainment abroad. Ambassadorial wives routinely brought fine linens, china, crystal, and silver along to their diplomatic posts. Moscow was a tricky assignment. Marjorie and Joe were instructed to bring along their best linens and china, but not their silver services or bowls. These, FDR warned the Davieses, were considered too ostentatious, too "capitalistic" to be appropriate for the USSR. Instead Marjorie was to set the table "entirely with crystal." To supplement her dinnerware, Marjorie bought glassware at Bloomingdale's for the ambassadorial mansion in Moscow.

The question of what food to put on the table was even more problematic. It was no secret that the Soviet Union had severe food scarcities. As recently as 1933 and 1934 the country had suffered one of the worst famines in history. Even in good years the brief Russian growing season made fresh fruits and vegetables difficult to obtain.

Remembering C.W.'s belief that fruits and vegetables were essential for health, Marjorie had no intention of doing without them even in Soviet Russia. She was, as E.K. observed, "a stickler about nutrition." Bolstering that determination was the fact that Joe had chronic stomach problems, which Marjorie believed could be kept under control with a "proper" diet. As a result, the heiress once again turned to the use of Birds Eye frosted foods. By late fall twelve food lockers stuffed with frozen foods and two thousand pints of frozen cream were loaded aboard the *Sea Cloud* for a voyage to Leningrad.

To those already critical of Davies's appointment, the transportation of frozen foods to the USSR was an egregious faux pas, the ultimate snub to a hungry Communist nation that already sneered at the excesses of American capitalism. It was, as *Fortune* observed in a portrait of Ambassador Davies, "about as tactful as presenting a cripple with a pair of ice skates." The incident—and particularly the two thousand pints of frozen cream—elicited angry headlines across the nation. Among them was one from the ordinarily circumspect *New York Times* that read AMBASSADOR HAS 2,000 PINTS OF FROZEN CREAM FORWARDED TO MOSCOW FOR FAMILY USE.

Marjorie passionately defended the decision. In the Soviet Union, as on *Sea Cloud* voyages, the cream was to be defrosted and mixed with water to produce milk, which was used for drinking and cooking. "It was hard for people to understand that frozen cream would be needed in Russia," she said. "Actually, it was terribly needed because they were just ending a dreadful famine . . . [and] had to rebuild their cow herds."

For months thereafter the image of the fabulously wealthy heiress and her ambassador husband sending what was essentially a 350-foot "refrigerator ship" to the Soviet Union with their own private food supply rankled many Washingtonians. Even in April 1937, when Marjorie returned home on her first leave from Soviet Russia, people refused to let the issue go. At a dinner following a White House reception, a guest cornered the ambassadress. "Is it true that you took two thousand jars of cold cream to Russia?" she asked. The question infuriated Marjorie. "I knew . . . that she was thinking of the frozen cream, but I couldn't get into that," Marjorie later said. "So I merely looked at her and said, 'Does my face look as if I needed two thousand jars of cold cream?' "

In Moscow the diplomatic community was awed by the variety of foods served at Marjorie's table. Upon arrival the ambassadress had ordered a dozen food storage bins installed in the basement of the American ambassadorial residence, Spaso House. But the mansion was ill equipped to handle the heavy electric load of Marjorie's twelve freezers. At the first party the lights blew out. Later, when Marjorie had Spaso House rewired, the freezers became a critical accessory to her weekly schedule of diplomatic dinners. They were, the inveterate hostess explained, "a great comfort . . . so we wouldn't be caught short as many embassies were." While fellow diplomats living in Moscow routinely sent abroad for groceries and fresh produce, their arrival was often delayed. "Sometimes, we would be asked to dinner and there would be carrots and turnips and potatoes and that would be all because the car didn't . . . come back in time."

Special clothing was also needed for the Russian sojourn. With so little time between the public announcement of the ambassadorship and the Davieses' early January departure to the USSR, warm clothing had to be ordered months ahead. To do so, Marjorie went to Bergdorf Goodman and instructed the founder's son Andrew Goodman to have her tweed coats lined with chamois for extra insulation. Since Joe's appointment was not yet announced, she had not explained why she needed the clothing. Shortly after the press reports appeared, Andrew Goodman presented Marjorie with the clothes—and a confession.

"Well, I see what this was all about," he said. "I thought maybe you had gone crazy."

Marjorie and Joe arrived in Moscow by express train on January 19, 1937, with fifty pieces of hand luggage and thirty trunks. The transatlantic crossing on the *Europa* to Bremen had been stormy, "the roughest that I think I ever had—terribly heavy winter seas," Marjorie recalled. With her usual positivity, the ambassadress nevertheless refused to consider the voyage a bad omen. By the time the *Europa* landed in Germany, Marjorie was "in a lather of excitement" about what lay ahead. Though Dina had been left behind in boarding school, Marjorie and Joe were accompanied by E.K., a former Vassar student who now planned to study at the University of Moscow. In addition, there were one of Joe's cousins, who was to serve as his secretary, and Marjorie's masseur and maid.

After passing through Germany by train, the Davieses were met in Poland by the American chargé d'affaires, Loy Henderson, who escorted them in a Pierce-Arrow to the fabled Russian capital. The first thing that struck Marjorie was the biting cold. The second was the blinding whiteness of Moscow. From the embassy car the snow-covered rooftops of the buildings glistened in the noontime sun upon streets packed high with snow. Beyond them and not far from a stately section of imperial mansions loomed the onion-dome rooftops and minarets of the Kremlin palace, suggesting the influence of the Orient upon Russia's long, sad history.

This magical vision was soon enhanced by the Davieses' arrival at the American ambassadorial mansion. Marjorie's first impression was that Spaso House, located near a small park, was "magnificent" in a world where "everything around us was pure white." The mansion was an elegant three-floor building once owned by a prominent prerevolutionary fur merchant. At its center was an enormous marble hall open to the roof and surrounded by a balcony leading to second-floor rooms. Within a few days Joe reported that Spaso House was "run-down" and in need of more renovations to fit American standards of comfort.

After months of diplomatic briefing the Davieses had arrived in Moscow as determined to encourage the American embassy staff as to charm the Russians. The first night of their arrival they hosted a reception at Spaso House for 125 members of the embassy staff. The next evening they held a second party for 175 people. This time their guests were Americans, most of them engineers employed by the Soviets as industrial consultants.

Despite the seemingly spontaneous nature of their hospitality, the Davieses had planned the parties weeks ahead. From the States, Marjorie had dispatched a butler, an interior decorator, and four other members of her staff to clean and furnish Spaso House. With them had come tapestries, paintings, and furniture from Mar-A-Lago. Fifty family pictures were placed in the living room to give the mansion a "homey" feel. Also arrived were dozens of electric gadgets and American equipment, among them freezer units, electric razors, and bathtubs, the last of which were temporarily stored in Spaso House's backyard until they could be installed. "The Russians were agog," said Dina. "They couldn't understand why these Americans needed so many bathrooms."

On January 25, 1937, Joe was officially presented to President Mikhail Kalinin as the American ambassador. That same day he and Marjorie were invited to return to the Kremlin for an important historical event, the last session of the USSR's Constitutional Convention.

From a diplomatic box, Marjorie and Joe gazed down upon an assembly of state officials and twenty-eight hundred delegates from various sections of the USSR. The diversity was remarkable; among the delegates were Mongolians, Eastern Europeans, Siberians, military men, and others in colorful provincial costumes.

To Marjorie's surprise there were many female delegates. The ambassadress wrote Eleanor Roosevelt that in the USSR they "are recognizing very much the ability of women, in many instances they are taking their places right along side of the men, . . . in executive positions and in . . . manual work." What impressed Marjorie most, though, was the diversity and vitality of the Russian people. In early March, she wrote Eleanor Roosevelt that it was "a great privilege to be allowed to have this experience."

There was, however, a dark side to the "triumph" of the Communist regime that disturbed the new ambassadress: the fact that the Soviets lived in a police state. Not far from Spaso House were a number of apartment buildings. In the dead of night Marjorie and Joe were often awakened by the bells on the wagons of the secret police. Inevitably this was followed by "the screams of the individuals and their friends and their families." Afterward there was silence, interrupted by the bells and the rumble of the wagons taking citizens "to jail and probably to death." What was most appalling, Marjorie later said, "was that no one could ever find out what had happened to an individual."

Even on the streets of Moscow in the full light of day, Marjorie wrote Eleanor Roosevelt, "there would be many things that would wring your heart. . . . Many, many faces bespeaking years of struggle and hunger and fighting for very existence. All this, of course, one finds in the faces of older people. The younger ones are better than they were a few years back and there is no question . . . but what they are making a very gallant effort to bring order out of chaos: but it is such a tremendous undertaking that one really wonders how they can keep up their courage."

That Marjorie and Joe had arrived at the Soviet capital at a moment of high political intrigue was obvious in other ways as well. Ostensibly, the highest officials in the land were President Kalinin and the prime minister, Vyacheslav Molotov, but the real power was held by Stalin, secretary of the Communist party. To ensure his supremacy, that crafty strategist had already engineered the "liquidation" of enemies in the 1934–35 "Reign of Terror."

By the winter of 1936, Stalin had plunged the USSR into a second purge. This one involved a group of men that included some of his most bitter enemies, among them the high party leader Karl Radek, former Trotskyites Grigory Sokolnikov and Leonard Serebryakov, and the former director of the State Bank, Grigory Pyatakov. The trial's star witness was Radek, who was accused of sabotage, conspiracy to assassinate Soviet leaders, and an international plot involving Germany and Japan.

It was no accident that Stalin demanded that the Radek trial be held in public, for he was eager to perpetuate the image of a just Communist state. With that in mind, Moscow's international diplomatic community and press corps had been invited to the sessions. What immediately struck Davies was the one-sided nature of Soviet justice. As he wrote Secretary of State Cordell Hull, "The most extraordinary part of this trial, from a Western outlook, is that there should have been such a trial at all. The accused had all entered the plea of guilty. There remained nothing for a court to do but to hear possible pleas for clemency and to . . . sentence the accused. . . ."

Off the record, Davies asserted that the trial had been carefully choreographed for the benefit of diplomats and reporters. The Radek trial, he wrote Hull, was intended to be a "warning to all existing and potential plotters and conspirators within the Soviet Union." It was also meant to discredit Trotsky to foreign governments and solidify Russian sentiment against the Germans and Japanese.

Despite the unilateral nature of the proceedings, Davies was convinced that the conspirators were guilty. Nevertheless, he found the Soviet justice system "quite as horrible in the impression it made upon my mind as the . . . Constitutional Convention was inspiring."

The same police-state mentality that sparked the Radek trials affected the lives of ordinary Soviet citizens. Young Russians were rigorously drilled in Communist party doctrine and expected to fulfill its ideals above any loyalty to family or friends. From childhood they had been taught that the USSR had a superior way of life that had no equal in the rest of the world. Among them were party spies ready to seize anyone who was disloyal to that doctrine. Those who disobeyed were taken to the forced labor camps of Siberia or "liquidated" by firing squads. As a result, frightened Soviet citizens hung pictures of Stalin in prominent places in their homes and lit candles beneath them when guests arrived. Others left volumes of Marxist writings on their tables to underscore their commitment. In public, people spoke carefully and in keeping with party doctrine. Anyone who disobeyed party rules or challenged the supremacy of the Communist way of life was considered a traitor.

One result of this fearful existence was rigidity in the thinking of the average Russian, an inflexibility Marjorie immediately noticed. Shortly after arriving in Moscow, the ambassadress and E.K. hired an Intourist guide to acquaint them with the city. One of the sights was the park of "Culture and Rest," a recreational center with roller coasters and other amusements. The park, Marjorie remarked, reminded her of Coney Island. From the front seat the guide asked what she meant, but when the ambassadress tried to explain, he interrupted her. "It's not true," the guide insisted. "There's nothing like this outside of Russia or anywhere in the world." Marjorie and E.K. exchanged glances. "Well, we had been taught not to discourage silly remarks like that, just to take them and go ahead with it. So we didn't say anything," the ambassadress recalled.

The same rigidity of thinking pervaded even the highest diplomatic circles. Early in her visit Marjorie had been introduced to Paulina

Molotova, commissar for cosmetics and wife of the Soviet prime minister. The attractive, Paris-trained commissar had immediately interested Marjorie by her ability to run the Soviet cosmetics industry. The ambassadress in turn had similarly fascinated Madame Molotova because of her interest in American business as well as in the more traditionally feminine aspects of life. The two hit it off so well that Madame Molotova even invited Marjorie to tour one of her factories.

On March 14 the commissar paid Marjorie the ultimate Russian compliment: She invited her to a luncheon at her dacha with the wives of the ten Soviet commissars. During the meal Marjorie's interpreter inquired about the "white stone" on her hand. "Why, it's a diamond," Marjorie replied. "It can't be. It's not round," the interpreter retorted. Patiently the ambassadress explained that it was indeed a diamond, but one cut in a "kite" shape. "It's not true. Diamonds grow round," the interpreter protested. Marjorie "let it stay at that." From a diplomatic perspective, even the usually forthright ambassadress knew better than to say anything that would contradict the rigid ideas of her Soviet hosts.

Other aspects of the Soviet police state under Stalin affected Marjorie even more directly. Soon after the United States had acquired Spaso House from the Russian government, a wing had been added to make it suitable for an American embassy. Within it were an oval-shaped dining room, a drawing room, and an enormous reception hall with pink marble pillars. Like most well-built Russian homes, Spaso House had been "furred in," built with an extra layer of wall between the exterior and interior to provide additional insulation against the cold.

The inner wall not only kept out the cold air but enabled the secret police, or NKVD, as they were then called, to have instant access to Marjorie and Joe's conversations. Before the trip William Bullitt had warned them that Spaso House was "bugged"—and hopelessly so, despite his efforts to prevent it. During his tenure Bullitt had hired an electrician to remove all microphones and wires from the inner walls of the house. Regardless of the electrician's care, the devices were back in place the next morning.

From their briefings Marjorie and Joe had learned that one way to ruin microphone receptivity was to tap a spoon on metal or glass as they spoke. Yet so many microphones were hidden in Spaso House that it was impossible to foil them all. "We found them in the fireplaces, we found them in the little vents, in the inner walls," Marjorie recalled. As if that were not intimidating enough, the Davieses also discovered that an unknown man and woman were secretly living with them in the Spaso House attic as spies.

Moreover, the secret police constantly shadowed the ambassador, alleging that their presence was a Soviet "courtesy" for foreign diplomats. Privacy, as Marjorie and Joe had known it, was essentially impossible in the USSR.

Even the Russian Spaso House domestic staff watched Marjorie and Joe. Virtually all of them had been handpicked and trained by the Soviet police to double as workers and as spies. This situation created tensions on all sides. Should a member of the Spaso House staff fail to report what he saw—even the most mundane activities of the American ambassador and ambassadress—he might be arrested by higher Soviet authorities. Knowing this, Marjorie and Joe maintained a guarded attitude toward the Russian staff. "They were all so tense and so nervous and so scared for themselves, for their families . . . it was really quite a terrifying thing."

What rankled Marjorie the most was the brazenness with which the Spaso House staff listened to her phone conversations. It was not uncommon for a phone call to be interrupted by spy intervention. Once, just before the *Sea Cloud* was to arrive in Leningrad with a load of food, the captain called Marjorie to arrange a meeting. Three times the phone call was interrupted because of listeners. Finally, in utter disgust the ambassadress went to the phone room and cornered the Soviet phone operator. "Get through again to Captain Lawson in Leningrad and you stay in this room and listen to my conversation so you can repeat it," she ordered the frightened woman. Significantly Marjorie noticed that she "wasn't cut off that time."

Even more unnerving was the mysterious disappearance of high-ranking Soviet officials. Sometimes a diplomat met with a Soviet official one day and expected him for dinner the next night only to find that he never appeared. When inquiries were made about the missing guest, one of his associates might explain, "Oh? You didn't hear? He was liquidated this morning. Would you please pass the soup?" One of the missing was the Soviet chief of protocol, who had been a favorite of the diplomatic community. Another was Marshal A. I. Yegorov, the Soviet chief of staff. Still another was Stalin's old friend Sergo Ordzhonikidze, whose sudden death was alleged to be from natural causes. "It happened a great deal that people disappeared. In my youth it seemed like a spy novel," E.K. said of those years.

. . .

There was, however, one benefit to living in the Soviet Union on the eve of the Bolshevik revolution's twentieth anniversary that Marjorie and Joe had not anticipated: an opportunity to purchase prerevolutionary art. Shortly after their arrival Joe began acquiring religious and contemporary Russian art with the idea of donating it to his alma mater, the University of Wisconsin. He also purchased contemporary works for his own collection. One of these was an oil painting of Ukrainians on a collective field that he presented to Marjorie for her fiftieth birthday.

By 1937 the Soviet Union was still so hard pressed for cash and eager for European and American currency that state officials decided to dispose of some of the prerevolutionary art that was still kept in state-owned storerooms and palaces.

There was nothing new about this trend. On the eve of the Bolshevik revolution fleeing émigrés had already sold some of their priceless art treasures to wealthy Europeans and Americans in exchange for cash or boat tickets. In the ensuing frenzy to destroy every remnant of life under the tsars, the Bolsheviks burst into palaces and churches to seize the gilded and bejeweled symbols of the old regime. Among them were centuries-old icons, statues, porcelains, china, crystal, gemstones, and tapestries owned by the Romanov family and other aristocrats. These Soviet authorities locked in warehouses or sequestered in boarded-up imperial palaces and estates as the collective property of the state.

Later, American millionaires like Andrew Mellon and Joseph E. Widener and businessman Armand Hammer (who made a separate career as a purveyor of Russian art to the wealthy) purchased priceless art treasures from state-owned Soviet museums like the Hermitage, Tsarskoye Selo, and the Gatchina. In 1933 government authorities had temporarily closed their storerooms, but by 1937 an abundance of Russian objets d'art were again available, primarily through the commission shops, or secondhand stores, where Russians hard up for cash often placed family heirlooms.

By March 22, 1937, Joe had written Eleanor Roosevelt that he and Marjorie had begun to frequent those shops, which sold "all manner of things brought in by the owners, from pictures to bedroom sets and from jewels to china. . . . We have all had a lot of fun doing a little shopping in these places."

The "little shopping" that Joe alluded to was the kernel of what later became Marjorie's Russian art collection, which is still on display at her last Washington home, the current Hillwood Museum.

Until the late 1920s Marjorie had almost exclusively collected eighteenth-century French antiques for her New York homes, among them Aubusson rugs, Beauvais tapestries, Sèvres porcelain, and Louis XVI furniture. In 1927 the heiress made her first foray into Russian antiques with the acquisition of a rare Fabergé snuffbox in amethyst quartz from the collection of Prince Feliks Yusupov, murderer of Rasputin. On tours of the storerooms of the Kremlin, Moscow's Tretyakov Gallery, and Leningrad's Hermitage and Winter Palace, Marjorie and Joe became impressed with the quality and scope of Russian art still available for purchase. Free to explore it on her own, Marjorie began to dabble in its vast varieties.

One of the most memorable places to find the spirit of "old St. Petersburg" was the commission shop of the master craftsman and jeweler Karl Fabergé. There, objects from Fabergé's workshop were thrown together haphazardly, "masses of icons stacked together . . . paintings . . . books and everything one could think of. Wonderful gold tea or coffee services, silver . . . trays, thousands of things . . . in the most dreadful disorder."

Marjorie's curiosity quickly outstripped her sense of dignity. Before long the fifty-year-old ambassadress was crawling on her hands and knees through the dusty, poorly lit storerooms to examine Fabergé's work at close range. She had, as she admitted, "a field day."

Among her acquisitions from the commission shops were silver chalices, ecclesiastical vestments, icons, imperial wineglasses, a pair of turquoise vases, a white imperial porcelain factory Bariatinsky vase, china from Catherine the Great's service for the Order of St. Andrew, and an ebonized lapis lazuli chest. Later she acquired other priceless examples of Russian art through European and American antiques dealers to round out the treasures that still later were considered "the finest such collection outside the Soviet Union."

What surprised Marjorie most of all was that the Soviet authorities paid little attention to the fine craftsmanship of the objects. Without batting an eye, the art dealers coolly placed antiques on a scale and sold them by the value of their raw weight or materials—despite the fact that the pieces were often centuries old, delicately enameled, or intricately carved. By 1937 Soviet standards, mementos of Russian history before the 1917 revolution were irrelevant. Even the suggestion that china, jewelry, or furniture created for the imperial palaces of the tsars was worth more than its weight in gold might be construed as anti-Soviet propaganda.

Decades later Marjorie still enjoyed describing the Soviets' blasé attitude to prerevolutionary Russian art as she showed guests cases of the Fabergé and imperial art at her Washington home. The Russian collection, as Marjorie's last beau, Fred Korth, observed, pleased her not only because of its beauty but for its romantically tragic story. Out of the Soviets' wholesale disregard for Russian history, the heiress had reaped "a real bargain and some wonderful work[s] of art."

19

"An Invaluable Asset
to This Mission"

By the end of March 1937 Marjorie and Joe had charmed the Soviets, separately and together. Marjorie's beauty and style were unparalleled, while her warmth and diplomacy won many friends.

The luncheon Paulina Molotova gave at her dacha for Marjorie had augured so well for Soviet-American relations that Joe told the White House about it. "Marjorie," he wrote Eleanor Roosevelt, "has made a great hit with the wives of the Commissars here." Later Madame Molotova showered gifts upon Marjorie, among them a pair of Russian imperial vases, sable pelts, and a full-length silver fox cape.

Other diplomats living in Moscow were similarly impressed. On March 10 they were awed by the splendor of a dinner given at Spaso House in honor of the Italian ambassador, Agosto Rosso, and his bride, Frances Bunker Rosso. So enchanted was the British ambassador, Lord Chilston, that he took Marjorie aside and said, "Madame, for the first time when I enter the dining room in the American embassy I see tables that are really worthy of your country. While Mr. Bullitt was here I was never impressed with American elegance that I knew existed."

A few days later, when Chilston heard about the Molotova luncheon, he was overwhelmed by the ambassadress's success. "You Americans are remarkable!" he told Marjorie. "I have been here seven years and haven't been able to get so much as a toe in their house—and you come and after only a few weeks you have a luncheon given there in your honor." In return, Marjorie hosted a luncheon for Madame Molotova on March 19 at Spaso House.

On the official diplomatic front Joe made even greater strides. Within days of his arrival he had held conferences with President Kalinin, Prime Minister Molotov, and Foreign Trade Minister Arkady Rosengoltz. In a show of good faith, those officials soon paid Marjorie and Joe the ultimate Russian compliment by inviting them to dine at their dachas. Kremlin officials opened storerooms at the Hermitage and Winter Palace for the ambassador to view art that he could purchase. Party members also provided Joe with a map of the USSR showing its major industrial regions. In late February the Soviets went even further: They granted the ambassador permission to tour the industrial cities and factories of the Ukraine. To facilitate the journey, they offered Davies a private railroad car to make the two-thousand-mile journey with E.K., staff aides, and a cadre of American reporters.

To show their appreciation, Marjorie and Joe reciprocated with a party at Spaso House for the Council of Commissars. The reception was unique in the history of Soviet-American relations to date, not only for its lavish food and the showing of the Hollywood musical *Naughty Marietta* but for the implication that a diplomatic thaw between the two countries was imminent.

Several days later the Davieses hosted another unprecedented affair, this time a reception for leaders of the Soviet army, with a traditional American cocktail hour and other "capitalistic trimmings." So enthusiastically was it greeted that it seemed still another indication of improved Soviet-American relations.

Despite those festivities, the exotic collections of Russian art, and the new diplomatic friendships, Marjorie and Joe yearned to return to the United States. It was true that Marjorie had penned cheery notes to the first lady about her daily "snappy walk around the Kremlin" and assured her that "it has been such fun to get back to the cold winters of our childhood." Still, Soviet Russia was literally and figuratively a chilling locale, relentless in its police-state mentality, terrifying in its inscrutable "liquidation" of political enemies, and muted in its social life. The truth was that Marjorie and Joe craved the glamour and freedom of a European appointment—particularly the one FDR had promised in Berlin.

In that hopeful mood Marjorie and Joe returned to the United States on April 7, 1937, laden with Russian gifts. For the president there was a fur-lined greatcoat. For Mrs. Roosevelt there was one of moleskin, curiously reminiscent of the one Marjorie as a child had sewn for her dolls. For friends and family there were Russian soaps, perfumes, furs, native fabrics, and Russian art. And in a gesture that was announced to the press, the ambassador donated a collection of Russian paintings to the University of Wisconsin.

To outside observers, Marjorie and Joe seemed to have arrived in Washington aglow with the sense of a mission well done. In compliance with FDR's order, Joe had softened relations with Soviet leaders. As ambassador he had been utterly politic, while simultaneously toeing a hard line on American expectations.

In a February 25 summary of a meeting with Prime Minister Molotov, Joe had written FDR that "I . . . emphasized again . . . that the President of the United States . . . had contributed immeasurably to . . . recognition of the Soviet Union; that the two countries had one great purpose in common . . . to preserve the peace of the world; that personally I felt . . . it would be a very great pity . . . if a situation should develop that would cast a cloud upon the confidence which the President . . . had in the good faith and integrity of the men . . . responsible for the . . . Government here. . . ."

That Davies had conscientiously studied the USSR's industrial strength was also apparent, for that February he toured the Don Basin and other major factory districts, including Leningrad and Kharkov, and the Cooper Dam. On March 5 he wrote FDR that the "plants and the equipment which I saw are first-class, the result of the synthesis of the best engineering judgement of the capitalist countries. . . ." Even more surprising was his discovery that the "communistic principle here has been completely abandoned. The profit motive and self interest is [sic] the main spring . . . production is stimulated by premiums and extra wage for service above the 'norm.' " As a result, Davies predicted, "my judgement confirms the general impression here in the Diplomatic Corps . . . that [with] . . . five or ten years of peace, extraordinary results will be developed by this industrial program."

While Joe traveled, Mesdames Molotova and Krestinskaya, the latter the physician wife of the Soviet undersecretary of state, had given Marjorie a tour of Soviet day-care centers and factory restaurants. When the unusual nature of the Davieses' activities reached the American press in March 1937, *Time* hailed Marjorie and Joe as having "definitely hit their stride in Moscow."

Shortly after Joe returned to Moscow, he emphasized the "capitalistic" similarities between the USA and USSR. To a group of journalists, he explained that his "most striking impression . . . was the universal use of the profit motive throughout Soviet industry as an incentive to workmen." The USSR was, he added, "a wonderful and stimulating experiment" which was led by an "extremely capable, serious, hardworking, and powerful group of men and women." Moreover, as an international power the Soviets would be "a resolute supporter of peace."

FDR was delighted with the news. The president gleefully told UP Washington bureau chief Raymond Clapper that Davies, unlike his predecessor, William Bullitt, "got around . . . and seemed to find out what the Russians were doing." Not only had the new ambassador been invited to the dachas of party leaders and enjoyed their luxurious lifestyle up close, but he himself had "lived in capitalist style and they [the leaders] ate it up."

Hopeful that Davies's impression of the Soviet Union would soften America's negative view, FDR decided to reward the ambassador. In the fall of 1937 he and Marjorie would be assigned to Germany.

But all was not well within the Department of State. With the exception of the chargé d'affaires, Loy Henderson, State Department aides in Moscow resented Davies. To them he seemed an arrogant political appointee whose knowledge about Soviet Russia was negligible. "He thought very well of himself. Moreover, he didn't seem to trust his staff," said Fanny Chipman, who, with her husband, Norris, a Foreign Service officer, was stationed in Moscow at the time.

Among others who held Davies in contempt were Charles "Chip" Bohlen and George Kennan, both already seasoned Russian-speaking experts. Exacerbating that contempt was Kennan's observation in his memoirs that "Mr. Davies's constituents in Moscow—those who received his confidence, before whom he aired his views, and whose opinions he consulted—were not members of his official staff, they were the American journalists stationed there."

Equally offensive to aides was Davies's insistence that the Americans had common ground with the Russians because of the "capitalist" methods they employed to increase productivity on farms and factories. Nor did they trust Davies's conclusion that the Soviets would be faithful allies in the event of a "long war" because of their underlying sympathy with capitalistic principles, their vast natural reserves, and industrial strength.

By the time Davies returned home in April 1937 a "cold war" had

already ensued between State Department aides and Roosevelt's appointee. Added to these tensions was Secretary of State Hull's preference for taking advice from his Moscow-based professional State
Department staff instead of the newcomer Davies.

The ambassador paid little heed to these critics. Davies's primary ob-
jective, according to his biographer Elizabeth Kimball MacLean, was to
have the ear of the president, who, like Davies, put little stock in the advice of State Department "careerists." Ultimately the ambassador
would do more than brush his underlings aside. While on leave in the
United States, he suggested to Robert Kelley, then director of the Division of Eastern Affairs, that in spite of Kennan's "splendid" performance in Moscow, the aide was ill and had probably stayed in the USSR
"too long for his own good." Shortly thereafter Kennan was sent home
to run the Russian desk of the European Division of the State Department. Kelley's division was folded into the new Department of European Affairs, and Kelley himself transferred to a diplomatic post in
Turkey.

With State Department aides thus in check and only a few months
before Davies's anticipated assignment to Berlin, FDR appointed his
friend to become an "ambassador-at-large." Though Davies was still
based in Moscow as ambassador, his new job was to visit a dozen Eastern European countries and examine their views on the tense international situation. Before doing so, Davies was given permission to attend
the coronation of George VI in England with subsequent stopovers in
Paris and Berlin.

To Marjorie this was a bittersweet reward. As an Anglophile she had
longed to attend the coronation. After three months in Moscow—
despite attendance at the Great Opera Theater and the Bolshoi Ballet—
she was eager to spend time in the more fashionable cities of Paris and
Berlin. Though the prospect of returning to the USSR was daunting, it
would be softened by a summer cruise on the *Sea Cloud* in a reunion
with her daughter Dina.

All winter Marjorie had been apart from her youngest daughter. At
the time of Joe's appointment she had decided to leave Dina in the
States, out of fear for her well-being. "Mother had this strange idea in
her head that I would get some peculiar disease. She didn't think it [the
USSR] was safe. Also, she didn't entirely trust the Russians, so she
wouldn't let me go," Dina recalled.

During her first few months in the USSR Marjorie had missed her
daughter terribly. "You see, Deenie was then still a very young girl, and

there was that tremendous pull to be with her," said E.K., who became a kind of surrogate daughter to Marjorie during the Soviet residence.

On May 5, 1937; Marjorie and Joe sailed on the SS *Bremen* to England, traveling in an "unofficial" capacity to view the coronation. For the occasion the ambassadress had rented for ten thousand dollars an enormous London mansion owned by the second Mrs. Marshall Field. There she and the ambassador were treated hospitably by the American ambassador, Robert Bingham, and his wife, and were soon mingling with dukes, duchesses, and other members of the British aristocracy.

During that visit, as throughout their stay in Russia, Marjorie and Joe did not hesitate to demonstrate their affection for each other in public. As *Fortune* noted, "They go out of their way to speak of each other in terms that can fairly be called flowery, to greet each other in terms that can only be called demonstrative." From England an impassioned Joe had written his daughter Eleanor that Marjorie "looked very beautiful and stunning." At the court ball she was more dazzling than other bejeweled guests "not only because of her distinct beauty but . . . [also because of] her carriage and general modesty."

By that time Marjorie and Joe were as sensitive to negative press reports about their lifestyle as they were to comments on their public declarations of love. Their stay in England was appropriately tempered. Whenever possible, Marjorie and Joe avoided splashy parties and balls, spending their time instead entertaining guests aboard the *Sea Cloud*, which was moored in Southampton. "Marjorie and I have not done anything social here to speak of," Joe wrote FDR on June 10 from London. "We have had a pleasant time and rest and I have done a job, I think, in picking up information for the Department. . . ."

In reality the chance to mingle with British leaders was a prelude to the role that Joe and Marjorie later played as apologists for Russia to the rest of the world. During their London sojourn, Joe met with several statesmen, among them David Lloyd George, Ivan Maisky, the Soviet ambassador to the U.K., and Commissar Litvinov. The most memorable meeting was a formal luncheon at Winston and Clementine Churchill's small London apartment. When Churchill plied Joe with questions about the purge trials, Davies "told him the truth as I saw it." The ambassador's response came as a "great surprise to the [other] diplomatic guests," who were stubbornly biased against the USSR. Although it was immediately obvious that Churchill had "no love for the Communists," he queried Joe about his analysis of Soviet industrial strength and its potential impact upon the coming military struggle. On May 26 Joe wrote about Churchill in his diary, "Too bad this man isn't more effective in the government here. Peace would be safer! He impressed me as a great man."

The next day Marjorie and Joe were stunned to hear that the Soviet military leader Marshal Mikhail Tukhatchevsky and seven Soviet generals had been condemned to death for betraying military secrets to "a certain hostile Fascist power." Four days later there was more unnerving news from Moscow. Arkady Rosengoltz, the Soviet commissar for foreign trade, had been dismissed from his station and taken into custody by the police. An incredulous Davies wrote in his journal, "Poor Rosengoltz! I hope he is not involved. It was only a few weeks ago that we were invited to his *dacha* . . . to spend the day."

In contemplation of the tense world situation and the growing Nazi threat, a worried Davies wrote FDR that not only Great Britain and Germany but "all parties are playing poker. The tragedy is that the enormous waste of mounting armament costs is leading to economic cataclysm and disaster." After stopping in Paris and Berlin, where Joe delivered FDR's plea for disarmament to Finance Minister Hjalmar Schacht, he and Marjorie returned to Moscow on June 24.

The ambassador's absence had done nothing to heal the rift that had opened between him and State Department aides. At issue was Davies's unshakable faith in the Stalin government, even in the face of the most recent purges.

By summer Stalin's campaign to destroy his enemies had accelerated. On July 13 he ordered the death of another sixty-one Soviets who had allegedly spied for the Japanese. Despite these horrors and reports from *New York Times* Russian correspondent Harold Denny about Stalin's duplicity, Davies continued to support the Kremlin. Anything party leaders did—even their having placed a microphone directly over the desk where the ambassador dictated letters to Washington—was excused in the name of maintaining good Soviet-American relations. If the Soviets chose to spy upon him, Davies told his astonished aides, they would learn that the United States wanted nothing more than their friendship.

Just a day before the ambassador's arrival in Moscow, Loy Henderson wrote Cordell Hull that "not one diplomatic mission [or] single foreign observer . . . believed that the executed Red Army officers were guilty of the crimes attributed to them." Yet within four days of Davies's return the ambassador wrote Sumner Welles that while "conditions here, as usual, are perplexing . . . the best judgement seems to believe . . . there was a definite conspiracy . . . to a coup d'état—not necessarily anti-Stalin, but antipolitical and antiparty and that Stalin struck with characteristic speed, boldness, and strength."

Whatever doubts Marjorie herself had about the conspiracy were quickly put to rest by Joe's analysis. He, after all, was the ambassador and privy to information Marjorie heard only secondhand. The ambassadress trusted Joe's judgment completely. Any independent thinking Marjorie would do about her Russian years did not occur until much later. For as a *Fortune* article from that era observed, the Davieses were in that early stage in marriage "when two people with dominant personalities still don't really know each other and try their very hardest not to step on each other's toes."

In the meantime, Marjorie's job was to conduct herself as neutrally and diplomatically as possible to win friends for the United States. For the ambassadress, who had been groomed in the art of conversation in Mrs. Stotesbury's drawing room at El Mirasol, the role was a familiar one. On June 30 the Davieses attended a soirée at the Bulgarian Legation in honor of the birth of an heir to the throne. One of the guests was Madame Litvinova, who, as Joe proudly recalled in a letter to his daughter Eleanor, "immediately singled out Marjorie and the two went into a huddle and had a long visit."

A week later the ambassadress left for Leningrad, where she was finally reunited with Dina. On July 17 Joe joined them from Moscow to begin a journey on the *Sea Cloud* to countries adjacent to the USSR.

Accompanying them were several guests—among them Ambassador Agosto Rosso and his wife, Frances, who soon became one of Marjorie's closest friends. Yet even outside USSR borders, the Russian bear was omnipresent—this time in the form of a Soviet naval destroyer that followed the *Sea Cloud* through foreign waters as "protection."

One night when the yacht was moored off an island in the Gulf of Finland, Marjorie and Joe invited the crew of the destroyer aboard for a movie. While Soviet rules prohibited the Russians from having anything to do with the capitalists, the sailors were pleased. And, to Marjorie and Joe's delight, so were their officers. "Well, there was the biggest running back and forth that you've ever seen on that little boat and it was at least an hour and a half before they could arrive at a decision as to whether they should go . . . [or] shouldn't go, if they'd be punished," Marjorie recalled. "Finally, they all trooped over and saw the movie and thoroughly enjoyed it." To the ambassadress it was a small but important victory—a subtle way of proving that American capitalism had its own unique rewards.

Later in the summer Marjorie and Joe traveled to Memel, Stockholm, Danzig, Prague, Riga, and finally Paris. From talks with leaders in the Eastern European countries, Joe concluded that they believed that "Russia is . . . at least for the present . . . a sincere advocate of peace." Yet Britain and France still regarded the USSR so suspiciously that they were unwilling to consider it a potential ally. Instead their primary concern seemed to be securing protection from fascism at Czechoslovakia's expense, which was then serving as a "buffer zone" between Germany and the USSR.

Most disheartening of all, Davies wrote Secretary of State Hull, virtually every country he visited seemed to "discount Russia's development and economic progress or the present strength of her government." There was no trust between the democracies and the Soviets. As Joe later told Marjorie, "Europeans and Americans did not seem to appreciate that the Soviets were as fearful of an invasion of Russia as were the Europeans of a Russian invasion."

The side trip to Paris was a temporary distraction from these worries. It also gave Marjorie and Joe a chance to have lunch with FDR's mother, the eighty-three-year-old Sara Delano Roosevelt, who, in the company of several senators and members of the American press, was also visiting Paris. For Joe this was another opportunity to ingratiate himself with the president. From Paris on August 30 he cabled FDR that "your noble and beautiful mother is lunching with Marjorie and me . . . we want to tell you that she is looking extraordinary [*sic*] fit and well. We are enjoying our visit with her so much and are having a grand time talking about our great president and her great son."

While the elderly Mrs. Roosevelt may have been the picture of health in the early fall of 1937, Marjorie was not. In late August she had fallen ill. Exactly what ailed her is not clear. To Europeans the affliction was known as "Moscow malaria," a flulike infection that waxed and waned over a period of months.

On September 5, Davies wired the State Department requesting two weeks' leave without pay because of Marjorie's "indisposition." To speed her recovery, the Davieses went to Vichy for the "cure." Even there they continued their search for Russian art. In an antiques shop near the spa the ambassadress was shown a tea service that once be-

longed to Prince Orlov, lover to Catherine the Great. Joe, according to
his daughter Eleanor, gave Marjorie this service as a gift.

Despite the excitement of traveling the Baltic, meeting heads of state,
and gathering art, Marjorie's trip aboard the *Sea Cloud* had a unique set
of tensions. Chief among these was Joe's inability to befriend Dina.
From the start the girl had taken a dislike to her stepfather, who, in her
eyes, could not compare with E. F. Hutton.

In one sense such resistance was predictable, for Joe had come into
Dina's life at a time when E.F. was shut out. Moreover, the pubescent
girl had just spent June with her father—the one month a year she was
allowed by court order—and his memory was fresh in her mind. From
her perspective, "Daddy Joe," as Davies liked to be called, lacked the
sense of fun and irreverence Dina found so appealing in her real father.

What added to Dina's pain was that summers aboard the *Sea Cloud*
seemed different. To start with, the ship was now registered in Joe's
name, probably, as Dina later came to understand, through a dollar-a-
year lease arrangement with Marjorie so that, as the future movie star
put it, "he could say it was *my* ship." Instead of cruising for fun to exotic islands like the Galápagos and Tahiti, the *Sea Cloud* now toured various Eastern European countries, where Marjorie and Joe were greeted
by state officials in what Dina remembered as a dull series of ceremonies. Equally annoying were "Daddy Joe's" constant recitation of love
poetry to Marjorie—and her mother's enthralled response. "I guess he
was a romantic soul in his way. He certainly didn't seem to be a romantic figure to me, but then I was prejudiced," Dina admitted many years
later.

While Dina was outwardly polite, her distaste was obvious to Marjorie, who had been far more successful charming Joe's grown daughters
than he had been in winning over hers. Try as he might, there seemed
no way for Joe to change Dina's reaction. The warmer his behavior, the
farther Dina seemed to retreat. Still, Marjorie remained hopeful that
time would mitigate her daughter's resentment. The end of summer
was fast approaching, but the ambassadress planned to prolong Dina's
time with her and "Daddy Joe" on a tour through the Black Sea. To do
so, Marjorie received permission from the headmistress at the Mount
Vernon Seminary, where Dina was then a student.

The *Sea Cloud* sailed east through the Mediterranean toward Nice.
Suddenly while they were out at sea, the ship's radio went dead. Unwittingly the 316-foot yacht had ventured into an area patrolled by Italian
submarines, and their radar was jamming the radio waves. Contact

with land was finally reestablished after forty-eight hours of silence. Shortly afterward the U.S. Navy advised Davies to cancel the Black Sea journey; there was too much submarine activity for the voyage to be feasible.

From the port of Monte Carlo the Davieses and Dina traveled to Vienna. Marjorie's health had not improved. In fact, it had so steadily declined that the ambassadress decided to sail to the States with Dina immediately, rather than return with Joe in November.

In the ensuing weeks of their separation Joe fretted continually about Marjorie's condition. A stream of telegrams and love letters followed the ambassadress across the Atlantic, many signed with the acronym WAMHILY: "with all my heart I love you." From Moscow on November 1 Joe wrote Steve Early about his concern: "Of course it's hell to be alone and have her away, but the vital thing is for her to regain resistance before making a winter crossing of the Atlantic and then the long cross-country trip here. . . . I miss Marjorie tremendously and am eagerly awaiting her return. I'm only half a man without her. . . ."

In response Early had rushed to Marjorie's side to ensure that she had good medical care. On November 12 the ambassador wrote his friend again: "You have been a great comfort to Marjorie. Her cables and letters tell me how fine you have been. She is so gallant about herself that for days, I didn't know she was as ill as she was on the ship and in New York. However, I am reassured now."

Marjorie, recalled her daughter Adelaide, had returned to the States so ill that even her hearing was impaired. Although it was years before Marjorie suffered permanent hearing loss, the side effects of "Moscow malaria" were a harbinger of the handicap that became the curse of her later years.

On November 6, 1937, *The Washington Post* announced that Marjorie had returned from Russia with a severe infection that had "seriously depleted" her strength. According to that newspaper, the ambassadress had arrived for the centennial of the Mount Vernon Seminary, where she was to receive a bronze medal for "distinguished service to her alma mater." In the end Marjorie did not appear; she was too ill to engage in "active participation in the ceremonies."

At the same time Marjorie was being honored by the Mount Vernon Seminary, the Washington press corps was giving her husband black marks. After taking leave of Marjorie, Joe had meandered back to Soviet Russia, stopping first in Hungary, Austria, and Germany to meet with state officials. What he learned underscored his previous reports to the White House: that the Europeans would probably cede Czechoslovakia to the Germans rather than confront fascism head-on.

In August 1937 Joe wrote FDR's secretary Marvin McIntyre about the importance of his travels: "I have had an interesting, but hard summer. . . . By the time I have returned, I shall have visited twelve countries. . . . It has given me insight on the forces at work in Europe today. . . . I do not hesitate to say that no one in Europe will have a wider and more up to date line on the forces at work here than I. . . ."

But some members of the stateside press corps were not convinced. In a scathing newspaper column Drew Pearson and Westbrook Pegler criticized "our freshman ambassador" Davies for abusing his diplomatic privilege by cavorting around Europe with his multimillionaire wife on the *Sea Cloud.*

The timing was diabolical. FDR, ever sensitive to public opinion, instructed McIntyre to have Davies postpone his return to the States for several months. In a September 22 letter McIntyre broke the news as tactfully as possible:

> I know how anxious you are to get back to the States. . . . Nevertheless, Joe . . . [y]ou know there have been . . . some very unwarranted and unjustified criticisms of the amount of time you have spent away from Russia—your brief visit home last Spring, your stay in London afterwards and your recent trips to other capitols. We, and I say "we" advisedly, realize just what you have been doing but you are a shining mark for the President's opponents. . . . [F]or the next three months you should stay in Moscow or at least not leave Russia. . . . I am writing you as one of your friends and to one of the best friends I have ever had. . . .

A few days later, Joe received a cable from Cordell Hull demanding that he remain at his post. The order, combined with his anxiety about Marjorie, was almost more than Joe could bear. Although he dutifully cabled Hull that he would "fully and gladly comply with suggestions," the ambassador was seething. Privately he wrote McIntyre that "it gripes me a bit to have some gutter-snipe distort the facts." Simultaneously he promised that out of respect for "the greatest man I have known in my life," he would take no revenge until the president gave him the "green light."

Although Davies subsequently complained to Westbrook Pegler, he failed to appreciate the depth of animosity he had engendered among State Department careerists. In despair he called Marjorie and asked her to send him five trunks of winter clothes.

By November 10 the political climate had eased enough for FDR to rescind his orders. The ambassador could come home for the holidays. From Washington, Marvin McIntyre wired Davies. "We see no reason why you shouldn't get home before Christmas personally suggest about December fifteenth. This much better than having Marjorie returning now."

Within a few days the good news was shattered by another telegram, this one from Secretary of State Hull. The current ambassador to Belgium, Hugh Gibson, was to be assigned to Berlin. Davies was to be posted to Brussels.

Joe was devastated. He and Marjorie had virtually been promised the Berlin post twice and now were being passed over for a State Department favorite. Behind the scenes the current German ambassador, William E. Dodd, had vehemently opposed Davies's appointment on the grounds of Davies's political naïveté and lack of fluency in German. But all Davies could see was the loss of a coveted diplomatic post.

When Joe heard about Gibson's appointment, he telegrammed Hull that he was returning home immediately. In the interim Gibson declined the appointment, and the State Department lobbied for one of its own, the assistant secretary of state Hugh Wilson. Ultimately Joe's friend Steve Early convinced FDR to wait at least until Davies's return to the States before making the appointment official. Joe's December 8 lunch meeting with FDR changed nothing. It was, the president explained, essential to send a professional diplomat to a country as troubled as Germany. To appoint someone known to be a friend to the president would send the Nazis the wrong message.

When the news broke, Drew Pearson and Robert Allen rushed in for the kill. In a "Washington Merry-Go-Round" column, they claimed that Davies had been assigned to Belgium because his marriage was in jeopardy. The proof of it was that Marjorie, "a very captivating, if somewhat dominating woman," had arrived in Washington without Joe and been escorted around by "a handsome Swedish manager of a shipping line. . . . [S]ince Mrs. Davies will not go back to Moscow, and since the State Department insists that he work at his job, Joe has asked for a transfer to another post—which, he hopes, will please the lady."

For Marjorie it was a terrible blow. In spite of her efforts to serve diligently as an ambassadress and in spite of the illness that brought her home, the twin "blessings" of her life—enormous wealth and the capacity to enjoy it—had engendered jealousy. It was not the first time reporters had carved her up, nor would it be the last, but the incident exacerbated the ambassadress's distrust of the press once again.

Joe was beyond rage. According to his biographer, Elizabeth Kimball MacLean, he was so upset by the vicious report that he vowed to throttle Pearson and Allen himself until Steve Early calmed him down. To help the ambassador save face, Early prevailed upon Washington's UP chief, Raymond Clapper. In a December 27, 1937, column appearing in the *Washington Daily News*, Clapper pointedly observed that while "some career diplomats have been sniping at . . . Davies, the White House is in his corner." The president, Clapper assured his readers, "does not share in the criticism that has been made of Davies in some quarters."

In February 1938 Marjorie and Joe returned to Moscow, even more determined than before to fulfill their Russian assignment before leaving for Brussels. Although both of them were ailing, Marjorie with "Moscow malaria" and Joe with gastrointestinal complaints, the Davieses left the States promptly to avoid more adverse press criticism.

Once again FDR had assigned Davies a difficult task, this time to work out a pact with the Soviets to share military information about Japanese penetration into East Asia. On the surface the plan seemed reasonable, for the Soviets were worried about a Japanese invasion. Nevertheless, Foreign Commissar Maxim Litvinov now rejected Davies's overture. Military information, he claimed, would be dangerous to share unless there was "a definite pact or agreement." Such an arrangement was out of the question inasmuch as American opinion against the Soviets still ran so strongly that FDR could not consider an official treaty.

By March 1938 the third of the Stalin "show" trials, the so-called Bukharin treason trials, had begun. To Marjorie and Joe's horror the trial again involved Soviet officials they knew personally. Among them was the lead defendant, Nikolai Bukharin, as well as the commissar for foreign trade, Arkady Rosengoltz, the undersecretary of state, Nikolai Krestinsky, and Dr. Dmitri Pletnev, a heart specialist who had treated Joe the year before. These men, it was alleged, had conspired to destroy the Soviet state. "It was difficult to look upon the prisoners in the box without shrinking," Joe wrote in his diary on March 2, 1938.

". . . There these men sat not more than ten feet from me in the prisoner's box. I hope they saw in my eyes the sorrow which I felt in seeing them again."

Nevertheless, as Joe wrote Secretary of State Hull on March 17, he was forced to agree with the tribunal's conclusion that the accused were guilty of treason. "Notwithstanding . . . a prejudice against a judicial system which affords practically no protection for the accused . . . it is my opinion so far as the political defendants are concerned, sufficient crimes under Soviet law . . . were established by the proof and beyond a reasonable doubt to justify the verdict of guilty of treason. . . . "

Marjorie echoed her husband's conviction. She wrote Eleanor Roosevelt (also on March 17) that "There would seem to be no question but what there was a tremendous plot. . . . Certainly the heads of the Government have been very clever in uncovering it just when they did."

Yet the trial was profoundly disturbing to her and the ambassador. "Joe has come back from the trials every day looking worn to the bone. . . . You see we had known several of these men. . . . To see a man standing there in the prisoner's dock with whom you had lunched and dined many times . . . gave a personal touch to it all that made it so much more realistic. . . . The trials recall . . . that Lenin advised his Bolshevik confreres that they must be more clever than the French revolutionaries . . . they must not follow in their footsteps and destroy each other, but here it is, the revolution eating its own children again."

Even worse than these signs of sabotage within the USSR was Davies's fear of fratricide outside it in Western Europe—especially in Britain's and France's indecisive hands. The Nazi invasion of Austria on March 12, 1938, brought the issue to a crisis. Four days after that conquest an anxious FDR asked Davies to extend his mission in Moscow for several more months.

The ambassador complied, although, as he wrote Steve Early, the delay was a "tough break" that meant he and Marjorie would not move to Brussels until after the muddy Russian spring. By March the Soviet situation had become more than a professional duty for the ambassador. It had become a personal cause célèbre, one he and Marjorie were to espouse throughout World War II.

On March 23, eleven days after the Nazis' conquest of Austria, Maxim Litvinov warned Davies that Europe was in danger of establishing a "fascist peace" created by Britain's and France's indifference to Czechoslovakia as a security buffer for the USSR. Should Germany persist in its imperialistic goals, the Soviets, Litvinov implied, would have little choice but to retreat into isolationism.

In a series of dispatches to Secretary of State Hull and Undersecretary Sumner Welles, Davies now pleaded for a reassessment of Soviet strength on the basis of its potential to save Europe from Nazi fascism. To Welles on March 26 he wrote, "From the viewpoint of the struggle for the survival of democracy . . . and in view of the fact that England and France are being imminently threatened by . . . domination of Fascism in Europe, it is rather difficult to understand why the strength that is here available should not be fostered and used. . . ."

In 1938 Davies's warnings had little impact on State Department policy, even though his observation that the USSR was too large a power to be ignored was a cold fact. It took the Nazi occupation of France and the air war over Great Britain for Davies's predictions to be recognized as the key to world peace.

Marjorie and Joe's remaining months in Moscow were consumed in cementing relations with the Soviets and scouring state warehouses for art. On Marjorie's fifty-first birthday she acquired other treasures to add to her collection. Among them were an imperial tea set made by the Gardner factory and, from Joe, a pink enamel and gold Fabergé clock. By May the Davieses had boarded the *Sea Cloud* again, this time for a tour of the Black Sea, the Ukraine, and the Caucasus—and another search for Russian art.

Writing to Dina, "Daddy Joe" (who was determined to win over his stepdaughter) reported on that farewell trip. His June 10 letter was filled with praise for Marjorie and for her "great and distinctive success" as "the first American Ambassadress to Russia since World War I." As he wrote:

> You and I, of course, understand how that would be . . . and I wish I could have had your arm tucked into mine so that you might have seen it all and shared with me the great pride and joy I found in "Mumsie" during these lovely tributes to her.
>
> During our sojourn in the Caucasus, Ukraine and Black Sea area—on the occasion of practically all of our "inspections"—"Mumsie" would . . . completely win over the officials by her simplicity, modesty and kindly human interest. So, it always happened . . . that either the director or the children or the nurses . . . or the officials in charge would come up and present her with an armful of flowers. It was like a triumphal procession.

What Davies failed to mention was that he had been honored in an even more significant way. On June 5, while Davies was paying a farewell call on Prime Minister Molotov at the Kremlin, Stalin had appeared and invited the ambassador to a private interview. The Soviet leader seemed shorter and slighter than Davies had envisioned. As he later reported in a memorandum, Stalin did "not look robust, nor strong as he appeared to be on the occasion of the May Day Celebration. There was a suggestion of the sagginess of an old man in his physical carriage. His demeanor is kindly, his manner almost deprecatingly simple; his personality an expression of reserve strength and poise very marked."

After an initial exchange of pleasantries, Stalin got down to business. First, he expressed the hope that a battleship that the United States had promised to the Russians but that had been delayed by U.S. Army and Navy opposition could be realized through Joe's friendship with FDR. There was also the matter of the old Soviet debt, which Stalin now insisted could be cleared in exchange for $200 million in credit from American bankers. A third issue was FDR's proposal for a Soviet-American military liaison. This, Stalin assured Davies, could be accomplished through the ambassador's selection of Colonel Philip Faymonville, an embassy military attaché, to be the American liaison officer. He demanded that communications about these issues be kept secret and discussions limited to FDR and the U.S. secretary of state.

Davies returned to Spaso House in a daze. Not only had he seen Stalin, but he had talked international policy with him. Eventually it would become clear that Stalin had conceded nothing but had merely demonstrated his desire to bypass traditional political channels by asking Davies to appeal directly to FDR.

Initially, though, the meeting with Stalin, Davies observed, created "nothing short of a sensation in the Diplomatic Corps here. It was regarded as a unique occurrence in diplomatic history. . . ." Thereafter the ambassador was flooded with requests for interviews. In America newspapers carried accounts of Davies's meeting with Stalin to discuss "world affairs."

Two days later Maxim Litvinov hosted a "large dinner" in honor of Marjorie and Joe that epitomized the opulence of Old Russia. The table was set with the finest china, silver, and crystal of the tsarist regime and was matched by an equally lavish menu. Afterward, over dessert and champagne, Litvinov characterized the farewell dinner as a sad occasion "for the simple reason, that using plain, undiplomatic language, we all like both Mr. and Mrs. Davies, we continually felt their friendship and good will toward our country and its peoples. . . . You, Mr. Ambassador, have done your best to understand our country. . . . If you will . . . pass on the results of your study and observation an unbiased judgement to your government and to your countrymen, you will certainly contribute much more to the strengthening of friendly relations between our two countries than by any other purely diplomatic activities."

Afterward the Soviets invited the entire diplomatic corps to attend a ball at Spiridonovka 17, the official Foreign Office house for entertaining. There, in a white marble ballroom, the party lasted until 3:30 A.M., when the Davieses came home "with the dawn breaking over the Kremlin."

Marjorie, as Davies enthusiastically wrote his daughter Eleanor, was "the belle of the ball. The Foreign Minister opened the party with her and he dances very well. So what with the ambassadors, ministers and young secretaries, the old man 'hisself' [Litvinov] was sorely put to it to get a dance. But the dear girl, my Marjorie, bless her heart, saw to that." She had, he added, been "a great Ambassadress" and an "invaluable asset to this mission."

The next day Marjorie was brought to the Kuskovo Museum of Ceramics, an old Sheremetev family palace, to choose a pair of antique vases as a present from the Soviet government. The gift, Joe noted in his diary, "was presented by Madam Molotov and was a tribute to the first Ambassadress of the United States to the Soviet Union."

20

Mission Fulfilled

*A*s ambassadress, Marjorie was to enjoy the grandeur and pomp of the Belgian kingdom only sporadically. To start with, the ambassadorial mansion was still being renovated when she and Joe arrived in Brussels on July 12, 1938. Nor, as Washington had promised, was the home furnished sufficiently for the lavish entertainments that were expected of an American ambassador. Even such rudimentary objects as a dining room table and dishes were missing.

"When I say no equipment, it's with a big *N* for the table. There was no table linen, no table silver, or glass or china. And the answer from the department was that 'it was ordered,' " Marjorie recalled. Without further delay the ambassadress had sent from the States some of her own furniture, among which were the marble dining room table from Mar-A-Lago and the Boucher tapestries from 2 East Ninety-second Street. Since it would be months before the renovations would be complete, Marjorie and Joe lived on the *Sea Cloud*, moored in nearby Ostend.

The natural amenities of life in Belgium more than compensated for the temporary lack of a home. One of the country's charms was the year-round availability of flowers, a decorative feature that Marjorie had sorely missed in the USSR. Another was the rich foods—heavy creams, cheeses, veal, and fresh vegetables—that flowed from the fertile farmlands and pastures of the lush countryside in an abundance reminiscent of the paintings of van Eyck and van der Weyden.

Belgium was also a country with royalty and an attention to the ceremonial pomp that always thrilled Marjorie. "Thank God! At least it's got a king!" she had exclaimed when Joe first told her about the assignment. To Marjorie's delight, the Belgian court retained rituals that evoked an earlier, more romantic era. On the day that Joe was to present his diplomatic credentials to King Leopold III, custom dictated that he appear in full evening dress. Footmen, outfitted in the scarlet and gold livery of the royal family, escorted the ambassador to the meeting in an ancient tandem coach drawn by a team of thoroughbred horses and surrounded by a parade of outriders.

Nearby Luxembourg, to which Joe also served as ambassador, was similarly steeped in tradition. After his July 26 presentation to the tall, stately grand duchess, Charlotte of Nassau, footmen in royal blue knickers and scarlet coats fluttered around Joe and Marjorie at a luncheon resplendent with gold dishes under the turreted roof of the palatial Château de Berg. The spell of royal splendor was shattered only when the grand duchess observed to Marjorie that "your domain in Texas is larger than all of Luxembourg." Although the ambassadress was taken aback by the comment, she answered as diplomatically as possible. The comment was indicative of the grand duchess's envy of her elegant American guest. Squeezed as Luxembourg was between the borders of France and Germany, there was good reason for Charlotte to feel vulnerable, for her principality was on the edge of what Joe was already referring to as the Nazi "volcano." Daily, Marjorie and Joe took trips into the Luxembourg countryside and peered across the Moselle River into Germany to see Nazi troop movement and other forms of "saber rattling." And from those daily excursions, it was clear that the volcano was about to explode. "It was frightening to see. I was scared. We all were," said Dina, who joined her mother and Joe in Luxembourg and Belgium for part of that summer.

Marjorie, Joe, and Dina also listened to Hitler's speeches on the radio every day. Since Joe spoke German, he was able to translate those speeches on the spot. Invariably the message was upsetting, and the ambassador began to fear not only for Belgium and Luxembourg but for all Europe. To him the Belgium assignment, distanced as it was from the vortex of European politics, was a lookout from which he could keep watchful eyes on the rest of the continent.

While Joe befriended King Leopold III and eventually even became his golfing partner, he admitted to Steve Early in September that the Belgium assignment was "not nearly as stimulating as was Moscow." It was, however, "equally interesting from . . . many angles. As a matter of fact, I think that both here and in Luxembourg, I've been able to pick up some information that had not reached the Department."

One of the Führer's "purposes," warned Davies, was to take Czechoslovakia as a first step toward domination of Europe. Publicly Hitler was demanding a small strip of Czechoslovakian territory known as the Sudetenland in exchange for peace. Privately he had designs on the rest of the country and would go to any extreme to obtain it. If, Davies observed, Hitler can "absorb Czechoslovakia or make it a vassal state," the Führer would have a "jumping off place against the Ukraine." Should he also seize the Romanian oilfields, the Nazi demagogue would have gained control of the Balkans and the Danubian basin.

The irony was that if Britain, France, and Italy engaged in a nonaggression pact with Hitler at Russia's expense for the sake of achieving peace, the treaty would probably be worthless. What value, Davies wrote Early, could such a pact have? After all, the 1936 "agreement" to preserve Austria's independence had been "thrown into the ashcan in May, 1938." There were only two possibilities for peace in Europe: either Great Britain would concede to Hitler's demands to occupy the Sudetenland, or Britain, France, and Russia would finally stand up to the Nazi leader.

By the end of September 1938 the first of Davies's predictions had come true. On September 29 Great Britain's prime minister, Neville Chamberlain, in a "last last" attempt to maintain peace, arrived in Munich for a conference with the leaders of France, Germany, and Italy. After a round of timorous negotiations Chamberlain agreed to let Hitler absorb the Sudetenland into the Third Reich, a deal Churchill warned the British Parliament was "a defeat without a war." In Belgium Davies was equally disenchanted. "Well, it's all over," he unhappily wrote Early on October 7. "The information which I had from London, and which I reported . . . when the British Lion was growling loudest, that it would all end with Hitler having his way and that such was the real Chamberlain policy, has proven . . . well-founded."

On the eve of the Munich crisis, Davies was so worried about Marjorie's and Dina's safety on the *Sea Cloud* that he insisted they return to the United States. "We were so near the border and Hitler's antics were so alarming that [we made] a middle-of-the-night decision and [began] packing frantically," Marjorie recalled. By the time they got to London, the crisis had passed. Chamberlain's name was plastered all over the newspapers with the claim that he had brought "peace in our time" to Europe.

Nevertheless, on October 1 Marjorie sailed for the States on the SS *Duchess of York*. From her perspective, whatever temporary peace Chamberlain brought to Europe was better than no peace at all— particularly with her beloved Joe left behind in Belgium. As Marjorie wrote in one of her scrapbooks that day, "our minds much at peace now that Munich has been settled and the world can breathe again." The specter of war was still a reality, however, particularly when, that first night at sea, the *Duchess of York* sailed through the mined waters of the North Sea.

To avoid press attention, Marjorie arrived in New York quietly, but Manhattan was a difficult place to remain anonymous, especially when the ambassadress had rented a suite at the Plaza Hotel for her short stay instead of opening her apartment on Ninety-second Street. By October 14 the New York *Daily News* had discovered that "Marjorie Post Close Hutton Davies" had arrived from Europe "very secretly last week minus the fanfare which customarily accompanies the movement of any member of the Hutton clan." Her purpose, wrote Nancy Randolph, was "to put Nedenia in school here," after which she was "to rejoin Joe in Brussels."

Before long Marjorie had left again for Belgium, without even staying for the opening night of the Metropolitan Opera. As the disappointed Randolph observed on November 14, "Mrs. Joseph E. Davies is one of the most conspicuous absentees on this year's list. . . . [She] could usually be depended on to be one of the most elaborately dressed women at opening nights."

By winter, renovations at the American ambassadorial residence in Brussels were complete, and the ambassadress began hosting parties of her own.

The Davieses' new home, the nineteenth-century Hôtel d'Assche, had a coincidental Russian connection, for it had been built by a Russian princess married to the marquis d'Assche. Constructed in the style of an Italian town house, the Hôtel d'Assche was graced with a courtyard surrounded by a garden of flowering chestnuts and other tall trees. At the center of the courtyard an elegant steel and brass staircase led to second-floor drawing rooms, a ballroom, and a private family suite, where Leopold III had been born. Among other unusual features of the house were a Russian malachite fireplace mantel and an enormous library with a cathedral window overlooking the courtyard.

The setting was enhanced by Marjorie's furniture from the States and especially the antiques and paintings of prerevolutionary Russia she and Joe had collected in the USSR. The first diplomatic dinner on December 14 was served on a china service of the royal Order of St. George, which Marjorie had gathered "piece by piece" in Soviet Russia. The plates were bordered in the order's colors of brown, black, and gold, and at the center of each was a gold star. To enhance their beauty, the table was set with lace place settings and a yellow satin brocade cloth upon which were bowls of brown and yellow orchids.

Already Marjorie's identity as a hostess was evolving into one with a distinctly "Russian flavor" as she often had stories to tell about the history of her furnishings and recollections of life in Moscow under Communist rule.

The history of Russia not only dominated the decor of the Davieses' ambassadorial home but also preoccupied Marjorie and Joe in the midst of their new diplomatic duties. As the ambassadress wrote Steve Early on January 26, 1939, "We have just come back from the festivities attendant upon the birthday of the Grand Duchess of Luxembourg and we really feel as if we have been living a story book tale for this last few days. That small, happy, successful country does not seem to be a part of the world that is wrangling and snatching and biting at each other. . . ."

By late March that "wrangling and snatching and biting" could no longer be ignored, as Hitler stormed into Prague and took the rest of Czechoslovakia with it. For months, in spite of Davies's efforts to convince Secretary of State Hull that the USSR could be a potential ally against fascism, the United States—and its allies, Britain and France—had ignored his advice.

Only now, with Czechoslovakia's absorption into the Third Reich, had Britain and France finally been stirred to action, but it was, as Davies observed, too little too late. "It looks pretty dark to me now. In fact, it looks worse to me than at any time," he wrote Steve Early. "Britain and France are making violent efforts now to establish a clear, countervailing axis by bringing Moscow into an agreement for common action. England has shown a genius in the past two years to wait until the procession has gone by. It has almost missed the caboose. If they had done two years ago what they are doing now, Czechoslovakia would still be on the map."

Actually, the situation was even worse than Davies suspected. Britain had already "missed the caboose." Simultaneous with talks among the USSR, Britain, and France, Stalin was negotiating with Hitler to see which side would offer him a better deal for expansion of Soviet territories into Eastern Europe.

The first signs of Stalin's shifting allegiances were subtle. On May 3, 1939, the Soviet premier removed Maxim Litvinov as commissar of foreign affairs. The official reasons for the dismissal were never made clear. Even the usually astute Davies, who knew that Litvinov was Jewish, failed to perceive that Stalin had removed Litvinov in preparation for a pact with Hitler. In Litvinov's place as foreign minister, Stalin appointed Vyacheslav Molotov, a man whose force of character, Davies predicted, would "project a hard, realistic front" in negotiations with Britain and France. With Molotov's steely manner, France and Britain would either join forces with the USSR or break altogether, forcing the Soviets into isolationism.

"God help the Western Powers over here if they do not bring Russia in . . . that situation right now does not look too good. They have been cuffing the Bear around so hard that the first thing they know he'll go back into his cave and ensure peace for himself on the easiest terms possible," Davies wrote FDR's appointments secretary, Colonel Edwin M. "Pa" Watson, on June 8.

The Russian bear was more resilient and less reclusive than Davies had surmised. On August 20 the USSR and Germany shocked the world by announcing a trade and credit agreement. Three days later Nazi Foreign Minister Joachim von Ribbentrop flew to Moscow to sign a nonaggression pact in which both countries agreed to avoid attacks upon each other or "any grouping of powers whatsoever that is directly or indirectly aimed at the other party." Secretly they were bound in an even more collusive agreement to divide Poland and the rest of Eastern Europe between them.

At dawn on September 1, 1939, German troops crossed over the Polish border, leaving burning villages, corpses, and swastikas in their wake. A few hours later the Luftwaffe passed overhead, dropping bombs of death and destruction upon the Polish countryside. Two days later, honoring their promise to protect Poland, Britain and France declared war on Nazi Germany.

News of the Polish invasion reached Marjorie and Joe while they were on leave in the United States. In August 1939 they had left Brussels for a vacation at Camp Topridge in the Adirondacks. It had been almost three years to the day since FDR had first called Joe to Washington to study the Russian question. In those three years, despite the ambassador's repeated warnings that the USSR would be a key player in the coming world struggle, anti-Soviet sentiment ran so strong in America that Roosevelt could not offer the Russians any support until it was almost too late.

In late August 1939 Marjorie received a chilling order from the Department of State: No member of an ambassador's family was to return to his European post, even to recover his personal belongings. Years later the ambassadress recalled that her initial reaction to the order was to "pack fast because I knew that it was going to be some mess." Besides Marjorie's clothes, jewelry, and furs, the Hôtel d'Assche still had the Boucher tapestries, the marble table from Mar-A-Lago, and the Davieses' priceless Russian art collection. The worried ambassadress immediately dispatched "packers" to Brussels to recover her things and have them returned to the United States.

Yet even Marjorie's vast wealth and ability to send members of her staff overseas could not protect her possessions from the vicissitudes of war. To reduce the chance that her clothes, art, and furniture would be destroyed in a single attack, Marjorie had them sent to the States on several ships. On the way back one of her assistants watched, first with horror, then with relief, as two torpedoes barely missed his ship.

Nor could Marjorie's fortune ensure protection for her husband in the international crisis. It was incumbent upon Joe as ambassador to Belgium to return to Brussels at the beginning of September regardless of the Polish invasion. "The only time in my life I ever saw Mother cry was when he had to get on that boat," said Dina. "Never, never did I see her in tears because she usually kept her emotions from us." Yet sea travel, even on civilian ocean liners, was becoming increasingly perilous. As Joe's ship, the RMS *Nieuw Amsterdam,* approached the English coast, the radio operator received a steady stream of SOS messages from British ships that had either been shelled or torpedoed. "Yesterday," Joe wrote Steve Early on September 11, "we passed a burning English tanker which had been shelled and deserted by her crew. Today, we see ships being conveyed by cruisers which were accompanied by airplanes scouting for submarines."

In the wake of the Polish invasion, Joe's expertise on the Soviets was suddenly seen in a new light. Earlier that year the ambassador had begged FDR to "bring Russia back before it is too late." But the president, facing reelection in 1940 and blocked by an American public that stubbornly adhered to an isolationist policy, had been powerless to change anything. What, FDR's constituents constantly reminded him, "did we get out of the first world war but death, debt and George M. Cohan?"

In the face of such opposition, Davies proposed an unusual solution. Would it not be better, he asked FDR, if he relinquished his ambassadorial post and worked for the Soviet cause as a private citizen? "What is your judgement? Should I get out and carry on a lone fight— or wait?"

Now, with Hitler's invasion of Poland and the announcement of the Berlin-Moscow trade pact, Davies's analysis of the USSR's industrial and military strength had a new importance. In answer to a query about the availability of Soviet oil, Davies assured Secretary of State Hull on October 12 that the USSR would not be able to supply Germany with "substantial quantities . . . for some time." The USSR's 460,000 tractors consumed essentially all the oil that the nation was able to produce. Still, it was possible that geologists could use high-pressure drilling methods to tap stores of oil in the USSR's Baku district.

Davies also used that opportunity to rub Hull's face in the Soviet-German alliance. "The Russian Bear has taken handsome revenge for being thrown out of Munich," he wrote. "In diplomatic circles here the Moscow-Berlin pact is generally conceded to be the greatest tragedy in the development of this war. . . ." While it was still not clear that the USSR would aid Germany on the western front, Davies insisted that the Soviets were motivated primarily by self-preservation.

Soviet policy "may be exactly what she proclaims it to be, namely a desire to establish peace in Europe if she can, and particularly on her eastern border and . . . to develop her own resources secure from attack of the capitalistic western nations. . . . Stalin's whole plan since 1926 has been to develop an internal economy that would be self-sufficient and create a socialistic communistic community that would be a model for the world . . . he said to me himself . . . they figured . . . for him and his associates to achieve that was a man-sized job and as much as they could do without trying to run the whole world."

Four days later Hull responded: "The president authorizes me to let you know that he is willing to have you relinquish your post and return to Washington for duty in the Department of State . . . should you feel that the time has come when you desire to make this change."

By late 1939 Joe had resigned as ambassador to Belgium and accepted a position as special assistant to the secretary of state in charge of war emergencies and policies. In that capacity he was to return home and serve as liaison between his European contacts and the Department of State to monitor the war's progress.

For Marjorie this was welcome news. From Brussels Joe had written in the autumn of 1939 about the flight of the wealthy from Bavaria, Belgium, and Luxembourg and the upheaval among ordinary citizens in the shadow of an imminent Nazi attack. On October 24 Joe wrote that he had "been out to Laeken quite frequently with the King. . . . He is trying his best to maintain a strictly honorable neutrality between the belligerents on all sides. . . . It is a thankless situation. . . . Then, this enormous army of six or seven [hundred] thousand men are practically idle . . . with nothing happening. . . . [T]here are quite a number of the unemployed. . . . There is also great difficulty . . . in the harvests, the gathering of the fruits . . . caused by the dislocation of man power through being called to the colors."

On November 3 he noted that "there is practically no social life here. Europe is virtually in an entire blackout. Thoughtful people are all desperately cognizant of the fact that . . . if this keeps up, their manner of life is ended."

Even more worrisome to Marjorie were Joe's references to the mysterious stomach attacks that often laid him low for weeks at a time but that he seldom mentioned until after his recovery.

Typical of these was a letter the ambassador sent on October 20, 1939. "Dearest Beloved," the letter began, as did most of his communications, "I had the staff for dinner on Friday night a week ago and on the Saturday morning following, I just cracked up [became violently ill]. . . . It was a characteristic attack. I am practically all right now again and have spent several hours in the office the last two or three days. . . . It has been pretty devilishly lonesome but I felt like a sick pup and was quite happy to lie in a corner and be undisturbed."

It was thus understandable that when Davies finally handed in his resignation in November 1939, Marjorie was overcome with joy. "Dearest-dearest—" she wrote on the train from Washington to Manhattan. "Am I an excited so & so! With you coming home on vacation! I shall be counting the hours & minutes—& clawing the air with impatience!"

In early January 1940 Marjorie and Joe were reunited in Washington. And on the twenty-second of that month FDR praised Joe for the "excellent work you have done . . . your reports from your recent posts, as well as those sent previously from Moscow, were extremely valuable.

"You exercised a happy faculty in evaluating events at hand and determining with singular accuracy their probable effect on future developments. . . . On this account I feel it is particularly fortunate that we are to have the continued benefit of your guidance and counsel in foreign affairs."

Although State Department officials still regarded Davies with disfavor, the fact that the former ambassador had presidential approval made members of the department wary of offending him.

For the first time since their marriage Marjorie and Joe put down roots in Washington. They had initially rented a large brick estate on Foxhall Road while looking for a house of their own. Rental, Joe had advised Marjorie from Brussels, was preferable to an immediate purchase, "for the reason that . . . possibly . . . you would not enjoy Washington. Then we would have it [a house] on our hands."

Joe could have spared himself that worry. Already by the autumn of 1939 Marjorie had ingratiated herself in Washington just as she had in Palm Beach, Moscow, Brussels, and Luxembourg. "She was very charming, very natural and very easy to talk to," said Fanny Chipman, who knew Marjorie from their Moscow years. "People liked her. And I don't think it was so much because she was a wealthy woman, but because she was very friendly and outgoing."

Once released from observing the State Department order that prohibited the wives of American ambassadors from giving newspaper interviews, Marjorie made friends with members of the Washington press. According to the Albany, New York, *Knickerbocker News*, Marjorie was a "changed woman" once Joe resigned as ambassador. "Always before extremely shy of the newspaper reporters, Mrs. Davies is now most friendly and cooperative," the paper observed on December 20, 1939. "Before no reporter could interview her. . . . Now, however, Mrs. Davies not only will be interviewed but telephones newspaper women when they have left their names." Mrs. Davies, the *Knickerbocker News* could not resist adding, is a "beautiful woman" who appeared at FDR's annual Christmas reception for diplomats at the White House in a "simple black velvet evening dress" with no hair ornament. Long earrings of diamond and crystal dangled from her ears. "Or were the large drops diamonds too? Your correspondent didn't ask."

Early that winter Marjorie was honored by the Women's National Press Club for her work as ambassadress. On January 24, 1940, she reciprocated with a luncheon at the Foxhall Road estate, which, noted the *Washington Star*, was decorated like a "springtime bower." Scrapbooks containing photographs from the Davieses' travels in the USSR and Belgium were on display in the drawing room and "were of particular interest to the newspaper women who remained . . . after the luncheon to look through them."

To become a consummate Washington hostess would require the acquisition of a permanent homestead. Within a few months Marjorie and Joe bought the old Parmelee estate, a Georgian Colonial mansion on twenty acres of hilly land near Rock Creek Park in northwest Washington. As with Spaso House and the Hôtel d'Assche, the Parmelee mansion was in need of renovation, and it was not until the spring of 1942 that Marjorie and Joe finally moved in. By then the mansion had been renamed Tregaron, in honor of Joe's ancestral town in Wales.

The former ambassador left another mark on the palatial three-chimneyed estate: his name on the deed as its sole owner. At the time of the purchase Joe made the down payment, and Marjorie agreed to pay the monthly mortgage. In 1941 the technicality of whose house it was meant little to the former ambassadress, for she was deeply in love, and still willing, as she had told members of the American embassy in Moscow four years earlier, to "follow that pair of black eyes to the ends of the world."

For Joe, ownership of the house was a matter of masculine pride. In spite of his ambassadorships and prominence in the Democratic party, the attorney bristled at any hint that he was the "kept" consort of a wealthy heiress. Years before he met Marjorie, Joe had admired the Parmelee estate. Moreover, recalled Marjorie's granddaughter Ellen MacNeille Charles, "He told Grandmother that it would be embarrassing to have the house put in her name. And Grandmother was the kind of person who would do anything to keep her husbands happy."

Joe was not the only one Marjorie wanted to make happy. After returning to the States, she had addressed herself with new vigor to her extended family. By 1939 she was the grandmother of three girls. In addition to Marjorie, called Marwee, who had been born to Adelaide and Tim Durant in 1928, Adelaide had given birth to two girls with her second husband, Merrall MacNeille: Ellen, born in 1938, and Melissa, born in 1939.

Whatever enjoyment Marjorie had from her new granddaughters was almost inevitably shattered by the worrisome and often deliberately disruptive behavior of their older sister. The problem was deeper than sibling rivalry. Long before Ellen and Melissa were born, Marwee had been a difficult child, subject to violent rages. Her nickname was a result of one of those tantrums. "Once at Hillwood [Marjorie's estate in Brookville] I opened a Christmas present that said 'Marjorie' on it and had a large diamond in it, and I had a major tantrum when it was taken away from me," Marwee recalled. Thereafter everyone in the family was careful to make distinctions between the elder Marjorie and her granddaughter. Subsequently Marwee became the girl's spoken and written name.

As Marwee grew, she became even more obstreperous, kicking guests in the shins and swearing at her mother, Adelaide. "We were like oil and water. . . . I guess I was a rebel. I don't know if I was born one, but I sure became one fast living with my mother. I hated to be with her. She was like a dictatorial mean aunt, and I brought out the worst in her and vice versa. . . . She used to tell me I reminded her of my father, and that didn't help."

By the time Marwee was eight or nine, her behavior had become truly alarming. Several times she tried to run away from her mother's home on the Hillwood estate, a separate house Marjorie had built for Adelaide at the time of her marriage to Tim Durant. Charming though that cottage was, complete with a nearby playhouse—the Deen-wee—that she shared with her young aunt Dina, Marwee thought of the Brookville homestead as a "paradise jail." Try as she might, though, the girl never got farther than Route 25A before she was surrounded by Hillwood's private watchmen and local police.

Only her grandmother Marjorie could seem to make Marwee obey. "I never listened to my mother," Marwee recalled. "The only one who could get me to mind was my grandmother because I loved and respected her."

Nor after Adelaide and Merrall MacNeille moved to the horse country of Maryland did Marwee become any happier. By late 1939 or early 1940 Adelaide had become so exasperated with Marwee that she sent her to California to live with her father, Tim Durant. By then Adelaide's ex-husband was one of Charlie Chaplin's writers and personal assistants. Living in a back apartment in Beverly Hills, he rented the front to movie stars like Greta Garbo and Olivia De Havilland. The glitzy, careless atmosphere was hardly nurturing for a pubescent girl, particularly because Durant, though devoted to Marwee, was a womanizer.

Marwee developed an unfulfilled longing for a mother figure and on holidays and in the summer traveled East to live with Marjorie. Even when Marjorie "drew her long red fingernail" down Marwee's back with orders to "stand up straight" or ordered her to dress for a cotillion, the tall, lanky girl promptly obeyed. "My grandmother," Marwee recalled many years later, "was the only one I tried to please, because although she was not my biological mother she was unmistakably my psychological one."

Although the girl was still unruly and was continually being expelled from schools, including Marjorie's alma mater, the Mount Vernon Seminary, her spunk secretly tickled the heiress. "She got a kick out of some of my capers and, when I was a lot older, once told me that I was to her a breath of spring," Marwee recalled. Although she believed that Dina was always Marjorie's favorite daughter, she maintains to this day that she was Marjorie's "undisputed second choice."

In the early 1940s Dina was rapidly developing into a beautiful young woman who bore a striking physical resemblance to Marjorie. To the former ambassadress, Dina's graduation from the Mount Vernon Seminary was a momentous event not only because it meant that Dina had grown up but because it signaled the end of her own child-rearing years. As she wrote an old Battle Creek friend, "My baby Deenie is growing up. The excitement is terrific."

Despite Dina's close attachment to her mother and their shared enjoyment of pretty clothes, the girl had little interest in following Marjorie's social path. Already, in decorating her rooms at Mar-A-Lago and at the Hôtel d'Assche, the adolescent Dina had chosen furniture as dramatically different from Marjorie's taste as possible. "It was the typical reaction of a child, rebellion, I was into austere modern. . . . And we got bleach blond birch furniture. It was okay, but it took me a while to learn to appreciate the finer stuff."

Moreover, by adolescence Dina had serious intentions to become an actress in spite of Marjorie's frank disapproval. Although she had had friends who were actresses, like Billie Burke, Marjorie had drummed into her daughters that their major life role was to be wives and mothers. The theater, she warned Dina, was no career for a woman who wanted to be married. "And I must say that when I went to drama school that thing was so firmly ingrained in my head that . . . when I married, I was going to quit," Dina recalled.

By that time Marjorie was attracting press attention of her own through her charities and kindnesses to others. With the threat of a Nazi invasion of Luxembourg, Marjorie helped the grand duchess spirit her six children out of the country and send them to the United States. By the spring of 1940 they had arrived in New York and were taken to Hillwood on Long Island. "Mother took one look at the boys in their heavy wool serge jackets and the girls in their middy blouses and heavy wool serge skirts and said, 'By God, this won't do. Come on, we'll go to Garden City.' Then she piled them into the car and took them to Best and Company to buy them new clothes," Dina recalled. "For months the children lived at Hillwood and that summer visited Marjorie and her family at Topridge." (One of the royal refugees, Jean, is now the grand duke of Luxembourg.)

For her kindnesses Marjorie was awarded the Order of the House of Savoy of the Grand Duchy of Luxembourg in March 1940. The following month she hosted a recital at Mar-A-Lago with Metropolitan Opera contralto Doris Doe for the Guild of St. Agnes of the Holy Trinity Church. That same year the former ambassadress also threw herself back into fund-raising for the American Red Cross. At her rented estate on Foxhall Road, Marjorie hosted several receptions. And in May 1940 she persuaded Eleanor Roosevelt to speak on the radio and appear in a film for the cause.

By the end of the year Marjorie's husband had become so frustrated by American isolationism that he decided to resign as special assistant to the secretary of state and return to private law practice. No sooner had he announced the decision than FDR appointed him head of his third Inaugural Committee.

As a result, Marjorie resumed her duties as a hostess for several inaugural events. On January 21, 1941, she was making headlines again, this time in a syndicated column by Nancy Randolph that described the problems of limiting the guest list for the presidential celebration. "As wife of the committee chairman, the good-looking Mrs. Davies this afternoon entertained the state Governors and their wives . . . with as much of Washington's resident officialdom as could be packed into the palatial Davies residence on Foxhall Road."

The problem, according to Randolph, was that "Mrs. Davies wanted to invite everybody of note, including her own personal friends. In the glow of resuming the duties of an official hostess—which she had not been since Davies resigned as Ambassador to Belgium—Mrs. Davies made out a tentative list of 4,500 names. After all, she reasoned, the inaugural reception to the Governors has almost a European-like tradition behind it—the custom is 100 years old. So why not do it up in grandiose style?

"But 4,500 guests is an impossible order in anybody's drawing room."

In the end Marjorie pared her list to five hundred, then "upped it here and there" with another five hundred, who, including thirty-three governors and their wives, constituted a sizable gala.

By April 1941 Marjorie's place in an exalted niche of Washington society had been assured. No longer was she primarily remembered as Emlen Knight Davies's "husband stealer" or even as the spoiled heiress who had haughtily packed her yacht with frozen cream and foods so she could live in style in Soviet Russia. Now, according to Associated Press reporter Sigrid Arne, Marjorie was the most revered hostess in Washington.

A month earlier Joe had become involved in another project that soon dominated Marjorie's life. In March 1941 FDR asked Joe to head the President's Committee for War Relief. And although the attorney was still suffering from chronic stomach trouble and in obvious need of a vacation, he felt it was a request that he "couldn't refuse." On June 22, 1941, FDR's reasons for keeping Joe "on retainer" became clear when Hitler invaded Russia.

At the time, Marjorie and Joe were at the University of Wisconsin, where the former ambassador was receiving an honorary degree. When asked by a reporter how long the Soviet army could hold out, he replied that the "extent of the resistance of the Red Army would amaze and surprise the world." It was just common sense, he added, "for us to give the Soviets all the aid we possibly could, because they were fighting the greatest danger to our security in the world." Davies's comments attracted national press attention. But while Secretary of State Hull and Secretary of the Interior Harold Ickes now agreed with Davies's assessment, most Americans remained adamantly anti-Soviet.

Faced with such opposition, there was little Roosevelt would do. Nor could he say little more than "Any defense against Hitlerism . . . from whatever source . . . will . . . benefit . . . our own defense and security." In lieu of an outright pledge of aid—as Churchill, who had succeeded the feckless Chamberlain in Great Britain a year earlier, now offered— FDR could only promise oblique tokens of support: the removal of a money embargo, a request for the war materials needed by the Soviets, and a promise that the Neutrality Act would be ignored so that Soviet ships carrying American-bought supplies would be protected.

Davies, meanwhile, launched a private campaign to convince the administration to commit itself to a program of prompt aid. By July 7 he had talked to the new acting secretary of state, Sumner Welles. The next day he met with White House aide Harry Hopkins, then in charge of Washington's lend-lease program. By July 9, Joe's message had gotten through, for FDR ordered Sumner Welles to ensure that supplies would be delivered to the Soviets before October 1.

After a luncheon that same day with the Soviet ambassador, Konstantin Oumansky, at the Davies estate, Joe offered to serve the State Department as unofficial liaison between the Russians and the Roosevelt administration. Ultimately FDR approved the plan because the State Department found Oumansky more difficult to deal with than did Joe. Later, after Hopkins visited the USSR and had assurances from Stalin that the Soviet army could last until winter, Davies's plea for prompt Soviet aid was fulfilled. In August 1941 at the Atlantic Charter Conference off Newfoundland, FDR and Churchill assured the Soviets that they would send large quantities of war equipment.

Although government leaders were now convinced of the importance of sending aid to the USSR, the American public was not. Ever since the Nazi invasion of Soviet Russia, Joe had been giving talks to support aid to the Soviets. By November 17 Marjorie had begun to campaign with him.

That summer, in the name of "mothers of America," female antiwar protesters had appeared at the White House and burned a scroll listing Roosevelt's promises to keep America out of war. To ensure publicity, they had placed bits of that scroll in a funeral urn and labeled it "Ashes of FDR's Promises." Another group of protesters, veiled and dressed in black, sat on a bench in an outer office of the Senate chamber for days on end, weeping as if in mourning over dead husbands and sons.

This sentimental "motherly" appeal for noninvolvement in the European war so disturbed Marjorie that she decided to address America's women herself. In a talk before two thousand at the Council on Soviet Relations in Manhattan, the former ambassadress noted that the status of women in the United States, Great Britain, and the USSR was higher than in other countries. "To none in this world is the outcome of this war more vital than to women," she said, her words reported in *The New York Times*. "If the Nazi totalitarian system should dominate our world, the status of women would be horrible to contemplate. It would be reduced to that of the breeder and the housefrau [sic] for an ordained super male in a world dominated by a so-called Nordic master race. Under such conditions, idealism, freedom, self-respect and opportunity for women would find no place."

For all of Marjorie's poise and prominence, she hated to speak in public. "It used to make Mother terribly nervous. She'd practice a speech for days before she'd give it," Adelaide recalled. Marjorie, like Joe, had become so passionate about the Soviets' good intentions that she had even overcome stage fright to promote their cause.

Joe had still another plan to win popular support for Soviet aid. That September it was suggested that the former ambassador collect his dispatches, journal, and diaries describing the strength of the Soviet military and industrial resources and publish them in the form of a popular book. Exactly who suggested it and to whom—Joe, FDR, or Steve Early or some combination thereof—is not clear. The result, however, was the subsequent publication of *Mission to Moscow*, a collation of Davies's papers attesting to the USSR's industrial and military might, its police state mentality, and its failing "communistic" system rejected in favor of "capitalistic" incentives.

The book, published in late December 1941, could not have been timed more brilliantly, coming as it did on the heels of the Nazis' invasion of Soviet Russia and immediately after Pearl Harbor. *Mission to Moscow* was virtually an overnight success and climbed to the top of the nation's best-seller list. To Joe, as to a beaming Marjorie, it was of little importance that the State Department had dubbed the book *Submission to Moscow* or that the literary critic Edmund Wilson later characterized Davies as the "greatest master of bad official English since the late President Harding."

What counted was that Davies now commanded the attention of an American public that was becoming increasingly sympathetic to the plight of the Russian people. Within the next eighteen months his message would reach millions more Americans with Hollywood's help. In 1943 Warner Bros. released the movie *Mission to Moscow*, starring Walter Huston as Joe Davies and Ann Harding as Marjorie Hutton Davies.

Shortly before the publication of *Mission to Moscow* there were rumors that a new Russian ambassador would be appointed to the Washington post. As Davies hoped—and told Konstantin Oumansky before he left the States—it would be best if the Kremlin appointed a man long considered a friend to the United States: Maxim Litvinov.

Although it had been two years since Litvinov had been left to cool his heels in the back corridors of the Kremlin after his dismissal as prime minister, party leaders reconsidered and assigned him the American ambassadorship. While it had taken the Nazi invasion to move them, Kremlin leaders now recognized the benefit of sending an amiable Soviet to Washington—especially one friendly with FDR's buddy Joe Davies.

In the meanwhile, there were ominous rumblings from Japan. In September 1940 that island country had invaded northern French Indochina and in July 1941 overran the entire country. In retaliation FDR had initiated a trade embargo and frozen all Japanese assets in the States. After weeks of discouraging talks the militant Japanese prime minister, Hideki Tojo, set a December 1941 deadline for an American resumption of free trade. By November 29 negotiations had broken down completely. American commanders in the South Pacific accordingly braced themselves for a Japanese attack that was expected in the Philippines or British Malaya.

On December 7, 1941, the Japanese bombed Pearl Harbor in Hawaii. Coincidentally, it was the same morning that Maxim Litvinov and his wife, Ivy, arrived in Washington. That noon Joe and Marjorie's old friends lunched at their estate and listened to the radio reports. In the space of a mere three hours the Japanese had created the worst military disaster in American history, resulting in the deaths of more than 2,000 soldiers and the destruction of 8 battleships and 188 airplanes. December 7, 1941, as a shaken Roosevelt told the American public, was "a date which will live in infamy."

After years of alienation and distrust, the United States and the USSR had a compelling new reason to become allies: a second enemy common to them both. At that cataclysmic moment, when both countries were threatened from the east and the west, the friendship between Davies and Litvinov assumed a new prominence that all their years of diplomatic talk had failed to achieve.

Nor, in the wake of Pearl Harbor, could leaders in Washington or the Kremlin question the necessity for a new American-Soviet alliance.

CAPITAL HOSTESS

21

"Since I Have No Son . . . I Will Offer the *Sea Cloud*"

*T*he war years strengthened Marjorie's position as the quintessential Washington hostess. On January 19, 1942, she and Joe invited all of official Washington to a reception in honor of Maxim and Ivy Litvinov. The party at the Davieses' antiques-stuffed Foxhall Road mansion was described by *Life* magazine as "the biggest blowout since the war began." Among the guests were Supreme Court justices, cabinet members, senators, foreign diplomats, Mrs. Cordell Hull, and the vice president's wife, Mrs. Henry A. Wallace. So packed was the house with dignitaries that the *Washington Times-Herald* observed: "If anyone stayed away, we should like to know who he was."

Until well after 7:00 P.M. Washington's best and brightest juggled teacups and champagne glasses and nibbled cucumber sandwiches and petits fours in drawing rooms lined with Russian art. Then they stood in line to meet the new Soviet ambassador and his wife, whose friendship had suddenly become so vital to the security of the United States. "All the Allied nations, the signers of the most important pact of the century, were well represented in the throng, either by . . . envoys or . . . the next man in rank . . ." noted Hope Ridings Miller of *The Washington Post.*

Marjorie, Miller observed, was "smartly turned out in a full-skirted frock of gray taffeta, set off with inserts of net in a leafy pattern—all very lovely." Several of Marjorie's friends and Washington's most important women, the reporter also noted, had assisted the hostess pouring tea: Mrs. Hugo Black, Mrs. Felix Frankfurter, Mrs. William O. Douglas, Mrs. Harold Ickes, Mrs. Paul McNutt, Secretary of Labor Frances Perkins, Mrs. George C. Marshall, and Mrs. Sumner Welles. To Marjorie, those friendships were far more than political conveniences. In the eighteen months since her return from Belgium, she had won the respect of these women through charity and community service work. One of her closest friends in this group was Kathleen McNutt, the wife of a member of Roosevelt's war cabinet and a fellow Christian Scientist.

By 1940 Marjorie had also joined Washington's Sulgrave Club, an elite women's art and charitable organization located in an elegant town house on Dupont Circle. Among its members were prominent women like Alice Roosevelt Longworth, the novelist Mary Roberts Rinehart, Eleanor "Cissy" Medill Patterson (owner of the *Washington Times-Herald*), Alva Vanderbilt Belmont, Florence Jaffray Harriman, and Helen Herron Taft.

In the months since Marjorie's return even formerly disapproving women of old Washington's "cave dweller" set, like future society columnist Betty Beale, had grown to admire the former ambassadress for her "generosity" and "sincerity." What Beale found especially refeshing was Marjorie's enjoyment of people for themselves, rather than for their titles or roles. "She entertained and gave important dinners because that was Joe Davies's interest. But really Marjorie didn't care," said Beale. "Marjorie would also have the 'little people.' . . . If she worked and was interested in a cause and she got to know the people . . . she would include them."

Adding luster to Marjorie's reputation was the confluence of two events of late 1941: the arrival of the Litvinovs and the appearance of *Mission to Moscow* on the nation's best-seller list. These catapulted her and Joe to a position of national prominence. Declared *Life* magazine: "To do honor to [Litvinov] no host could be more suitable than his good friend, shrewd Joe Davies, who predicted the unsuspected strength of the U.S.S.R. in battle . . . and his handsome wealthy wife."

Over the next four years Joe was repeatedly thrust into the nation's limelight as an expert on Soviet-American relations. In this, as in Marjorie's earlier role as ambassadress, her duties would necessarily be ancillary: as hostess and devoted wife who provided her husband with an elegant backdrop for his political activities. That secondary role, as David Brinkley pointed out in *Washington Goes to War*, was virtually all that a "rich and socially well-connected married woman" of that era was permitted to be. And for Marjorie, who was already sensitive to the power of her money to deflate her husband's ego, that role was all she would permit herself.

Enamored with Joe as she was, Marjorie accordingly devoted herself to his daughters. By the war years E.K., like Joe's second daughter, Rahel, was married and lived out of town. In their absence Marjorie doted especially upon Joe's eldest daughter, Eleanor, now long since married to Maryland's senior Democratic senator, Millard Tydings. There was, of course, nothing really new about Marjorie's friendship with Eleanor. From the moment of her 1935 engagement to Joe, Marjorie had treated the newly divorced Eleanor with kindness. When Eleanor married the aristocratic Tydings, then considered Washington's most eligible bachelor, just a few days after Marjorie's own wedding, the heiress had adopted Eleanor and her husband as if they were children of her own.

Later, although there were some strains resulting from the conservative-minded Senator Tydings's criticism of Roosevelt's New Deal policies, Marjorie, Joe, Eleanor, and Millard remained a warm family unit. In 1939, when the newspapers headlined stories announcing a movement to have Tydings run against Roosevelt at the end of his second term, Joe had shrugged off the embarrassment. Marjorie had reacted with similar discretion. "Funny the turns life can make," she later wrote beneath the news articles she pasted in her scrapbooks about Tydings's proposed nomination.

Marjorie made life easier for Eleanor and Millard in many ways: by buying tables for Eleanor's Red Cross and war relief benefits, through generous gifts, furs, vacations to nearby resorts, and flowers on the Tydingses' anniversaries. Nor did Marjorie seem to expect anything in return that might put a strain on the Tydingses' budget. At Christmas, for instance, she routinely gave them a list of what she knew they could afford.

Marjorie's generosity extended to Eleanor's children from her first marriage, young Joe and Eleanor Cheesborough, who were subsequently adopted by Senator Tydings. While Marjorie showered young Eleanor with dresses, dolls, and toys, she had a special fondness for young Joe. "As a boy I was a rarity in the family," explained Joe Tydings, who later became an attorney and a Maryland senator, "and this put me in sort of a special category with Aunt Marjorie." At the time of Marjorie's wedding there were no other boys in the family. Both she and Joe Davies had three daughters apiece, and although they both were grandparents, they had no grandsons other than seven-year-old Joe.

As a result, Marjorie "spoiled" young Joe with gifts and often invited him to stay at her homes. And as with Marwee and Barbara Hutton, she soon ingratiated herself with the youngster and had a strong influence upon him. "She was always patting me on my back, just like my grandfather," Joe recalled. "One of the great things she did was to give me self-confidence and a real sense of balance. Thanks to her, I'm not impressed by material things, but [by] the human values which are really important in life."

While Marjorie may have seemed to be just a glamorous and supportive figure who enhanced Joe's personal and professional life, she remained a strong woman in her own right. Imbued with a sense of civic duty, Marjorie felt compelled to leave her own mark on the war against fascism as she had done nearly twenty years earlier during World War I.

After the United States declared war on Japan and the Axis powers, Marjorie leased the *Sea Cloud* to the U.S. Navy for a dollar a year. "Since I have no son to give to the war, I will offer the *Sea Cloud*," the former ambassadress said in early 1942. After Marjorie removed the yacht's antiques and furnishings, naval engineers stripped the 316-foot *Sea Cloud* of its sails, rigging, and masts. The schooner's handsomely paneled staterooms were then converted into sleeping quarters for two hundred men. Guns were placed in strategic positions. The yacht's vast food storage areas were redesigned so it could serve as a military convoy ship in the North Sea.

In that same period Marjorie also attempted to convince her adolescent granddaughter Marwee to join the WACs after graduation from high school. "My grandmother was a very patriotic woman," Marwee explained. "She wanted me to go into the service, to train for the army. I was horrified at the thought."

As it happened, it was Marjorie's own daughter Dina who volunteered to serve—not as a WAC but as an actress. Toward the end of the war Dina, having completed a round of study at the American Academy of Arts, begged her mother to let her join the USO. Marjorie, who had always been overprotective of Dina, initially refused. Dina ultimately had her way by using the same reasoning that had motivated Marjorie to lend the Navy the *Sea Cloud*. "Mommy, you have no son; at least let your daughter go," Dina pleaded. By 1945 Dina was in a USO production of *The Man Who Came to Dinner* in the South Pacific.

At home Marjorie worried constantly about Dina's safety. A stream of letters found the young actress wherever she was stationed. Marjorie also sent her daughter packages. One of these was entrusted to Millard Tydings, who, as chairman of the Senate Armed Services Committee, had to make an inspection tour of the Marianas. En route to his destination, the senator gave Marjorie's package to a naval officer, explaining its "importance" to the receiver. To accommodate the senator, the officer had the parcel sent posthaste to Dina via special delivery plane to Saipan, where she was then stationed. The young actress opened it with curiosity—and promptly howled with laughter. "And sure enough, dear Mom had sent me two rolls of toilet paper, which she was sure I didn't have out there, a box of Kleenex, and a girdle. With the girdle came a note: 'Do tell those fool jeep drivers not to drive too fast, and wear this because it will bounce your insides out if you don't.' "

In Washington, meanwhile, Marjorie immersed herself in war work. Even before Pearl Harbor she had again been involved with the American Red Cross. Afterward she hosted a free canteen in Manhattan for military men on leave. By 1942 Marjorie was a committee member for the National Symphony Orchestra's "Sunset Symphonies" on behalf of Army-Navy Relief. "I think the orchestras are making one of the most vital contributions to morale," Marjorie observed. "And England knows it. Symphony music has never ceased in London."

Still, it was Soviet Russia to which Marjorie devoted most of her energies. As a hostess she repeatedly opened her house to the Litvinovs and other Soviet dignitaries, among them Soviet general Lvidmilla Pavlichenko and young Andrei Gromyko, who, in 1943, became the Soviet ambassador to the United States.

Soon after her arrival in Washington, Marjorie began rallying food, money, and clothing on behalf of Russian War Relief. Overcoming her reluctance to speak in public, she addressed a radio audience requesting funds on behalf of the Union of Red Cross and Red Crescent Societies of the Soviet Socialist Republics. "In all this Red Cross work in Russia which . . . is doing so much to help us defeat Hitler, the American people have played a share," explained Marjorie. "They have given splendidly in the past, they are still giving. I know that they will continue to give."

In the course of her war-related work, Marjorie became acquainted with a sister Sulgrave Club member, Julia Cantacuzene, first grand-daughter of Ulysses S. Grant, who had once been married to Prince Michael Cantacuzene, aide-de-camp to Grand Duke Nicholas of Russia. After fleeing the 1917 Russian Revolution and returning to Washington, the petite Princess Cantacuzene had started the Russian Relief Program to help refugees.

By the spring of 1943, inspired by Madame Cantacuzene's early efforts and her own belief in the importance of Soviet-American friendships, Marjorie lent Russian paintings, porcelains, jeweled Easter eggs, and other imperial art treasures for a Manhattan exhibition to benefit Russian War Relief. The following winter, Marjorie purchased four rare pieces of American sandwich glass, which, along with other domestic antiques, she planned to send to Moscow's Kuskovo Museum in a Soviet-American cultural exchange.

In July 1944 Marjorie also organized an exhibit of American nursery furniture that was sent to the USSR in the name of the Women's Committee of the National Council of American-Soviet Friendship. "We look forward to the day of victory, the establishment of a durable peace, when all children may enjoy their rightful heritage of health, plenty and happiness," read the scroll Marjorie presented on that occasion to Mrs. Eugene D. Kisseleve, wife of the Soviet consul general.

In 1944 the "durable peace" that Marjorie hoped for still seemed questionable, its course complicated by tensions among the USSR, the United States, and Great Britain. After that one incandescent moment of Soviet-American friendship at Marjorie and Joe's reception for the Litvinovs in January 1942, relations between the two countries had become strained. At the root of the tension was Roosevelt's earlier promise to Soviet Foreign Minister Molotov that the Allies would support a "second front" in Western Europe against the Nazis before the end of 1942. But in the summer of 1942, when Libya's port city of Tobruk fell to the Nazis, Churchill pressed so hard for a second front in North Africa that Roosevelt had conceded.

Litvinov was none too pleased with that decision. The United States and Great Britain, he complained, were determining the course of the war, while the USSR did all the fighting. Eventually the Soviet ambassador even accused Churchill of intentionally delaying a second front so that the USSR would be "bled white by fighting the Germans alone." By war's end, Litvinov gloomily predicted, Great Britain would thus be

well situated to "dominate and control" all of Europe. To this, Joe—
who was still acting as unofficial liaison between the Soviets and the
White House—could only reply that the Allies were doing the best they
could to crush the Nazi war machine.

By the spring of 1942 Marjorie and Joe had moved to Rock Creek Park
into the old Parmelee estate, now Tregaron. There, on twenty lush
acres of wooded land in northwest Washington, the sprawling mansion
had been redesigned as a showcase for the Davieses' Russian art collection. At Marjorie's orders, a dacha was built on the property. Within
the house was a special room filled with display cases of Easter eggs, imperial porcelains, chalices, and icons. Above them were dozens of Soviet
paintings that *Life* called the "best U.S. collection" of modern Russian
art. Tregaron, said the *Evening Star*, was a "veritable museum, with its
many fine collections of French furniture . . . and . . . a Russian room
with . . . objects of art."

No other Washington setting could have been more appropriate for
the two-day "congress of American-Soviet friendship" that took place
in September 1942. But in contrast with Marjorie and Joe's warm reception for the Litvinovs nine months earlier, the congress at Tregaron
was a frantic effort to assure disgruntled Soviets that their friendship
with the United States was intact.

In introductory remarks Joe praised the USSR as one of America's
bravest allies. "Today we pay tribute to that great people who are holding the fort. Tomorrow, God willing, we will be fighting physically by
their side," he told an audience of senators, congressmen, federal officials, and reporters. Vice President Wallace heaped similar accolades
on the USSR, predicting the Allies were "over the hump" in the war.
When asked by a midwestern reporter about the significance of the
Nazi attack on Stalingrad, Wallace said that "Stalingrad is Chicago's
first line of defense." The Tregaron conference, reported *The New York
Times*, was only the first in a series of pro-Soviet programs that were to
culminate in a rally at Madison Square Garden that November.

Despite the Davieses' two-day congress at Tregaron and other quasi-
governmental efforts to assure the Soviets that the United States was
still sympathetic to their needs, Stalin was incensed. Even after three invitations from FDR, Stalin refused to meet the American president face-
to-face. Nor did events in early 1943 improve the deadlock. During a
January 1943 meeting with Churchill in Casablanca, FDR agreed to
delay the second front again, further deepening Stalin's suspicions of an

American-British alliance that would exclude the USSR from a share in
the conquered lands of postwar Europe.

By early spring FDR was so anxious about the tenuous state of
Soviet-American relations that he decided to send Joe back to the Soviet
Union as ambassador. For the first time FDR's "ace in the hole" balked.
His hesitation had nothing to do with politics. By the spring of 1943 the
sixty-seven-year-old man's chronic stomach trouble was becoming so
severe that it could no longer be ignored.

To Marjorie, the prospect of another grueling assignment that could
endanger her husband's increasingly fragile health was upsetting.
From the first years of her marriage to Joe she had fretted about her
husband's delicate stomach and had tended carefully to his diet. Now
she found herself experimenting with many of the cautionary measures
once practiced by her father, C.W., for his troubled digestion. "As a result," recalled E.K., who lived with her father and Marjorie in Moscow
and Belgium before her marriage, "Marjorie was very careful to have
him eat a lot of puréed foods and cream and dairy products, a lot of soft
foods."

FDR, a sick man himself, insisted that Joe's presence was crucial to
an improvement in Soviet-American relations. If his doctors believed
that a second ambassadorship was inadvisable, could Joe at least travel
to Moscow for a few weeks to see Stalin? The purpose of the trip would
be to deliver a letter inviting the Soviet premier to meet with the president. Since the Soviets had "confidence" in Joe, FDR believed he could
assure Stalin that the United States had no secret alliance with Great
Britain.

Before agreeing to the assignment Joe visited Boston's Lahey Clinic
for a thorough medical checkup. There, doctors explained that while
his digestive problems were not life-threatening, he needed to be monitored and to avoid undue stress. From the hospital Joe wrote FDR explaining his inability to accept the ambassadorship but his willingness
to make a brief trip to the USSR.

By late April FDR had prepared the promised letter for Stalin. The
press immediately promoted the high hopes raised by Joe's journey.
"Reports from British and American diplomats stress the discontent of
the Russian leader with the American-British war policy of 'nibbling' at
the fringes of Europe. . . . Mr. Davies is believed by many officials to
be the one man who could get the ear of the Russian Premier," wrote
the *Evening Star*. Because of Davies's "unstinted efforts to make the

American people Russian conscious," he had "almost become a second Russian Ambassador to the United States."

On May 6, 1943, amid a flurry of press speculations about the content of FDR's letter to Stalin, Davies left for Moscow with a private physician, an aide, and a supply of dehydrated food. The mysterious purpose of Joe's assignment, the tenuous state of Soviet-American relations, and the daily arrival of wounded veterans, missing-in-action telegrams, and flag-draped coffins in the United States added drama to Davies's mission. As *Time* put it, "The plane carrying America's No. 1 Russophile on Mission II to Moscow circled down at the Soviet capital with an escort of five fighters. . . . Under his arm he tightly pressed the brief case holding a private letter from Franklin Roosevelt to Joseph Stalin. No one but the President and a secretary-typist knew what the letter contained."

The complex emotions Marjorie felt about Joe's refusal to accept a second ambassadorship to Moscow—relief that they were not going on another "hardship assignment," disappointment at the lost opportunity for being at the center of the international crisis—were eclipsed by her anxiety about Joe's health. As a result, he was greeted at every port en route to Moscow with messages from her, inquiring about his health and assuring him of her love. Because of German U-boat activity in the North Atlantic, the envoy was flown to Moscow on a C-54 Douglas Skymaster along a southern route through the Caribbean and the Mideast. To Marjorie, who had a morbid fear of flying, the transoceanic flight was an additional anxiety on a journey she already considered dangerous to the health of her beloved "Joey."

To cheer him along the way, she had roses and tulips sent to Dakar. In response, Joe wired Marjorie: "Messages comfort, joy, tulips, kit fine. . . . Wamhily." In a long letter of May 12, the envoy assured his wife that the trip "is much more comfortable than I had anticipated. The ship is the object of constant comment from all the officers of the Air Transport Command. It is the consensus . . . that it is the finest, most comfortable and best airplane as well as the largest for use in luxurious travel. . . . I don't mind sleeping on the plane and manage to get in at least two or three hours of rest and sleep in the daytime."

By the time Joe arrived in Cairo on May 14, he was writing Marjorie that "While tired I feel pretty well. . . ." From Teheran Joe confessed that "all this, my beloved . . . has been so difficult, if only you had been 'along.' . . . It would have given color, girl, and . . . pleasure to what has otherwise been only a hard gruelling job. . . . I miss you my glorious . . . and beloved wife beyond and above words. . . ."

Although Joe's mission was to prove successful, the former ambassador's arrival in the USSR on May 19, 1943, created resentments in Moscow's American embassy. The current U.S. ambassador, William H. Standley, was, after all, already in residence at Spaso House and, as aides pointed out, could far more easily have delivered the letter to the Kremlin himself. Nevertheless, Standley held his temper, and on May 20, Stalin agreed to meet him and Davies at the Kremlin at 9:00 P.M. After a brief greeting to the Soviet premier, Standley tactfully took his leave, and for the next two and a half hours Davies explained FDR's position toward the Soviets.

The president, Davies said, was willing to accede at least in part to the USSR's claims on lands retained by Poland at the end of World War I—the so-called Curzon Line. Further, FDR had been contemplating the likely political balance in the postwar period and concluded that the United States and the USSR would be the world's wealthiest—and dominant—powers. Thus the two nations had the potential to create an atmosphere of international cooperation and permanent peace.

The length of the meeting itself, observed *Time* magazine several weeks later, "was an extraordinary honor for any visitor." Equally extraordinary was the meeting's outcome. As Davies spoke, Stalin sketched aimlessly upon a piece of paper. When Joe finished, the Soviet premier finally looked up from the desk. "I think your President is right. He is a great man. You may tell your President I will be very glad to meet with him." So conciliatory was Stalin that he even offered to meet the crippled FDR on American soil—either in Fairbanks or Nome, Alaska. Two days later Joe was given an elaborate state dinner by Stalin that lasted four and a half hours and included twenty-two dishes and nineteen toasts.

Before Joe's return to the United States, the Douglas Skymaster had been gaily decorated with the words *Mission to Moscow* painted in yellow in English and Russian. When the envoy arrived in Washington on June 3, he presented FDR with a letter from Stalin sealed in wax and an account of the premier's offer to meet him in Alaska. Virtually none of what was discussed, however, was publicly disclosed. The only thing Joe would say to the press was "There is every indication that all of the contents of the President's letter were entirely agreeable and that Mr. Stalin is completely in accord with its contents."

What was also kept confidential was that the mission had exacted a toll upon Joe's health. On May 28, on his way home from the USSR, he wrote Marjorie: "It was not surprising that I had to stay in bed Thursday. . . . Friday again I was laid up in bed. . . . I was unable to return his [Sir Archibald Kerr's] call because of illness."

Shortly after Joe's return, Marjorie whisked him away from Washington for a rest at one of her favorite American spas, the elegant Gideon Putnam Hotel in Saratoga Springs, New York.

Meanwhile, the spark of friendship that Davies had managed to kindle anew in Moscow exploded into a full-scale, less friendly conflagration in the United States. Months earlier, in an effort to bolster American confidence in the USSR, Davies had allowed Warner Bros. to make *Mission to Moscow* into a motion picture. Upon its release in the spring of 1943, some critics assailed the film as war propaganda and claimed that Hollywood had been goaded into the project by FDR. In early May *Time* characterized the movie as "Hollywood's most controversial film ever." Part of that controversy was engendered by the Office of War Information's endorsement of the motion picture, an endorsement given additional credence by Joe's personal appearance in the beginning of the film. To members of the State Department, Davies's cameo appearance, coupled with the movie's portrayal of the Stalin purges as a necessary evil, was nothing short of a travesty. *Mission to Moscow* was, said Chip Bohlen, Moscow embassy officer during Davies's tenure, "one of the most blatantly propagandistic pictures ever screened." During a private showing of the film for the Office of Strategic Services, Bohlen said he and other State Department staffers had "recorded sixty-seven factual errors."

When *Mission to Moscow* was finally shown to the public, Anne O'Hare McCormick of *The New York Times*, Manny Farber of *The New Republic*, and Dorothy Thompson of the *New York Post* sharply criticized it. Fifty-two educators, historians, writers, and trade union leaders sent a statement to the *Evening Star* contending that the movie was "the first full-dress example of the kind of propaganda movie hitherto confined to totalitarian countries . . . it falsifies history and glorifies dictatorship." Philosopher John Dewey and author Suzanne La Follette condemned the movie in a letter to *The New York Times* as the "first instance in our country of totalitarian propaganda for mass consumption." Roosevelt's enemies, among them the Republican National Committee, noting that film critics had denounced the movie as "phony propaganda," wondered if the New Deal had "implicated" itself by allowing Hollywood to make the picture in the first place.

A few voices did, nevertheless, praise the film, if not for its accuracy, then at least for the friendly feelings it was meant to engender between Americans and Soviets. "It is not necessary to agree with all of the Ambassador's findings," wrote a columnist for *The Saturday Review.* "But the work he has been doing to cement good feeling between Soviet Russia and ourselves deserves better...."

During his visit to Moscow, Joe had aired the film for Stalin and other high Kremlin officials at the state dinner given in his honor. The Soviet premier, Joe recalled, had particularly enjoyed Walter Huston as Davies; both Stalin and Molotov had been "warm in their congratulations." Despite subsequent reports in the U.S. press that Stalin had enjoyed the film "immensely," the American ambassador, William Standley, claimed that the Soviet premier had done little more than sip his champagne and grunt a few times and that he had left as soon as the screening ended. According to reports Chip Bohlen received from Moscow, Kremlin leaders were embarrassed by the movie. Even so, Stalin allowed *Mission to Moscow* to be distributed throughout the USSR, where it was greeted with wild enthusiasm. Suddenly Marjorie's and Joe's names became household words that were vitally linked to the Allies' struggle against fascism.

The return from the USSR, armed with Stalin's promise for a meeting with FDR and with *Mission to Moscow* in movie theaters from Kalamazoo to Kiev, found the former ambassador at the peak of his powers.

Davies's triumph was, however, to be short-lived. During his absence FDR had met with Churchill and British military chiefs of staff at the White House, in the Trident Conference of mid-May 1943. Despite Davies's warnings that still another cancellation of a second front might do irreparable harm to Stalin's faith in the Allies, Churchill persuaded FDR to postpone the opening of the second front again in favor of the long-planned invasion of Sicily.

In Moscow Stalin reacted to this latest slight by recalling his pro-Western ambassador, Ivan Maisky, from Great Britain. Nor did pro-American Soviet ambassador Maxim Litvinov, who had returned temporarily to Moscow that spring, reappear in Washington. After weeks of silence, on August 8, Stalin finally informed FDR that because of his involvement at the Russian front, he was unable to attend a face-to-face meeting with the president. The Soviet premier would, however, be happy to have either FDR or representatives from his country and the USSR meet in Astrakhan or Archangel. Stalin was also willing to have Churchill or his aides attend such a meeting.

To Davies and FDR, the Soviet premier's reaction was a slap in the face. Still, the prospect of a meeting of lower-level ministers of the Big Three in the summer of 1943 seemed better than nothing at all. The conference, which was ultimately held in Quebec from August 14 to 24, solved nothing. At its conclusion, FDR was still jockeying with Churchill for Stalin's trust and still uncertain about Soviet territorial claims after the war. For months thereafter Joe continued to press Roosevelt to concede the Curzon Line to Stalin as a condition for a three-power meeting. To encourage détente, he even went to Mexico City to meet with Konstantin Oumansky, then Soviet ambassador to Mexico.

Finally, in November 1943, FDR, Stalin, and Churchill met in Teheran. In private meetings the president assured Stalin that while he intended to honor some of the Soviet premier's claims for Polish territories that went back to the 1919 Curzon Line, a reelection year and the importance of the American Polish vote prevented him from granting Stalin all the disputed territories. By the end of that conference Churchill had promised to proceed with the long-awaited second front in France that spring. To FDR's way of thinking, as he subsequently wrote Stalin, the conference had been "an important milestone in the progress of human affairs."

With the achievements at Teheran, Joe's job as unofficial liaison between the White House and the USSR was finished. Thereafter, save for an attempt to extradite the Soviet defector Victor Kravchenko, Joe Davies faded from the international spotlight.

During the frenzied period of international intrigues that alternately thrilled and frustrated Joe during World War II, Marjorie maintained an image of composure and dignity. To the former ambassadress, her "Joey" remained a hero, albeit one who was often misunderstood by the American press, the State Department, and even, upon occasion, by President Roosevelt himself. Long before, Marjorie had learned to ignore negative press reports, no matter how scathing or critical.

Now, during the remaining war years, she devoted herself entirely to the Allied victory. When the United States declared war, Marjorie closed her house in Palm Beach. Her parties became benefits and fundraisers. In allegiance to the Office of Price Administration's slogan "Use it up, wear it out, make it do, or do without," menus were restricted to foods that could be purchased with ration tickets. When society reporter Betty Hynes of the *Washington Times-Herald* observed that a Tregaron benefit for the National Symphony reminded her of an earlier reception at the Davieses' estate on Foxhall Road, Marjorie quickly corrected her. "O yes, but this is different. . . . We can't do things that way any more. It's all going to be simple with its rationed menu."

However, even during periods of international crisis, the wealthy have always lived better than less privileged people, and Marjorie was no exception. During the war she was able to supplement her menus with extra milk, meat, and vegetables from the dairy farm and extensive victory gardens she maintained at her Long Island estate.

To save fuel, Marjorie also purchased a coach and two horses for transportation around Washington. But finding a driver for the quaint vehicle in 1943 was nearly impossible. To a snooping reporter from *The Washington Post* who disguised himself as a candidate for the job, Marjorie said, "I don't care what the coachman looks like, what color his skin is, I am just interested in knowing that he can drive and take care of the horses. I like riding in a carriage, did a lot of it years ago and most likely before your advent." Undoubtedly Marjorie must have remembered with nostalgia the stagecoach ride through England she had once enjoyed with C. W. Post.

Curiously, memories of Marjorie's father surfaced in another way, too, in 1944, when the U.S. Maritime Commission named a 10,500-ton Liberty ship in his honor. The dedication had come about at the recommendation of James Merrill, president of the St. Johns River Shipbuilding Company of Jacksonville, Florida. According to a General Foods press release, Merrill, long impressed with C.W.'s contribution to America's breakfast food industry and his creation of the model city Post, Texas, had decided to name a Liberty ship in his honor. Coincidentally, Jacksonville was the same port where the *Sea Cloud* docked in peacetime. Like other local residents, Merrill must have been familiar with the yacht and its owner.

While the *C. W. Post* was the 2,504th built by the U.S. Maritime Commission and the 68th created at the Jacksonville shipyard, its dedication was a moving moment for Marjorie. On November 8, 1944, she, her daughter Eleanor, and granddaughter Marwee arrived in Jacksonville for the christening.

As they stood on a tiny launching platform before the towering gray hull, Marjorie later recalled:

Through my mind ran a swift series of images—various tableau [*sic*] in the life of the man—my father, in whose memory this ship was being dedicated. . . . Mr. Merrill smiled, 'all set, Mrs. Davies,' he said. The silken enmeshed bottle crashed against the hull. Slowly the huge bulk began to move down the greased ways towards the quiet river water. The shipyard now accompanied by the voices of two impertinent tugboats in the river, became a steady drone. Faster and yet faster the C. W. POST traveled down its track. Suddenly there was a glistening spray of water. . . . At the same moment the entire C. W. POST was outlined by hundreds of electric lights. She stood reflected in the quieting waters of the river. The tugs hushed their crying and hastened to her side. . . . In only a few days, the POST will join similar ships—taking her place in the convoy line steaming to far-off ports.

For Marjorie, a family legacy had been fulfilled. A ship named after C. W. Post, pioneer of America's breakfast food industry, would now be carrying food and supplies to a younger generation of Americans who were pitted in the largest struggle for individual liberties that the world had ever known.

22

Transformations

*T*o Marjorie, as to the rest of America's civilian population that clamored to bring twelve million GIs "home alive in '45," the end of World War II was a vast relief. No longer were the great cities of North America blacked out at night. No longer was Washington a corridor for wounded veterans or coffins bound for Arlington National Cemetery. Ration tickets for gas, rubber, meat, and cheese disappeared. So did throngs of single women who had dominated the office buildings and restaurants. Songs like "We're the Janes Who Make the Planes" and "They're Either Too Young or Too Old" went out of fashion. In the factories and shipyards of North America, Rosie the Riveter relinquished her hard hat to returning "vets." In the last months of 1945 the national mood swung from war to love, marriage, and baby making, to the reestablishment of home and hearth as Americans had known them in the years before the war.

Marjorie was swept up in the mood. To her, finding happiness in love was one of life's greatest achievements, the sine qua non without which a woman could not be complete. Once the war ended, she became eager to help the single women in her acquaintance find mates. In that spirit Marjorie invited Alden Sibley to Topridge in the summer of 1945.

To Alden, there was nothing unusual about this invitation. The young army officer was not only the nephew to Pearcie—Adelaide's and Eleanor's old nurse—but was Marjorie's godson. From the time he had moved east from Nevada and become a West Point cadet, Alden was repeatedly invited to Marjorie's homes in Manhattan, the Adirondacks, and Palm Beach. What was unusual about Aunt Marjorie's invitation this time was that she asked Alden to stop at her Long Island estate on his way from Washington to the Adirondacks.

"Now, dear, will you get my car from Stanley at Hillwood and drive it up here for me? I need it," Marjorie had requested. "And after you get the car, can you pick up a friend for me, a widow?" Alden had dutifully agreed to both requests. Assuming Aunt Marjorie's friend was elderly, Alden drove to Bedford, New York, in his godmother's maroon and black Packard. To his surprise, the widow was an attractive young woman named Elvira "Ellie" Trowbridge. "The demon Marjorie had in the back of her mind a nefarious proposition!" Alden (later Major General Sibley) laughed years later. "She needed me to bring the car up there like a hole in the head."

To be polite, Alden offered to have Ellie sit in the back while he acted as her chauffeur. Amused, the young woman declined and instead rode with him in the front. By the time the couple reached Albany, they had become acquainted and were beginning to enjoy each other's company.

When they climbed out of Marjorie's enormous Packard and stopped at a roadside hotel for a Coke, people gaped. "We decided," said Ellie, giggling with the memory, "that they thought we were somebody's chauffeur and maid." The car, with its Rolls-Royce engine, maroon body, and black patent leather fenders, was, as Alden put it, "a breathtaker," and his delight in it was second only, at that moment, to his growing infatuation with his passenger.

Once they arrived at Topridge, Alden and Ellie were thrown together by their hostess at "every possible opportunity." After five days of swimming, canoeing, and hiking, Alden had to return to Washington. Nevertheless, he volunteered to drive Ellie back home to Bedford. The ever-tactful Marjorie said nothing. Ellie, however, was sure that her hostess must have "had her suspicions" about the couple's budding romance.

The introduction was a brilliant stroke. By November 1945 Ellie and Alden were married. "Marjorie was very pleased with her matchmaking," Ellie recalled. For a wedding present Marjorie gave Ellie a pair of sapphire earrings. And the following summer, when Marjorie again invited Alden and Ellie to Topridge, she insisted they stay at the camp's Honeymoon Cottage.

From the moment they were wed, Marjorie considered the Sibleys part of her family. Whenever they were in the States, she invited them to Washington and Palm Beach. On birthdays and anniversaries she sent them gifts. She asked Ellie to accompany her on cruises and to spas. Once, while renovating her new estate in Washington (the current Hillwood Museum), Marjorie gave the Sibleys its linenfold paneling for their Manhattan apartment. When Alden was stationed in France, she volunteered to keep the Sibleys' poodle, Cocoa. Later, when she learned the dog was getting old, she had a special screen made for his bed to keep out drafts. "That," said Ellie, "was the generous kind of thing Marjorie would do."

Even late in life Marjorie continued to take pride in the match. In the summer of 1970, when the Sibleys were visiting Topridge, Marjorie insisted that they stay again in the Honeymoon Cottage. While neither Ellie nor Alden had said a word, their hostess remembered that it had been twenty-five years since the couple met on the way to her Adirondacks camp.

Within a few months Marjorie celebrated another romance, this one within her immediate family. In January 1946 Dina became engaged. Her fiancé was a tall, handsome Yale graduate, the Colgate heir Stanley Rumbough, Jr. Years earlier, the youth had met Dina at Mar-A-Lago through one of his college roommates who was then her beau. Yet it was not until late 1945, when Stan was discharged from the Marines and Dina was back from the South Pacific, that the two met again. In January 1946 Stan had proposed, but the wedding was delayed until the Broadway show Dina was then in—*The Mermaids Singing*—closed.

To Marjorie, Dina's fiancé was an ideal prospective son-in-law: well bred, good-looking, and ambitious. "Mother," said Dina, "was crazy about him." And Stan returned the feeling. "She was a wonderful mother-in-law. I can't remember any episode whatsoever where I crossed swords with her or a time when she was not supportive or interested in what I was doing," he said.

What pleased Marjorie most of all at the time of the marriage was that Dina had agreed to give up the theater. "Mother didn't really discourage me or encourage me," said Dina, who had been acting in school plays since childhood. Still, when she announced her engagement and her intention to give up the theater, Marjorie exclaimed, "Thank God."

Years later Dina regretted her decision. Simultaneous with her engagement, the young actress had been offered a lead role in the Chicago road company production of John Van Druten's *The Voice of the Turtle*, but had turned it down. With Stan's daytime hours and her nocturnal ones, it seemed an unlikely schedule for a marriage. "I really didn't think I had any choice," said Dina. "The times were different, and also because of my parents' divorce, I was bound and determined that I was married for life."

The wedding underscored the bitterness of that divorce. While planning it, Marjorie vowed she would not attend the ceremony if E. F. Hutton was in the church. "Oh, it was awful," Dina recalled. For days she begged Marjorie to listen to reason. E.F. was, after all, her father, and Dina wanted him to walk her down the aisle and give her away. But much as she loved her beautiful daughter, Marjorie would not concede the point. What made it all the more ironic was that the heiress must have remembered her own feelings forty years earlier as a young bride about to marry Ed Close. On that occasion Marjorie's mother, Ella, had threatened to boycott the wedding if C.W. attended. Only at the end had Ella relented.

Ultimately, so would Marjorie, but only after Adelaide had sat her down and given her a "long talking-to" about what was proper. "All right, I'll be in church," Marjorie finally conceded, "but E.F. can't come to the reception." On that issue neither Adelaide nor Dina dared push their mother any further. "She was very resentful. Very resentful," Dina recalled. "I think she still had a sneaker for him, that's why. Well, he was the love of her life."

The wedding was held on March 24, 1946, at Trinity Church in Roslyn, Long Island, not far from Marjorie's country estate. "Miss Hutton," wrote society editor Margaret Hart of Washington's *Evening Star*, "made an exquisite picture as a bride. Her blonde loveliness was set off by her white satin gown and beautiful rose point veil that extended the length of her train. . . . The off-the-shoulder neckline followed the petals of appliquéd white satin flowers embroidered in pearls . . . clusters of tube roses formed her headdress and held her veil in place." The small reception was at Hillwood.

Although the wedding was scheduled to start at 4:00 P.M., the ceremony was delayed. Seventy-year-old and still handsome E.F. was apparently so nervous about the affair that he misunderstood the arrangements. Instead of arriving at Hillwood, which was only a few miles from his own estate, Hutfield, the former broker went directly to the church to wait for the bride. At Hillwood, meanwhile, Dina paced nervously about, waiting for her father's arrival. "Everybody had gone to church, and there I was in my wedding dress, wondering where was my father," Dina recalled. Finally E.F. called the house and was informed that the bride was waiting for him. "So poor Daddy climbed into the car and came bustling up and picked me up and took me down to the church."

Dina's wedding and the Sibleys' marriage were the first in a series of events that signaled the postwar return to "normalcy" in Marjorie's life. A third was Marwee's imminent graduation from high school. By adolescence Marjorie's oldest grandchild had blossomed into a statuesque blonde with extraordinary athletic skills.

What the pretty girl needed most of all, the heiress believed, was a sense of stability, an anchor to which she could tether her volatile disposition. "After high school my grandmother told me to get married, get a career, or go to college," Marwee said. Marjorie's preference was that her granddaughter marry and have a baby. Her annual question, according to Marwee, was "when I was going to give her a great-grandchild." Marjorie even offered to pay for full-time nannies and governesses if Marwee would wed and produce a baby.

But Marwee assiduously avoided any long-term commitment. Instead she elected her grandmother's third option. For several semesters she enrolled at the University of Southern California and swam competitively for the Los Angeles Athletic Club. Later, when Marwee no longer swam for that club, Marjorie hired a famous Oregon swimming coach for her granddaughter. Soon the training, combined with the young woman's natural athletic talent, began to pay off. By the early fifties Marwee was ranked by the Amateur Athletic Association as a world-class swimmer in the backstroke and a three-year champion for rough water. There was even talk of her competing in the Olympics.

But Marwee was restless. After an alleged involvement in a cheating scandal at USC, she transferred to the University of Miami, where she took courses and swam for two years. In between, Hollywood scouts began testing her for the movies and discovered she was photogenic. Eventually she appeared in small roles in six movies, including *Friendly Persuasion* with Anthony Perkins and Gary Cooper.

Still, nothing seemed to stick. By the early 1950s Marwee was back at USC to complete her degree. After her experiences in Hollywood she had all but forgotten her ambitions as a swimmer. The best thing, Marjorie decided, was for Marwee to get married. "At one point, when I complained that one of my boyfriends snored, my grandmother encouraged me to marry him anyway. She told me that if I did, she would build him a 'snoring' room next to Hillwood so I wouldn't be disturbed at night."

Nearly simultaneous with Marwee's final years of high school was the release of the *Sea Cloud* from naval service. To Marjorie's pride, the luxurious pleasure craft she and E.F. had designed fifteen years earlier had distinguished itself during the war as a sturdy and heroic ship. From 1942 to 1944 the *Sea Cloud*, painted battleship gray and stripped of its masts and sails, had served as a U.S. Coast Guard convoy weather ship sailing from the Azores to Greenland. It also made runs to Murmansk, Russia, where, despite Nazi U-boat activity in the North Atlantic, it escaped unharmed.

Although the boat was deep within "submarine wolf pack country" it may have been saved, according to its captain, Lieutenant Commander Carlton D. Skinner, because the "Germans were trying to break our weather code and may have been content to leave us alone and listen." Later, in June 1944, the yacht served in the Battle of Normandy, where it destroyed one German submarine and assisted in the sinking of a second.

That fall, when the Navy completed construction on a series of specially built weather boats, the *Sea Cloud* was decommissioned. James Forrestal, secretary of the navy, wrote Marjorie: "It will no doubt be a matter of pride . . . to you to know that the *Sea Cloud* gave valuable and excellent service in the important duties assigned to her, thus contributing greatly to the successful prosecution of the war effort." In recognition of its service, the secretary awarded the *Sea Cloud* five chevrons to be placed on its stack near the bridge to represent each six months of service to the U.S. Navy.

By the time the *Sea Cloud* was returned to civilian waters in July 1945, the U.S. Navy had partially restored it to its former condition by replacing the wood paneling and gold bathroom fixtures in the staterooms. Still, war service had taken a toll upon the luxury ship. The placement of gun mounts on the teakwood decks of the *Sea Cloud* had destroyed its intricate rigging system. Its four stately masts, the largest of which towered 190 feet in the air, had been removed for military service and had to be replaced. So did the *Sea Cloud's* 55,000 square feet of custom-made sail and eight miles of rope. Even the frame of Marjorie's antique painting of the frigate SS *Constitution*, which hung over the mantel in the yacht's living room, was filled with dart holes.

When the newly decommissioned *Sea Cloud* first pulled into port in Alexandria, Virginia, Marjorie and Joe were so thrilled that they immediately planned a cruise to the Caribbean. Another year went by, however, before they could undertake that journey because they were unable to purchase enough rope and sail to restore the square rigger to its prewar condition.

Money had nothing to do with it. Business was booming at General Foods with net sales of $330 million and profits of $18 million in 1946. In the immediate postwar period Birds Eye products were becoming increasingly profitable. Moreover, major oil reserves had been discovered on C.W.'s old properties in Texas. Ultimately the *Sea Cloud* cost $3 million to renovate, a sum that came out of Marjorie's own pocket.

Yet availability of yacht supplies was something that no amount of cash could buy. On June 4, 1946, Marjorie pasted a picture of the unmasted *Sea Cloud* into her scrapbook. "Our beloved 'Sea Cloud' arriving home to her family after her tour or duty for the war," she wrote. Two pages later she had fastened another picture of the *Sea Cloud* in its prime. "Some day again, she will look like this ——, but we can't get the 8 miles of rope needed for rigging," she wrote on the opposite page. It was not, in fact, for another ten months, until April 1947, that Marjorie and Joe again enjoyed the *Sea Cloud* in its prewar glory. By then the yacht had been fully restored to its original splendor, its masts, sails, ropes, and rigging replaced.

In celebration Marjorie and Joe hosted a cocktail party aboard the *Sea Cloud* for guests that included Mr. and Mrs. Alfons Landa, Mr. and Mrs. Harold Fitzgerald, Mrs. Joseph W. Wear, Hugh Dillman, and Joe's son-in-law and daughter Senator and Mrs. Millard Tydings. A day or two later the Davieses slipped out of the port of Palm Beach on the yacht for a trip to the West Indies.

"This initial journey is merely a 'shake-down' cruise," Marjorie explained to a cortege of newspaper reporters. What she did not mention was that the trip was also a family reunion, a chance for Marwee, Eleanor Tydings, Dina, Stan Rumbough, and the Rumboughs' new baby (also called Stan) to enjoy the palatial yacht that had long been one of Marjorie's favorite homes.

Nor did the former ambassadress disclose that the cruise would retrace part of the journey she and Joe had taken on their honeymoon eleven years earlier. That the war and its aftermath had exacted nearly as severe a toll on the Davieses' marriage as it had on the *Sea Cloud* was something Marjorie was not yet ready to acknowledge. "Mother was funny, she never showed things like that," Adelaide explained. Instead she either braved them out herself or discussed them with her Christian Science practitioners. More often than not, what was recommended was a positive attitude. "Mother used to say that you get out of life what you put in, and if you put joy and love and friendship and warmth into your life, you get back the same kind of thing. If you go around with a sour attitude and a sour face, you'll probably get sour lemons back," recalled Dina.

Strains were already obvious in the relationship. At times Joe was unaccountably short-tempered. He could also be overbearing, particularly about what he considered "proper" for Marjorie's children and grandchildren. Less than two weeks after his marriage to Marjorie, he had already tangled with her two eldest daughters. When Eleanor stopped by to visit her mother at East Ninety-second Street, Joe lectured the then thrice-married young woman about "what she should and should not do." A few minutes later Adelaide arrived at 2 East Ninety-second Street, where she found her sister in tears. When she learned about Joe's heavy-handed approach, Adelaide was, as she put it, "ready for blood. I told him off right in front of Mother. His parting remark was 'Someday you will find I'm your best friend.' That didn't endear him to me in any way."

Later, during the war years, he criticized Dina because of what he considered the "ordinary" quality of the people she brought home as her friends. Dina's profound dislike for Joe was, according to her sister Adelaide, one of the reasons that she went into the theater at such an early age. "Deenie started to go to summer theater to get away from him," Adelaide observed.

On several occasions Joe also scoffed at Marwee's desire to become an athlete. Once, after he told the young woman that it was not ladylike to be a swimmer, she retorted that "it was better than becoming my first choice, which was a track and field star and letting the hair grow under my arms." Appalled, Joe almost left the table. Later, when Marwee did take up competitive swimming and was participating in the nationals, she claimed that Joe continually "put my swimming down to my grandmother."

Long after Joe Davies's death his grandson Joe Tydings admitted there was some truth to reports that Davies behaved dictatorially to Marjorie's staff. "Well, Granddad could be a little unrealistic, I guess, and, you know, irascible as he got older," said Joe Tydings. "And my mother was very upset with him that he would be critical of Mummyda's [Marjorie's] children." As the former ambassador aged, he became ill and, as Eleanor Tydings put it, was "not as pleasant as he always had been."

Moreover, Joe's passion for Marjorie was gradually assuming an alarmingly possessive quality. Often he accused Marjorie of flirting with other men when she was simply making conversation. One of the most memorable arguments was occasioned by Marjorie's and Joe's attendance at a war bond rally at Madison Square Garden where steel magnate Henry Kaiser was the keynote speaker. At the end of the rally Kaiser passed by the Davieses' box, and Marjorie leaned over to shake his hand and congratulate him. By the time the Davieses got home, Joe was steaming. "I was kept up half the night wrangling over this: that I was making a pass at Kaiser," Marjorie recalled.

Still, the many years of happiness Marjorie had enjoyed with Joe were not something she would easily dismiss. Only a few years earlier, in December 1939, she had written in her scrapbook, "Three joyous happy busy years, the best of all my life. How blessed I am to have found Joe." The memory of those attentions was not something to be casually tossed aside, especially for a woman, even an enormously wealthy one, who had already been twice divorced.

Moreover, Joe's deteriorating behavior had coincided with other stresses in his life: declining health and declining respect for his advocacy of the importance of the Soviet Union for world peace. With Roosevelt's April 1945 death and Harry Truman's ascendancy to the presidency, Joe's role as a liaison between the White House and Moscow was suddenly called into question. The subsequent free fall from presidential grace in 1945 and 1946 was understandably traumatic, a disappointment that Marjorie doubtless took into account.

It was true that within two weeks of taking office, Truman had consulted Joe about the Russians, but the new president was poorly informed about FDR's view of a postwar world dominated by the United States and the USSR. Neither was he aware of the discussions that had taken place at Yalta, where the USSR had agreed to accept Anglo-American influence in Italy and Greece in exchange for a Soviet presence in Poland.

Prompted by hard-liners like Averell Harriman and Secretary of State Edward Stettinius, Truman greeted Vyacheslav Molotov politely at the White House on April 24, 1946, but with the avowed purpose of setting guidelines. This first official meeting between the two men ended on a sour note when Truman bluntly insisted that the Soviets relinquish control of the Polish government. "I have never been talked to like that in my life," an appalled Molotov said at the time.

After that meeting Truman listened anxiously to Davies's analysis of Soviet fears about a postwar alliance between the United States and Great Britain. Now that the president had won the respect of the Soviets, Joe diplomatically coached Truman, it was necessary for him to "command their confidence as well" by treating them with "reciprocity and respect." Thereafter, Chip Bohlen noted, Truman "tended to ease up on the Soviets and rejected Churchill's power-politics approach to diplomacy."

During that spring Davies counseled Truman about the Soviets, emphasizing their heroic sacrifice of millions of soldiers against the Nazis and their fears that the United States and Great Britain were conspiring against them. To straighten out any misunderstandings, Truman finally suggested that Davies make a third trip to Russia. But the former ambassador would not risk it. Earlier that spring he had been so ill with digestive problems that he had been hospitalized. Instead Davies agreed to send Stalin a personal telegram suggesting that he meet with Truman separately, before a meeting of the Big Three could occur.

Churchill, who was facing general elections in July 1945, became nearly apoplectic when he heard about those proposed meetings, but finally he agreed to a mid-July meeting in Potsdam. There it was decided that Truman, Stalin, and Churchill would meet informally in private discussions before the official sessions between the Big Three began. Temporarily, at least, Davies had achieved his goal of bringing Truman together with Stalin, in much the same way that he had negotiated for FDR's meeting with the Soviet premier in Teheran.

And for that contribution the president was grateful. In fact, Truman now insisted that Davies be present at the Potsdam Conference. His presence, according to Davies's biographer, Elizabeth Kimball MacLean, was an implicit "symbol of the American effort to cooperate with the Soviets and [he served] as a personal channel of communication to the Soviet delegation."

Other statesmen were considerably less enthusiastic about Davies's appearance at Potsdam. Shortly after his arrival Secretary of State James Byrnes told the former ambassador that some officials were disgruntled that the Potsdam meeting had been achieved through Davies rather than through official government representatives. That night, after arranging Truman's first meeting with Stalin on July 17, Joe

asked the president about the propriety of his presence at the conference. Truman assured Davies that from his perspective at least, the former ambassador was a critical element in the conference, one he
depended upon to represent FDR's thinking.

The next day another salvo was fired at Davies. This one issued from
Averell Harriman, then ambassador to the USSR, who venomously observed that it was preferable for Truman to work through him, rather
than through Davies, who, after all, was only an unofficial liaison to
the Soviets. Just as coolly Davies responded that he had come to Potsdam as a presumably positive influence, one who was meant to stop
any further erosion in Soviet-American relations. After a bitter inter-
change in which Harriman denied the implication that he had a hostile
attitude toward the Soviets, the meeting ended abruptly.

A chastened Davies consequently sat near Truman during the thirteen plenary sessions and rarely spoke aloud. Although he occasionally
offered the president his opinion and encouraged a friendly attitude
toward the Russians, Davies's role at Potsdam was minor; primarily he
was a behind-the-scenes facilitator for Soviet-American meetings.

Nor did Davies leave the conference with a sense that the key issues
had been satisfactorily resolved, despite the fact that Truman seemed
genuinely pleased with what had been accomplished.

During Potsdam the United States had successfully exploded its first
atom bomb at a remote New Mexico test site. Through most of the
negotiations Truman was considering using the bomb to end the war in
the Pacific. To Davies the use of nuclear weapons had momentous
ramifications for world peace. Was it not, he finally asked Secretary of
State Byrnes, in the best interests of the United States and the USSR to
come to terms at Potsdam about the future of their use? Byrnes dismissed Davies's idea as premature.

That summer Joe tried again to gain Truman's ear. From Topridge
the former ambassador extended an invitation to the president to join
him and Marjorie in the Adirondacks. "Do come if you can, and bring
your own crowd," Davies wrote him. But Truman did not accept.

Finally, on September 29, the frustrated Davies wrote the president
a long memo, pleading for the continuation of a conciliatory attitude
toward the Soviets in the interests of long-term peace. Above all, Truman should consider a "spheres of influence" policy for Europe; such a
concept, Davies argued, would give the USSR the sense of security it
desperately needed on its borders.

For a few months Davies's viewpoint seemed about to prevail. In December 1945, at the second meeting of foreign ministers established by the Potsdam Conference, James Byrnes agreed to allow the Soviets to sponsor the governments of Romania and Bulgaria in return for American influence in Japan.

Byrnes's victory was short-lived. Truman, infuriated that his secretary of state conceded to the Russians without his clearance, declared in a letter that he was "tired of babying the Soviets." By early 1946, despite earlier promises to the contrary, the Soviets had still not withdrawn their troops from Iran. They had also reneged on a promise to retire from the government of Azerbaijan. The coup de grâce came on February 9, 1946, when, in a radio broadcast from Moscow, Stalin warned of an irreconcilable clash between capitalism and communism and the inevitability of another war.

From Moscow on February 15 George Kennan sounded an alarm. In what later became famous as "the long telegram"—an eight-thousand-word cable dictated in five parts to the Department of State—Kennan testified to the intractability of Soviet ideology and to that government's resolve to destroy the capitalistic system. The solution was "long-term, patient, but firm and vigilant containment of Russian expansive tendencies." Years later Kennan wrote in his memoirs: "Had the message come six months earlier, it would probably have been received in the Department of State with raised eyebrows. . . . Six months later, it would probably have sounded redundant." But coming as it did at the crest of American discontent with the Communists, Kennan's analysis was widely circulated in Washington.

On February 27 the ranking Republican of the Senate Foreign Relations Committee, Arthur Vandenberg of Michigan, railed against Soviet behavior in Europe and Asia and demanded that the United States "draw the line" with the Russians.

A week later, after being introduced by Truman, Churchill told an audience at Westminster College in Fulton, Missouri, that "from Stettin in the Baltic to Trieste in the Adriatic an iron curtain has descended across the Continent. Behind that line all the capitals of the ancient states of Central and Western Europe, Warsaw, Berlin, Prague, Vienna, Budapest, Belgrade, Bucharest and Sofia . . . and all are subject in one form or another, not only to Soviet influence, but to a very high . . . and increasing measure of control from Moscow."

The influence of the Communist parties of Eastern Europe and their attempts to seize totalitarian power, he added, had resulted in a political situation that was "certainly not the Liberated Europe we fought to build up. Nor is it one which contains the essentials of permanent peace."

By then neither Washington nor the American public gave heed any longer to Joe's plea for cooperation with the Soviets. Truman himself now adopted a tougher approach, first by sending part of the Sixth Fleet to the Black Sea, then by threatening to dispatch combat soldiers. That spring the president also presented the United Nations with an atomic energy control plan. Only if the USSR promised to cease work on atomic energy would the United States relinquish its atomic arsenal.

As tensions mounted between the United States and the USSR in the ensuing cold war, a pro-Soviet stance came to be considered treasonous to the American way of life. *Communism* became a dirty word. In 1947 and 1948 the House Un-American Activities Committee conducted hearings to expose Communist influence upon American life. In his inauguration day speech on January 20, 1949, Truman asserted that "actions resulting from Communist philosophy are a threat to the efforts of free nations to bring about world recovery and lasting peace." In 1949 eleven leaders of America's Communist party were tried and sentenced to prison.

By the end of the decade Joe Davies had good reason to feel discouraged and depressed.

Knowing that, Marjorie remained keenly sympathetic to Joe and tolerant of his moods. To her children and closest friends, she revealed nothing. With time and kindness, the optimistic Marjorie hoped that Joe would become philosophical about his fall from political grace.

Meanwhile, sixty-year-old Marjorie began to look to other aspects of her life for happiness. In the immediate postwar years that meant expanding activities that had always given her pleasure: friendships, philanthropy, and family.

In the winter of 1948 Marjorie was chairman of the "New Look Ball" for the Everglades Club on behalf of the Good Samaritan Hospital. The March 19 affair was not only festive but profitable, raising $176,000 from a "Chinese auction." One of the fund-raiser's subcommittees was headed by Wallis Windsor, who, a few days later, showed up with her husband, the duke of Windsor, at the *Sea Cloud.* To the astonishment of Palm Beach gossipers, the royal couple's arrival was not merely for a luncheon but for a cruise on the *Sea Cloud.*

Later the duke wrote Joe that "words are quite inadequate in trying to thank you and Mrs. Davies for the wonderful time you gave us. . . . The Duchess and I could not have enjoyed the cruise more, whether at sea especially under sail or ashore in Nassau and Havana. It was an ideal combination of rest and quiet and then the interest and excitement of visiting the historic and picturesque capital of Cuba for the first time. You are both perfect hosts and I derived great stimulation from our talks. . . . Your charming hospitality will always be a high spot in my memories."

What was left unmentioned was Wallis's previous good deed for Marjorie's granddaughter Marwee. Just a few months earlier Marwee had been expelled from the Mount Vernon Seminary. Marjorie was so disgusted that she considered sending Marwee back to her father, Tim Durant, in Beverly Hills. But at a New York restaurant the duchess had spent time talking with the unhappy girl. Later, when the duchess was alone with Marjorie, she praised Marwee's attributes to her hostess. "As a result, my grandmother was so proud she reconsidered and said I could try to finish school again," Marwee recalled.

That same February Marjorie and Joe sailed south toward South America, crossed through the Panama Canal, and stopped in the Dominican Republic. There Rafael Trujillo gave his old attorney friend and wife a royal reception. Parties were hosted on their behalf, the symphony orchestra gave a special concert, and Marjorie was presented with the Order of Duarte, the same honor presented to Joe a dozen years earlier on his honeymoon trip with Marjorie.

In the postwar era the sponsorship of cultural events—music, art, and dance—was to assume increasing importance in Marjorie's life. But in order to cultivate those interests, Marjorie felt that she had to be rooted in one place: her adopted hometown, Washington.

Shortly after the Davieses had purchased Tregaron, Marjorie decided to sell her Manhattan apartment. To do so during the war was nearly impossible. By 1944 the newspapers noted that Marjorie's enormous triplex was essentially a white elephant that had been vacant and unused for most of the year. "The largest and probably the most luxurious apartment known to realty men—an imposing fifty-four room suite at 1107 Fifth Avenue, corner of Ninety-second street—is available for rent, in case anyone is interested," announced *The New York Times* in March 1944.

The lack of interest in a sale was attributed to changing times—specifically higher taxes, restricted incomes, and the servant problem.

Exactly what effect the story had upon Marjorie's decision to sell her apartment after the war is not clear. But the *Times* had pinpointed her feelings about its obsolescence with deadly accuracy.

By late 1946 Marjorie's children were grown and married. Her permanent residence was in Washington with Joe. Although she needed a place to stay when she came to New York for General Foods meetings, there was no need for fifty-four rooms. A more practical solution was the rental of an apartment at Manhattan's luxurious Sherry-Netherland Hotel.

In the same period, and for similar reasons, Marjorie saw no need to continue to maintain her Long Island estate, Hillwood. The heiress had retained the home until Dina's 1946 marriage, but thereafter the 122-acre estate was seldom used. Coincidental with Marjorie's desire to sell the property was a search by the trustees of Long Island University for a new site. A mere year after World War II, returning GIs were marrying and producing babies so rapidly that real estate developers began snatching up parcels of land in Long Island upon which to erect suburban homes, schools, and shopping centers.

By late 1946 the trustees of Long Island University decided that Marjorie's Hillwood was an ideal site for expansion of their Brooklyn campus. The property was centrally located, just off the old Hempstead Highway, and accessible to public transportation. Moreover, the residential buildings were in fine condition and could easily be converted into classrooms. The estate also had a swimming pool, sports fields, stables, and greenhouses. And with rolling hills and woods that extended over 122 acres, there was plenty of room for future expansion.

Nor was the trustees' decision to convert Marjorie's Gold Coast estate into an educational institution an unprecedented idea. By the late 1940s the era of pre–income tax abundance that had given rise to Long Island's mansions and elite sporting fields had ended. In its place was something the owners of the Gold Coast mansions had always deplored: an influx of the middle and working classes. For decades the barons of Long Island had protected themselves from these populations with thickly wooded buffer zones, servants, high walls, watchdogs, and guards.

By 1946 the sheer number of returning World War II veterans had created a national housing shortage. In the fifteen years between the onset of the Depression and the end of the war, thousands of young people had postponed marriage, and now they were making up for it with a vengeance. In 1946 alone, there were 2.2 million weddings in the United States, twice as many as in any other peacetime year. In 1947 a record 3.3 million babies were born.

This latest incarnation of the working and middle classes was thus an eager crop of returning veterans with brides and infants—either in tow or in the making—whose homes and college educations would be subsidized by the new GI Bill. To the landed gentry of Long Island's Gold Coast, there was little to be done about the influx except retreat behind the stone walls of their mansions.

On June 12, 1947, Long Island University signed a contract to purchase Marjorie's estate at an alleged price tag of $200,000. The moment word got out that Marjorie was planning to sell Hillwood to a university, a "vocal minority" of the town of Oyster Bay's residents protested. Their fear, according to Long Island University president Tristram Walker Metcalf, was that the tranquillity of Oyster Bay would be shattered by an influx of "Brooklynites," a code word for populations of largely poor or minority students who frequented that borough. Moreover, the same protesters discovered that by a quirk in zoning regulations, while the old Hillwood estate could be turned into a school or a college, there was no provision for its becoming a "university." To resolve the issue, it was necessary for the Oyster Bay zoning board to hold a special meeting.

On the eve of the July 10 hearing, tempers were running so high that the beleaguered Metcalf told *The New York Times:* "We are an American institution and conduct ourselves in the American way. We will graciously accept the judgment of the community. Maybe we are wrong, thinking that our institution would be a worth-while addition to Oyster Bay. But before we decide that Oyster Bay does not want us we would like to know how most of you feel about us."

More than one thousand residents turned out for the July 10 meeting, which lasted until 2:00 A.M. So heated was the hearing, and so thorny the issue, that a second hearing was scheduled for later in the month. On July 31 the zoning board came to a decision. A variance would be granted so that Long Island University could acquire Hillwood for the use of Long Island students and veterans returning to school. Within a few days of the Oyster Bay zoning board decision, the protesters found other loopholes. The fight to turn Hillwood over to Long Island University dragged on for another four years.

During the controversy Marjorie remained silent, assiduously avoiding newspaper reporters, who clamored for quotes about the disposition of her old estate. Her behavior implied that Marjorie was annoyed by the snobbery of her old neighbors, just as she had been years earlier when snubbed by the relatives of Ed Close.

Even so, the usually conservative Marjorie was gambling with slippery social chips. Many of her friends still lived on Long Island's Gold Coast when they were not in residence in Palm Beach. It was people of her own "class" that Marjorie was theoretically threatening by the sale of Hillwood to Long Island University.

Publicly Marjorie sidestepped the issue by turning it over to her attorneys and financial managers, but privately she ordered those same men to continue the fight for Long Island University. In the interim, Marjorie turned her attention wholly to Washington, where she refined her role as one of that town's most dazzling, democratic, and original hostesses.

23

The Duchess
of the District of Columbia

*I*n postwar Washington one of the most coveted events of the social season was an invitation to a Marjorie Davies garden party. "That was one of the most glamorous things that happened every year," recalled Lady Bird Johnson, who was then a junior congressman's wife. "I was delighted to be invited. It was a signal to buy a new hat, a fancy hat."

Already by the end of the war Marjorie was widely recognized as one of Washington's social arbiters, a hostess whose invitations to the powerful—and would-be powerful—members of the political community were an important seal of approval. To young congressional wives like Lady Bird, Marjorie was a legendary figure whose bearing and behavior could only be described as regal. Lady Bird's first impression was that Marjorie was "sort of a duchess." And over the years that first impression never wavered. "She was very erect, had beautiful white hair which she wore mostly up in soft curls around her face," recalled Lady Bird. "She looked like she was just ready to have her portrait painted practically every time I saw her."

When Lady Bird and Lyndon Johnson were invited to their first dinner party at Tregaron, they were both impressed by Marjorie's aristocratic aura. As the Johnsons walked into the dining room, they were stunned to see that the table was large enough to seat one hundred guests. "And it was set with gold plates, knives, forks, spoons, the whole array of implements. Gold! My eyes were out on stems," said the future first lady. In the hall was a "heroic"-size, beautifully executed portrait of Marjorie by Frank O. Salisbury. The whole house, with its priceless French and Russian antiques, tapestries, and furnishings, was nothing short of a "dream."

Lady Bird and Lyndon Johnson were not the only ones who were awed. By the late forties all of Washington was fascinated by the patrician atmosphere Marjorie had created at Tregaron. Even the president and his wife were impressed. "Dear Mrs. Davies," wrote Bess Truman from the White House after a dinner party at Tregaron. "I can't tell you how greatly Harry and I enjoyed your and Mr. Davies' delightful dinner for us. . . . It was extremely kind of you to do that for us and it is an evening we shall long remember with the greatest pleasure.

"Thank you sounds very mild and meager, but I don't know any other way of saying it."

It was upon the judgment of her gardening that Marjorie's legendary garden parties hinged. Perfectionist that she was, the hostess expected to hold her outdoor parties at the peak of the spring bloom. To do so, she consulted head gardener Hugh McRae, who in turn looked to nature itself for the answers. Everything depended upon when Tregaron's solitary yellow dogwood came into full bloom. Thirty days later, according to McRae, the garden would be at its peak. With that date in mind, Marjorie sent out invitations for the two garden parties she hosted each spring.

Occasionally the timing was off. In the spring of 1948 the yellow dogwood burst into bloom on February 14, but for the next six weeks the weather turned so cold that the garden failed to flower on schedule. Marjorie seldom left things to chance. The same woman who had "lifeboats for her lifeboats" also had rainy-day flowers for her garden parties. When it poured for the first of Marjorie's 1950 outdoor parties, guests spent time indoors admiring the Davieses' art collection and a profusion of orchids, lilies, and pink flowering cactus blossoms that decorated Tregaron's sunroom and other parts of the house.

In her quest for the ideal, Marjorie was no less precise about the quality of her refreshments. One of the staples of her garden party was fresh strawberries, served in silver bowls with powdered sugar and whipped cream. The fruit, Marjorie insisted, had to be flawless. So did the lemonade and the macaroons. Years later Fred Korth, former secretary of the navy and Marjorie's last beau, recalled that the day of a garden party, the hostess "tested out the macaroons herself" with painstaking care. If, when dropped from a certain height onto a dish, the macaroons failed to land a certain way, Marjorie proclaimed them unsatisfactory. "Take them away," she would tell her staff.

Oddly enough, in spite of Marjorie's extensive travels and acquaintance with international leaders, she never lost her nasal midwestern twang. At times, to the amusement of Washington's people watchers, she peppered her speech with down-home phrases and even expletives. The first time journalist Liz Carpenter interviewed Marjorie she was struck by the incongruity of sitting in the former ambassadress's eighteenth-century French drawing room and hearing her use expressions like *golly* and *gosh* and *gee whiz*. Others, like family friend George Floyd, were similarly amused to hear Marjorie greet Mrs. Floyd as "Possum" as she walked across a tapestried hall filled with exquisitely gowned and bejeweled guests.

Nor, according to other Washington friends, like Anne Frailey Braverman, did Marjorie put on airs. Behind the glittering aura that enveloped the heiress and contributed to her sometimes "remote" image was a warm person whose naturalness won her many friends.

"She was very open," observed Anne Frailey Braverman. "She didn't pretend. For instance, if a guest admired a plate at the table, and it was an imitation, she would admit it. She was also open about her clothes. If someone complimented her on a dress, she would tell them what dressmaker made it."

Some of Marjorie's ingenuousness spilled over into an occasionally risqué sense of humor. Once, for instance, when a friend expressed horror that a woman of their mutual acquaintance had received an overly generous settlement from a divorce, the heiress had defended the divorcée. "Why, she deserves it!" Marjorie exclaimed. "Just imagine sleeping with that man every night!" Another time in a restaurant, when a waiter appeared at the table with an enormous pepper mill, Marjorie, thinking about her niece Barbara Hutton's latest marriage, exclaimed, "That's the Porfirio Rubirosa of pepper mills." A third time, when a taxidermist in the Adirondacks asked Marjorie whether she wanted a male and female monkey mounted for her display at Topridge, Marjorie quipped, "No, just shaking hands!"

Still another time, while shopping in Saks, Marjorie, realizing she had very little money with her, summoned her chauffeur. "Jimmy," she asked, knowing he traveled with large bills, "can you lend me some money?" In response, the chauffeur opened his trousers to get to his money belt. "My, my, Jimmy what are you doing? I'm only looking for money!" she cracked.

The informality of the summers at Topridge also revealed Marjorie's love of entertaining. One of her favorite Adirondacks rituals was the portage—a combination canoe trip and hike that took her and her guests through seven nearby lakes, culminating in a grand cookout. After a meal of grilled steak, ham sandwiches, and salads, the dessert traditionally consisted of Adirondacks pie—a huge batch of pancakes covered with maple sugar and syrup. At night there were occasional surprise costume parties and other group games.

As a midwesterner growing up in the late nineteenth century, C.W.'s daughter had probably been introduced to square dancing as a child. With the exception of one "barn dance" she hosted as a Greenwich matron, Marjorie seems to have avoided square dancing altogether for many years. Instead she devoted herself to ballroom dancing. Long after her childhood lessons at Professor Irwin's school in Battle Creek, Marjorie continued to improve her ballroom-dancing technique, and while still married to Ed Close, she learned the tango. That sexy South American dance was, in fact, her favorite. "If anybody could tango with her, she was happy as could be," said her daughter Adelaide. Once, while vacationing at the Virginia resort The Homestead, Marjorie created a sensation on the dance floor doing the tango with John D. Rockefeller. As dance styles changed and new dances like the samba and rumba appeared, Marjorie quickly learned them. To speed the process, she hired teams of dance instructors for Mar-A-Lago and Topridge to teach her and her friends the latest steps.

One of those teams was George and Elizabeth Montgomery, who first arrived at The Breakers in 1949 and were hired by Marjorie that same winter. "At that time she'd have two dances a week at Mar-A-Lago, one on Wednesdays and the other on Saturdays," recalled Elizabeth Montgomery. On those nights guests arrived at the estate at seven for drinks and dinner. Included in the guest list were the Montgomerys and several other instructors who were subtly "tagged" with identification buttons but mingled freely with Marjorie's guests. After dinner footmen rolled up the rugs and a small orchestra appeared. As the music began and couples moved out onto the dance floor, the Montgomerys and their staff invited guests to dance. Should someone be unfamiliar with a step or a new dance, he or she received an on-the-spot dancing lesson.

For years Marjorie followed a similar routine at Topridge with dancers from the local Arthur Murray school. As a result, nearly every youngster in Marjorie's family became a good dancer. Even Marjorie's stepchildren benefited. "You learned to dance. I learned to do the Viennese waltz the way the Viennese men would do it. Because of Mummyda, I'm a damn good dancer [today]," recalled Marjorie's stepgrandson, Joe Tydings.

After the war Marjorie had begun to tire of the traditional dinner and ballroom dancing routine. Yet the newest dances of the youth—the jitterbugs of early rock and roll—did not quite suit the spirit of the sixty-three-year-old socialite. By the summer of 1950, Marjorie had a new idea—the introduction of a "round and square" dance—ballroom music that alternated with square dancing. At Camp Topridge, the idea had been an immediate hit. To the folksy, fast-talking drawl of a square dance caller, the "sober-faced" secretary of agriculture Charles F. Brannan had amazed his friends with the lithesome way he "swung his partner" around the dance floor at Topridge's main lodge. Associate Justice Tom Clark "grinned and sashayed with Texas know-how" along with guests General Wade Hampton Haislip, Virgil Petersen, Max Truitt, and Jack Logan.

Square dancing subsequently became so popular that Marjorie integrated it into the normal flow of her Washington parties. Thereafter rarely a week went by in Marjorie's life without a "round and square" dance at one of her estates. Sometimes the "round" part—ballroom dancing—was left out entirely. To highlight the informal spirit, Marjorie appeared in a full skirt and peasant blouse. Accordingly, invitations were issued to guests suggesting "day dress" or "square dance costume." Before long Marjorie's women friends were appearing in cotton dresses or peasant skirts and blouses, while the men, grateful to toss their dinner jackets aside, donned brightly colored shirts, bow ties, and lavalieres.

Over the next two decades innumerable Washington politicians, diplomats, and "cave dwellers" hopped, shuffled, and do-si-doed at Marjorie's square dance parties. Among them were luminaries like General Anthony "Nuts" McAuliffe, Lady Lewis, Billie Burke, Clark and Marney Clifford, Senator and Mrs. William Fulbright, Prince and Princess di Bisignano, the Hubert Humphreys, the Drew Pearsons, Serge Obolensky, General Omar Bradley, Mrs. Robert Guggenheim, Admiral and Mrs. Lewis Straus, and Sherman Adams. The square dances began at 7:00 P.M. sharp with a dinner buffet. At 11:00 P.M., after soft drinks, cider, and cookies, the party—like all of Marjorie's affairs—came to an abrupt end.

. . .

When she held square dances at Tregaron, Marjorie took special precautions. Noticing that the estate's fine hardwood floors were torn up by women's heels after a square dance, Marjorie left a large bowl of heel covers in the front hall. To accommodate the various shades of her guests' shoes, the hostess had these made either in black or white. Not everyone understood what they were. On one occasion a male guest, mistaking them for candy, dug his hand into the bowl and, after pulling out a black heel cover, promptly popped it into his mouth. "I just love licorice," he said enthusiastically.

In time nearly everyone in Marjorie's acquaintance—not only Washington's best and brightest but Marjorie's friends, daughters, sons-in-law, and grandchildren—learned to square-dance. "I must say I don't think a single daughter or granddaughter liked square dancing, but we all did it," admitted Marjorie's granddaughter Melissa MacNeille Cantacuzene. There were others in Washington who undoubtedly felt the same way. By the late fifties, Marjorie's square dances had become so integral to her hospitality that few people dared turn down her invitations for fear they would be permanently cut from her formal dinners.

From an entertainment perspective, Marjorie's square dances were refreshing. The fast pace, the group spirit, and the amusing patter of the callers were natural icebreakers, useful not only in the politically intense atmosphere of Washington, D.C., but also at Palm Beach and the Adirondacks. The genius of the square dance, as Marjorie used to tell her friends, was that everyone—young or old, male or female—could participate.

Marjorie also had personal reasons for enjoying square dancing. By 1950 she was in her early sixties and already worried about the rigidity that sets in with advancing years. Like her father, Marjorie had remained a dedicated believer in physical exercise. Her mornings traditionally began with a program of stretches and calisthenics, followed by a rubdown from her masseuse. Square dancing, she came to believe as she aged, was a complement to that regimen because it exercised the muscles of the entire body.

Only one person in her family disagreed: Joe Davies. Although an expert ballroom dancer himself, the seventy-four-year-old attorney adamantly refused to learn to square-dance.

. . .

In March 1955 Betty Beale observed in the *Sunday Star* that while only half of those invited to Mamie and Dwight Eisenhower's White House receptions ever appeared, invitations to Marjorie's parties were "grabbed up with ill-concealed eagerness." That response, said others who knew Marjorie well, was merely a reflection of her gregarious spirit and her passion for showing others a good time. So comfortable was she about her reputation that she even invited other reigning Washington hostesses to her parties, among them Perle Mesta, Kay Shouse, and Gwen Cafritz. Rarely, if ever, did these women invite one another to their affairs. Removed from the internecine rivalries of her peers, Marjorie was different, if for no other reason than that she refused to dwell in petty jealousy or open competition with anyone. Such thoughts, like gossip and ill health, were, by the teachings of Christian Science, to be avoided at all costs.

As a result of Marjorie's open-spirited hospitality, younger members of Washington's political and diplomatic set began to model themselves after her style. Among her followers were Ruth and Wiley Buchanan, the latter an official in the State Department with aspirations to an ambassadorship. Shortly after attending one of Marjorie's garden parties, Ruth began emulating Marjorie's style at her own parties. "My husband kept saying he was going to make me Washington's poor man's version of Marjorie," Ruth Buchanan recalled. Being fond of the Buchanans, Marjorie took the young woman under her wing and instructed her in the protocol of diplomatic life, just as Mrs. Stotesbury had done for Marjorie years earlier at Palm Beach. "Marjorie taught me a great deal. I learned all about flowers and tables and crystal from her," Ruth Buchanan reminisced. By the time Wiley was appointed ambassador to Luxembourg, Ruth was thoroughly accustomed to entertaining in the manner appropriate to diplomatic life abroad.

Still another admirer was Gladys Heurtematte, then the wife of the Panamian minister consulate to the United States, Julio Heurtematte. What impressed Gladys most about Marjorie was her thoughtfulness. A typical sign of that caring was the special flowers that she ordered placed in Gladys's room when she visited Mar-A-Lago. Or she left a fresh bottle of Gladys's favorite perfume upon her dresser. In her quiet, understated way, Marjorie carefully noted her guests' needs and desires at every juncture. Should they mention they had forgotten a shawl, wanted a car for the afternoon, or enjoyed a late-night snack before retiring, Marjorie made arrangements. It was the "little details like that," recalled Gladys, that touched her friends most of all.

To reign as one of the District's leading doyennes, hostess to diplomats and political leaders, was not enough to satisfy Marjorie. Observed her daughter Dina: "Had she been born later, Mother would have been head of a major corporation." But in the mid-twentieth century such an ambition was still impossible to fulfill, even for someone as vastly wealthy as Marjorie.

Increasingly, as her relationship with Joe deteriorated, she began to search for other areas of personal satisfaction. One of these was to improve the lackluster cultural life of the city of Washington. It was to this cause that Marjorie now began to address herself with almost singular devotion. In 1950 the heiress hosted a garden party on behalf of the National Symphony Orchestra. People turned out in droves for the affair, according to Gerson Nordlinger, who was then a new member of the Symphony Board, because "there was so much interest in those gardens." It was during that event that Marjorie befriended Nordlinger and discovered that he was a cultured, single man, an important commodity for any Washington hostess. Before long she had begun inviting him to parties.

Though he was from one of Washington's oldest families, Gerson Nordlinger, who was only thirty-five, was initially "awed" by Marjorie. Well into her sixties, Marjorie was still "a woman of dazzling beauty" and one who lived on a scale he "had never encountered before." A year or two later, when Nordlinger, as treasurer of the National Symphony, reported on the orchestra's deficit at a meeting of the National Symphony Orchestra Association, Marjorie motioned him over. "I'll take care of that," she whispered. "The whole thing?" he asked incredulously. "Yes, the whole thing," she said. The sum was ninety thousand dollars.

Before long Marjorie did even more. By then she was involved in improving the financial and artistic stability of the National Symphony Orchestra. In 1954 she was honorary chair of the symphony's first benefit ball. And the following year, in the spring of 1955, she became its foremost "angel." That year Marjorie decided to treat the high school students of America to free concerts at the National Symphony.

Dr. Howard Mitchell, conductor of the National Symphony Orchestra, had originally proposed the idea. At a meeting at orchestra president Carson Frailey's home, he mentioned that 500,000 teenagers arrived in Washington for high school tours each spring. While the trip was an important part of their education, most of them had never attended a live performance of an orchestra. This was an ideal opportunity to introduce America's youth to symphonic music. To make it even more relevant, a musical competition for talented high school students could be linked to the performances.

Such a series, Dr. Mitchell continued, would have other benefits as well, among them an additional five weeks' work for members of the symphony. The resulting thirty-one-week-long season would then be exceeded by only two other leading orchestras: the Boston and Philadelphia orchestras. With more work to offer, the National Symphony would draw some of the country's most talented musicians to its ranks.

During Dr. Mitchell's presentation Marjorie had listened quietly. Then she excused herself from the room and placed a long-distance call to her Manhattan financial manager, Meyer Handelman. A few minutes later she returned smiling. She would fund the program with an initial donation of $100,000.

The result was a series called "Music for Young America." By the following April 1956 the National Symphony had presented its first "Music for Young America" concert at Washington's Pan-American Union. Attended by thirteen hundred students, the program was an immediate hit. When friends congratulated Marjorie on opening night, the beaming benefactress quickly downplayed the significance of her contribution. "It's all Howard's baby," she insisted. As usual, Marjorie remained modest about her contributions, seeing them as her duty rather than as a means of gaining praise, another instance of having her money "work" for the betterment of humanity.

By the end of that year more than 50,000 teenagers had heard the National Symphony. High schools across the country were pressing the National Symphony business office for tickets for the following season. In addition, winners of the Marjorie Merriweather Post musical competition had received scholarships to prestigious institutions like Juilliard. By the mid-1960s the "Music for Young America" series was so highly regarded that its concerts were shown on national educational television.

To Marjorie, the success of "Music for Young America" remained a source of intensely private but deeply felt pride. When interviewed about her reasons for supporting the series, Marjorie reminded reporters that she had once supported a soup kitchen in Manhattan during the Depression. "I suppose nothing will ever match that in the satisfaction it gave me," she mused. "But this—well, it's been a thrill to watch these youngsters, to hear their comments, to get their letters. One was even kind enough to write that her class felt this was the highlight of their entire trip to the Capital."

Ironically, Marjorie never had a music lesson in her life. Yet she was an avid listener at an early age. C.W. had given her piano rolls as a child that she could play in his Pianola whenever she wanted to hear music. "Why take music lessons," Marjorie once said, "when I could play anything I liked and it came out so beautifully on that marvelous thing?"

While music may be the food of love, it can also serve as solace for love's demise. For Marjorie in the mid-fifties it served that sad purpose. In spite of a public image of connubial bliss, she had been living unhappily with Joe for several years. The estrangement had begun slowly, almost imperceptibly in ways that only lovers can know—chagrin for an unkind word or an unreasonable demand.

What had once drawn Marjorie so passionately to Joe—the fervor of his political vision, his ease with world leaders, and his passionate attachment to the heiress at a time when she was in the depths of disillusionment over E. F. Hutton—was no longer as compelling as it used to be. By the early 1950s, at the height of the McCarthy era, Joe had become a political nonentity, a man whose earlier pro-Soviet stance now made him a dubious figure. Already Joseph McCarthy had destroyed the career of Joe's son-in-law Senator Millard Tydings, former head of the Senate Foreign Relations Committee, and it was only because of Joe's many friends in Congress that he had managed to escape a similar prosecution.

Although Marjorie's daughters believed that the glamour of international politics was an important factor in her initial attraction to Joe, there was more to her disillusionment than the demise of his career. What bothered Marjorie most of all was Joe's moodiness, his "whiplash" temper, and his incessant critiques of her children, grandchildren, and friends. From the beginning of Marjorie's marriage, her daughters had avoided their stepfather whenever possible. Even old friends of Marjorie's like Hunter Marston, while polite to Joe, had never warmed to him. "I saw him only on account of Marjorie. We did not want to give up our friendship and love of Marjorie because of a bad husband," Hunter Marston once remarked.

According to other observers, Joe's political decline, compounded with Marjorie's increasing prominence in Washington, filled him with jealousy. The former ambassador, noted Anne Frailey Braverman, always seemed "overly impressed with himself" and "stood on ceremony" with people. In contrast were Marjorie's warmth and openness, for she was "much more democratic to people than he was. He wanted to be more important than Marjorie Merriweather Post. But she outshone him."

In the early fifties the former ambassadress only occasionally revealed the depth of her unhappiness to others. When she did, it was usually over something quite superficial. One of her classic gripes, for instance, was Joe's obsession with cards. "Here it is, a perfectly beautiful day, and he's sitting there playing bridge and missing everything," Marjorie used to complain to Adelaide and her daughters when they were cruising on the *Sea Cloud.*

Only once did she reveal to her family her real despair over Joe's cantankerousness. One spring day when Adelaide boarded the *Sea Cloud* in Bermuda, the yacht's radioman asked her to see Marjorie in her stateroom immediately. "Could you please go and tell Joe not to come into my room again?" Marjorie begged her daughter from her bed. "He's been very difficult, and I've been sick and fainted. I don't want to see him now." Another time, in an unguarded moment, she told Gerson Nordlinger, "You know, Joe Davies should have been an actor. His whole life was an act."

The older Joe got, the more possessive he seemed to become. This may have been a reaction to his own sense of decline and his perception that Marjorie was still desirable to other men. Finally he became so obsessed that he began to heckle Marjorie regularly. If she talked or danced with anyone for any length of time, Joe accused her of ignoring him. "At the end of the evening he'd come in and grill her. 'Who is that person?' 'How did you know him?' until Mother would finally say, 'Look, for God's sake, I was just dancing,' " Dina recalled.

As a newlywed Marjorie had rejoiced in Joe's attachment to her, and even later she had seen it as a reminder of their first, happily married years together. As late as 1947 she told Betty Beale that "that man has given me the twelve happiest years of my life." But the possessiveness of new love was no longer endearing when it became mixed with rages and accusations. To Marjorie, Joe's possessiveness seemed not only stifling but at times even frightening. "As a result," Dina recalled, "Mother began to spend more time away from him."

Privately Marjorie was caught in a terrible bind. In 1950 Joe had been diagnosed with intestinal cancer, and although he was treated with apparent success, Marjorie felt obliged to remain by his side. "I think she felt that she made her bed and she'd better lie in it," said Dina. Humbled by the memory of the happiness they once shared, Marjorie consequently tried to tolerate Joe as best she could.

Marjorie's final alienation from Joe, according to his daughter Eleanor, may have resulted from a malicious story told by a member of Marjorie's staff. Allegedly Margaret Voigt, the heiress's efficient but conniving social secretary, somehow convinced Marjorie that cancer was contagious and even made people homicidal. This may have made Marjorie—who already had odd ideas about illness and often used unconventional, even "quack" doctors to cure her own aches and pains—grow even more fearful of Joe.

Said Eleanor: "I can't imagine Marjorie swallowing that. She was too smart a woman. She must have been getting old, too. It's the only way I can explain it to myself . . . because I've never seen a woman more in love than she was with my father and he with her."

There was at least one element of truth to that observation. Throughout her life, whenever she was faced with unpleasantness, Marjorie's instinct had been to flee—spiritually, if not physically. Whatever natural tendencies she already had in that direction had been strengthened by the teachings of Christian Science, which encourages followers to emphasize the positive. Through her own interpretation of Mary Baker Eddy's teachings, Marjorie consistently shunned people who were negative or overcritical of others. For that reason, too, she scrupulously avoided discussing her own illnesses or those of people in her acquaintance—even close friends and relatives.

Had Joe been kindly, had his relationship with Marjorie been consistently tender, she might have reacted differently, but ill health combined with ill temper was too much for her to take. Fearful of being dragged down into her husband's dark moods, Marjorie began to pull away. Her mother, Ella, had died of what Marjorie called a "broken heart." She had vowed that would not happen to her.

To fill the ensuing emotional void, Marjorie drew her family around her. In the summer of 1953 she rented Sutton Place in Guildford, England, and invited her daughters, their husbands, and their children to visit. The splendid Elizabethan manor house, owned by the duke of Sutherland, was conveniently near the residence of one of her closest friends, the artist Lady Alice Clifford, wife of the former governor-general of Nassau, Sir Bede Clifford.

Even in that bucolic setting just south of London, surrounded by friends and family, Marjorie seemed anxious that Joe would interfere. So obsessed, in fact, was she with the idea that one night she awakened Adelaide. "He's here," Marjorie announced, convinced she had heard Joe coming through the front door. "Mother, who's here?" asked Adelaide. "Joe is here," Marjorie insisted. "Mother," the younger woman pleaded, "calm down." With that, Adelaide picked up the phone and called the night watchman. The person who had walked through the front door of the manor house had not been Joe Davies, but rather the cook, who had forgotten his key.

Marjorie's worries were not as irrational as they sounded. That same summer Joe had also traveled to England, but the former ambassador had stopped only briefly in London before going on to the Continent to visit various heads of state with his grandson, Joe Tydings. It was only then, the younger man recalled, that he began to suspect there was something wrong between his grandfather and Marjorie.

The last straw occurred the following summer, when Marjorie crossed the Atlantic again to see her friends Ruth and Wiley Buchanan, the latter recently named the American ambassador to Luxembourg. In the course of conversation Wiley remarked that when preparing for the Luxembourg assignment, he had examined Washington residential housing records. He had done so, he explained, so as to make an accurate assessment of his own home for the federal government. As the newly appointed ambassador flipped through the files and came across Tregaron, he was surprised to see that the owner of the estate was Joe Davies. "Why did you put it in his name?" Wiley asked Marjorie. The hostess showed—or feigned—surprise that the estate was not listed in both their names. In fact, she was so furious, recalled Ruth Buchanan, that she announced she was going to divorce Joe at once.

The reality, according to Marjorie's granddaughter Ellen MacNeille Charles, may have been that Marjorie was embarrassed at her earlier generosity. Wiley's question, coming at a time when she was already contemplating divorce, gave Marjorie an "official" reason to act out her intentions.

Hating confrontation as she did, Marjorie was afraid to break the news to Joe herself and left the job to Adelaide. At first Joe begged Marjorie to stay. When she refused to give the marriage another chance, Joe's anguish turned to anger. He had purchased Tregaron, he reminded Marjorie. It was his house, and it belonged to him. He had no intention of giving it up.

A bitter fight ensued. For years, as Marjorie later told her friends, she had the sense that Joe was grabbing everything he could from her. The fact that he insisted upon "renting" the *Sea Cloud* from her so he could say it was "my yacht" had been only one example. Other things, like some of the jewelry and art Joe purchased for her as "gifts" and even a birthday party he threw in her honor, had allegedly been paid for with Marjorie's money. With deliberate myopia, Marjorie had looked away, but Tregaron was too much.

Finally, two attorneys were brought in. Joe retained his son-in-law Senator Millard Tydings, who had received so many kindnesses and been a frequent guest in Marjorie's homes. The heiress, meanwhile, retained Charles Littlefield. In the end, after a series of exhausting negotiations, Marjorie agreed that Joe could keep Tregaron.

Another equally acrimonious fight soon occurred over the division of the Davieses' Russian art collection. So vituperative were the couple's arguments that in the end the icons, imperial china, paintings, chalices, and Fabergé objects were arbitrarily divided in half. Ultimately Joe gained certain items that Marjorie claimed she had originally purchased for herself at her own expense. One was her favorite portrait of Catherine the Great by Dmitri Levitsky. After Joe's death Marjorie was able to buy it back through Joe Tydings. Today it hangs in the front hall of Marjorie's last home in Washington, the current Hillwood Museum.

In revenge Marjorie stripped Tregaron of virtually every improvement she had made. Recalled her friend and attorney Henry Dudley: "She took everything that belonged to her prior to her marriage." One night, when she knew Joe was away, she sent a truck over with her staff to repossess the Oriental rugs from her old homes in New York and Connecticut. The coup de grâce came on another dark, moonless night. In the wee hours of the morning a large truck pulled up in front of Tregaron. Armed with heavy shovels, several gardeners methodically stripped the grounds of Marjorie's prize azaleas.

Despite the bitterness of the negotiations, the divorce was kept secret until after it was effected on March 8, 1955. Even members of Tregaron's household staff were ignorant of the impending separation. "She called me up in the bedroom one day and said, 'From now on, wherever I go, you should be at the wheel,' " recalled Marjorie's chauffeur, Jimmy Sottile. Simultaneously Marjorie instructed Jimmy to tell Tregaron's second chauffeur, Carl, to become Mr. Davies's chauffeur. "I figured there was something in the wind, but I didn't know what it was all about," Jimmy recalled.

Nor, for fear of a leak to the press, did Marjorie tell her friends about the breakup until she was already in Sun Valley, Idaho, for the requisite six weeks' residency before the divorce. From there Marjorie's social secretary, Margaret Voigt, wrote to friends like Mrs. Axel Johnson, General and Mrs. Conger Pratt, the Paul McNutts, Lady Braebourne, and Lady Birley announcing Marjorie's plans. "It has taken great courage for her to arrive at this decision," observed Voigt, "but it seemed the only real and honest solution. And I think you would like to know that your staunch and very sweet friendship, particularly through this trying period of several years past has meant a very great deal to her and been the greatest comfort and joy."

For months Marjorie had been searching for a new house. To preserve her anonymity, the heiress asked young David Close, cousin to her first husband, to assist in the search. In this, as in everything else in her life, Marjorie had exacting requirements. The new house had to be stately, have fifteen-foot ceilings, and be situated on a large, thickly wooded site. Ultimately, Marjorie settled upon a Georgian Colonial estate in northwest Washington called Arbremont. To maintain Marjorie's anonymity, David Close listed himself and his wife, Margaret, as the prospective buyers. Only when the divorce was final was the title to the estate registered in Marjorie's name.

After three divorces the heiress had come to a new understanding about her identity. No longer would she memorialize her unhappy marriages in her name. Though no feminist, Marjorie had evolved into an individual with a strong sense of her own identity and a history that would no longer be linked to the name of any man.

Henceforth she would be known as Marjorie Merriweather Post.

24

Vital Contributions

$\mathcal{N}$ews of Marjorie's divorce from Joe Davies stunned Washington. For weeks rumors had circulated that something was amiss when Marjorie canceled a world cruise and went instead to Sun Valley, Idaho. Still, only a few Washingtonians had suspected a divorce. "Thus ends a marriage which has so often been described in diplomatic dispatches as 'a great love story.' Joe and Marjorie were not only very much in love, but they acted it in public," stated the *New York World-Telegram and Sun*.

No less newsworthy were the grounds on which Marjorie won the uncontested divorce: "extreme mental cruelty." According to *The New York Times*, "Mr. Davies to whom she had been married nineteen years ago was jealous and . . . his activities and attitudes had made her unhappy, upset, and nervous." The former ambassador, reported *Newsweek*, had a "whiplash temper" and was jealous of anybody or anything that won Marjorie's affection: "children, business, men and women." Ultimately Marjorie had divorced him because of "a lack of basic, straight thinking that was very hard to live with."

A few journalists were more cynical. By the time Marjorie returned to the East Coast, said *Time*, she looked "as well preserved as a frozen peach." The *New York World-Telegram and Sun* made a point of mentioning that Marjorie had been wed twice before and had married Davies in the thirties, when she had been "bitten by the diplomatic bug." Later, when the pro-Soviets, or "parlor pinks," were no longer fashionable, Davies had been "placed on the shelf." Now the former ambassador may well have gotten what he deserved: retribution "for the time when he left his first wife and mother of three daughters."

Criticisms like these were soon overshadowed by the appearance of a story headlined MARJORIE THE MAGNIFICENT that appeared in the Washington *Evening Star*. The newly single Washington heiress, proclaimed columnist Betty Beale, was "the most fabulous hostess in all America. She is the last of an age of opulence and she knows it." Beale's story, which emphasized the dramatic background of Marjorie's life and her philanthropic contributions, noted that while she never sought publicity for her entertainments, she was widely acknowledged as America's "No. 1 hostess." Now, under her maiden name of Marjorie Merriweather Post, she intended to entertain at her new estate, Arbremont, which, like its owner, had also been renamed. Henceforth the sprawling estate on the edge of Rock Creek Park would be known as Hillwood, after Marjorie's former property in Brookville, Long Island.

It was to the reconstruction of this new Hillwood that the sixty-eight-year-old Marjorie now applied her energies. Foremost in her mind was the thought that the estate would be not only a home but a museum in which her art collection could be enjoyed by the public after her death. In many ways the twenty-four-acre property was ideal for such a monument. The Georgian Colonial mansion perched majestically upon a hill overlooking Rock Creek Park and the valley of the District of Columbia. Beyond it were spacious grounds for gardens, greenhouses, and outbuildings.

To the keenly aesthetic heiress, the thirty-six-room house—built in the twenties by the Washington "cave dweller" Mrs. Delos Blodgett for one of her daughters—needed extensive renovation. "Grandmother," as Marjorie's granddaughter Ellen MacNeille Charles put it, "had very strong ideas about the way a house should be organized." And one characteristic of that organization, added journalist Liz Carpenter, "was to turn every place she lived into a palace or a museum and sometimes both." A house, in Marjorie's view, had to be built with magnificence. Should it lack certain amenities, they should be added at once.

Given her high standards, it was perhaps inevitable that when Marjorie first saw the old Arbremont estate, she would be displeased with its interior. "Mother," as her daughter Adelaide recalled, "was not enchanted." What Marjorie objected to most of all was the English linenfold paneling in the living room. She also disliked the heavy stone fireplace and other stonework details over the door. "Mother hated anything that was dark," Adelaide recalled. Only after seeing the other properties then available in Washington and reassessing Arbremont's potential did Marjorie finally decide to buy it. "But I am not going to keep that paneling," she told Adelaide.

One of Marjorie's first actions was to have the offending paneling removed and replaced with a lighter one that was made in France. As noted earlier, the old linenfold paneling was shipped off to Marjorie's godson and his wife, the Sibleys. With similar efficiency, Marjorie had the living room stripped of other heavy features. Among them was the stone fireplace, which was replaced with a white marble mantel from the period of Louis XVI.

To accomplish the transformation, Marjorie hired the New York architectural firm of Alexander McIlvaine. In the course of the next two years Hillwood was gutted and rebuilt. The kitchen in the east wing was enlarged and equipped in stainless steel for the preparation of banquet-size meals; the bathrooms, plumbing fixtures, and electrical wiring were updated; and dozens of display cases were built to show off Marjorie's art collection to its best advantage.

Hillwood eventually emerged as an airy, regal estate that was hailed by *Architectural Digest* for its evocation of the "elegance and style of France's *belle époque* and all the romance and barbarism and rich acquisition of Russia's imperial past." As in earlier renovations, Marjorie incorporated some of her favorite architectural features from previous homes into Hillwood. Years earlier, when she sold the East Ninety-second Street apartment, she had retained the windows and fretwork from the breakfast room. Now she brought them out of storage and incorporated them into a small breakfast niche attached to the south side of Hillwood's dining room.

The result—a sunny, orchid-lined addition graced by a green and transparent crystal chandelier from Russia's Catherine Palace— became Marjorie's favorite room, one in which she often dined with friends or family for breakfast or lunch. It was here that she once invited her dancing instructor Elizabeth Montgomery to lunch. When the teacher admired the pretty colored glass dishes that lined the sunroom walls, Marjorie said, "I bought them at Woolworth's."

Other renovations similarly reflected Marjorie's preferences. To the energetic heiress the estate had to be more than a showcase for art. It was also to be a house for parties, balls, and square dances. To accommodate those activities, Marjorie ordered the creation of a "party" room, or pavilion, built onto the west side of the estate. And because she liked to show guests first-run movies at the end of her dinners, two state-of-the-art movie projectors, a screen, and a sound system were built into the pavilion.

At Hillwood, as at all her other residences, Marjorie demanded perfection. Nor did she want to wait an undue amount of time to achieve it. Being a firm believer in planning ahead, she expected to know when the estate would be complete. "I really have been quite disgusted with the progress of the new house here. Both the architect and the contractor can't seem to make their minds up as to when it should be finished," she complained to Don Handelman, son of her financial manager, Meyer Handelman, in October 1955. "Each time I press for an answer they give me a vague reply or something completely different to what I have had before. Accordingly, I have asked Commander Clyde Ault to come to Washington and act as my representative on the job." While the commander—a stalwart gray-haired gentleman who had been Marjorie's chief engineer on the *Sea Cloud*—acted as her proxy, all major decisions about the house were still left to Marjorie. When gardeners cleared trees on the estate's south lawn and discovered a view of the Washington Monument, they immediately brought it to Marjorie's attention. She was thrilled; what better symbol for her long association with the city of Washington and the government of the United States than a view of its premier monument?

The glint of the Washington Monument at six miles' distance, its white spire pointing heavenward by day, backlit with spotlights at night, was too inspiring a sight to ignore. Such a view, Marjorie insisted, simply had to be seen within the house as well—particularly from the glass-paneled doors of the library, which were just beyond the front entrance hall. At the time those doors were just a few inches off line from the view. To move them so that they would frame the monument perfectly would be not only difficult but exorbitantly expensive.

To Marjorie neither the expense nor the difficulty of the task was important. The new Hillwood was to be a showcase for the history of her life, a repository for her memories, and a museum for her art collection. To provide a perfectly aligned view of the Washington Monument, the glass-paneled library doors—and anything else that got in the way—would have to be moved.

The story has become part of Marjorie's legend. Even today a joke still circulates in Washington that Marjorie found another solution: Rather than touch the paneled doors of the library, she simply moved the

Washington Monument. However it was accomplished, the result was a perfect view. One of the first impressions guests had as they entered Marjorie's palatial white-marbled hallway at Hillwood was, and still is, the dramatic sight of the Washington Monument in the valley beyond the trees of Rock Creek Park.

By 1956 Marjorie's extensive renovations had transformed Hillwood into an imposing visual experience. The grounds of the once heavily wooded estate had been cleared of decaying vegetation and overgrown vines. In their place was Marjorie's springtime signature: thousands of azaleas, rhododendrons, magnolias, flowering cherry and crab apple trees, and four kinds of holly. As at Tregaron, Hillwood's grounds now bloomed in brilliant abundance from thousands of hybrid tulips, narcissuses, and other flowers. In addition to the bold swaths of color, Marjorie created a series of unusual plantings on the estate reminiscent of her world travels. In one corner was a rose garden, in another a topiary garden, in a third a pet cemetery with weeping dogwoods. There was also a formal French garden with boxwood planted in the shape of a fleur-de-lis and a Japanese garden with fountains and waterfalls. "For sheer quality," proclaimed the *Evening Star* soon after the estate was opened, "this place is in a class by itself."

The inside was no less magical. As guests entered the white marble entranceway, they stood beneath a huge French pear-drop rock crystal chandelier. The hall itself was decorated with family portraits and pictures of tsars and tsarinas, including one of Catherine the Great by the Swedish painter Alexander Roslin. Several pairs of Russian imperial vases stood on eighteenth-century commodes, two attributed to the renowned French cabinetmaker Jean-Henri Riesener and one obtained from the Parisian collection of the marquess of Hereford. In the men's coatroom Marjorie had interjected sly humor with the display of *Night*, a large painting by Adolphe Bouguereau featuring a female nude draped in black chiffon.

To the right of the main hallway, guests could peer into the octagonal Russian Porcelain Room through a door flanked by the two vases Madame Molotova had presented to Marjorie when she left the USSR in 1938. The Porcelain Room contained shelves displaying the gilded and decorated dishes of the tsarist court. From there guests could enter the cream-colored French drawing room with its Beauvais tapestries featuring the cartoons of François Boucher, its antique French sofas and chairs with tapestries from the Gobelin factory, and an eighteenth-century desk that may have been made for Marie Antoinette.

In other alcoves off the Porcelain Room was the core of Marjorie's Russian art collection: jewel-studded chalices from the Russian Orthodox church, eighteenth-century icons, Easter eggs, silverwork, *kovshi* or ornamental ladles, enameled or encrusted with jewels. The crowning glory was the Fabergé collection, which included picture frames, a pink enamel clock, nephrite snuffboxes, and two Easter eggs encrusted with diamonds and other precious gems.

From the Icon Room, Marjorie's guests could wander through an alcove containing cases of porcelains from the imperial, Gardner, and Popov factories to the Norwegian pine-paneled library. From there one could enter Hillwood's forty-four-foot dining room. There the walls were lined with French Regency paneling hung with four Dutch paintings of hunting scenes. The floor was covered with an enormous Aubusson rug said to have belonged to the Mexican emperor Maximilian.

Not until May 1957 would Marjorie finally open Hillwood to guests. To curious columnists like Betty Beale, the wait had been worth it. "Don't ever say there's no such thing as magic. Yesterday an invisible wand was waved and I stepped into a palace right here in Washington. It is easy to see why it took Mrs. Merriweather Post two years to finish her new home. . . . It takes time to create beauty. It took infinite care and planning to provide . . . for the kind of perfection of craftsmanship that came out of the palaces of czars, of Mme. Pompadour, or the estate of an English lord."

On July 4, Marjorie hosted her first big party at Hillwood, a home, as *The Washington Post* now called it, that "is a little less than a museum of magnificent art objects." Independence Day had been deliberately chosen to enhance the uniqueness of the Hillwood site. After senators, ambassadors, and other Washington dignitaries assembled on the flowered terrace overlooking Rock Creek Park for dinner, they watched the nation's most famous fireworks display light up the sky from the mall of the Washington Monument.

Within a year Hillwood had gained a reputation as one of Washington's most extraordinary estates. So much praise was heaped upon the estate that *The Washington Post* noted that Marjorie's "refurbishing of Hillwood from 1955 to 1957 so quickly exhausted all the adjectives, over-eager society writers began to make up stories about it."

The same rumormongering was directed at Marjorie's social life. While no one questioned her role as one of Washington's leading hostesses, some speculated about who would become her fourth husband.

To Washington society watchers, there was no doubt whatsoever that there would be a fourth—despite Marjorie's initial attempts to refute the idea.

By the time she returned from Sun Valley with her divorce from Joe Davies, Marjorie seemed relieved of a terrible burden. Virtually all her friends applauded the decision, among them her closest companions, Kathleen McNutt and Frances Rosso, in whom she had long confided her unhappiness. Even those who were little more than social acquaintances congratulated Marjorie on her divorce. "My dear, I wondered what took you so long," observed fellow Sulgrave Club member Alice Longworth Roosevelt. An old Battle Creek schoolmate quipped, "Well, you've been three times around the track, and now I see you've returned to the post."

To a slew of calls from prying newspaper reporters, Marjorie insisted that she had no intention of remarrying—in spite of rumors that she was dating a Texas millionaire. "Why are people so sure I'm about to change my name again right away? Why does everybody think I went to all kinds of trouble to change my name to one I haven't used in forty years if I intended to take another immediately?" she finally complained to a *Washington Post* society editor. "And believe you me, it's a chore to change your name for all the things that surround me; for everything I have to sign! For every record; for every account." As for the alleged love affair with a Texas millionaire, Marjorie said, "I'd like to know who he is and I'd like to meet him."

Indeed, she was not yet ready to remarry. Relieved to have finally obtained a divorce from Joe Davies, she had reached a turning point in her emotional life, a time in which she needed solitude to sort out an independent identity. In the spring of 1955 other events conspired to give Marjorie even more cause for self-contemplation.

In February 1955 Marjorie's first husband, Ed Close, had suddenly died at his home in Greenwich, Connecticut, at the age of seventy-three. Had Marjorie been on the East Coast rather than in Idaho she probably would have attended his funeral. Months earlier Marjorie had startled her daughters Adelaide and Eleanor by reminding them that in December 1955 she and their father, Ed Close, would have been married fifty years. While no longer in love with Ed, Marjorie still had intensely sentimental feelings about her youth and her first marriage. "Grandmother was a romantic and thought it would be perfectly wonderful if they reenacted the wedding. All of us, Mother [Adelaide], Aunt

Eleanor, and I were just horrified at the idea," recalled Marjorie's granddaughter Ellen.

Whatever misplaced emotions led Marjorie to contemplate such a celebration, the idea was impossible. To start with, Ed Close's second wife, Betsy, had always been jealous of Marjorie. Betsy had produced twin sons for Ed Close and was a well-liked and respectable member of Greenwich society. It may have been that despite all her devotion, Betsy knew that Ed remained enamored of Marjorie. When he died, Betsy anxiously asked Adelaide if Marjorie was planning to attend the funeral. When she heard that Marjorie was out west "on business," Betsy seemed relieved.

Nevertheless, Marjorie's presence seemed to loom over the funeral. To start with, she had an enormous bouquet sent in Ed's memory. After the service Betsy Close's Irish maid claimed that she had seen a handsome middle-aged woman wearing a hat step out of a chauffeur-driven maroon and black Packard. The woman had entered the front of the church during the service, bowed her head for a few minutes, and then disappeared. Oddly enough, the maid had never met Marjorie or seen her car. The story so chilled Marjorie's daughters that they called their mother in Idaho, where she was obtaining a divorce from Joe Davies. "Mother, were you there?" they asked her. "In spirit," Marjorie replied.

If Ed Close's death forced Marjorie to scrutinize the history of her marriages, it also forced her to reevaluate the scope and significance of her life. With her divorce from Joe Davies, Marjorie was no longer a diplomat's wife. Although Marjorie maintained friendships with members of Washington's diplomatic corps, prime ministers, and U.S. presidents to the last years of her life, she was no longer a political insider.

The removal from a worldview and proximity to political power that Marjorie had enjoyed for nearly two decades created a void in her life. Journalist Roy Meacham, who first met Marjorie after her divorce from Joe Davies, sensed that the heiress was searching for something "to define her life," something to replace "being at the center of things, some vital contribution she could make."

Marjorie accordingly plunged into a series of philanthropic activities. For years she had maintained that "Wealth is a greater responsibility than a privilege," and now she set about illustrating that maxim with renewed munificence.

The focus of Marjorie's largesse was young people—especially those in schools, colleges, and citizenship training programs. By April 1956 her establishment of the National Symphony Orchestra's "Music for Young America" program had become the cornerstone of her new commitment. Six months later, on November 15, 1956, Marjorie donated a new building to her alma mater, the Mount Vernon Seminary and Junior College, where she was a member of the board of trustees. The Georgian Colonial redbrick structure, which was to house the library and a formal reception room for the new campus on Foxhall Road, had been named after Marjorie's parents. At the time of its construction, friends claimed that they "could have recognized Post Hall by its reception room even without identification," for it bore a striking similarity to Hillwood's drawing room.

In contrast with Marjorie's active support of the Mount Vernon Seminary was her passive sponsorship of the new college created in New York by Long Island University. By 1951 the battle had finally been won for the university to purchase Marjorie's old estate. Yet it was not until 1954, after still more litigation that ended with the assignment of Marjorie's old estate to the village of Brookville, that Long Island University could finally open its doors.

In the spring of 1954 Dr. Gordon Hoxie, the newly appointed dean and later president of the Brookville campus, was approached by one of Marjorie's old friends and a Long Island University board member, Grover Whalen. "I'll bet that Marjorie would be interested in this as a new college if it bore the name of her father," Whalen proposed. He was right.

To Marjorie it was a timely idea. That year happened to be the one hundredth anniversary of C. W. Post's birth. What better way to memorialize her father than by naming a college after him? In November 1954 Marjorie appeared with her three daughters and members of General Foods for the dedication of the Brookville campus as C. W. Post College. By the following September a class of 102 men and 19 women had enrolled for its first classes. A year later, when Dr. Gordon Hoxie's wife, Dr. Louise Hoxie, established two sororities on campus, she asked Marjorie to become a sorority "mother." The philanthropist not only agreed but subsequently invited "her" girls to visit her in Washington each year.

Eventually, as the heiress watched the tiny C. W. Post College grow into the most popular undergraduate campus of Long Island University, she began making annual donations—first in sums of fifty thousand dollars and later in allocations of one hundred thousand dollars.

By the early sixties C. W. Post College had outstripped even the dreams of its original founders by becoming one of the fastest-growing colleges in the nation. It was then that Marjorie decided to leave a bequest to the C. W. Post College in her will.

Schools were not the only beneficiaries of Marjorie's largesse. For her granddaughters Ellen and Melissa there were debut parties at the Chevy Chase Club. For Marwee, on April 19, 1956, there was a wedding at the Shoreham Hotel, complete with hundreds of guests and a police escort. And for Alden Sibley's sister, Julia, there was tuition for the Union Theological Seminary. Although it was not yet possible in that era for women to be ordained ministers in the Episcopal church, Julia Sibley, who was already in her thirties, longed to become a member of the lay clergy. "Aunt Marjorie was thrilled and supportive and made it possible for me to go," recalled Julia Sibley, who subsequently began her theological career as a hospital chaplain. "Aunt Marjorie was very much for anybody who was pulled together, was upbeat, and wanted to do well."

Increasingly, "doing well" for Marjorie came to mean fulfilling one's obligations, even in times of duress. In September 1957 Marjorie was asked to participate in the golden jubilee celebration of the founding of C. W.'s model city, Post, Texas. To open the festivities, Marjorie had agreed to appear in a parade with several celebrities who advertised products for General Foods. On the designated morning a heavy sandstorm blew over the city. The celebrities, among them Jack Benny, refused to leave their hotel. Yet Marjorie was undaunted. Donning a pair of sunglasses and a scarf, the seventy-year-old heiress marched down the street in the parade and later dedicated a statue to her father.

That same public-minded philosophy led Marjorie to support citizenship programs for youth. For years she gave money to the Boy Scouts of America. To the South Plains Area Council in Post, Texas, Marjorie donated four hundred acres for a camp in her father's name. She also gave money to the Boy Scout Council at Saranac Lake. And in Washington, D.C., the heiress donated tens of thousands of dollars for the creation of new headquarters for the National Capital Area Council. So constant was the outpouring from Marjorie's pocketbook that in 1959 the Washington Council announced it planned to create a camp in her name. In April 1960, on the golden anniversary of the Boy Scouts of America, Marjorie was honored with a bronze plaque.

Other organizations heaped similar honors upon Marjorie in that period. Among the prizes were the Washington Board of Trade Award for Music in the Nation's Capital, the American Symphony Orchestra League Award, the People of Garza County, Texas, Golden Jubilee Award, the American National Red Cross, an award from the National Society Children American Revolution, and the National Conference of Christians and Jews' Brotherhood Award. What thrilled Marjorie the most was the bestowal of the French government's highest civilian award, the cross of a chevalier of the Legion of Honor. At an embassy dinner on October 31, 1957, the French ambassador Hervé Alphand presented Marjorie with that award (which had been announced in April of that year) on behalf of her "long demonstrated friendship towards France." Forty years earlier she had contributed a three-thousand-bed military base hospital in World War I. More recently, in the spring of 1955, Marjorie had raised funds for the Versailles Exposition on the bicentennial anniversary of Marie Antoinette's birthday.

Distinctive as was the red ribbon and white and golden cross of the French Legion of Honor, it was too cumbersome for even the jewelry-loving Marjorie to wear on most of her formal clothes. Thereafter the philanthropist ordered hundreds of tiny embroidered red ribbons symbolic of the award to be sewn onto her gowns and evening dresses.

Shortly after Hillwood was completed, Marjorie received another tribute, this one even more personal and touching. For years friends who had enjoyed Marjorie's parties and invitations to the Adirondacks and Mar-A-Lago had debated how to show their gratitude. On March 15, 1957, when Marjorie turned seventy, Lady Birley and Lady Braebourne hosted a surprise party in her honor in Palm Beach. That event was only prelude to a more permanent testimony of goodwill.

Secretly a committee of friends that included Frances Rosso, Lady Constance Lewis, and Sadie Pratt had been preparing plans for the creation of Friendship Walk—a secluded and landscaped pathway that would wind through the grounds at Hillwood from the estate's rose garden to a crest overlooking Rock Creek Park. All winter the committee worked with Marjorie's gardeners and landscape architect and in March 1957 sent letters to Marjorie's closest friends asking for their signatures and donations.

By November the path, shrubbery, and statues had been put in place. On the third of that month friends gathered at Hillwood to lead the astonished philanthropist to the rose garden. There a marble plaque had been set in the ground. It read, "Friendship Walk—Hillwood—

Prepared by her friends—a tribute to Marjorie Merriweather Post for her generous nature, love of beauty, and devotion to human needs."

Marjorie's friends then led her along the path to the crest of a hill where the walkway ended in a circular terrace. At its center was another marble stone inscribed with the words of one of Russia's most tragic characters, the last tsarina, Alexandra Feodorovna: "Friendship outstays the hurrying flight of years and aye abides through laughter and tears." Around the terrace were statues of the four seasons copied from eighteenth-century Carrara marble originals in Florence.

At the end of the tour, members of the Friendship Walk Committee presented Marjorie with a parchment scroll. Upon it were a copy of the inscription placed in the rose garden and the signatures of the 181 people who had contributed to Friendship Walk.

"Oh, my goodness, I'm so thrilled!" was all the usually articulate Marjorie could say at the time. Thereafter she often showed Friendship Walk to visitors. And rarely a week went by when Marjorie did not slip away by herself on the private path created by her family of friends.

FOR THE

COMMON

GOOD

25

Mrs. Herbert May

"*F*riendship," the poet Byron once wrote, "is Love without his wings!" By the time Friendship Walk was dedicated in November 1957, Marjorie's heart had already taken flight.

Among the contributors to Friendship Walk was a handsome, silver-haired Pittsburgh businessman named Herbert A. May who often escorted Marjorie around town. For months Washington had buzzed with rumors that the philanthropist would marry either him or another escort, Jack Logan. So heated was this debate between Marjorie's friends that they were divided into two camps, some favoring a "May" marriage, the others a "Logan" one. By the spring of 1958 the issue had been settled. On June 18, in a quiet ceremony at the Maryland home of Marjorie's daughter Adelaide, Marjorie became the bride of Herbert May.

The next day, when the wedding was announced, gifts and telegrams poured in from well-wishers. Among those who cabled their congratulations was Marjorie's granddaughter Ellen, who was stationed in a Texas army camp with her new husband, George Iverson. In reply Marjorie wired back an unforgettable message: "Walking on fluffy pink clouds." At seventy-one years of age, the still-lovely Marjorie seemed to have at last found the love she had been searching for all her life.

How or where Marjorie first met Herb May is not clear, but it was more likely in Washington than Palm Beach. As executive vice-president of Westinghouse Air Brake International, May often commuted to Washington from his home in Pittsburgh, Pennsylvania. During World War II he had visited the capital on business even more frequently.

At the time of her wedding Marjorie told friends that she had first met Herb thirty years earlier. Yet it was not until after her divorce from Joe Davies that she was reintroduced to the handsome businessman. Coincidentally, Herb, like Joe Davies, had been born in Watertown, Wisconsin, and during the war had done business with the Soviets. He also belonged to the Burning Tree Golf Club and was invited to many of Perle Mesta's parties. There the resemblance between him and Joe Davies ended.

While Joe often seemed pompous and abrasive, Herb was soft-spoken and diplomatic. "He was a very attractive person, very well liked and kind," recalled Marjorie's daughter Adelaide. Moreover, he had many interests in common with Marjorie. "He was a charming man, loved to dance and loved to entertain, and he and Mother knew a lot of the same people. We all thought it was going to be just wonderful," said Dina.

In addition to his position with Westinghouse Air Brake, Herb was a member of the board of directors of the New York, Chicago & St. Louis Railroad Company as well as the Wheeling & Lake Erie Railroad. He was a close friend of Richard Mellon's and served on the Mellon National Bank and Trust Company's advisory board. He was also an avid equestrian. Marjorie's beau was so fond of riding that he was an early secretary of the Rolling Rock Hunt and a member of suburban Pittsburgh's Rolling Rock Club.

Dashing, witty, and popular, Herb had become a widower in 1937, when his wife died of pneumonia, leaving him with four young children and a twenty-eight-room mansion in Pittsburgh. In spite of his good looks and prominence, he had not remarried. For years Herb had dated two Pittsburgh socialites so steadily that his children were convinced he would wed one of them. Yet by 1957 his three sons and adopted daughter were grown and Herb was still single. Once he met Marjorie, Herb's attitude toward marriage changed. When Herb first brought Marjorie home to meet his grown children, his daughter, Peggy, expected an elderly woman.

"I was totally undone. Marjorie was wearing an off-shoulder, form-fitting evening gown and the Russian imperial emeralds," recalled Peggy May Maryn. "My first impression was 'Dear God, when I get to be that age, let me look like her.'"

In addition to her beauty, Peggy was impressed with Marjorie's intelligence. "And she did not talk around things. She had an ability to cut right through to the meat of the matter but did it very diplomatically." Though four years older than Herb, Marjorie still seemed like a much younger woman—lovely, vivacious, and eager to dance, party, and travel.

By late 1957 Marjorie and Herb had become fond companions who were often seen together at Washington parties and receptions. That is not to say that the gregarious executive was in the same financial league as Marjorie. Far from it. Few men or women were. While Herb commanded a large salary as one of the top executives of Westinghouse Air Brake, he was a bon vivant who spent money almost as fast as he made it. "Don't count on me leaving you any inheritance," he used to tell his son Phil. "I like to smell the roses along the path."

The disparity in their financial resources did not seem to bother Marjorie. Long ago she had accepted the fact that it was unlikely that she would fall in love with someone as wealthy as she. By 1957 Marjorie was again being touted in newspapers and magazines as one of the richest women in America. Her wealth was said to be in excess of $250 million. Even with allowances for exaggeration, the likelihood of her finding the "right" man in a similar category was improbable. For Marjorie, edging toward seventy, the crucial thing was to find someone she could love. Despite the pain of the Davies divorce and the memory of her previous marriages, Marjorie still longed for a grand passion—and an adoring, compatible husband to fulfill it.

"Grandmother was a romantic. And if you didn't have a man, there was something wrong with your life," explained her granddaughter Ellen MacNeille Charles. Once she had found that man, his financial status was relatively unimportant. Should he be less wealthy than she, as indeed all Marjorie's husbands were, she simply set up a trust fund for him. "Money," Herb once told his son Phil after his marriage, "is the least of our problems."

Herb, like Marjorie, was thoughtful, intelligent, and outgoing. He, too, was a committed patron of the arts, serving as head of the Pittsburgh Civic Opera at the time of his wedding. His long career in railroads and banking had made him an astute business manager whose skills Marjorie respected. Yet what most attracted her to Herb was his warmth, his enjoyment of people, and his obvious pleasure in her company.

Months before the engagement was announced, Herb confided to his son Phil that he was wild about Marjorie. "She's the first woman I've met since your mother who really cares for me." That interpersonal glow, combined with their mutual interests, made Marjorie and Herb seem ideally paired. Physically they were also well matched, for both were tall and elegant. "Herb May was a handsome silver-haired man. If you ever saw a king and queen, together he and Marjorie looked like it," recalled Marjorie's attorney, Henry Dudley.

Simultaneous with Marjorie's and Herb's courtship, Joe Davies's health took a turn for the worse. On May 9, 1958, he died at Tregaron of bronchial pneumonia. Three days later the former ambassador was buried with great pomp from Washington's National Cathedral.

Coincidentally, it was the same day that Betty Beale announced Marjorie's forthcoming marriage to Herbert May in the *Evening Star*. "Although I didn't do it intentionally, people blamed me for the timing," Beale recalled.

While Joe Davies's death had little impact upon the timing of Marjorie's wedding, the circumstances of their divorce resonated through her new marriage. For months before the private June 18, 1958, ceremony at Adelaide's country home, Marjorie and Herb had debated which city would become their common residence: Washington or Pittsburgh. The memory of the Davies divorce and Marjorie's displacement from Tregaron was still too fresh in her mind. While she was happy to relinquish her maiden name socially and be known as Mrs. Herbert May, she was still psychologically Marjorie Merriweather Post. No man, no matter how adoring, would again subsume her identity or threaten her possessions. Nor did Marjorie intend to give up Hillwood for a home in Pittsburgh.

For his part, Herb was equally reluctant to relinquish his Pittsburgh estate, Rosewall. As a compromise, Marjorie and Herb decided to maintain homes in both cities and commute between the two.

When Marjorie visited Rosewall, in Pittsburgh's elite Squirrel Hill district, to scrutinize it as her future residence, she was appalled by its rundown condition. As she recalled later, "Herb had been a widower for twenty-one years. I don't think he stopped to stay in the house [more than] overnight or to give a big party, there were so many things to be done. The first, of course, was the fixing of quarters for me, which he suggested just before we were married."

The week after Marjorie and Herb were married, they hosted two receptions for their friends. The first, on June 23, 1958, was planned for

Pittsburgh. Under Marjorie's exacting eye, Rosewall had been spruced up with paint and wallpaper. In keeping with the nuptial theme, a new garden, containing white lilies, petunias, and snapdragons, had been planted on the grounds. As a Washington newspaper put it, "Blue skies decided not to quarrel with a picture pretty Victorian setting of larger-than-life-size white plaster cherubs holding massed white flowers, white and blue tables around a pagoda buffet of tiers of white carnations, garlands on blue ropes today as industrialist Herbert A. May introduced his bride, the former Marjorie Merriweather Post of Washington, to business associates and friends."

To greet their 350 guests, Marjorie and Herb stood at the head of a staircase leading to Rosewall's drawing room. Over the mantel hung a dramatic portrait of Marjorie in a black evening gown. By the end of that afternoon the seventy-one-year-old bride had not only charmed many of Herb's closest friends—among them the W. King McCords of Westinghouse Air Brake, the Roy Hunts, and the Frederick Blackburns of the Mellon Bank—but had unequivocally established herself as the new mistress of Rosewall. That night the newlyweds accompanied friends to a performance of Les Ballets de Paris at Pittsburgh's Civic Opera.

Within three days Marjorie and Herb had returned to Washington for a second wedding reception. This one, held at Hillwood on Thursday, June 26, was an even more opulent outdoor tea. Background music, provided by Sidney and his orchestra, wafted through the air. Among the three hundred guests were Washington luminaries like Justice and Mrs. John Harlan, Assistant Secretary of State and Mrs. Walter Robertson, Director of Defense Mobilization and Mrs. Gordon Gray, Senator and Mrs. John McClellan, and Ambassador and Madame Hervé Alphand of France. One of the women who poured tea for the occasion was none other than Marjorie's friend and rival Perle Mesta.

The pièce de résistance was to be a performance by the Washington Ballet. To accommodate the dancers, Marjorie had a stage built on the lawn and decorated it with green satin curtains and flowering orchids. Weeks earlier, after fretting over the possibility of rain, Marjorie arranged for a huge white tent to be placed over the stage, seats, and party area.

On the appointed day Marjorie's worst fears were realized. June 26 dawned damp, hot, and humid, and Hillwood's staff, hoping to protect the green satin and fresh orchids, swathed the tent in plastic sheets. By the time Marjorie and Herb were receiving their guests at Hillwood's Russian Room, it had begun to pour. Undaunted, the newlyweds and their guests adjourned to the tent for tea and refreshments.

Though the tent protected Marjorie and Herb's guests, the plastic sheeting trapped the humidity. The dampness, combined with the heat from the stage lights and the body heat of three hundred guests, had a disastrous effect on the performance. "It was like putting the dancers in a fish bowl." Mary Day, artistic director of the Washington Ballet, laughed years later. "Everything drooped, the girls drooped, the flowers curled, and all the costumes stretched."

Despite that inauspicious introduction, Marjorie's marriage to Herb May initially was happy and ushered in a time in which the heiress was at the peak of her powers. A year before the marriage society editors had debated which hostess was Washington's most brilliant; Gwen Cafritz, Perle Mesta, or Marjorie Post. While it was generally acknowledged that Perle Mesta's parties were often the largest, few were more lavish than Marjorie's. Nor were any of Washington's reigning hostesses more interested in the culture of that city than Marjorie Merriweather Post. And no one, as Marie McNair of *The Washington Post* observed, recalling an engagement party Marjorie hosted for her granddaughter Ellen at the Chevy Chase Club that included a dance performance, had "ever put on a ballet for their guests."

Those who knew Marjorie well understood that she had no consuming ambition to outshine Perle Mesta or Gwen Cafritz as Washington's leading hostess. Far more important, journalist and National Symphony publicist Roy Meacham observed, "was to be taken seriously and make a significant contribution to humanity." To the spirited septuagenarian Marjorie, that contribution was increasingly to be of a cultural nature, something that would give other people pleasure and live beyond her. As her daughter Dina once explained, "She felt a very strong compulsion to share her material means with individuals less fortunate than she and institutions, both arts and social, she felt deserved support."

By the 1950s it was obvious to Marjorie and a cadre of Washington's elite that the capital was a cultural wasteland. For years there was talk about replacing Washington's Constitution Hall with a new auditorium, and in September 1955 President Eisenhower finally appointed a District of Columbia Auditorium Commission to search for a location. By 1958 the concept of a National Capital Center for the Performing Arts—the future Kennedy Center—was already in the works.

Marjorie believed that one of the hallmarks of a cultured city was a top-quality dance company. Without it, she felt, Washington would never achieve the cultural preeminence of other national capitals like London, Paris, or even Moscow. To create such a company would require years of work. By the late 1950s, with the interest and support of Jacqueline Kennedy and patrons like Marjorie, the remarried Gladys Heurtematte Johnston, and Gerson Nordlinger, a Washington Ballet Guild was established.

Under the auspices of that organization a new Washington School of Ballet soon began giving performances. To increase the visibility of the fledgling guild, Marjorie hosted teas and receptions at Hillwood. For a 1958 Christmas performance of *The Nutcracker* at Constitution Hall, she even donated nine of her gowns as costumes.

Behind the scenes members of the Washington Ballet Guild were quarreling. At issue was board chairman Mrs. Richard Riddell's insistence that a National Ballet Company be established at once. In direct opposition to this concept were artistic director Mary Day, Gladys Heurtematte Johnston, and Marjorie, who wanted to create a professional school from which a company would evolve. After an acrimonious debate the guild fell apart. Mrs. Riddell and her supporters pulled away and independently established the National Ballet Company. Meanwhile, Mary Day, Gladys Johnston, and Marjorie devoted themselves to the establishment of a full-time ballet academy.

The result was a new Washington National Ballet Foundation, under whose auspices was the Washington School of Ballet. The school was the first of its kind in the United States and offered, according to artistic director Mary Day, a "combined curriculum of dance and academics, the same kind they had in the Bolshoi, which Marjorie admired so much." To establish the academic requirements for certification in Washington, D.C., Marjorie called upon her associates at the Mount Vernon Seminary and Junior College. She also continued to contribute funds, give teas, and act as a behind-the-scenes source for publicity.

By the early sixties Marjorie had overcommitted herself. In 1958 she had "retired" from the board of General Foods, and had almost immediately assumed a directorship of Washington's National Savings and Trust Company. Her days were further divided among philanthropic activities, a heavy schedule of entertainment, and travel. There was little time to give the Washington National Ballet Foundation the attention it deserved. Instead she entrusted it to her husband, Herb May, who subsequently became chairman of its board.

. . .

That Herb was willing to wage cultural battles for the betterment of Washington was only part of his appeal. His businessman's emphasis on efficiency also impressed Marjorie. Herb took pride in being au courant, in utilizing the most current technological innovations of the era. Although an inveterate "railroad man," he often traveled by air.

To Marjorie the idea of flying was terrifying. For years she had avoided air travel whenever possible, and now, even with her marriage to Herb and the necessity of traveling between Washington and Pittsburgh, she preferred to stay on the ground. Trains, she insisted, were one of the few dependable modes of transportation, and it was by train that she still intended to go.

In 1953, during the waning years of her marriage to Joe Davies, Marjorie sold the *Sea Cloud*. No longer was the yacht practical to run. High taxes and the exorbitant cost of maintenance and labor had made it impossible to justify. Bidding on the boat was a handful of potential buyers, among them Cuban dictator Fulgencio Batista, the crown prince of Saudi Arabia, a Swedish industrialist, the Greek shipping magnate Aristotle Onassis, and the governments of Iran, Portugal, and Argentina. In the end Marjorie sold the boat for a mere $550,000 to Jacksonville ship owner George W. Gibbs. Before long Gibbs in turn sold the *Sea Cloud* at a $50,000 profit to Joe Davies's old friend Dominican Republic dictator Rafael Trujillo.

To Herb May, Marjorie's refusal to fly was another impracticality left over from the Davies years. Determined to help Marjorie overcome her terror, Herb arranged for a Lockheed Lodestar owned by Westinghouse Air Brake to take her from Pittsburgh to Washington. To ensure her comfort, he insisted that the flight occur on a calm, sunny day.

The takeoff was flawless. Twenty minutes into the smooth, sun-filled flight Marjorie turned to her husband. "Herb, I like this," she said. Her husband smiled but said nothing. A few minutes later she turned to him again. "Herb, I want one." "Marjorie," the executive gently explained, "a plane like this costs several million dollars." "Herb," Marjorie replied in an equally soft but firm voice, "I didn't ask how much it costs. I want one."

By February 1959 Marjorie and Herb had purchased a Vickers Viscount turboprop jet once owned by Nicaragua's Lanica Airlines. The British-made plane, which was capable of carrying forty-four passengers, was powered by four Rolls-Royce engines and had a traveling speed of 335 miles an hour. At first Marjorie and Herb planned to give the plane a name that reflected both of their own. But one day Herb realized that his wife's middle name was the most fitting of all: Merriweather.

Having acquired the jet, Marjorie and Herb remodeled its interior as a living room. In lieu of a traditional row of seats, they outfitted the cabin with tables, chairs, and a couch. Hot meals were prepared in a nearby cabin by a stewardess. A three-man crew, consisting of two pilots and a backup, was hired—more manpower than on most commercial airlines. Henceforth the *Merriweather* flew regularly into Washington's National Airport and became Marjorie's favorite mode of travel. It was, in fact, such a convenience that Marjorie was soon using it to chauffeur friends and family from Washington to Palm Beach and the Adirondacks. Only occasionally—usually for long overseas flights—did Marjorie resort to commercial airliners. In her view, they were neither as comfortable nor as safe as her beloved *Merriweather*.

Marjorie's early fear of flying was only one of several foibles Herb found frustrating. Another was her intolerance of alcoholic beverages. For half a century Marjorie had restricted the cocktail "hour" before dinner parties to twenty minutes. Although wine was served at dinner, the glasses, as guest Dick Pearson later recalled, "were not constantly filled." In Herb's view, Marjorie's abbreviated cocktail hour seemed inhospitable. Moreover, as a businessman accustomed to staying in fine hotels and the homes of other executives, he found it peculiar that Marjorie provided no liquor for her guests in their rooms at Topridge and Palm Beach. Through patient exhortation, Herb lobbied to change Marjorie's policy. By the early sixties the cocktail hour had been extended to half an hour. And those who came to Topridge and Palm Beach were surprised to see that their rooms had been amply stocked with liquor.

Despite these changes, Marjorie's attitude toward liquor remained puritanical. C.W.'s old admonitions against drinking, those of the Christian Science church, and her youthful memories of the "inebriated" Ed Close could not be forgotten. Under Herb's tutelage, Marjorie became more tolerant of liquor, but she never learned to enjoy it herself. On occasion, and mostly for appearances, she would sip a little rye and nibble upon a cracker, but she never became tipsy.

Marjorie's natural warmth almost immediately won over Herb's children. Among them were three sons—Herb junior, Phil, and Ted—and

Herb's adopted daughter, Peggy. Shortly after the wedding, Marjorie
went out of her way to "adopt" Peggy as her new stepdaughter—just
as she once had with Joe Davies's daughters, Eleanor, E.K., and Rahel.
"Mother was terrific like that," said Dina. "As soon as she married
someone, she took his kids in as if they were her own."

For that, Peggy was particularly grateful. Being the only girl in
the family and having lost her adoptive mother at a tender age, Peggy
had grown up without an intimate female model. To make matters
worse, her relationship with her father, Herb, was awkward, and as she
grew into adolescence and young womanhood, it became even more
strained. By the time Marjorie and Herb wed, Peggy was in her late
twenties, divorced, and in need of womanly counsel. Sensing that, Marjorie promptly took Peggy under her wing. "What the world often saw
was a lot of glitz, but the truth was that Marjorie was very real," Peggy
explained. "We had a relationship where I felt free to go to her and ask
her advice." When, for instance, Peggy fought with her father about
the men she was dating, she confided in Marjorie. The heiress, in turn,
mediated.

From the start the young woman did not refer to her stepmother as
Marjorie. "I called her Mother," Peggy recalled. And in many ways
Marjorie earned the title through her love, advice, gifts, and invitations
to her various homes. To Peggy, Marjorie was the closest thing to a beloved mother she would ever know.

With similar warmth, Marjorie reached out to Herb's other children.
When his oldest son, Herb junior, decided to marry a second time, Marjorie welcomed his bride-to-be, Jan, into the family. "Now, I want you
to be married at my house, here at Hillwood," she told the future bride.
The young woman was awed by the thought. Not only did Marjorie intend to host the wedding, but she lent her own silver, crystal, china,
and linens for the affair.

For her engagement Marjorie gave Jan a gold bracelet and at the time
of the wedding presented her with a pearl necklace with a diamond and
sapphire clasp. Later, when the couple had settled into married life,
Marjorie invited them to parties at Hillwood and weeks at Topridge and
Palm Beach. "I thought she was a wonderful woman. She had a unique
warmth about her," Jan May said. "My only regret is that I didn't see
more of her than I did."

Other children in the May family expressed similar affection. Phil
May, Herb's middle son, recalled that Marjorie invited him to go on a
cruise with her and his father at Christmas 1958. It was only then that

Phil began to appreciate Marjorie's sensitivity toward others. Gradually, as Phil talked about his problems, Marjorie shared some of her Christian Science philosophy with him.

Shortly afterward a leather-bound volume of Mary Baker Eddy's *Science and Health* arrived at his home. The inscription read "To my new son, with my love from Mother Marjorie." Around the same time she sent Herb's youngest son, Ted, a car. "I felt that I got the better of the gifts," said Phil, who subsequently became a Christian Scientist. "I saw love in that inscription and in that book."

The initial happiness of Marjorie's marriage to Herb May also caused her to reexamine her roots. Although it had been twenty years since her stepmother, Leila, died, Marjorie had assiduously avoided leaving her philanthropic mark upon Battle Creek. Coincidentally, by the early 1960s Battle Creek school superintendent Harry Davidson was attempting to raise funds for a new athletic stadium. When he realized that so many local institutions were already named after W. K. Kellogg—a community college, a school, an auditorium, and the airport—it occurred to him that it would be fitting to name a stadium after the city's other major industrialist, C. W. Post.

By the early sixties virtually nothing in Battle Creek stood as a memorial to Marjorie's father except a statue and the old Post Tavern. A medical center had been named the Leila Hospital after C.W.'s second wife. A recreation field was called Post Park. But that was all. C.W.'s once larger-than-life presence in Battle Creek had all but vanished from the town he made famous at the dawn of the twentieth century.

Through Davidson's friendship with George Lambeer, director of the Post Division of General Foods, the superintendent broached the stadium idea to Marjorie. To his surprise, the heiress, encouraged by her sports-minded husband, Herb, responded enthusiastically. By early 1961 she had donated $150,000 to give Battle Creek a superb athletic stadium—the first large donation she had given the city in forty years.

Simultaneously, General Foods' Post Division donated $100,000 to the twenty-five-acre athletic facility. Using those combined gifts, the Battle Creek schools installed a professional press box, an electric scoreboard, concession stands, and an all-weather track—all in all, according to Davidson, "a much better stadium than we would have otherwise planned."

In November 1961 Marjorie, her daughter Adelaide, and Herb flew into Battle Creek for the dedication of the C. W. Post Field. To Battle

Creekers, Marjorie's arrival was a momentous occasion. Although she toured the Post factory from time to time, her visits were infrequent and rarely publicized, but November 3, 1961, was different.

The city of Battle Creek turned out en masse to greet her. At the airport the Battle Creek Central High band stood in formation awaiting Marjorie's arrival. As soon as the door of the *Merriweather* opened and the silver-haired benefactress emerged, the band struck up an arrangement of "Margie." Dignitaries, school officials, and members of the press rushed forward to welcome her. Marjorie, Adelaide, and Herb were then whisked off to have their first look at the stadium. Above the handsome facility stood a twenty-foot pylon with the name of Marjorie's father upon it. "It's a wonderful field! I couldn't be more pleased with it," Marjorie exclaimed.

That evening after a formal dedication of the C. W. Post Field, the Battle Creek Bearcats played against the Muskegon football team. Although the weather had turned cold and drizzly, Marjorie, wrapped in a Russian sable coat and extra blankets, sat cheerfully through the game. Hovering around her and Herb May was an "honor guard" of high school students, who held umbrellas, fetched blankets, and provided their guests with hot drinks.

The benefactress did not fail to notice the students' ministrations. Before leaving for Washington, she asked for their names. A few days later each of them received a wristwatch. So touched was Marjorie by the hospitality of her hometown that she extended an invitation to have some of the students from the Battle Creek High School visit Washington the following year.

A year later Marjorie kept her promise to the students of Battle Creek. On May 3, 1963, twenty-four high school students—members of the football team, student council members, and those with honors grades—accompanied by high school teachers and chaperons arrived in Washington.

For three days the youngsters, many of whom had never been out of the state of Michigan, were treated to a whirlwind tour of Washington that included the White House, the Capitol, and a special lecture at the National Gallery of Art. In the evenings they attended a National Theater production of the Jerry Herman musical *Milk and Honey* and a "Music for Young America" concert. It was, said Janet Disbrow, one of the students on that trip, "like a fairy tale come true. I was amazed to see that the concert was sponsored by Mrs. Post. That seemed to be her style, yet she never made you think she was a . . . very wealthy person because she was . . . down-to-earth." Throughout the trip Marjorie mingled freely with the students, asked about their interests, and even rode the tour bus with them. "What she seemed to want was to be remembered as a person, not as Mrs. Post," Janet Disbrow observed. "And she thought of every comfort."

That Marjorie seemed to think of everything was neither coincidental nor solely the result of her natural thoughtfulness. From the time C.W. first established Marjorie in her own household at The Boulders, she had been given an expert staff of servants. Over the years as that staff aged or retired, Marjorie had trained others in their places. Requirements were strict. Good health, a sterling employment history, a desire to please, and a perfectionistic streak were essential. So were a good disposition and a willingness to work hard. In return, Marjorie rewarded her staff with salaries as high as or slightly higher than others in similar positions earned. She also provided them with room and board, health care, and uniforms. In contrast to the way servants were often treated in other "great houses" of the rich, Marjorie's servants ate the finest quality food and had a special cook of their own to prepare it. Their living quarters were also comfortable. Nearly all staff members had private bedrooms with private or semiprivate baths. At Mar-A-Lago and Topridge staff members even had their own recreation rooms and dining halls. (Although friends insist that Marjorie was not biased against minorities, all her staff members were white. Many were European, often from Britain or the Scandinavian countries.)

There were standard procedures for everything—for serving meals, setting tables, preparing guest rooms, even for mopping up spills and removing stains. "But everything was done pleasantly, without the slightest upheaval or confusion," said one man who worked for Marjorie in the mid-sixties as a footman. Nor, in the two years that he was employed by Marjorie, did this man (who prefers to remain anonymous) ever see her become upset with a staff member. If a newcomer made a mistake, a servant higher up in the chain of command reprimanded him to "protect" Mrs. Post from the trouble. So devoted, in fact, were members of Marjorie's staff that privately they referred to her as "Mother."

When Marjorie reached her mid-seventies, her staff wanted to express their appreciation and warmth in a direct and permanent way. On October 20, 1962, fifty staff members traveled from Palm Beach and the Adirondacks to dedicate a flagpole at Hillwood in honor of their seventy-five-year-old mistress. "Those of us who have been with the organization for many years will always recall the many kind things you have done. Your deeds speak far better than I can say," former employee Charles Cronk told Marjorie on that occasion. "On behalf of all the employees over the years, I ask you, Mrs. May, to accept this flagpole as a token of our esteem and gratitude."

Nevertheless, there remained a vast gulf between Marjorie and her staff that very few dared to breach. Only a handful were given that privilege. Among them was James Griffin, Sr., the original carpentry supervisor of Mar-A-Lago and later its superintendent. Another was Mar-A-Lago butler Frank Moffat. At Hillwood his counterpart was head butler Gus Modig. The closest of all to Marjorie was Margaret Voigt, the social secretary who had been with her since the 1940s and who, by the 1960s, ran virtually all of the heiress's social affairs.

In that capacity Margaret not only screened Marjorie's mail and phone calls but also wrote letters, made travel arrangements, accepted and refused invitations, and organized the calendar. Explained the Reverend Julia Sibley: "Margaret was a manager type and almost served as Aunt Marjorie's alter ego."

While she greatly facilitated the complex duties of Marjorie's life, some of the heiress's friends and family thought that Margaret was too powerful. What offended them most was Margaret's insistence that they treat her with nearly the same reverence accorded Marjorie. Should they refuse, or treat Margaret merely as a secretary, the woman took her revenge: by giving Marjorie their messages late, by refusing their invitations on Marjorie's behalf, or by omitting them from guest lists. "In a sense she decided who was going to be at court and who wasn't, and I am not using that term *court* loosely," observed Phil May.

If anyone, even Adelaide or Dina, complained that Margaret was officious or haughty, Marjorie brushed the protester aside. "You mind your business and I'll run mine," she once told Dina when the latter criticized Margaret. By the early 1960s everyone who was close to Marjorie knew that Margaret had a powerful hold on the heiress. Once, when Margaret returned from an overseas vacation, Marjorie stayed up past her usual bedtime to await her arrival. Then, recalled Phil May, she "fussed over her just like she was a child, went out to the kitchen and got her things to eat, and brought them in herself."

Exacerbating Marjorie's attachment was the fact that her hearing had begun to degenerate. By the 1950s the hearing loss that Marjorie had complained about when first returning home from Russia had become noticeable to others. "Speak up! Don't mumble," she often said to her grandchildren Ellen and Melissa when they were growing up. By the end of the decade Marjorie's hearing had deteriorated so badly that she began experimenting with hearing aids. Some were put at the side of her ear. Others were hidden in earrings. But it was no use. "She certainly tried every known one, but there really weren't any that helped her," Adelaide recalled.

Nor, unfortunately, did Marjorie's physicians hold out much hope for a surgical intervention. After innumerable consultations and tests, they concluded that she had incurable nerve damage. By the early 1960s she was beginning to miss bits of conversation. Yet when Adelaide suggested that her mother learn to lip-read, Marjorie bristled. Instead she persistently reminded others to speak louder—especially women, whose voices tend to be softer and higher-pitched.

Sometimes people overreacted. At one memorable luncheon Phil May's former wife and mother-in-law spoke in deliberately loud voices. After a few minutes Marjorie put her fork down and looked them both square in the eye. "You don't have to talk so loud," she said. "I can hear both of you perfectly fine."

In a world of encroaching silence a substitute set of ears—such as Margaret Voigt's—became essential. Yet it was not only Dina, Adelaide, and some of Marjorie's friends who disliked Margaret Voigt and distrusted the heiress's dependence upon her. Early in their marriage, Herb also raised objections. Margaret, he believed, was too familiar and had too much power over Marjorie's life. Since she was a member of the staff, it was hardly appropriate, he said, for her to eat with Marjorie. Moreover, he did not think Margaret's office was run as efficiently as it should be. In fact, he suspected the social secretary was sometimes careless and wasteful. Finally, Herb talked to Margaret about ways to streamline her office procedures. A bitter argument ensued.

From the start Margaret had resented Herb as an interloper, one who was drawing Marjorie in new directions and increasingly out of her sphere of influence. Clearly she hoped to get Herb May out of her life— and Marjorie's affairs—altogether.

By 1963 events had conspired in such a way that Margaret's wish came true. That spring Marjorie received one of the worst shocks in her life. A set of photographs arrived that left no doubt that Marjorie's husband, Herb May, was a homosexual.

26

"Her Step Is Firm,
Her Stamina Discouraging"

*T*he storm that broke around Herb May came as no surprise to members of Marjorie's family. To Dina it was obvious from the start that her stepfather was gay. "But he was also a charming man and very companionable and loved to do the things Mother did, and so we thought, well, isn't that a great match for later years," she observed.

Before the marriage a friend warned Marjorie's daughter Eleanor that Herb was a homosexual. Since there was no proof, Eleanor knew that Marjorie would brush it off as malicious gossip. Some of Marjorie's friends also had their suspicions. Gladys Heurtematte Johnston observed that Herb seemed to have unusually close relationships with men—among them a secretary he brought on his honeymoon and a dancer at the National Ballet. "People tried to tell her what he was, and she just wouldn't believe it," recalled Estelle Vesugar Needham.

Gradually, and only after she had been married a few years, Marjorie began to listen more closely to those rumors. Still, with her usual determination to think positively, she dismissed whatever suspicions she had. By mid-1963 the truth could no longer be denied. One of Marjorie's attorneys was presented with incriminating photographs of a nude Herb and boys and young men cavorting at Mar-A-Lago's oceanside swimming pool. Moreover, a blackmailer who claimed to have written a book exposing the unsavory side of Washington's elite was threatening to devote a chapter to May with those same photographs.

Simultaneously, Marjorie's daughter Eleanor, who still lived in

France and was married to the conductor Leon Barzin, had boarded the *Normandie* and crossed the Atlantic to visit her mother in the States. As the ocean liner drew close to port, a friend contacted Eleanor and urged her to tell Marjorie the truth about May before the photographs were published.

When Eleanor broke the news, Marjorie was stunned. At first she said nothing, staring at her daughter in disbelief. "I guess I knew because he was acting so strange," she finally replied. It was true that Herb had been drinking more than Marjorie thought appropriate. On at least one occasion she had thrown out all the prescription drugs he popped at whim. Moreover, one night, when Marjorie, Eleanor, and Herb were having dinner in a Montmartre restaurant, he had seemed unduly "interested" in the waiters. At the time, Eleanor recalled, Marjorie had mumbled to herself, "Not natural, not natural." Yet, in spite of such incidents, it had not dawned on Marjorie that her husband was homosexual.

"You mean, you didn't know?" an incredulous Dina asked her mother when the truth was finally out. "Of course I didn't. I wouldn't have married him," Marjorie retorted. And then to Dina with equal astonishment: "You mean, you did?" For all her sophistication, Marjorie had not recognized Herb's sexual proclivities. "It was very strange. Mom was in some ways very unworldly," Dina mused. "It wasn't that she didn't know any homosexuals. She knew a lot of them—'pansies' she called them. It just never occurred to me that she didn't realize he was like that."

Marjorie's incredulity was not entirely irrational. Herb had, after all, been married and fathered three children. His physical relationship with Marjorie at the beginning of the marriage had been normal enough for her to have sent the "fluffy pink clouds" telegram to her granddaughter Ellen. Gradually, though, their relationship seems to have become somewhat one-sided. "My god," Herb once complained to a friend, "she wants to do it every night." Her mother, Dina subsequently surmised, was really a "very earthy lady. And we didn't give her credit for that. Why she didn't try it [sex] beforehand, I'll never figure, but she was a very old-fashioned person in those ways."

Everyone in the family had a different explanation. From the start Adelaide believed that Margaret Voigt and certain members of Marjorie's staff who disliked Herb because he suspected they were embezzling funds had had the photographs doctored. The May children attributed their father's alleged homosexuality to his declining health, fears about losing his potency, or simply an aberration. Until the very end of their marriage, observed Herb's son Phil, he and Marjorie seemed to be happy. When, for instance, Phil visited them at Camp Topridge, he often found them sitting cozily together in the evenings, looking through Montgomery Ward catalogs for casual shoes. "You can't be unhappy with somebody and sitting there and doing that," said Phil. "Somebody had to put their finger in the pie."

According to Peggy May Maryn, Herb may well have felt threatened by Marjorie—in spite of her attempts to make him feel important. Yet Marjorie's natural gifts, coupled with the fact that she simply was more powerful than he, somehow undermined his ego. "My father learned early on that when it came to brains and business acumen, she was way ahead of him. . . . [T]hrough no fault of her own or his own, he was rather second fiddle. And I think he was the type of man who would find that difficult to deal with. He liked being master in his own house."

Whatever the psychological dynamics actually were, the mere existence of embarrassing pictures of a naked Herb with boys and young men in Palm Beach—and a blackmailer waiting to be paid off—was more than Marjorie could stand. The guiding principle of Marjorie's life, a friend once said privately, was "that anything was good, and if it isn't, you turn your back on it." Being unwilling to accept May as merely a "companionable" husband or the possibility of Margaret Voigt's culpability, Marjorie retreated from the controversy altogether. "She was mortified and so upset that she was bound and determined that she was going to get rid of him," Dina recalled.

Soon after the accusations were made, Herb's mental state began to decline alarmingly. A psychiatrist was brought in. When Herb's "confusion" got worse, his son Phil accompanied him on the *Merriweather* to the Institute, a private psychiatric facility of the Pennsylvania Hospital. During the ordeal Marjorie continued to treat Herb with kindness, paying his medical fees and living expenses for a private suite at the hospital, sending him flowers, and keeping him informed of her whereabouts.

By September 1963 Herb had recovered sufficiently to write, "I want you to know from my heart how grateful I am to you for the courageous, generous, loyal and loving support which you have given to me during my illness. I am more than grateful to you for all of these things and without them I would not have been able, in my opinion, to have come through to the extent that I have."

Later, when Herb suffered a stroke, there were other medical expenses. Marjorie quietly paid for those as well as an apartment in Fort Lauderdale, where Herb lived until his death in 1968.

Nor did she turn her back on his children. After her separation from the Pittsburgh executive, the socialite continued to invite Peggy to Hillwood for dinners and garden parties. And occasionally Peggy attended them. "I felt no animosity. They were big people and had to make their own decisions," she recalled. Herb's treatments at the Institute of the Pennsylvania Hospital lasted nearly a year, during which time Marjorie took steps to initiate a Mexican divorce. By August 1964 Herb had signed the papers as well. The same month Marjorie announced that she was again assuming her maiden name.

The divorce was a blow to Marjorie's pride from which she would never fully recover. Despite her beauty, brains, and wealth, Marjorie never had a marriage that remained happy for very long. Twice she had suffered the indignity of being jilted by her husbands—first for other women and now for other men.

At the time of Marjorie's divorce from Herb May and for years thereafter, friends speculated about her four marriages. To some, Marjorie's passionate adulation of her father, C. W. Post, was responsible. To others, like Marjorie's daughter Adelaide Riggs, she just had "bad luck" choosing husbands. There may have been some truth to that analysis. According to Roy Meacham, who knew only Marjorie's last husband, "There was twice the life force in her than in Herb May." Years earlier Marjorie's old friend Hunter Marston had said the same thing about Ed Close.

Others believed that Marjorie's physical and financial assets were just too much for any man to handle. Moreover, as Marjorie aged, her lifestyle became increasingly ritualized and less likely to allow her husbands to carve out "space" for themselves. "On one hand, she would do everything she could to make her husbands happy, and on the other, she had a lifestyle that didn't accommodate them," observed her granddaughter Ellen. A remark Herb once made seemed to suggest the validity of Ellen's comment. "Gee, you have a nice house, Herb," said a friend at a party. "Living in Hillwood is like living in a goddamn museum," he replied.

Marjorie's granddaughter Marwee maintained that Marjorie had a romantic blind spot. When confronted with men who were bright and dominant, like E. F. Hutton and Joe Davies, she ended up fighting with them. "And the sweet ones," Marwee concluded, "either got no respect or became emasculated."

Marjorie herself seemed to have few insights into her "husband problems." Once, some years after Marjorie's divorce from Herb May, General Foods chairman Clare Francis asked her about them outright. "Marjorie, you could run General Motors. You could run U.S. Steel. You could run anything. You're the smartest woman I know. But why do you have so much trouble with husbands?" "Clare, I honestly don't know. Ain't it hell?" Marjorie said, and shrugged her shoulders.

Soon after deciding to divorce Herb, Marjorie invited his sons to Topridge to discuss the situation. "I saw a very sad woman when I visited her in her island home off Saranac," recalled Phil May. "I saw a woman who really looked like the world had come down on her and that she had lost her last good chance for happiness."

That same summer Marjorie's friend Gladys Heurtematte Johnston visited her for two weeks at Topridge. By then the seventy-six-year-old heiress had had time to contemplate the peaks and valleys of her life and examine her own culpability in them. "I had many lovely things," she told Gladys, "but in choosing a husband I never had much luck."

Yet Marjorie was not prone to indulge in self-pity for long. During the winter of 1963–64 she consulted regularly with her Christian Science practitioner, Katherine Ross. Although the divorce was not yet announced to her friends, Marjorie devoted herself almost single-mindedly to emphasizing everything that was or had been positive in her life. It was probably not coincidental, then, that a project she had been working on for years—a biography of her father, researched and written by Marjorie's on-staff genealogist, Nettie Leitch Major—was finally finished in 1963. The resulting book, a vanity publication entitled *C. W. Post: The Hour and the Man*, appeared in February 1964. Before long hundreds of copies of the flattering profile of C.W.—with an equally praiseworthy chapter on Marjorie—were sent to her friends.

In March 1963 the heiress went on a Mediterranean cruise with her friends Lady Alice and Sir Bede Clifford. The trip, Marjorie wrote her friend Princess Cito di Bitetto, "was a mess from the beginning. I had been under considerable nervous tension and strain with Herb's illness so was not at my best when we started off. We had a bad crossing with very heavy seas and rain and . . . throughout the entire time, the weather was not particularly good." By May Marjorie had returned, regained the six pounds she had lost, and—despite rumors of her separation from Herb May—hosted her annual garden party at Hillwood.

By the summer of 1964 Marjorie seemed to have recovered her equilibrium. In her newly reinstated identity as Mrs. Merriweather Post, she hosted a series of five-day house parties at Camp Topridge. Distinguished guests, such as Ambassador and Mrs. Jawaharlal Nehru, the Greek ambassador and Mrs. Aleco Matsas, Brigadier General Godfrey McHugh, and the Leonard Carmichaels, were flown up from and back to Washington on the *Merriweather.* It was Marjorie's first "solo" summer at Topridge in many years, and it was so flawless, so seemingly effortless that her guests were awed.

By autumn 1964 Marjorie had recovered enough of her confidence to reemerge in Washington as an independent woman—still lovely and still regarded as one of the city's premier philanthropists and hostesses. On October 5 she appeared for the opening night of the National Ballet "looking youthful and charming in a short evening gown . . . with a new escort." Ten days later she hosted a round and square dance for one hundred friends at the Army-Navy Country Club. On November 12 she traveled to Manhattan to attend the Daiquiri Ball benefit for the New York Girls Club. At the end of that month ninety-five friends held a dance in Marjorie's honor as "one collective expression of thanks" for her hospitality in the Adirondacks.

Nor did Marjorie's social pace slacken in the new year. A decade earlier, during the last years of Marjorie's marriage to Joe Davies, she had deliberately kept Mar-A-Lago closed for the winter season, thinking that it was hardly worth the effort or expense as a single woman. She did not open it again until 1961, after her marriage to Herb May. Now that she was again alone—perhaps permanently—the seventy-eight-year-old Marjorie thought there was every reason to enjoy her Florida home in the winter months, with or without a man.

"The tremendous feeling here this season that Palm Beach has been reborn to new brilliance could well be due to the return of Mrs. Marjorie Merriweather Post, multimillionairess, to her oceanside Spanish palace, Mar-A-Lago," wrote her old advocate, New York *Daily News* society editor Nancy Randolph. "Mostly absent for some years past, Mrs. Post told your reporter yesterday that she will never again miss a season at her fabulous stone pile. 'It's so strong a fortress that not even a hurricane can shake. I've decided to spend the rest of my winters here,' Mrs. Post said."

In February 1965 Marjorie invited forty guests to the Snow Ball benefit. Among them were several ambassadors and their wives, and Palm Beach notables like Rose Kennedy, Charles Munn, Mary Sanford, and Colonel Serge Obolensky. The last gentleman, the septuagenarian White Russian once married to Alice Astor and later the manager of Manhattan's St. Regis Hotel, would soon be linked to Marjorie as the man most likely to become her next husband. Although Obolensky— Oboe, as Marjorie called him—was one of her favorite escorts, romance never blossomed between them. When confronted by prying reporters, the tall, gallant Obolensky brushed off rumors that there was anything more than a friendship between them.

It was true that from the time the White Russian first arrived in Palm Beach in the twenties he and Marjorie had been friends. They had many things in common—a keen aesthetic sense, a love of Russia and Russian art, and a fondness for ballroom dancing—yet their relationship was and would remain merely one of friendship.

By late 1965 there was a new beau in the wings: Fred Korth, a silver-haired, recently divorced Washington attorney and former secretary of the navy under President Kennedy. Shortly after Marjorie's return to Washington as a single woman she had invited Korth to a dinner party. The attorney was only one of a myriad of Washingtonians Marjorie casually knew through her social network. A dozen years earlier Korth, then assistant secretary of the army, had attended Marjorie's garden parties with his first wife. Now that he was single, the bespectacled Texas-born attorney, although twenty years Marjorie's junior, began to see her in an entirely new light—not only as one of Washington's most renowned hostesses but as a potential sweetheart. "She was one of the greatest ladies I have ever known. She was highly intelligent, beautiful, charming, and attractive," he said. "She had the attributes of a beautiful female, a desirable female, a lady with it all."

Almost all. The one thing that Marjorie lacked was good hearing. Fortunately Fred had a booming voice that she could easily hear, and it may well have contributed to their attraction. By early 1966 Fred had become Marjorie's constant companion, not only at Washington parties but also at Topridge and Mar-A-Lago. When the legendary hostess showed a film after one of her dinner parties, it was "the attractive and amusing Korth," noted a reporter, "who sits beside her." And in May 1966, after a dinner dance given in Marjorie's honor by the Kuwaiti ambassador, a friend predicted there would soon be "wedding bells" for Marjorie and the Texas attorney.

Although Marjorie and Fred were mutually adoring, they made no commitment. They attended parties and balls together. They played golf at Mar-A-Lago and on the putting green at Hillwood—usually with Marjorie beating Fred badly. Whenever possible, they traveled together: to Palm Beach, to California to see Marwee and Barbara Hutton, to Europe to visit with Eleanor and Leon Barzin, to St. Croix to see their friends Jack and Polly Guggenheim Logan. They also celebrated each other's birthdays, teasing each other about the advancing years. On one occasion Marjorie gave Fred an exquisite pair of silver cuff links and a cake with four candles. On another, the attorney delighted Marjorie with the presentation of a tsarist bank note.

When they were apart, affectionate letters floated between them attesting to a sturdy and caring relationship that often included Fred's children. "Darling: . . . I'm looking forward to next Thursday when I come down [to Palm Beach] with Fritz, Penne, Gary and Nina [Korth's son, daughter-in-law, son-in-law, and daughter]. I have already served notice on them that they are going to have to pretty well take care of themselves, since I'm going to be with *you*," Fred wrote in one of those letters. In another, while on a business trip to Portugal: "I miss you and wish I were at Mar-A-Lago with you instead of 3,000 miles away. I'm saving lots of hugs and kisses for your return."

And in 1967: "You should be glad that you left Washington because it started raining immediately upon your departure, but I might expect the weather to get gloomy when you left."

Eventually the relationship reached the point where it demanded clarification. Months earlier Marjorie had confessed to her friend Gladys Heurtematte Johnston that "if Fred Korth proposed to me, I would accept." Despite her advancing age and four unhappy marriages, Marjorie was ready to try matrimony again.

When Marjorie finally raised the possibility that she might wed a fifth time, Adelaide, Eleanor, and Dina had thrown up their hands in horror. "Look, Mom, why complicate things at this stage of your life? Why not just move him in?" the three younger women suggested. Marjorie regarded them with disbelief. "What, my own daughters are telling me to live in sin?" "Yes!" Marjorie's daughters nodded in emphatic agreement. "We are." "Well, I never thought I would hear that from any of you!" Marjorie exclaimed indignantly, and swept up the stairs. For nearly a week she refused to speak to any of them.

The thought of marrying Marjorie had crossed Fred Korth's mind more than once, but he was also well aware that he was twenty years Marjorie's junior. And while she looked and acted much younger than her nearly eight decades, the disparity in their ages was an irrefutable biological fact. Moreover, Fred, being imbued with normal masculine pride and highly sensitive to public opinion, feared that if he did marry Marjorie, people would think he had done so for her money.

Finally the attorney shared his reservations with Marjorie. They talked it over for a while. And finally, if reluctantly, the heiress agreed. She and Fred would continue to enjoy each other as sweethearts but would remain unmarried.

"And we were perfectly happy with that. Our relationship remained very close through the end of her life," Fred Korth later reminisced.

As a septuagenarian, Marjorie had come to feel that she was running out of time, and this had stirred her to make provisions for her death. Even before Hillwood was complete, she knew that the house and museum she was building would be an example of an era whose elegance and opulence would likely not be seen again. As Dina subsequently explained, Hillwood was part of her mother's "wish to show a certain way of life that was dying, that wouldn't exist again, and to share the collections that she made and loved."

Those collections had grown over time. After Marjorie's return from Soviet Russia and residence at Tregaron, she continued to add to her art collection, and the process had accelerated at Hillwood. The criterion for her new acquisitions was straightforward: Anything she purchased had to be beautiful as well as important. To assist her in this task, Marjorie was constantly in touch with leading art and antiques dealers in New York and Europe. In 1958, when insurance appraisers insisted that she catalog her collection at Hillwood, Marjorie hired a Byzantine art specialist named Marvin Ross. With his encouragement, Marjorie began to acquire certain pieces over the years to make it truly "the finest collection of Imperial Russian treasures" in the United States. Among them were early imperial porcelain from the period of the Tsarina Elizabeth, a gold and jeweled chalice commissioned by Catherine the Great for the Alexander Nevsky Monastery, and the nuptial crown set in eighteenth-century diamonds worn by the last tsarina, Alexandra.

As early as December 1962, when Marjorie was still married to Herb May, the press announced that she planned to leave Hillwood and its furnishings to the Smithsonian. Included in this arrangement were Marjorie's entire art collection, antique furnishings, rugs, tapestries, and the Hillwood estate itself. The only exceptions were the majority of

Marjorie's jewelry. Nevertheless, several pieces she purchased from the jeweler Harry Winston, such as a 31-carat antique diamond from the Rovensky collection, a 31-sapphire blue heart-shaped diamond ring, and a 275-carat diamond necklace Napoleon had given his wife the Empress Marie-Louise, as well as other gems in Marjorie's collection, were willed to the Smithsonian. "This means that the Government's huge and famous museum that embraces in its aegis the National Gallery of Art, will receive the second greatest private bonaza of its history," predicted the *Sunday Star.* Noting that the first had been Andrew Mellon's gift, which established the National Gallery, "Marjorie Post May's collection by itself is worth in the millions."

Marjorie's decision had been made through her friendship with Dr. Richard Howland, president of the National Trust for Historic Preservation. When, however, in 1960, Dr. Howland left the National Trust to chair the Smithsonian's Department of Civil History, he brought the idea of establishing Hillwood as a museum with him. By 1962, the Smithsonian had accepted Marjorie's gift and an alleged seven-million-dollar endowment that went with it.

By 1964 Marjorie, fearing that Mar-A-Lago would fall victim to a wrecking ball—as had Mrs. Stotesbury's El Mirasol after her death—decided to bequeath Mar-A-Lago to the state of Florida. That arrangement was not to be. When Florida governor Farris Bryant arrived at Marjorie's fabled estate for a tour, he asked how much it cost to maintain Mar-A-Lago and its staff per year. After examining the 1962 ledgers, Marjorie presented him with a precise figure: $259,512.47. C. W. Post would have been proud. His daughter had learned her lessons in household accounting well.

But so had Governor Bryant. Mar-A-Lago was too expensive for the state of Florida to maintain. Politely, and with regrets, the state passed on the offer.

The honors were now accruing as fast as the years. And with them, any hopes that Marjorie had for anonymity were dashed. In November 1965 *Life* magazine ran a major story on Marjorie and her three estates with photographs by Alfred Eisenstaedt. "To set foot inside Hillwood, the Georgian mansion in Washington, D.C., Marjorie Merriweather Post calls home, is like turning back the clock to a time of formal elegance," began the article. "Mrs. Post, at 78, resembles a Dresden doll, but gives the strong impression of being woven of steel wire. Her step is firm, her stamina discouraging."

Marjorie would soon need that stamina to withstand the blizzard of letters that began to pile up at Hillwood's front door. "People have been writing in from all parts of the world, wanting this, wanting that . . . they do not seem to stop and this is almost a year," Marjorie complained to Clare Francis, chairman of the General Foods board, the following July. "Now as I approach my eightieth birthday, I am looking for calm and quiet, and no more publicity."

That was already impossible. For years Marjorie had opened Hillwood for charity teas, educational groups, and art lovers. At times as many as five hundred people toured her home each week. A group of volunteer docents—especially friends like Estelle Vesugar Needham, who wanted to repay Marjorie's kindness—guided visitors through the house. In May 1966 *The New York Times* published a complimentary profile on the philanthropist, describing her as having "patrician features" that hid a "salty down to earth manner." The following February *Time* magazine featured her in another story. "At 79, Marjorie Merriweather Post Close Hutton Davies May is still slender and pridefully erect—but she is far more than merely a remarkably handsome woman. . . . Mrs. Post is a grande dame of high society. . . ."

A month later Marjorie received similar accolades from the National Symphony Orchestra. The date was March 15, 1967, Marjorie's eightieth birthday. On that occasion Marjorie's son-in-law Leon Barzin had flown in from Paris with Eleanor to conduct the symphony in her honor at Constitution Hall. The program included some of Marjorie's favorite music: Beethoven, a Handel organ concerto, and Hindemith's *Hérodiade*. The highlight of the evening was the National Symphony's "Happy Birthday" serenade to its most important benefactress. During it Marjorie "stood erect and regal beneath a blinding spotlight in her garlanded box as the audience at Constitution Hall applauded and smiled at her. She smiled back happily." Surrounding her were her three daughters—Adelaide Riggs, Eleanor Barzin, and Dina Merrill—and several grandchildren.

Hundreds of friends had turned out for the event. A day earlier nearly three hundred of them had assembled in the Sulgrave Club's gold and white ballroom to give Marjorie a "private" birthday celebration. Among them were such luminaries as Madame Nehru, Mrs. Searle Whitney, General McAuliffe, and Admiral George Anderson, who joined former Metropolitan Opera singer Anna Case in "Happy Birthday."

Douglas R. Smith, chairman and president of the National Savings and Trust Company, then presented Marjorie with an unusual birthday gift: a pair of lapis lazuli and ormolu imperial Russian candelabra. The benefactress's beauty, he noted, "is more widely known and admired than any other woman's in the world." And so was her "elegance." In a final touching tribute, Supreme Court Justice Tom Clark presented Marjorie with a red Moroccan leather portfolio listing the names of those who had contributed to the gift.

Marjorie interrupted the Supreme Court justice. "May I have a word? There's never been a birthday like this—all those dear faces. It's really an emotional binge—a joyous and marvelous one." She had, Marjorie went on to explain, her own little surprise for National Symphony Orchestra conductor Howard Mitchell. "I was waited on today by two men who came down from New York from a certain large bank that I've been doing business with since 1914. They brought me a check for $5,000 for my birthday," she said with glee. "It's made out to the National Symphony."

Though she was growing deafer, the magic of live orchestral music was something Marjorie was determined to share with future generations.

27

Careful Housekeeping

*T*o the octogenarian Marjorie, the spectacle of an angry generation burning draft cards, staging sit-ins, and picketing universities because of American involvement in Vietnam was a travesty, but the social turbulence of the late sixties and early seventies would change neither Marjorie's lifestyle nor her loyalties. For the philanthropist it was a time of consolidation, contemplation, and renewed charitable contributions.

With friends in Congress and the military, Marjorie remained staunchly supportive of the American "cause." As the Vietnam War wore on and reports of casualties mounted, she grew baffled by the duration of the struggle. To the orderly, take-charge heiress, it seemed, as she once lamented to the Long Island University president Gordon Hoxie, that "things were getting very much out of focus."

What dismayed Marjorie most were the young lives lost or maimed by the war. From her serene Louis XVI bedroom at Hillwood, where she conducted business every morning, Marjorie sent contributions to organizations honoring Vietnam veterans. When, in May 1969, Marine Sergeant Robert J. Chicca, described by the Marines as "one of the few entirely undisputed heroes of the U.S.S. *Pueblo* affair," returned to a welcoming crowd of a thousand, Marjorie donated money for the celebration. At Washington benefits each year she bought two tables for enlisted marines. And every spring she invited veterans from Walter Reed Army Hospital and the Bethesda Naval Hospital to a garden reception at Hillwood. By the late sixties the guests at these affairs were almost exclusively Vietnam veterans, many of whom arrived on crutches, in wheelchairs, and even on stretchers.

One of them was a marine officer who later met Marjorie's grandson-in-law Rody Cantacuzene in Naples. "I'm going to buy you a drink," he insisted to the surprised young man. "You have no idea what it was like to be recovering from an injury in a war where nobody cared about you and then taken to Hillwood. We were amazed by the grounds, the food, and the house. We didn't know what we were seeing inside, but we knew it was good. We were all so moved."

Other veterans were incredulous that Marjorie recognized the unpopularity of the war and their own untenable situation. "You mean she has all this, nothing to worry about but living it up, and she still cares about us guys?" one veteran told a member of Marjorie's staff at another garden party. Invariably some of the soldiers also noticed that Marjorie's hearing was so bad that she had difficulty conversing. "I wish I could give her both of my ears; this is all in the world she could use," said another.

Over the years letters, cards, and notes of appreciation poured in. In 1969 the Marine Corps awarded Marjorie the Dickie Chapelle Award for her "demonstrated concern and solid support for the American hospitalized servicemen and for her lifetime of philanthropy and public service."

Marjorie's gradual envelopment in a nearly soundless world would not make her any less conscientious about other civic causes. Even when totally deaf, she remained a determined donor to organizations she deemed worthy.

To maintain contact with the outside world, Marjorie had to develop a system of substitute "ears." The first of these was a special amplification device attached to her phone. Though initially helpful, it became less so as Marjorie's hearing deteriorated. In its place she relied even more completely on Margaret Voigt. Now, instead of merely screening calls, as Margaret had for many years, the secretary was forced to take most of them herself. Later she recorded them in memo form along with the time and date and often the speaker's "mood." Efficient as the system was, it inevitably strengthened Marjorie's dependency upon Margaret and, much to Adelaide's and Dina's distress, gave the secretary nearly absolute control over their mother's life.

As her daughters feared, the result was that Marjorie was additionally "protected" from certain people and invitations—sometimes contrary to what she would have chosen herself. For instance, when Joe Davies's eldest and by then widowed daughter, Eleanor, invited Marjorie to her wedding to the Reverend Dr. Lowell Ditzen, Margaret Voigt telephoned Marjorie's regrets. A few days later, when Eleanor saw Marjorie at a party, she said, "I'm so sorry you can't come to my wedding." "What wedding?" Marjorie asked. Eleanor explained that she had written Marjorie a note with an invitation. "Well, I never saw it. I never got it. Of course I'm coming," her former stepmother replied. That same week Marjorie invited Eleanor to dinner at Hillwood.

Marjorie often heard people better in person than on the phone. This was especially true on certain "good days" and when she was with only one or two people. Although Marjorie stubbornly refused to learn lip-reading, she probably acquired some of that skill on her own, for when friends sat directly in front of her, she seemed to understand them. Marjorie also heard people better while traveling in a car, particularly when they sat nearby. What astonished her friends most of all, however, was Marjorie's performance at her round and square dances. Even when nearly totally deaf, the sprightly octogenarian maintained perfect rhythm while dancing. Perhaps, as Marjorie's granddaughter Nina Rumbough Craig later speculated, "she sensed the vibrations of the instruments" on the dance floor from the live orchestra.

Although Marjorie was not a "cuddly" type of grandmother, she was thoughtful about her grandchildren and grandchildren-in-law. When Melissa and Rody returned to the States after being stationed overseas, Marjorie seconded a nomination for her grandson-in-law to become a member of the New York Yacht Club. Knowing Rody was not only half Russian but also a descendant of Ulysses S. Grant, Marjorie selected presents that honored his heritage, among them a portrait of the famous general, an imperial platter once owned by Nicholas I, and a Cossack hunting knife.

As a grandmother Marjorie also had no qualms about telling her seven grandchildren what they "should" do and offering them the means to do it, whether they wanted to or not. When, for instance, her granddaughter Ellen's husband, George, was sent to Vietnam, leaving Ellen home in Chevy Chase with three young children, Marjorie summoned the young woman to Hillwood. "I'm sending over a watchman for you," she told Ellen. Embarrassed by the idea, the young woman automatically grimaced. "I know." Marjorie smiled. "I felt the same way about my father when he insisted I have one. He was right, and I am doing the same thing for you."

Nor was she any less dutiful or insistent when it came to honoring significant events in her grandchildren's lives. Although she seldom saw Eleanor's son Tony de Bekessy because he lived abroad, Marjorie looked forward to attending his wedding. Just before that event she was in Capri and from there planned to fly on the *Merriweather* to Paris. On the appointed day the plane was temporarily grounded in Naples with mechanical trouble. In despair Marjorie instructed Margaret to contact her diplomatic connections in the Italian navy and explain that she needed a helicopter from Capri to Naples. "And for some reason they delivered it," recalled Tony. From Naples Marjorie flew on the now-repaired *Merriweather* to Paris in time for the wedding. Afterward Tony, his bride, and Marjorie boarded the *Merriweather* together. "My grandmother," Tony explained, "insisted on taking me and my wife off to honeymoon in Rome."

Marjorie was no less attentive to Dina's children: Stan junior, David, Nina, and Heather—the child Dina had with her second husband, Cliff Robertson. Marjorie's favorite among these was David, a handsome boy whose high spirits were tempered only by the fact that he had juvenile diabetes. Despite obvious musical ability and other talents, David was a restless youth, who never settled into any one activity for very long. He had, as his sister Nina put it, "fast cars, fast boats and lived his life very fast. Yet he was incredibly charming." Moreover, David knew just how to please Marjorie by cavorting with her on the dance floor, telling stories, and relating some of his own adventures in an amusing way.

Once, when David asked to spend the entire summer at Topridge, Marjorie agreed on one condition: Her grandson could not spend the entire summer loafing; he would have to be trained as a footman and work in that capacity when Marjorie had houseguests. David agreed. By summer he had, in fact, learned his job so well that Marjorie's guests were not even aware of his identity. One night, as she swept out of the dining room after dinner, she stopped before a liveried footman and kissed him. Only then did Marjorie's guests realize that their hostess was saying good night to her grandson. "It was," Dick Pearson recalled, "very moving for us."

Marjorie exercised similar discipline toward her granddaughter Marwee. For years, when the girl got into scraps, Marjorie had bailed her out, sending her from school to school, until she was finally graduated from the University of Southern California. When Marwee got into a brawl over her dog with her boyfriend and employees in a Los Angeles fruit store and the story made national news, her grandmother lost all patience.

To Marjorie, who prided herself, her family, and her staff upon upholding the finest standards of decorum, Marwee's behavior was unconscionable. "She cut me right out of her will," Marwee recalled. "She told me that I was the smartest one in the family and if she left me money, I wouldn't do anything with my life." Not that Marwee was to be left penniless. Some years earlier Marjorie had established a trust fund for her granddaughter. Although she subsequently gave the young woman a dazzling wedding in Washington, lavished generous gifts upon her at Christmas and holidays, and provided nurses for Marwee's five children—her "great-grands," Marjorie called them—she remained true to her word. Marjorie's will excluded Marwee from any major inheritance.

In the waning years of her life Marjorie continued to be conscientious about her civic obligations to Palm Beach. Until virtually the last year of her life she served as international honorary chair emeritus of the Red Cross Ball, shepherding statesmen and ambassadors to the benefit in the *Merriweather*. In the late sixties Marjorie hosted other charities as well, among them the Good Samaritan Ball, receptions for the World Wildlife Fund, and the Palm Beach Fine Arts Festival.

By the early seventies the strain of her hearing loss was beginning to tell on her. At a reception Marjorie gave at Mar-A-Lago for a benefit, she asked the younger Palm Beach philanthropist Sue Whitmore to receive the guests as they entered her drawing room. "You stand there and greet people," she said. And then, Mrs. Whitmore recalled, Marjorie uncharacteristically "walked off to sit in a chair."

One of Marjorie's fondest dreams was the preservation of Mar-A-Lago as a Winter White House. Since her daughters were not interested in maintaining the 115-room, tax-heavy mansion after her death, Marjorie sought its preservation through a government agency. After the state of Florida rejected Marjorie's offer in 1965, she developed a new idea. Why not turn Mar-A-Lago into an official American house of state, a resting place for international dignitaries arriving in this country before they traveled to Washington? Another possibility was to have Mar-A-Lago serve as a federally owned estate where the president, weary of Washington's cold winter, could escape for a few days.

To create a Winter White House would, however, require approval by the executive branch of the government and the Department of the Interior. In hopes of "selling" Congress on the idea, Henry Dudley invited members of the House Interior Committee and their wives to stay at Mar-A-Lago. A dinner was held in their honor. Marjorie herself walked them around the grounds. She urged them to play golf, swim, and climb the seventy-five-foot tower that provided a panoramic view of Palm Beach. Most of all, she talked with them sincerely and personally, not just about Mar-A-Lago but about her life and theirs, their home states, and their common interests. Before long they were wild about their hostess—and the mansion she wanted to give away. "I have never seen a lady of her stature more at home with the wives of the members of Congress. She slayed them," Dudley recalled.

The effort was worth it. Ultimately the House Interior Committee approved the idea. The next step would be considerably more difficult: enlisting support from the president's office and the National Park Service, which would ultimately be responsible for Mar-A-Lago's maintenance. On April 2, 1968, Marjorie invited Lady Bird Johnson and National Park Service director George Hartzog, Jr., to tour her beloved estate.

In her memoir, *A White House Diary*, Lady Bird Johnson later alluded to Mar-A-Lago as "that beautiful never-never land." To enhance that vision, Marjorie arranged for the first lady to stay in "Deenie's House," the fairy-tale suite once occupied by Marjorie's youngest daughter. In honor of Lady Bird's arrival, a twenty-person dinner party was held in Mar-A-Lago's paneled dining room. There was luncheon on the crescent-shaped veranda with Marjorie's and the first lady's mutual friend philanthropist Mary Lasker.

In between, as Lady Bird recalled, Marjorie "walked us through every inch of the house and told us where everything had come from."

By late 1968 the first hurdle had been cleared. In anticipation of Mar-A-Lago's transfer to the federal government, the National Park Service had selected it as its first architectural and photographic study for the Historic American Buildings Survey. In February 1972 Marjorie's famous estate was declared a National Historical Landmark. The following October, President Nixon signed a bill authorizing the Department of the Interior to accept title to Mar-A-Lago. The only step remaining was the president's signature on the proposal to have Mar-A-Lago adopted as a Winter White House. With that stroke of the pen, the imaginative talents of Urban, Wyeth, and Barwig expressed in steel, stucco, and stone would be preserved in perpetuity.

· · ·

With similar compulsivity, Marjorie confirmed arrangements for the Smithsonian to maintain Hillwood after her death. Although reports of an agreement had appeared in the papers as early as 1965, it was not until January 1969 that the regents of the Smithsonian actually voted for its ratification. By its terms, Marjorie had the right to use the estate throughout her life, after which ownership would devolve to the Smithsonian.

To celebrate the ratification, Marjorie hosted a dinner at Hillwood for twenty-three male guests, among them Smithsonian officials, the Smithsonian regent and current vice president, Hubert Humphrey, Marjorie's attorney, Henry Dudley, and her curator, Marvin Ross. During the meal Smithsonian director S. Dillon Ripley hailed Marjorie's generosity as "ranking with the generosity of Mr. Mellon and perhaps two or three others."

He then recalled his first meeting with Marjorie in the spring of 1965. On that occasion she had appeared at the Smithsonian "castle" with several friends and a granddaughter with a shopping bag in tow. Without further ado, Marjorie then unpacked an "irreplaceable collection of jewels and lace" from the shopping bag. Among them were a great emerald from the Hapsburg dynasty, Marie Antoinette's pear-shaped diamond earrings, and a blue diamond necklace that the empress Eugenie had once received from Napoleon III. Now, Ripley observed, the value of Marjorie's gift of Hillwood was inestimable. The mansion's collection of eighteenth- and nineteenth-century imperial Russian art "may be the finest in the world."

Given the high spirits of the event, there was every reason to believe that the Smithsonian was delighted with the arrangement, but beneath the surface were tensions. At an early stage in the negotiations Dr. Ripley had mentioned that when the Smithsonian did finally take over Hillwood, he anticipated using the mansion's dining room to entertain visiting dignitaries. When Marjorie heard about his plan, she became alarmed. A call went in to her attorney, Henry Dudley. "If we transfer my house to the Smithsonian, no food can be served there," she insisted. The kitchen and dining room were to be part of the museum. Should Smithsonian officials want to serve food at the estate, they would have to set up a tent outside.

On that point Marjorie remained adamant. As far as she was concerned, Hillwood was being given to the Smithsonian to be preserved. Any dinners at Hillwood would undoubtedly be catered. Since Marjorie's own veteran staff would no longer be around to supervise those dinners, the dishes, crystal, and furniture might well be ruined. Eventually, if somewhat reluctantly, the Smithsonian acceded to Marjorie's demand.

The debate had shaken Marjorie. To the ever-cautious heiress, nothing—especially the precious collection she had amassed at Hillwood—could be left to chance. It would be necessary, she told Henry Dudley, to develop an alternative plan to care for the estate independently should the Smithsonian balk. Moreover, despite encouraging steps toward the disposition of Mar-A-Lago as a Winter White House, the arrangement was not yet complete. Henry Dudley solved the problem by establishing the Marjorie Merriweather Post Foundation of the District of Columbia. By its terms, any gifted property that was not used in accordance with Marjorie's guidelines would revert to the foundation.

The only property not included in that arrangement was Camp Topridge. Originally Marjorie had considered giving the vast wooded property to C. W. Post College, but in the late sixties, when riots broke out at Long Island University and forced Dr. Gordon Hoxie's resignation, she changed her mind. Still, Marjorie remained convinced that the 207-acre Adirondacks property would be ideal for an educational retreat, a place where teachers and politicians could hold seminars. The Adirondacks camp was only eighty miles from Albany. With that in mind, she decided to leave Topridge to the state of New York, which was then under the leadership of her friend Governor Nelson Rockefeller.

Despite the gradual decline in Marjorie's vitality and hearing, she remained a handsome woman, whose beauty and style continued to intrigue newspaper columnists. She was not only the "queen of Palm Beach" and one of Washington's leading hostesses but was still considered one of the most alluring women in the world. Marjorie's photograph continued to appear regularly in newspapers, even when she was not making news herself. Often there were pictures of her in gowns, furs, and tiaras accompanying stories about fashion or beauty. In an age of jet-setters, rock stars, and "the beautiful people," Marjorie remained a famous face. Much like the Russian paintings on her walls at Hillwood, Marjorie had become an icon, representing physical beauty, fiscal preeminence, and personal grace in its most exalted form.

In 1970, on the occasion of her eighty-third birthday, Marjorie hosted ninety people for dinner at Mar-A-Lago. After the meal she invited her guests to join her in a round and square dance. She looked, wrote the syndicated columnist Suzy, "like a hundred million—for her that's easy—in a dear little peasant blouse with short sleeves and a deep ruffled neck, a flaring black velvet skirt embroidered in brilliants, her fabulous pearls, and a coral necklace. As she whirled and dipped in the tango (you go to Mrs. Post to dance or you stay home) her pleated red taffeta petticoat flashed and her red shoes twinkled. Wow! . . . Mrs. Post may well be the world's most beautiful and remarkable octogenarian."

28

Twilight in
Friendship Garden

*B*y 1970 rumors were once again afloat that Marjorie would be married—this time to a fifty-eight-year-old Palm Beach real estate developer named Robert Wilson. As the newspaper stories proliferated, Margaret Voigt took the matter into her own hands. The rumor, she told members of the press, "is all too ridiculous and inaccurate to even bear discussion." Finally, even columnist Betty Beale attempted to silence her peers. Although Marjorie was occasionally escorted by other men—among them Serge Obolensky, Victor Bowman, and fellow Palm Beacher Colonel C. Michael Paul—she assured them that "Fred Korth was still No. 1!"

By the summer of 1971 there were undeniable signs that Marjorie was failing. "Her poor health became noticeable. A lot of the time we worked around her," recalled Lawrence Lester, a staff member at Camp Topridge. Despite her weakened condition, Marjorie nevertheless insisted upon inviting groups of friends to the Adirondacks for four-day visits as usual. In the summer of 1971 she invited fewer of them. The inveterate hostess had done so, as Betty Beale reported in a column on August 25, because "four days of entertaining a large group every week was becoming a bit of a strain." Even this lighter schedule eventually took a toll upon Marjorie. At the end of the summer Marjorie became so ill that she had to be rushed to the nearby Saranac Hospital. Later she was transported back to Washington. Exactly what ailed Marjorie has never been clear, but at the time there were rumors of a mild heart attack.

According to Adelaide, her mother was beginning to suffer a series of strokes—small ones that left her increasingly infirm and occasionally forgetful. Moreover, Marjorie was now almost totally deaf. Still, the intrepid heiress was determined to maintain her old lifestyle as long as possible. In December 1971 she wrote Peter Pelham, president of the Mount Vernon Junior College (by then exclusively a junior college and no longer a prep school), of her arrival in Florida. "It is so nice to be back here at Mar-A-Lago in this warm and sunny south. I have been very quiet but am now looking forward to the arrival of Eleanor and Leon Barzin today and to Adelaide tomorrow. They will be here to spend Christmas with me and it will be a joy to have them."

That Christmas Marjorie invited Eleanor, Leon, The Miami Herald society editor Helen Rich, several couples, and members of her staff on a cruise to the Caribbean on the SS Gripsholm. Although the ocean liner was one of the most luxurious of the Swedish-American Line, the furnishings of its staterooms did not suit the ailing Marjorie. Before the journey began, she had the ship's furniture removed and her own bed, bureau, and chairs brought in to replace them. Nevertheless, according to a staff member of the Gripsholm who wishes to remain anonymous, she was a "wonderful passenger" who "never made any trouble" and "was very nice to the staff in the dining room."

Halfway through the cruise Marjorie became ill again, and so alarmingly that arrangements had to be made for her to leave the Gripsholm. By the time the ocean liner reached Antigua, the Merriweather was waiting to fly Marjorie, accompanied by her family and staff, back to Palm Beach. The ailing heiress, according to the newspapers, was suffering from a "virus."

In March 1972 Marjorie's eighty-fifth birthday was celebrated quietly at Mar-A-Lago by Dina, Cliff Robertson, Adelaide, Fred Korth, and several grandchildren. Despite a winter riddled with illness, Marjorie was eager to resume her old life. She had every intention, she now told her family, of returning to Washington before May so as to host her annual garden parties at Hillwood. Dina and Adelaide tried to dissuade her. Instead they suggested that she stay in Palm Beach a bit longer to rest and simply forget the parties that year. Ultimately Marjorie relented, but by early May she had returned to Washington.

In the ensuing months Marjorie still entertained occasionally at Hillwood. Now the guest list was arranged almost exclusively by Margaret

Voigt—sometimes with odd results. Among the usual roster of Marjorie's guests were friends of Margaret's. The care that Marjorie had taken in her prime to create a congenial guest list was missing. Once at a square dance Marjorie asked about a particularly good-looking female guest. "Why, Marjorie, you should be ashamed," a friend sarcastically replied. "That's Snow White, the most famous call girl in New York." "Good grief! How did she get here?" Marjorie inquired. The woman, it turned out, was a houseguest of some of the hostess's own friends.

Nor could close friends help noticing that in Marjorie's increasingly deaf and frail condition, she had trouble communicating with others. Gradually the legendary hostess was becoming a figurehead at her own parties, smiling and nodding cheerfully at the head of the lace-covered and crystal-laden table but understanding very little of what was actually being said. Yet a sense of decorum, an insistence upon punctuality, and a strict policy about drinking were still carefully maintained. For that reason, some guests who attended Marjorie's late-in-life parties found their hostess "remote" and her parties impersonal or mechanical.

As Marjorie's health waned, so did the frequency of her parties. At one of the last, when she suddenly became too ill to appear, her bed was wheeled to the window so that she could wave to her guests on the lawn.

By August 1972 Marjorie's memory loss was so severe at times that she no longer recognized her genealogist-secretary Nettie Leitch Major or even certain members of her family. That summer, for the first time since she had purchased Topridge a half century earlier, Marjorie did not open the camp. It was, recalled a staff member, "a sad time for everybody."

Still, Marjorie refused to give up visiting her beloved Mar-A-Lago. When her granddaughter Marwee came to visit her at Hillwood that fall, Marjorie was lying in bed. "Get me out of here," she told her granddaughter. By the winter of 1972, although now confined to a wheelchair, Marjorie took up residence at Mar-A-Lago again. Christian Science readers appeared daily at the estate. Friends and family gathered around. Dina and husband Cliff Robertson moved in with their young daughter, Heather. And so did Marwee.

By late February 1973 Marjorie had become ill again—this time with a serious chest infection. Before long Eleanor arrived from France. Adelaide flew down from Maryland. From Palm Beach there were frantic phone calls to Marjorie's doctors in Washington, to her Christian Science practitioner, to a surgeon friend of hers, Dr. Walter Newburn, to some of the "unconventional" doctors she favored, and finally to a young Palm Beach physician named Stanley Kuvin.

Upon examining Marjorie, Dr. Kuvin suspected that the octogenarian was suffering from pneumonia. On February 23 he moved her to Good Samaritan Hospital in West Palm Beach, the same hospital Marjorie had raised money to create a half century earlier. Despite the difficulty of communicating with the stricken and deaf Marjorie, and sensitive to her background in Christian Science, Dr. Kuvin explained that penicillin was a "natural" drug, derived from a bread mold. He also approved the idea that Marjorie wanted a Christian Science reader to visit her daily.

Marjorie responded to Dr. Kuvin's ministrations. By April 4 she had recovered sufficiently to return to Mar-A-Lago. As earlier, members of the family congregated by her bedside. Yet it was weeks before Marjorie regained her strength. The stress of the illness, combined with her inability to hear or walk, made Marjorie even more frustrated and impatient.

A personality change occurred. Increasingly, and not always for reasons that her caretakers understood, Marjorie had become difficult. The same iron will that had enabled her to contribute so meaningfully to society now began to emerge in unpleasant ways. Having been autonomous all her life, Marjorie deeply resented her dependency on others. Oddly enough, one of the few exceptions was Dr. Kuvin. "She smiled when I came in," he recalled. "But she could be obstreperous with others."

Finally, Adelaide and Eleanor urged Dina and Marwee to have Marjorie moved back to Hillwood, where, they believed, she would be more comfortable in summer. Marwee vehemently objected. "She'll be dead in three months," she predicted. Nevertheless, Adelaide and Eleanor prevailed, and in May 1973 the *Merriweather* brought their mother back to Washington. Marjorie's devoted butler, Gus Modig, stood waiting patiently at Hillwood's front door. As she and Adelaide entered the estate, Marjorie turned to her butler. "Gus, I'm home," she announced. A smile passed between them. Then the butler's eyes filled with tears.

Over the course of the next two months Marjorie seemed to rally. One of the people who saw her in that period was Gladys Heurtematte Johnston, who had been invited to dinner by Margaret Voigt. When she arrived at Hillwood, Gladys was pleasantly surprised to see her old friend looking quite well. "I found she had gained weight and was walking," Gladys recalled. Psychologically, too, Marjorie seemed like her old self—interested in others and what they were doing. When the widowed Gladys confided that she intended to be married again—this time to Champion International chairman Karl Bendetsen—the heiress expressed delight. Characteristically Marjorie made no allusions to her own health, and knowing that Marjorie assiduously avoided unpleasant topics, Gladys did not dare inquire about her friend's progress.

Fred Korth was another frequent visitor. Like Gladys, he talked about many things but seldom broached the subject of Marjorie's health. "We just didn't talk about it to any extent," he recalled. "I was trying to make her happy."

Nor did Marjorie discuss her condition with others who visited her that summer. Among them was her godson, Alden Sibley, and his wife, Ellie. Yet Marjorie must have had a sense that her time was short. As she passed through the library with Alden, she stopped to show him a book. "Here," she said, removing a volume from the bookcase and handing it to him, "you'd better take that." Then, in the deepening twilight, Marjorie sat with her godson in Hillwood's gardens for a long, wistful time.

That same summer Adelaide decided it was time to "retire" Margaret Voigt. Nettie Leitch Major, the genealogist who had written C.W.'s biography for Marjorie and now served as her "second" secretary, could handle the few office chores still needing to be done. For years Margaret had been secretly suffering with a heart condition. Now, having been dismissed, she planned a vacation in Vancouver and a reconciliation with her estranged husband, Frank Voigt, once a radio operator on the *Sea Cloud.* No sooner had Margaret arrived in Canada in mid-August than she died of a heart attack.

Later Marjorie's friends would say that there was nothing surprising in Margaret's death; she had simply gone ahead to prepare things for the arrival of her mistress.

Meanwhile, Marjorie's own health had again begun to decline precipitously. Part of the problem was that she had stopped eating almost completely. Most of the time she stayed in bed. And she did not always seem to recognize people, including the two doctors who attended her. In her last few weeks she spoke little, if at all. As in Florida, she became stubborn and uncooperative, even with her butler, Gus, her devoted personal maid, Eva, and two private-duty nurses.

Marjorie's children and grandchildren visited whenever they could. Weak as she was, Marjorie never forgot her sense of propriety or her expectations about it from other members of her family. Whenever her grandson-in-law Rody Cantacuzene came for a noontime visit, Gus prepared a sandwich and a cold beer. Once, when Rody entered Marjorie's bedroom with a beer can, she grabbed his hand and slapped it—so sharply that even the nurse recoiled. Rody immediately understood Marjorie's message. If beer was to be consumed at all, it should never be sipped from a can. Chastened, the naval officer went into Marjorie's bathroom, fetched a glass, and poured the beer into it. From the bed Marjorie smiled with approval.

On the morning of September 10, the nurses greeted Adelaide with surprising news. "Wait until you see your mother. She is absolutely beautiful. She looks like herself again," they said. As Adelaide approached the bed, Marjorie, who had not talked in several days, said, "Adelaide, you've always been a comfort to me." Tears came to her daughter's eyes. Her relationship with Marjorie had not been without its share of arguments and controversies, particularly as the heiress aged and fought to maintain her independence.

Those were the last words Marjorie spoke to any member of her family. Within a few hours she had lapsed into a coma. On Thursday, September 12, 1973, at 5:30 A.M., Marjorie Merriweather Post quietly died. Cardiac failure was said to be the immediate cause of death. With her death, an era of elegance and hospitality, of gaiety and splendor in their most ingenuous and original American form, faded forever.

On Monday morning, September 17, 1973, a funeral service was held at the National Presbyterian Church. Officiating were Marjorie's old friend Edward L. B. Elson, chaplain of the United States Senate, assisted by the church pastor, the Reverend Louis H. Evans, Jr. The church was filled with floral tributes from all over the world. As sunlight streamed through the stained-glass windows, members of the National Symphony Orchestra, led by Marjorie's son-in-law Leon Barzin, played selections from the works of Berlioz, Mozart, and Tchaikovsky.

Although the service was to last less than an hour, nearly twelve hundred people, including many from New York and Palm Beach, were jammed into the church. Among those who came to pay their respects were Marjorie's spiritual confidante and practitioner, Dr. Katherine Ross, Mamie Eisenhower, Clark Clifford, the Honorable John Clifford, Dillon Ripley, and the ambassadors of Romania, Italy, Peru, Turkey, Nicaragua, and the Soviet Union.

In a eulogy later published in the *Congressional Record,* Cliff Robertson praised Marjorie as "this patriot—whose life was resilient to the fortunes of her country . . ." a patron who was "aware of the artistic nourishment needed by all people" and a "lady" who recognized "man to be more important than anything he has acquired.

"This lady—recognized, decorated, admired throughout the world—retained her most beautiful virtue, a simplicity of faith and spirit—a belief in God and man, and country.

"This lady—this strong, yet gentle lady."

At three that same afternoon, in accordance with Marjorie's wishes, a simple service, led by a Christian Science "reader," was held in Hillwood's drawing room for her family.

By the terms of her fifty-page will, Marjorie left her family what the newspapers reported as an estimated $117 million in before-tax dollars. The sum, as her attorney, Henry Dudley, explained to the press, was exclusive of the value of Marjorie's properties—among them Topridge, Mar-A-Lago, Hillwood, and the property she owned in Texas. The remaining assets were to be divided primarily among Marjorie's daughters, Adelaide, Eleanor, and Dina, after large sums were subtracted for trust funds to maintain Mar-A-Lago and Hillwood. In addition, each daughter was to receive a one-third share on a "joint account" of the oil-rich Texas lands Marjorie owned with Leila's heirs.

Marjorie's daughters were also to divide an estimated $619,000 in jewelry, furs, porcelains, silver, and other "tangible property." Most of Marjorie's famous jewel collection, such as a $40,000 pearl necklace and a $25,000 sapphire diamond flower brooch, would be sold or donated to the Smithsonian because of their prohibitively high insurance costs.

Each grandchild was to inherit his or her mother's share of the estate upon her death. There were only two exceptions: Marwee and Tony de Bekessy. "I am," Marjorie explained, "making no provision for my grandson, Antal Post de Bekessy, for . . . I feel I would be doing him a disservice to add additional funds to those . . . he will inherit from a very large trust I created many years ago." Moreover, "I am making no provision in this Will for my granddaughter, Marjorie Durant Dye (Mar-wee), for the reason that it has been my pleasure to adequately provide for her during my lifetime."

To a few faithful servants like her business manager, Betty Cannella, Mar-A-Lago supervisor James Griffin, Jr., and the recently deceased Margaret Voigt, Marjorie had left $50,000 apiece. Others, including Marjorie's butler, Gus Modig, chauffeur Vincent "Jimmy" Sottile, and personal maid Eva Jackrisson, would receive only $10,000 or $15,000.

The executors of the will were Marjorie's friend and attorney, Henry Dudley, her beau, Fred Korth, and her financial manager, Meyer Handelman, all of whom received court-approved fees for their administration of the estate.

Not even in death would Marjorie forget the causes and charities she supported so faithfully in life. To her alma mater, Mount Vernon College, to the National Symphony, C. W. Post College, and the American Red Cross, she left endowments of $100,000 each.

A year after Marjorie's death, in a private family ceremony led by the Reverend Julia Sibley, Marjorie's ashes were consigned to a porphyry urn on a pink granite pedestal in Hillwood's rose garden. The day was rainy, and during the ceremony Julia Sibley and members of Marjorie's family were forced to huddle beneath umbrellas. "I am sure Mother was looking down on us amused at our umbrellas," Eleanor later wrote Julia Sibley.

Less amusing was the possibility that Marjorie's plans for the disposition of her two beloved estates would soon be washed away.

Although the House and Senate had approved adoption of Mar-A-Lago by the U.S. Department of Interior, its designation as a Winter White House was still not complete in August 1974, when President Nixon left office precipitously. In 1975 federal security agents determined that Mar-A-Lago was unsuitable as an official American "house of state" because it lay directly beneath a flight path from the West Palm Beach Airport. And in 1976, despite a $3 million trust fund left to maintain Mar-A-Lago's exterior, the newspapers reported that the estate was costing the federal government more than $268,000 in annual maintenance.

Moreover, the town of Palm Beach, which had long opposed opening Mar-A-Lago as a public museum because of the tourist traffic it would bring the area, claimed that its ownership by the federal government was creating heavy losses in tax revenues. Although Marjorie's attorney, Henry Dudley, later refuted those charges as a result of inflation rather than a skimpy endowment, the damage had been done. In 1980, after a protracted struggle, Mar-A-Lago was officially returned to the Post Foundation.

Five years later, after a parade of prospective buyers, Donald Trump purchased the estate for $10 million. Soon, however, he claimed that hefty Palm Beach taxes and the high cost of Mar-A-Lago's upkeep were making it impossible to retain the estate in its original condition. After an unsuccessful battle with the town of Palm Beach to subdivide the property, Mr. Trump, at this writing, has agreed to maintain Mar-A-Lago and convert it to a private club.

Marjorie's beloved home in Washington met a similar fate. Soon after her death, the Smithsonian began procrastinating about converting Hillwood to a museum. To do so, they maintained, would require many changes in the estate: special doorways, parking lots, and public facilities. By 1975 the Smithsonian was claiming that the $10 million endowment left for Hillwood's maintenance, which would have provided an alleged $450,000 annual income, was insufficient because of galloping inflation. Privately Marjorie's friends and family suspected that the heiress's original prohibition on dining had something to do with the Smithsonian's hedging. By April 1976 Hillwood too had been returned to the Post Foundation.

Today Marjorie's former home is operated and maintained by the foundation as Washington's Hillwood Museum, and is renowned for its magnificent collection of eighteenth- and nineteenth-century French art and its unique treasures from imperial Russia.

"Perhaps the greatest thing about having lots of money is the pleasure of giving a great deal of it away," said an editorial that appeared in Washington's *Star-News* two days after Marjorie died. "Marjorie Merriweather Post, who died here this week at 86, was superbly equipped to practice philanthropy, being perhaps the third wealthiest woman in America, if not the world, and beautifully endowed with good business sense—a must for philanthropists, if their largesse is not to be squandered. She also had time and taste."

Dozens of other obituaries about Marjorie appeared across America. Among the most representative was one in *The New York Times*, which observed that in addition to Marjorie's business achievements, she "gave generously of her time and money for a wide range of philanthropies. Her life-style, with its many estates, domestic staff of more than 40 persons, and many parties, often resembled royalty."

If Marjorie was regarded as an uncrowned American queen, whose footman changed livery for each meal and whose lifestyle inspired awe from real monarchs like the late Queen Maud of Norway and Charlotte, the grand duchess of Luxembourg, she was also remembered as a benevolent one. Though she was imperious in her demands for decorum and duty, Marjorie's gifts were meant to delight and beautify, to elevate and edify to the highest standards known to humanity.

It was this natural nobility of character, "her ability to give happiness to others," rather than the wealth she inherited from C.W., another friend told Representative James Fulton (the comment was recorded in the *Congressional Record*), that made Marjorie unique—a standard-bearer for excellence in a nation proud of its legacy of rugged individualism. To those who knew her well, Marjorie was a very human queen. Although she "entertained kings and queens, Presidents and diplomats, Cabinet officers and Members of Congress in her several magnificent homes . . . regal as she was, she always retained the earthly quality and capacity for friendship." This common touch, combined with Marjorie's very human attention to "the good life," not only drew but kept many admirers by her side.

Much of that warmth came from what her friend Anne Frailey Braverman referred to as Marjorie's "great zest for life." It was reflected in the pleasure she received from many sources: her homes, gardens, friends, and children.

If Marjorie's great wealth, imperious style, or temper sometimes intimidated others, this was counterbalanced by her heartfelt sympathy for those stricken with ill health, poverty, or bad luck. "There are people with money who don't do things to help others the way Marjorie did," Anne Braverman observed. "I think that altruistic streak was instinctive to her." As Marjorie herself once observed when hounded by newspaper reporters about being one of the wealthiest women in the world, she made her money "work" for those around her.

That Marjorie was criticized for her possessions, sneered at for her ostentation, and derided for the eclecticism of her art—which ranged from the sublime to the merely decorative—is also a fact. Yet Marjorie's aestheticism gave rise to two of America's most fascinating estates— one in Palm Beach and the other in Washington. By temperament, Marjorie was a lusty woman, so exuberant in her likes and dislikes and so enthusiastic about the varied expressions of beauty in life that she was never a purist. Despite her jewels, estates, and world travel, she remained an unequivocal product of her midwestern roots. As such, Marjorie collected things she found appealing, rather than merely for their intrinsic value.

Status merely for the sake of status was never Marjorie's game. Something or someone had to attract her personally in order for her to adopt it. It little mattered that critics scoffed at Mar-A-Lago as a bastardization of European decorative styles or that at Hillwood the priceless in art was sometimes displayed alongside the plebeian. "I don't care. I like it," she often retorted to her art expert daughter Eleanor when told that an object in her collections was either a forgery or of poor quality.

Marjorie's highly developed aesthetic spirit can still be felt today in her estates Hillwood and Mar-A-Lago and in cultural institutions like the National Symphony and the Kennedy Center for the Arts she so faithfully supported. As Lady Bird Johnson once observed, "Everything she touches turns to beauty."

In the obituary that appeared in the *Congressional Record*, Senator Jennings Randolph observed that "there was a gentleness yet firmness in Mrs. Post's life. She was thoughtful and helpful to thousands of people, yet she was a strong woman of sound business sense. . . . She achieved much for herself and for other people. She was a patron of the arts and a patriot of her country. Perhaps we shall never know again such a dynamic woman so devoted to beauty and so dedicated to wholesome service."

That Marjorie would be envied for her vast wealth was understandable. What was more remarkable was that she was seldom despised for it but ultimately admired—largely because she gave so much of it away with such benevolence and modesty. From a girlhood that began in the white barn with the hand gluing of labels to packages of Postum and their delivery in horse-driven wagons to an adulthood when she flew ambassadors to the Palm Beach International Ball on the *Merriweather*, Marjorie witnessed vast changes in scientific technology. Yet the human values she had learned at C.W.'s and Aunt Mollie's knees—the obligation to help others less fortunate than herself—were permanently stamped into her soul.

Thousands would never know that it was Marjorie Merriweather Post who was responsible for their well-being. Soldiers who survived World War I in the Number 8 Base Hospital in France, children who

were saved from starvation in her soup kitchens, Russians who benefited from her Soviet War Relief drives in World War II, Boy Scouts who
cavorted in camps she had contributed, music lovers who attended the
National Symphony, housewives who were freed from the chore of canning food, and students who received anonymous scholarships to colleges—all were objects of Marjorie's largesse.

These men, women, and children were Marjorie's proudest legacies,
far more than the chalices, Easter eggs, and gem-encrusted dishes of
imperial Russia she publicly displayed in her Washington home.

Nine years before her death Marjorie recalled that her father, C. W.
Post, had always believed that life was a series of spiritual gradations
that depended upon "how much you learn and how much you accomplish."

Marjorie would have made her father proud.

Sources

The author extends special thanks to the following: the Bentley Historical Library, University of Michigan, Post Family Collection; Robert Brier, Ph.D.; Colby Chester, Jr.; Margaret Truman Daniel; the Joseph Davies family; Orin Finkle; Foreign Service Spouse Oral History, Inc.; the Greenwich Historical Society; the Hillwood Museum, Washington, D.C.; the Historical Society of Palm Beach County; the Estate of Barbara Hutton; the Jacob's Pillow Dance Festival; Judge James R. Knott; Andra Kustin; Kraft General Foods Archives, Morton Grove, Illinois; Hunter Marston, Jr.; the Herbert May family; the New-York Historical Society Library; the Marjorie Merriweather Post family; the B. Davis Schwartz Library, C. W. Post Campus, Long Island University; Post Division, Kraft General Foods, Inc.; the Franklin D. Roosevelt Library and Museum; Professor Conrad Schoeffling; Patricia Ziegfeld Stephenson; the Harry S Truman Library; the Donald Trump Organization; and the Washington, D.C., Historical Society.

Acknowledgments

While the writing of a biography is a solitary venture, the research that precedes is often an intensely interpersonal experience. So it was for this book, which owes its existence to the contributions of dozens of thoughtful men and women. Many of them knew Marjorie Merriweather Post personally. Others were professionally familiar with her archives or the history of the places where she lived. Still others were engaged in the contemporary women's biography movement. It is to all these generous individuals, many of whom are listed below, that I am indebted for these pages.

My own interest in the life of Marjorie Merriweather Post coincided with the 1990 opening of her archives at the Bentley Historical Library of the University of Michigan and was one of those happy coincidences that delight authors and suggest that they were "meant" to write their books. I am grateful to research archivist Nancy Bartlett, reference assistant Karen Jania, administrative assistant Nancy Hatfield, and Francis X. Blouin, Jr., Bentley Historical Library director, for their help over many weeks in 1991 and 1992 as I sifted through the Post Family Collection.

While researching Mrs. Post's life, I was also privileged to be a member of the Women Writing Women's Lives Seminar at the New York Institute for the Humanities at New York University. The thought-provoking presentations and lively discussions that occurred at those meetings enriched my own sensitivity toward what constitutes a woman's life. My appreciation to the group, especially to Blanche Wiesen Cook, Elizabeth Harlan, Louise Bernikow, Nell Painter, and Sue Shapiro for their special interest in my work.

Nor could this book have been written without the generosity of the staff at the Hillwood Museum of Washington, D.C., Marjorie Merriweather Post's last home. In particular I want to thank curator Anne Odom for her expertise and patience with my seemingly endless questions, registrar Cara Seitchek, assistant director Mary Alexander, and director Fred Fisher, who warmly welcomed me to the museum and encouraged his staff to cooperate with me. My appreciation must also include curator emeritus Katrina Taylor, Wendy Lopes, Liana Paredes-Arend, and Priscilla Linn.

I am also indebted to Elizabeth Adkins, archives manager of the Kraft General Foods Archives in Morton Grove, Illinois, who thoughtfully attempted to answer my questions about the history of the Postum Cereal Company and General Foods. When answers were not easily obtainable, she persisted in teasing them out or pointing me in directions where they might be found. Archives staff members Becky Tousey, Steve Carvell, and Arlene Swedberg also offered expert assistance and lively companionship.

Nor will I forget the interest with which I was greeted by John Swarthout, division manager of the Post Division of Kraft General Foods, Inc., in Battle Creek, site of the original Post factory. Not only did he help me sift through old records and advertisements, but he arranged tours of the production facilities so I could understand how some of C. W. Post's original products were made. Special thanks to Deborah Calkins, Kevin Benner, Ray Dahlman, Tom Boyle, Mike Dunn, Mel Herzig, and Bob Hamilton for their contributions.

For information on Battle Creek, I am indebted to several local historians. Among the most generous were Mike and Dorothy Martich, who worked with a commitment and attention to detail rarely seen outside the university. Bob McCarty was another devoted historian who greatly enriched my understanding of Battle Creek. Duff Stoltz took time out of his busy schedule to find photographs and answer questions about the early days of the Battle Creek Sanitarium and the Kellogg brothers. Virginia and Ralph Moody generously shared their collection of Post memorabilia on behalf of the book. Bob Miller, Jr., chairman of the *Battle Creek Enquirer,* not only opened his newspaper files but lent me books on Battle Creek's colorful history—and offered words of encouragement along the way. My appreciation also to former Post employees Marjorie and Frank Jones, Willard reference librarian Marlene Steele, Diane Beckley of the Kimball House Historical Museum, Kenneth Montgomery, Peter Heydon, Ralph Heikkinen, and Bob Nealt.

In Palm Beach, Dr. Nan Dennison of the Historical Society of Palm Beach County persistently found answers, located photographs, and suggested other local historians. Among the most gracious were Judge James R. Knott, Olivia Morrish, and Buddy Galen. To Anne Anderson, Barton Gubelmann, Francie Dixon, and Bruce Bent I am also grateful. Linda Rawls, editor of the *Palm Beach Daily News*, greatly enhanced my knowledge of Palm Beach and Mrs. Post's role in it by opening her newspaper files on behalf of my search.

In Connecticut, the Greenwich Historical Society was indispensable to my understanding of Marjorie's Boulders years. I particularly want to thank archivist Susan Richardson and historian Bruce Finch for their help and guidance.

Dr. LucyAnn Geiselman, president of Mount Vernon College, and her staff unearthed information about the school's origins and Mrs. Post's contributions to it. Among those who replied to my challenging questions were Dr. Lucy Coche, Polly Surrey, and Dr. Nancy White. Alumnae such as Florence McElroy, Ainsley Mobley, Eleanor Gow, former president Dr. Peter and Isobel Pelham, and board member Walter Beach took time out of their busy schedules to tell me about Mrs. Post's dedication as a trustee.

For Long Island history, I was blessed with the dedication of Gold Coast expert Orin Finkle, who along the way has become a friend. Dr. Robert MacKay, director of the Society for the Preservation of Long Island Antiquities, and Henry Havemeyer extended themselves to provide information about life on Long Island in the nineteenth and early twentieth centuries.

On interpretations and the history of Christian Science I am indebted to David Robertson, chairman of the New York State Committee on Publications, Betsy Baumgarden of the Eighth Church of Christ Scientist, and Jim Bencivenga, senior associate of the First Church of Christ Scientist.

To the reference librarians of Westchester County I am deeply appreciative. For months Wendy Bloom and Linda Kurtz of the Mount Kisco Public Library and Dianne Hobbie of the New Rochelle Library checked facts, located newspaper and magazine articles, and conducted computer searches on behalf of the book, often into the evening hours. So did Judy Clark and Delys DeZwaan of the Mamaroneck Public Library, who also located hard-to-obtain books outside the Westchester system.

Several experts graciously shared their knowledge about Russian antiques, history, and American philanthropy with me. Without the help of Aleksandre Manic, Russian art appraiser; Paul Schaffer, president of À la Vieille Russie; Dr. Henry Huttenbach, professor of history at City College of New York; and my friend Dr. Kathleen McCarthy, director of the Center for the Study of Philanthropy at the Graduate School and University Center, CUNY, the book would have been far more difficult to write and place in a historical context.

As I explored Mrs. Post's life, I was aided by several research assistants: Laura Nisbet of Battle Creek, Mark Hurley of Washington, D.C., and Ken Pearl of Manhattan. These three gifted individuals relentlessly pursued questions, located articles, and greatly eased the burden of what, at times, seemed an insurmountable research task.

The spiritual generosity that flowed from Mrs. Post toward others was evinced in the efforts of her closest friends and associates to help me understand her personality. To Don Handelman, David Close, Fred Korth, and Henry Dudley for their thoughtfulness, extraordinary kindnesses, and suggestions about other sources I am truly indebted. That same warmth also emanated from other friends, among them Gladys H. J. Bendetsen, Estelle Needham, Major General Alden and Ellie Sibley, and Anne Frailey Braverman.

To the family of Marjorie Merriweather Post I am most appreciative. Without exception, her children, grandchildren, and stepchildren gave of themselves generously in interviews and meetings—sometimes in spite of illnesses, travel, painful memories, or other pressing concerns. Special thanks to Mrs. Post's daughters, Adelaide Close Riggs, Eleanor Close Barzin, and Nedenia Hutton Hartley, for their graciousness and cooperation.

To Cleveland Amory, for his generosity in reading the first draft of the manuscript, his suggestions and encouragements when I felt most insecure, I am indebted. Personally, as well as professionally, his wry humor often brought a smile to my face as I was writing.

I owe special appreciation to friends who stood faithfully by me during the long months of the writing process. Victoria Secunda not only took time from her own writing schedule to critique parts of the first draft but raised questions that heightened my awareness of important gaps. Robin Brancato and Sue Weiner accompanied me on a visit to the

Hillwood Museum and offered encouragement throughout the project. Joel Weiner directed me to his historical colleagues and even lent me his graduate assistant. I am also grateful to Shel Secunda, Alexandra Ballantine, Doris Bucher, Valerie and Hank Enders, Andra Kustin, and John Brancato for their warmth and friendship.

My agent, Agnes Birnbaum, has been a steadfast voice of encouragement and reassurance from the moment of the book's inception to its completion, a friend as well as a valued professional associate. Often it was due to her wise counsel that I pursued paths I thought had closed, which in turn led to surprising and sometimes rewarding revelations.

My editor, Diane Reverand, editor in chief and publisher of Villard Books, has been an unfailing source of encouragement and intelligence in spite of the other obligations that press upon her professionally. Her faith in my work, ability to envision the larger picture, and keen personal interest has made the creation of this biography an exhilarating process.

Notes

FOREWORD

ix. "The queen is back," "Suzy Says," *Dallas Morning News*, December 17, 1969.

x. "While she has always lived like a queen," "Mrs. Post Serves Tea—for 300," *New York Times*, May 26, 1967.

x. "Let's not make too much," Roy Meacham, NR interview.

xii. "was that they didn't lose their luster," Jim Griffin, Jr., NR interview.

xiii. "I had many beautiful things," Gladys Bendetsen, NR interview.

xiii. "We used to call her the train dispatcher," Dina Merrill, NR interview.

xiii. "her ramrod posture," "A Legacy of Grandeur," *Palm Beach Life* (September–October 1976).

xiv. "universally dreaded," "The Way They Were," *Connoisseur* (June 1991).

xiv. "Mrs. Post, who is often described as regal, or even imperious," "Palm Beach Is the Big Stadium," *New York Times Magazine*, March 21, 1971.

xiv. "she was so extraordinarily beautiful," Emlen Davies Grosjean Evers, NR interview.

CHAPTER ONE: "A HEALTHY, HEARTY, AND HANDSOME GIRL"

4. "American nervousness is the product," Beard, *American Nervousness*, 96; Lutz, *American Nervousness, 1903*, 4.

5. "remedial value," Numbers, *Prophetess of Health*, 82.

6. "the largest institution of its kind in the world," Schaeffer, *Legacy*, 128.

10. "healthy, hearty, and handsome girl," Post Col., Box 40, baby book.

11. "Papa down again," Post Col., Box 40, baby book.

11. "Mrs. Gregory, I am," Major, *C. W. Post,* 29.

12. "Mr. Post, go ahead," Ibid.

12. "hardly knew any disease," Post Col., Box 40, baby book.

12. "has been my strength," Post Col., Box 20, F. 4.

CHAPTER TWO: "THERE'S A REASON"

13. "I thought it over," Major, *C. W. Post,* 30.

17. "Oh, Mrs. Post," Post Col., Box 47, interview, December 30, 1964, 20.

18. "Do you see them?" advertisement courtesy of Kraft General Foods Archives.

19. "I come to your side," C. W. Post, *I Am Well,* 6–7.

20. "diversion of thought," Post Col., Box 47, interview, February 13, 1964, 10.

20. "Now, goddamn it," ibid., 12.

21. "perfectly furious," ibid., 7.

22. "Marjorie, I would prefer," Post Col., Box 47, Zeitlin, 7.

22. "full-fledged school girl," Post Col., Box 40, baby book.

22. "bright, winsome," Post Col., Box 40, letter, March 26, 1894.

23. "Maybe, Mr. Post had five dollars," "C. W. Post's $5 Check Once Was Questioned at Grocery," *Battle Creek Enquirer and News,* January 30, 1944.

23. "Another one for the padded cell," ibid.

23. "She would look at me," Adelaide Riggs, NR interview.

23. "mixed and browned," Major, *C. W. Post,* 34.

23. "an article of food-drink," ibid.

24. "Some years I sell," ibid., 37.

CHAPTER THREE: A BATTLE CREEK GIRLHOOD

27. "give me not 'jewels,' " Post, *Aunt Carrie's Poems,* 38.

27. "What shall we do," Post Col., Box 47, letter, November 18, 1964.

28. "This was playing," Post Col., Box 47, "Transcription May/Major," 15.

28. "Teacher is cross," Post Col., Box 40, baby book.

29. "She was really a delight," Henry Dudley, NR interview.

30. "I could walk anywhere," Post Col., Box 47, "Transcription May/Major," 18.

30. "My little girl was struck," Post Col., Box 5, letter book, 1895–99.

30. "worked like a little dog," Post Col., Box 47, interview, February 13, 1964, 28.

31. "I think I saw the manufacturing," Major, *C. W. Post,* 158.

31. "Dad, can you help," Post Col., Box 47, interview, February 13, 1964.

32. "were paying us a profit," Post Col., Box 3, F. 1, "Preliminary Training of an Advertiser," 10.
33. "Why, I wouldn't touch it," Post Col., Box 47, interview, February 13, 1964, 17.
34. "My bills for advertising," Major, *C. W. Post*, 38.
34. "On this side," ibid., 39.
35. "Can you cut," ibid., 48.
36. "The daily introduction," ibid., 42.
36. "Naturally, my business soon felt," ibid., 43.
36. "It was one of the most complete," ibid.

CHAPTER FOUR: "A LITTLE LIKE PLAYING HOUSE WITH DOLLS"

39. "That training," Post Col., Box 47, interview, February 13, 1964, 33–34.
41. "She was the kind of person," Anne Frailey Braverman, NR interview.
41. "Stay out of the sun," Gladys Bendetsen, NR interview.
42. "Mom had," Dina Merrill, NR interview.
42. "I have never had any," Post Col., Box 16, F. 42, letter, March 8, 1967.
43. "we both lacked mature judgment," Post Col., Box 5, Scrapbook 4, "Address to Postum Workers," December 31, 1904.
43. "left Dad and myself," Post Col., Box 48, taped interview, February 1962.
43. "a little like playing house," ibid.
43. "She was obviously very much taken," Dr. Gordon Hoxie, NR interview.
44. "best wages in Michigan," Burnett Organization, "Biography of Charles William Post," Post Col., Box 2, F. 29.
44. "knew something of his hopes," Post Col., Box 5, Scrapbook 4, "Address to Postum Workers," December 31, 1904, 1.
45. "the first requisite of a good citizen," Theodore Roosevelt, *The Works of Theodore Roosevelt: v. 13, Presidential Addresses and State Papers*, 200.
45. "all surplus revenues," Andrew Carnegie, "Wealth," *North American Review* (June 1889), 661–62.
45. "Mix altruism," Major, *C. W. Post*, 77.
45. "was getting heavy," ibid., 75.
46. "we would invent a better food," Powell, *W. K. Kellogg*, 90.
47. "Orders were coming in so rapidly," ibid., 93.
47. "would develop in such a manner," ibid.
48. "rest and be fed," Massie and Schmitt, *Battle Creek*, 69.
49. "fairy godmother," "Mrs. C. L. Post Dies in West," May 26, 1925, Ross Coller File, Post, Carroll Lathrop.
49. "beloved by every age," Post Col., Box 47, interview, February 13, 1964, 2.

49. "Oh, there were so many little things," ibid., 3.
50. "handle your employees," Post Col., Box 3, F. 3, letter, March 25, 1903.
50. "soft and balmy," Post Col., Box 5, Scrapbook 4, "Address to Postum Workers," December 31, 1904.

CHAPTER FIVE: "TWENTY-SEVEN BOILS"

52. "I... adored it," Post Col., Box 48, taped interview, February 1962.
52. Students were expected, Post Col., Oversized Scrapbooks 3.
53. "those young ladies," "Generations That Attend Centenary of School Founder," *Sunday Star*, October 31, 1937.
54. "very comfortably," Post Col., Box 48, taped interview, February 1962.
54. "a very charming," Post Col., Box 47, interview, December 30, 1964, 28.
54. "She had total recall," Betty Cannella, NR interview.
55. "There was this wonderful theatrical side," Dina Merrill, NR interview.
56. "Your Mother's whereabouts," Post Col., Box 13, F. 35.
57. "was talking love," ibid.
57. "It was a house," Post Col., Box 48, taped interview, February 1962.
58. "Well, there never in the world," Post Col., Box 47, interview, February 13, 1964, 30.
59. "decidedly in favor," Burnett Organization, "Biography of Charles William Post," 12, Post Col., Box 2, F. 29.
59. "It was many, many years," Post Col., Box 47, interview, February 13, 1964, 25.
60. "dear, sweet girl," Post Col., Box 13, F. 35.
60. "I wonder," ibid.
61. "Not on the ground," ibid.
61. "let anybody dare to," Post Col., M. Post Scrapbook 4.
62. "to keep a dozen families," Post Col., Box 5, "Address to Postum Workers," Scrapbook, 1904–05.
62. "Marjorie, I'm going to be married," Post Col., Box 47, Zeitlin interview, 8.
62. "if forced to be idle," "Brief Announcement of the Marriage of Mr. Charles W. Post to Miss Lila [sic] Young," *Kalamazoo Gazette*, November 18, 1904.
62. "this creature," Post Col., Box 47, Zeitlin interview, 9.

CHAPTER SIX: THE BRIDE

66. "You ask what I think," Post Col., M. Post Scrapbook 4.
66. "a very nice fellow," Post Col., Box 47, Marston interview, M-A-L, 6.
67. "Harry took it," Adelaide Riggs, NR interview.

67. "make it as lovely as possible," Post Col., Box 47, interview, December 30, 1964, 32.

67. "rest of the trousseau," ibid., 32.

67. "miles and miles," ibid.

68. "Well, she's a cute little thing," Cliff Robertson, NR interview.

68. "while the subdued harmonies," *New Yorker*, December 6, 1905, Post Col., Scrapbook 4, 1904–05.

69. "stuck off," Post Col., Box 47, interview, December 30, 1964, 34.

69. "Dear Little Sweetheart," Post Col., Box 4, F. 17.

69. "Be tender and kind," Post Col., M. Post Scrapbook 4, 1904–05.

70. "will occupy a prominent position," "Wed Heiress on Ancestral Ground in Grace Church," newspaper unknown, December 4, 1905, Post Col., Scrapbook 4, 1904–05.

70. "the bride, who," *New Yorker*, loc. cit.

70. "Well, I am very sorry," Post Col., Box 47, interview, December 30, 1964, 13.

71. "I'm sure both Leila and Marjorie," Kenneth Montgomery, NR interview.

71. "We were days," Post Col., Box 47, interview, December 30, 1964, 15.

72. "My God," ibid.

72. "I never saw," "Blue Norther Hit the Post Party," *Fort Worth Star*, February 6, 1906.

73. "It was an enormous house," Post Col., Box 48, taped interview, February 1962.

73. "just dumped," Post Col., Box 47, Zeitlin interview, 9.

75. "That course stood by," ibid., 11.

75. "She knew everything," Jim Griffin, Jr., NR interview.

75. "Gladys, please speak Spanish," ibid.

76. "I could have gone through the floor," Post Col., Box 47, interview, December 30, 1964, 48.

76. "Mrs. Close," Post Col., untitled Battle Creek newspaper, M. Post Scrapbook 2, 1898–1913.

76. "Perhaps no one," Major, *C. W. Post*, 92.

77. "lying and potentially deadly," "Futility," *Collier's* (July 27, 1907), 9.

77. "When a journal," Major, *C. W. Post*, 104.

CHAPTER SEVEN: "IT WASN'T DONE THAT WAY"

79. "marvelous waterfall," Post Col., Box 48, taped interview, March 1962.

80. "had better patronize," Post Col., Box 4, F. 18, September 9, 1908.

80. "Mom was wonderful," Dina Merrill, NR interview.

81. "I [am] glad," Post Col., Box 4, F. 18, September 6, 1908.

82. "... It beats H——," Post Col., Box 4, F. 18, December 24, 1908.

82. "Come on," Post Col., Box 47, Zeitlin interview, 24.

82. "Well, that kind of thing," ibid.
82. "Drugs, Cataplasmas," Eddy, *Science and Health*, 158.
82. "never seen a man," Post Col., Box 47, Zeitlin interview, 24.
83. "You've just got to," ibid.
83. "It made an exaggerated impression," Post Col., Box 47, notes, June 5, 1965, 4.
83. "Mrs. Post was not overly fond," Dick Pearson, NR interview.
84. "It wasn't done that way," Post Col., Box 47, interview, June 5, 1965, 1.
84. "I would be flabbergasted," Post Col., Box 47, interview, December 30, 1964.
84. "He was madly in love," Adelaide Riggs, NR interview.
84. "a very good mixer," Bruce Finch, NR interview.
86. "He [Ed] was a very good-natured person," Post Col., Box 47, Marston interview M-A-L, February 14, 1966.
87. "One got about," Post Col., Box 47, "Palm Beach Recollections," 1.
87. "would practically carry us off," Post Col., Box 47, February 1965, 5.
88. "She always said," Eleanor Barzin, NR interview.
88. "Shocked," Post Col., Box 13, F. 17.
88. "that we are and in part," Post Col., Box 13, F. 20.

CHAPTER EIGHT: THE POSTUM CEREAL COMPANY HEIRESS

89. "extreme nervousness," "Post Planned Killing Self," *Battle Creek Journal*, May 10, 1914,
90. "He'd have one," Post Col., Box 47, Zeitlin interview, 12–13.
90. "a race against death," "C. W. Post Races Death to Have Appendix Out," *Battle Creek Enquirer*, March 4, 1914, Ross Coller file.
90. "the worst looking thing," Post Col., Box 47, Zeitlin interview, 12.
90. "in the best of spirits," "Tells of Operation," United Press, May 9, 1914.
90. "sudden impulses," ibid.
91. "Forgive me," Post Col., Box 13, F. 25.
92. "In the portentous hush," "Multitude in Mute Grief Pays Touching Tribute to Memory of C. W. Post," May 14, 1914, Ross Coller file.
92. "That Mr. Post," "Battle Creek Citizens," newspaper unknown, June 14, 1914, Ross Coller file.
92. "The community took leave," "As Farewell Is Said," *Battle Creek Enquirer*, May 15, 1914.
93. "Mrs. Post was enamored," Dick Pearson, NR interview.
93. "She used to tell me," Henry Dudley, NR interview.
94. NO LITIGATION, "$6,000,000 Cash as Settlement," newspaper unknown, December 9, 1915, Ross Coller file.
94. "There is no trouble between," ibid.
94. "Mother hated," Eleanor Barzin, NR interview.

95. "the continuance of the great management," "Who Will Succeed Late C. W. Post?," *Journal of Commerce*, June 8, 1914.

95. "Mother was much too feminine," Eleanor Barzin, NR interview.

95. "Things became very active," Post Col., Box 48, taped interview, February 1962.

95. "She had to do all the thinking," Post Col., Box 47, Marston interview, February 19, 1966, 7.

96. "It seemed to me," Post Col., Box 48, taped interview, February 1962.

96. "the homes of New York leaders," Brown, *Valentine's City of New York*, 349.

97. "I was catapulated into this thing," Post Col., interview, February 13, 1964, 19.

97. "perfectly good cereals," ibid., 20.

97. "[I]t had so many by-products," ibid.

98. "My grandfather," Eleanor Barzin, NR interview.

98. "It was horrible," Post Col., Box 48, taped interview, March 1962.

98. "The trunk broke open," ibid., 4.

99. "My room was a mess," ibid., 5.

99. "silly to put it back," ibid.

101. "I am not the richest woman," "A Flair for Philanthropy," *Washington Post*, March 12, 1967.

CHAPTER NINE: DARING PROPOSITIONS

102. "My sister was forever," Adelaide Riggs, NR interview.

102. "I was full of mischief," Eleanor Barzin, NR interview.

103. "was promptly attacked," Post Col., Box 47, December 30, 1964, 12.

103. "I had to use it," ibid.

104. "I don't want to say good-bye," ibid., 10.

104. "My mother was one," Adelaide Riggs, NR interview.

104. "She was very definite," ibid.

105. "with all their gear," Brown, op. cit., 265.

105. "It must have been a terrible shock," Eleanor Barzin, NR interview.

106. "very gregarious, charming," W. E. Hutton, Jr., NR interview.

107. "The earthquake," ibid.

108. "The impression I had," Fred Korth, NR interview.

108. "She was madly in love," Eleanor Barzin, NR interview.

109. "Marjorie Post Close," "Let Them Eat Cake," *Fortune* (October 1934).

109. "change his life," Colby Chester, Jr., NR interview.

110. "a new generation," F. Scott Fitzgerald, *This Side of Paradise* (New York: Scribner's, 1970), 282.

111. "was losing its," Churchill, *The Upper Crust*, 237.

112. "grande dame of the winter set," Curl, *Palm Beach County*, 45.

112. "Pearls, in the daytime?," Knott, *The Mansion Builders*, 10.

113. "soul of graciousness," "Society," New York *Daily News*, February 28, 1935.

113. "an aunt to me," "Marjorie Merriweather Post . . . Reminiscences of Early Days," *Palm Beach Daily News*, 75th Anniversary Special, January 1969.

114. "so horribly noisy," Post Col., Box 48, taped interview, March 1962.

115. "We decided that we young marrieds," Post Col., Box 47, "Palm Beach Recollections," 4.

115. "the only way we were selected," ibid.

115. "was not asked to sing," ibid.

115. "That didn't bother me," ibid.

CHAPTER TEN: IT WAS "QUITE A PLACE"

120. "He and Marjorie," Post Col., Box 47, Marston interview, February 14, 1966, 1.

120. "My grandmother lived life," Marjorie Durant Dye, NR interview.

120. "Old? Don't mention," Gladys Bendetsen, NR interview.

121. "Mom had a bit of a fixation," Dina Merrill, NR interview.

121. "a small English country village," Sclare, *Beaux-Arts Estates*, 140.

121. "excellent duck (and snipe)," Post Col., Box 48, taped interview, February 1962.

123. "a country in which nothing," Mackay et al., *Between Ocean and Estate*, 130.

123. "Although E. F. Hutton made money," Vincent Sottile, NR interview.

123. "This has been our refuge," Post Col., Box 48, taped interview, February 1962.

124. "the most luxurious hotel in the woods," Kaiser, *Great Camps of the Adirondacks*, 47.

125. "They were always at home," Post Col., Box 47, December 30, 1964.

125. "inappropriate," Kaiser, op. cit., 209.

125. "noted for [their] beauty," ibid., 210.

126. "She used to come up here," Vincent Sottile, NR interview.

126. "*you*, my dear," Post Col., Box 13, F. 20, September 30, 1918.

126. "the lobby of a great hotel," Liz Carpenter, NR interview.

127. "is to get a glimpse into the life of a queen," "Camp Topridge Is Fit for a Queen," *Washington Evening Star*, August 16, 1964.

128. "I was named," Dina Merrill, NR interview.

128. "We had a perfectly lovely porte cochere," Post Col., Box 48, taped interview, February 1962.

129. "the largest and very possibly," Alpern, *New York's Fabulous Luxury Apartments*, 74.

129. "The apartment really offered," Post Col., Box 48, taped interview, February 1962.
130. "quite a place," Post Col., Box 48, taped interview, March 1962.

CHAPTER ELEVEN: VORACIOUS APPETITES

133. "The high standards of living," *New York Times*, November 30, 1925, as quoted in *The Handwriting on the Wall*, 70.
134. " 'Let Leila do it!' " Doris Lambeer, NR interview.
134. "In all the many years," MMP letter, May 9, 1941, courtesy Postum employee Mike Dunn.
135. "So with the war being over," Post Col., Box 47, interview, February 13, 1964.
136. "It is our opinion," *The Handwriting on the Wall*, October 26, 1926, 71 and 74.
137. "Will I have another?" *General Foods Family Album*, 19.
137. "That nearly finished me off," Post Col., *Annual Report 1922* and *Annual Report 1923*.
138. "will be used for extended cruises," untitled article, *Town and Country* (September 1, 1923).
140. "Bugs?," "Frozen Foods: From the Eskimo to Bing Crosby," *The Reporter*, October 24, 1959, 23.
140. "There was nothing very remarkable," "If I Were 21," *The American Magazine*, as reprinted in *Reader's Digest* (April 1951), 66.
141. "You've got to buy Birdseye," Dina Merrill, NR interview.
141. "Marjorie, listen to reason," ibid.
141. "Believe me, Ned," ibid.
142. "Tell me about Birdseye," "Fifty Years of Frozen Foods," *Quick Frozen Foods*, March 1980, 52.
143. "I am sure it has been gratifying," Post Col., Box 18, F. 11, March 25, 1927.
143. "The main reason prompting," Kraft General Foods Archives, Box H-5880, July 31, 1928.

CHAPTER TWELVE: "SUCH SCRAMBLING AS WE DID!"

145. "To understand the gala," Post Col., Box 47, "Palm Beach Recollections," 3.
146. "Mrs. E. F. Hutton," " 'Persian Ball' at Bath & Tennis," *New York Journal*, March 11, 1927.
147. "a most agreeable," Post Col., interview December 30, 1964, 41.
147. "For some unknown reason," ibid.
147. "half rose from her chair," Ziegfeld, *The Ziegfelds' Girl*, 123–24.

148. "would lose a hundred thousand," Post Col., Box 47, interview, February 1963, 1.

148. "It seems a strange thing," ibid.

148. "naturally quite a gambler at heart," ibid., 2.

149. "I almost fell out of the car," ibid., 3.

149. " 'If I ever hear,' " ibid.

149. "negotiated for an extremely," ibid.

150. "Hunter, you young snips," Post Col., Box 47, Marston interview, February 14, 1966, 3.

151. "was down to the ground," Post Col., Box 47, "Palm Beach Recollections," 2.

151. "Such scrambling," ibid.

151. "helped the other guests," Knott, *Palm Beach Revisited II*, 67.

CHAPTER THIRTEEN: MAR-A-LAGO

153. "determined to find," Post Col., Box 48, taped interview, February 1962.

153. "quite used to the idea," ibid.

153. "a Florida house," Post Col., Box 48, taped interview, February 1962.

154. "When we finally," ibid.

154. "ecclesiastical aspect," ibid.

155. "Gold is so much easier," *Mirabella* (August 1991).

155. "How much is that going to cost," "Sea to Lake Dream Becomes Marjorie's Second PB Home," *Palm Beach Daily News*, September 9, 1983.

155. "You've got to come back," ibid.

156. "not very fruitful," "Wyeth's History Built with PB's" *Palm Beach Daily News*, March 16, 1981.

156. "more than you really bargained for," Post Col., Box 48, taped interview, February 1962.

157. "more antique Hispano-Mooresque," Major, "Mar-A-Lago," March 1969, 2.

158. "perfectly exhausted," Post Col., Box 48, interview, February 1962.

159. "That was the most wonderful thing," Dina Merrill, NR interview.

160. "We refused to stop construction," Post Col., Box 47, "Palm Beach Recollections," 4.

161. "original," "Prominent Personages on Way Here," *Palm Beach Times*, January 23, 1927.

161. "unique," "Hutton Home Gains Rapid Unique Shape," *Palm Beach Daily News*, December 20, 1926.

161. "quite in keeping with," "Town Topics," newspaper unknown, March 17, 1927.

161. "The house here," Post Col., Box 18, F. 10, April 5, 1927.

161. "You know Marjorie said," Dina Merrill, NR interview.

CHAPTER FOURTEEN: ''DESPITE THE FORTY ADDED SUMMERS''

165. "You have been my inspiration," Post Col., Box 13, F. 31, April 25, 1925.

166. "tumors and complications," "Interment Made in California," May 26, 1925, newspaper unknown, Ross Coller file.

166. "stepped into the gap," Post Col., interview, December 30, 1964, 58.

167. "great-grandmother of the macadamia," ibid.

167. "I didn't loan it," Adelaide Riggs, NR interview.

167. "Mother looked after," Dina Merrill, NR interview.

167. "She was very much for anybody," Reverend Julia Sibley, NR interview.

167. "Adelaide, I don't care," Adelaide Riggs, NR interview.

168. "At one time Barbara told me," Dina Merrill, NR interview.

168. "Grandmother did not have a warm," Ellen MacNeille Charles, NR interview.

169. "the kindest and dearest," Post Col., Box 18, F. 7, telegram, August 27, 1941.

169. "I don't like big parties," Adelaide Riggs, NR interview.

170. "It took me about five minutes," ibid.

170. "All right, you don't have to go back," ibid.

170. "I went on a strict diet," ibid.

171. "I told Mother I didn't want to come out," ibid.

171. "Mother thought I was too young," ibid.

171. "to rival any in point of glamour," "Wedding Holds Many in North," *Palm Beach Times*, January 14, 1927.

171. "people who put the 'so' in society," "Miss Hutton and Tom Durant Wed; Are Coming Here," *Palm Beach Post*, January 20, 1927.

172. "The grandeur of the beautiful," "Adelaide Hutton Weds in Most Lavish Nuptials Ever Saw [sic]," *New York American*, January 20, 1927.

172. "a fortune in wedding gifts," ibid.

173. "quietly disturbed," Post Col., Box 16, F. 3, February 8, 1927.

173. "one of the most popular younger men," *New York American*, January 20, 1927.

173. "They [Adelaide and Tim] are back in town," Post Col., Box 18, F. 10, April 5, 1927.

174. "Their guests were seated," "Annual Affair Staged Amid Tropical Splendor—E. F. Huttons Give Dinner," *New York Evening Post*, March 2, 1927.

174. "lovely ensemble," "Huttons Entertain at Notable Dinner Party Preceding Masque," *Palm Beach Times*, March 2, 1927.

174. "You have no idea," Post Col., Box 10, F. 10, March 9, 1927.

174. "ballet-in-time," Post Col., "Mrs. E. F. Hutton Plans Large Party at Palm Beach," *New York Evening Sun*, March 12, 1927.

174. "promises to go down," "Hutton Party This Evening Large Affair," *Palm Beach Times,* March 13, 1927.

175. "just one more gesture," Post Col., Box 13, F. 7, March 27, 1927.

175. "had a very happy day," Post Col., Box 18, F. 2, telegram (undated, presumably March 16, 1927).

175. "My debutante child," Post Col., Box 16, F. 1, March 26, 1927.

176. "And that," Eleanor Barzin, NR interview.

177. "Mother had always wanted," ibid.

CHAPTER FIFTEEN: "LADY BOUNTIFUL"

179. "clean blue oilcloth," "1,000 Thank Hell's Kitchen Lady Bountiful," *New York Herald and Tribune,* June 10, 1932.

179. "To the needy," "Profiles: Lady Bountiful," *New Yorker* (February 11, 1939), 26.

180. "I like to think that," "Marjorie Merriweather Post, 86, Dies," *Washington Post,* September 13, 1973.

180. "Keep it moving," "A Flair for Philanthropy," *Washington Post,* March 12, 1967.

180. "If Marjorie was cast," "Post Hostess with the Mostest," *Time* (September 24, 1973).

181. "at precisely five," "Profiles: Lady Bountiful," loc. cit.

181. RICHEST GIRL IN THE WORLD, Van Rensselaer, *Million Dollar Baby,* 17–18.

182. "Barbara, you must forget," ibid., 82.

182. "I have refused," Post Col. Box 18, F. 10, April 5, 1927.

182. "I do not care," ibid.

182. "Once I became a reporter," Roy Meacham, NR interview.

183. "call off the Pinks," Dina Merrill, NR interview.

183. "That's pin money to her," Sturges, *Sturges,* 255.

183. "dig up a bad reputation," ibid.

184. "Of course these things," "Eleanor Hutton, Playwright Wed with Exactly $7," *New York Times,* April 15, 1930.

184. "still very much in love," Sturges, op. cit., 263.

184. "their romance is to end," "Strictly Disagreed," *New York Post,* May 28, 1932.

184. "Not that I was in love," Eleanor Barzin, NR interview.

184. "had devoted themselves," "Picks 10 Woman Over Age of 30 as Most Charming in Nation," newspaper unknown, December 23, 1932, New-York Historical Society, Edward F. Hutton file.

186. "even Mrs. Hutton's lifeboats," "A Legacy of Grandeur," *Palm Beach Life* (December 1977), 82.

186. "Saw ship," ibid.

186. "I was so excited," "The Sea Cloud—A Beautiful Dream," *Washington Sunday Star*, April 20, 1969.

187. "an exquisite suite," "A Cruise at the Top," *Washington Evening Star*, May 27, 1981.

187. "Why, Mrs. Hutton," "Mrs. Merriweather Post Food Heiress, Dies at 86," *Washington Star-News*, September 12, 1973.

187. "Mother was an explorer," Dina Merrill, NR interview.

188. "Life was fairly simple," ibid.

188. "The number of stockholders," *Annual Report of General Foods Corporation*, 1929.

189. "the last grand gesture," "Profile: Lady Bountiful," loc. cit.

189. "If all big-boat owners," Amory, *The Last Resorts*, 384.

CHAPTER SIXTEEN: A MERE CLASH OF WILLS

190. "one of the most socially," "Marjorie Post Hutton Gets Decree from Broker-Hubby Naming 'Siren' in Her Suit," newspaper unknown, September 10, 1935, Ross Coller file.

190. "there was Mrs. Hutton and his slippers," "Spends $5,000 on Orchids to Decorate Private Pullman for Wife's Journey," newspaper unknown, January 16, 1929, Ross Coller file.

191. "She loved him deeply," Estelle Needham, NR interview.

191. "I am thankful," Post Col., Box 18, F. 11, March 25, 1927.

191. "Dad was a real huggy bear," Dina Merrill, NR interview.

191. "fast marital pace," Amory, *The Last Resorts*, 331.

192. "She told me Ned," Marjorie Durant Dye, NR interview.

192. "There was no two ways about it," Post Col., Box 48, "Interview of Mr. Griffin," 11.

192. "That Ned Hutton!," Gladys Bendetsen, NR interview.

192. "Mother did not want," Adelaide Riggs, NR interview.

192. "Mother always felt sorry," ibid.

192. "Human affection," Eddy, *Science and Health*, 57.

193. "should improve," ibid., 66.

193. "Nobody fooled me," Ellen MacNeille Charles, NR interview.

194. "I took one look," Adelaide Riggs, NR interview.

194. "Grandmother was really terrified," Ellen MacNeille Charles, NR interview.

194. "I never saw any evidence," Dina Merrill, NR interview.

195. "the papers in the suit," "Marjorie P. Hutton Receives a Divorce," *New York Times*, September 8, 1935.

195. "five feet one inch," "Hutton Case Blonde Still a Puzzle," *New York Daily Mirror*, September 9, 1935.

195. "Until today's disclosure," "Marjorie Post Hutton Gets Decree from Broker-Hubby Naming 'Siren' in Her Suit," loc. cit.

196. "In my opinion," "The Business Man and Government," *New York American,* April 29, 1935.

196. "adopting as his own," "Rallying Cry Is Sounded in Defense of Recovery," *Detroit Free Press,* June 30, 1935.

196. "Personally I would be glad," "Hutton Offers All His Income to U.S. If Democrats Fulfill 1932 Pledges," *New York Evening Journal,* August 21, 1935.

196. "So I say, Let's gang up," "Interest of Business in Utility Controversy, Let Business 'Gang Up,' " *Public Utilities Fortnightly* (November 1935), 688.

197. "Chester informed the Commerce Department," "The Washington Merry-Go-Round," *Washington Herald,* November 27, 1935.

197. "General Food Corp has," " 'We Must Gang Up on Administration,' " *New York American,* November 20, 1935.

197. "All I had in mind," "Hutton Explains Remark," *New York Times,* December 11, 1935.

198. "Mr. Hutton had intended," "Hutton Resigns from High Post with Gen. Foods," *New York World-Telegram,* December 11, 1935.

198. "She loved him so much," Dina Merrill, NR interview.

198. "there was not the," ibid.

198. "I can't," ibid.

198. "as Mrs. Hutton is far wealthier," "Marjorie Post Hutton Gets Decree from Broker-Hubby, Naming 'Siren' In Her Suit," loc. cit.

199. "Ed told me," William E. Hutton, Jr., NR interview.

CHAPTER SEVENTEEN: MRS. JOSEPH DAVIES

203. "Now look, Robert," Dina Merrill, NR interview.

204. "a man of mature years," Post Col., F. 1, "My two dear big girls."

204. "a grand and glamorous woman," "Profiles: Lady Bountiful III," *New Yorker* (February 18, 1939).

204. "The guests were having cocktails," Eleanor Tydings Ditzen, NR interview.

205. "That's what," MacLean, *Joseph E. Davies,* 21.

205. "You're the man I want to marry," Liz Carpenter, NR interview.

205. "There was always somebody to take," Cliff Robertson, NR interview.

205. "She always wanted to get married," Melissa Cantacuzene, NR interview.

205. "You're not the one," Dina Merrill, Adelaide Riggs, NR interview.

206. "Mother was enchanted," Dina Merrill, NR interview.

207. "A poor settlement," *Washington Evening Star,* Davies obit, Davies file, Martin Luther King Library.

207. "one of those birds," *Milwaukee Journal,* May 29, 1952.

207. "dictator in the making," MacLean, *Joseph E. Davies*, 18.

207. "in the New Deal mold," Eagles, *Ambassador Joseph E. Davies*, 20.

207. "Davies was a charming," D. Pearson and R. Allen, "The Washington Merry-Go-Round," *Washington Herald*, December 27, 1935.

208. "corporation lawyer with a liberal viewpoint," "Joseph E. Davies Divorced in West," *New York Times*, March 10, 1955.

208. "likely to go up the ladder," "J. E. Davies, Local Attorney, Named Ambassador to Russia," *Washington Evening Star*, November 20, 1936.

208. "I was quite disconsolate," Post Col., Box 10, F. 1, March 18, 1935.

208. "Dearest, dearest, dearest," ibid., March 23, 1935.

209. "My dearest—" Post Col., Box 12, F. 21, April 6, 1935.

209. "I find it wonderful," Post Col., Box 12, F. 24, "My Joe darling."

210. "The first time I met him," Dina Merrill, NR interview.

210. "Mother was devastated," Eleanor Tydings Ditzen, NR interview.

210. "When I knew that my," ibid.

210. "I would not have any use," ibid.

210. "freedom rather than a life of lies," Post Col., Box 7, F. 7, "Dearly beloved."

210. "Mr. Davies is handling a tax case," "Mrs. Marjorie Merriweather Post Is Dead at 86," *New York Times*, September 13, 1973.

211. "She was a remarkably generous woman," Eleanor Tydings Ditzen, NR interview.

211. "We were absolutely honest," ibid.

211. "one of the finest and noblest," Post Col., Box 10, F. 7.

211. "simple, quiet and dignified," "Profiles: Lady Bountiful III," loc. cit.

211. "Mother felt," Dina Merrill, NR interview.

211. "You are the Best," Post Col., Box 10, F. 6, "At Home Thursday, Dec. 5."

212. "$7-a-Slice," "$7-a-Slice Cake Eaten as Mrs. Hutton Weds," *New York World-Telegram*, December 15, 1935.

212. "Mrs. Post Close Hutton Davies' luxurious," Wright, *Heiress*, 126.

213. "My father didn't need to be bought," Eleanor Tydings Ditzen, NR interview.

213. "a roaring scandal," Emlen Davies Evers, NR interview.

213. "most everybody, certainly the old ladies," Eleanor Tydings Ditzen, NR interview.

213. "I thought it was a terrible thing," Betty Beale Graeber, NR interview.

215. "I have been doing a little," Marjorie M. Post letter from the Arlington Hotel, December 1, 1933, Kraft General Foods Archives, Hj588 1933.

215. "Since our talk of Tuesday," Clare Chester letter, September 26, 1935, Kraft General Foods Archives.

215. "the first woman director," "Post Heiress General Foods Board Member," *Washington Evening Star*, April 9, 1936.

215. "altogether conversant," "Richest U.S. Women," *Fortune* (November 1936).

215. "a person respected," "Mrs. Davies: Business Chief," *Literary Digest* (April 18, 1936).

215. "until I understand," "Likes Her Job as Director," *New York Sun*, July 6, 1936.

216. "Again back into my Daddy's," *Sea Cloud Album 1936*, courtesy Nedenia Hartley.

216. "I always have to get dressed up," Ellen MacNeille Charles, NR interview.

216. "She wanted to show the world," Don Handelman, NR interview.

216. "She kept that steel-trap mind," Roy Meacham, NR interview.

216. "socially ambitious," "Richest U.S. Women," loc. cit.

217. "But whatever it was," Dina Merrill, NR interview.

CHAPTER EIGHTEEN: FIRST "AMBASSADRESS" TO THE SOVIET UNION

218. "the bleakest and dullest," "Profiles: Lady Bountiful III," loc. cit.

218. "ultimate plan," Davies, *Mission to Moscow*, xiv.

218. "touch of Rooseveltian humor," MacLean, op. cit., 24.

219. "put up," "Profiles: Lady Bountiful III," loc. cit.

219. "the one country on the," "Davies: Corporation Attorney Becomes Ambassador to Soviet," *Newsweek* (November 28, 1936).

219. "I said to Mr. Davies," Post Col., Box 47, interview, August 31, 1964.

219. "I had been living," ibid.

219. "almost embarrassingly so," Emlen Davies Evers, NR interview.

219. "I began to feel that," Post Col., Box 47, interview, August 31, 1964.

219. "She loved the idea of being a diplomatic wife," Dina Merrill, NR interview.

220. "an edged energetic participation," "Richest U.S. Women," loc. cit.

220. "Mother loved to entertain," Dina Merrill, NR interview.

220. "has no sense of guilt," "Mumsy the Magnificent," *Time* (February 6, 1937).

220. "this whole Russian question," Freidel, *Franklin D. Roosevelt*, 172.

220. "served to emphasize the importance," "J. E. Davies Named as Our Ambassador to the Soviet Union," *New York Times*, November 12, 1936.

221. "It is felt certain in official quarters," "J. E. Davies, Local Attorney, Named Ambassador to Russia," *Washington Evening Star*, November 20, 1936.

221. "peculiarly well fitted," "Soviet Envoy Is an Expert on Trade," *Washington Evening Star*, November 21, 1936.

221. "which go far to compensate," "Mr. Davies to Moscow," *Washington Post*, November 21, 1936.

221. "Am deeply moved," FDR Library, PPF, File 1381, telegram, November 22, 1936.

222. "He . . . went to the USSR," "Ambassador Davies," *Fortune* (October 1937).

222. "She learned not to wear so many jewels," Emlen Davies Evers, NR interview.

222. "more appropriate to the court of Versailles," Williams, *Russian Art and American Money*, 231.

222. "the most stunning woman," ibid., 231.

222. "They were absolutely goggle-eyed," Dina Merrill, NR interview.

223. "entirely with crystal," Post Col., Box 48, interview, March 1962.

223. "a stickler about nutrition," Emlen Davies Evers, NR interview.

223. "about as tactful as presenting a cripple," "Ambassador Davies," loc. cit.

223. AMBASSADOR HAS 2,000 PINTS, "Davies Ships Food to Use in Russia," *New York Times*, December 6, 1936.

223. "It was hard for people to understand," Post Col., Box 47, interview, August 31, 1964.

224. "Is it true that you took two thousand," ibid.

224. "a great comfort," Post Col., Box 48, interview, March 1962.

225. "Well, I see what this was all about," Post Col., Box 47, interview, August 31, 1964.

225. "the roughest," ibid.

225. "in a lather of excitement," ibid.

225. "everything around us was pure white," ibid.

226. "The Russians were agog," Dina Merrill, NR interview.

226. "are recognizing very much the ability," FDR Library, E. Roosevelt, PP 100, Personal Letters, March 3, 1937.

226. "a great privilege," ibid.

226. "the screams of the individuals," Post Col., Box 47, interview, September 1, 1964.

227. "there would be many things," FDR Library, E. Roosevelt, PP 100, Personal Letters, March 3, 1937.

227. "The most extraordinary part," Davies, op. cit., 42.

228. "warning to all," ibid.

228. "quite as horrible," ibid., 45.

228. "It's not true," Post Col., Box 47, interview, August 31, 1964.

229. "Why, it's a diamond," ibid.

229. "We found them in the fireplaces," ibid.

230. "They were all so tense," Post Col., Box 47, interview, September 1, 1964.

230. "Get through again," ibid.

230. "Oh? You didn't hear?," Dina Merrill, NR interview.

230. "It happened a great deal," Emlen Davies Evers, NR interview.

231. "all manner of things," Davies, op. cit., 131.

232. "masses of icons," Post Col., Box 47, interview, August 31, 1964.

232. "the finest such collection," "Mrs. Marjorie Merriweather Post Is Dead at 86," *New York Times*, September 13, 1973.

233. "a real bargain," Fred Korth, NR interview.

CHAPTER NINETEEN: "AN INVALUABLE ASSET TO THIS MISSION"

234. "has made a great hit," Davies, *Mission to Moscow*, 130.

234. "Madame, for the first time," Post Col., Box 47, interview, August 31, 1964, 13.

234. "You Americans," Davies, op. cit., 114.

235. "snappy walk," FDR Library, PSF Russia 1937, March 3, 1937.

236. "I . . . emphasized again," FDR Library, PSF Russia 1937–40, February 25, 1937.

236. "plants and the equipment," FDR Library, PSF Russia 1937–40, March 5, 1937.

236. "definitely hit their stride," "Russia: Babbitt Bolsheviks," *Time* (March 15, 1937), 20.

237. "most striking impression," ibid., 24.

237. "a wonderful and stimulating," MacLean, op. cit., 37.

237. "got around," ibid.

237. "He thought very well," Fanny Chipman, NR interview and Foreign Service Spouse Oral History.

237. "Mr. Davies's constituents," Kennan, *Memoirs: 1925–1950*, 83.

238. "too long for his own good," MacLean, op. cit., 38.

238. "Mother had this strange idea," Dina Merrill, NR interview.

238. "You see, Deenie," Emlen Davies Evers, NR interview.

239. "They go out of their way," "Ambassador Davies," *Fortune* (October 1937).

239. "looked very beautiful," MacLean, op. cit., 15.

239. "Marjorie and I have not," FDR Library, PSF Russia 1937–40, June 10, 1937.

239. "told him the truth," Davies, op. cit., 150.

240. "a certain hostile Fascist power," ibid., 152.

240. "Poor Rosengoltz!," ibid., 153.

240. "all parties are playing," FDR Library, PSF Russia 1937–40, June 10, 1937.

240. "not one diplomatic mission," MacLean, op. cit., 40.

240. "conditions here, as usual," Davies, op. cit., 161.

241. "when two people with dominant personalities," "Ambassador Davies," loc. cit.

241. "immediately singled out," Davies, op. cit., 162.

241. "Well, there was the biggest," Post Col., Box 47, interview, September 1, 1964, 6.

242. "Russia is," Davies, op. cit., 210.

242. "discount Russia's development," ibid., 218.

242. "Europeans and Americans," Post Col., Box 47, interview, November 2, 1964, 5.

242. "your noble and beautiful," FDR Library, PPF 1381, telegraph, August 30, 1937.

243. "he could say it was *my* ship," Dina Merrill, NR interview.

243. "I guess he was a romantic soul," ibid.

244. "Of course it's hell to be alone," FDR Library, S. Early Papers, Box 3, 1934–37, November 1, 1937.

244. "You have been a great comfort to Marjorie," ibid., November 12, 1937.

244. "distinguished service," untitled article, *Washington Post,* November 6, 1937.

245. "I have had an interesting," FDR Library, PPF 1381, August 28, 1937.

245. "our freshman ambassador," MacLean, op. cit., 44.

245. "I know how anxious you are," FDR Library, S. Early Papers, Box 3, 1934–37, September 22, 1937.

245. "fully and gladly comply," MacLean, op. cit., 44–45.

246. "We see no reason," FDR Library, PPF, 1381, telegram, November 10, 1937.

246. "a very captivating," D. Pearson and R. Allen, "The Washington Merry-Go-Round," *Washington Herald,* December 16, 1937.

247. "some career diplomats," MacLean, op. cit., 47.

247. "a definite pact or agreement," ibid., 50.

247. "It was difficult to look," Davies, op. cit., 266.

248. "Notwithstanding . . . a prejudice," ibid.

248. "There would seem to be no question," FDR Library, E. Roosevelt Papers, PP 100, Personal Letters, March 17, 1938.

248. "Joe has come back," ibid.

248. "tough break," MacLean, op. cit., 271–72.

249. "From the viewpoint," Davies, op. cit., 298.

249. "great and distinctive success," Post Col., Box 10, F. 19, June 10, 1938.

249. "You and I," ibid.

250. "not look robust," Davies, op. cit., 343.

250. "nothing short of a sensation," ibid., 339.

250. "for the simple reason," ibid., 364.

251. "with the dawn breaking over the Kremlin," ibid.

251. "the belle of the ball," ibid.

251. "was presented by Madam Molotov," ibid., 351.

CHAPTER TWENTY: MISSION FULFILLED

252. "When I say no equipment," Post Col., Box 48, interview, March 1962.

253. "Thank God!," untitled newsclip, courtesy *Palm Beach Daily News* morgue, and Dina Merrill, NR interview.

253. "your domain in Texas," Post Col., Box 47, conversation with M. M. Post, November 2, 1964, 31.

253. "volcano," FDR Library, S. Early Papers, Box 3, 1938–41, September 7, 1938.

253. "saber rattling," Post Col., Box 47, conversation with M. M. Post, November 2, 1964, 16.

253. "It was frightening to see," Dina Merrill, NR interview.

253. "not nearly as stimulating," FDR Library, S. Early Papers, Box 3, 1938–41, September 7, 1938.

254. "a defeat without a war," Gilbert, *Churchill*, 600.

254. "Well, it's all over," FDR Library, S. Early Papers, Box 3, 1938–41, October 7, 1938.

254. "We were so near the border," Post Col., Box 47, conversation with M. M. Post, November 2, 1964, 17.

255. "our minds much at peace now," Marjorie Post Scrapbook *Belgium*, vol. I.

255. "Marjorie Post Close Hutton Davies," "Society," New York *Daily News*, October 14, 1938.

255. "Mrs. Joseph E. Davies is one," "Jewels Dusted Off, Met Opens in Week," New York *Daily News*, November 14, 1938.

256. "piece by piece," Post Col., Box 47, conversation with M. M. Post, November 2, 1964, 11.

256. "We have just come back," FDR Library, S. Early Papers, Box 3, 1938–41, January 26, 1939.

256. "It looks pretty dark to me," S. Early Papers, Box 3, 1938–41, March 29, 1939.

257. "project a hard, realistic front," MacLean, op. cit., 67.

257. "God help the Western Powers," FDR Library, S. Early Papers, Box 3, 1938–41, June 8, 1939, letter to "Pa."

257. "any grouping of powers," McClellan, *Russia*, 176.

258. "pack fast," Post Col., Box 28, interview, March 1962.

258. "The only time in my life," Dina Merrill, NR interview.

258. "we passed a burning English tanker," FDR Library, S. Early Papers, Box 3, 1938–41, September 11, 1939.

258. "bring Russia back," MacLean, op. cit., 68.

259. "did we get out," Brinkley, *Washington Goes to War*, 27.

259. "What is your judgement?," MacLean, op. cit., 68.

259. "substantial quantities," Davies, op. cit., 464.

259. "The Russian Bear has taken," ibid., 465.

259. "may be exactly," ibid.

259. "The president authorizes me," MacLean, op. cit., 68.

260. "been out to Laeken," Post Col., Box 10, F. 29, October 24, 1939.

260. "there is practically no social life here," Post Col., Box 11, F. 1, November 3, 1939.

260. "Dearest Beloved," Post Col., Box 10, F. 29, October 20, 1939.

260. "Dearest-dearest," Post Col., Box 12, F. 28, November 21, 1939.

260. "excellent work you have done," FDR Library, FDR Official File, letter, January 22, 1940.

261. "for the reason that," Post Col., Box 11, F. 1, October 31, 1939.

261. "She was very charming," Fanny Chipman, NR interview.

261. "changed woman," "Joseph Davies Being Groomed for High U.S. Post," *Knickerbocker News*, December 20, 1939.

262. "springtime bower," "Mrs. Davies Hostess to Writers," *Washington Evening Star*, January 24, 1940.

262. "follow that pair of black eyes," "Ambassador Davies," *Fortune* (October 1937), 218.

262. "He told Grandmother," Ellen MacNeille Charles, NR interview.

263. "Once at Hillwood," Marjorie Durant Dye, NR interview.

263. "We were like oil," ibid.

263. "I never listened to my mother," ibid.

264. "drew her long red fingernail," ibid.

264. "She got a kick," ibid.

264. "My baby Deenie," Post Col., Box 16, F. 12, May 23, 1941.

264. "It was the typical," 446. Dina Merrill, NR interview.

264. "And I must say," ibid.

265. "Mother took one look," ibid.

265. "As wife of the committee chairman," "Mrs. Davies Official Hostess in Washington," *Palm Beach Daily News*, January 21, 1941.

265. "Mrs. Davies wanted," ibid.

266. "upped it here and there," ibid.

266. "couldn't refuse," MacLean, op. cit., 70.

266. "extent of the resistance," Davies, op. cit., 475–76.

266. "Any defense against Hitlerism," Freidel, op. cit., 374.

267. "mothers of America," Brinkley, op. cit., 30.

267. "To none in this world," "Need for Quick Aid to Russia Stressed," *New York Times*, November 18, 1941.

268. "It used to make Mother terribly nervous," Adelaide Riggs, NR interview.

268. "greatest master of bad official English," MacLean, op. cit., 77.

CHAPTER TWENTY-ONE: "SINCE I HAVE NO SON . . . I WILL OFFER THE
SEA CLOUD"

273. "the biggest blowout," "Life Goes to a Party," *Life* (February 9, 1942), 102.
273. "If anyone stayed away," *Washington Times-Herald* (as quoted in "Life Goes to a Party," loc. cit.).
273. "All the Allied nations," "Capital Whirl," *Washington Post*, January 19, 1942.
273. "smartly turned out," ibid.
274. "She entertained and," Betty Beale, NR interview.
274. "To do honor," "Life Goes to a Party," loc. cit.
274. "rich and socially well-connected," Brinkley, op. cit., 143.
275. "Funny the turns," Marjorie Post Scrapbook *Belgium*, vol. I.
275. "As a boy I was," Joe Tydings, NR interview.
276. "She was always patting me," ibid.
276. "Since I have no son to give," "Deenie Weds Stan Rumbough," *Palm Beach Daily News*, September 12, 1983.
276. "My grandmother was a very patriotic woman," Marjorie Durant Dye, NR interview.
276. "Mommy, you have no son," Dina Merrill, NR interview.
277. "And sure enough, dear Mom," "A Legacy of Grandeur," *Palm Beach Life* (December 1977).
277. "I think the orchestras," untitled newspaper clip, *Washington Times-Herald*, March 11, 1943.
277. "In all this Red Cross work," Post Col., Box 22, F. 44, "Address prepared for Mrs. Joseph E. Davies for Washington radio delivery."
278. "We look forward to the day," "Nursery Exhibit Given to Russia," *New York Times*, July 7, 1944.
278. "bled white by fighting," MacLean, op. cit., 89.
279. "dominate and control," ibid.
279. "best U.S. collection," "Russian Painting," *Life*, March 29, 1943, 44.
279. "veritable museum," "Davies Home Elaborate Setting for American Soviet Reception," *Washington Evening Star*, March 8, 1945.
279. "Today we pay tribute," "Second Front Is Urged at Gathering on Davies Estate," *Washington Evening Star*, September 25, 1942.
279. "Stalingrad is Chicago's first line of defense," "We Are over Hump," *New York Times*, September 25, 1942.
280. "As a result," Emlen Davies Evers, NR interview.
280. "Reports from British," "Davies Preparations to Return to Moscow Blocked by Ill Health," *Washington Evening Star*, April 28, 1943.
281. "The plane carrying," "The Missionary's Return," *Time* (May 31, 1943).
281. "Messages comfort, joy," MacLean, op. cit., 107.

281. "is much more comfortable," Post Col., Box 11, F. 12, May 12, 1943.
281. "While tired," ibid., May 14, 1943.
281. "all this, my beloved," ibid., May 16, 1943.
282. "was an extraordinary honor," "The Missionary's Return," loc. cit.
282. "I think your President is right," MacLean, op. cit., 104.
282. "There is every indication," "Moscow's Mood," *Newsweek* (June 14, 1943).
283. "It was not surprising," Post Col., Box 11, F. 12, May 28, 1945.
283. "Hollywood's most controversial film ever," "Hollywood Goes to Moscow," *Time*, May 10, 1943.
283. "one of the most blatantly propagandistic," Bohlen, *Witness to History*, 122–23.
283. "the first full-dress example," "Mission to Moscow," *Washington Evening Star*, May 1943.
283. "first instance in our country," MacLean, op. cit., 106–07.
283. "phony propaganda," " 'Mission to Moscow' Received White House Blessing, GOP Thinks," *Washington Evening Star*, undated.
284. "It is not necessary to agree," "The Phoenix Nest," *Saturday Review* (May 15, 1943).
284. "warm in their congratulations," MacLean, op. cit., 107.
285. "an important milestone," Freidel, op. cit., 490.
285. "Use it up," Boyer et al., op. cit., 946.
286. "O yes, but this is different," "Mrs. Davies Buys Coach and Two," *Washington Times-Herald*, March 11, 1943.
286. "I don't care what the coachman looks like," "Mrs. Davies Has Coach, Pair, No Driver," *Washington Post*, January 22, 1943.
287. "Through my mind," "Mrs. Joseph E. Davies Christens New Libery Ship," General Foods Press release.

CHAPTER TWENTY-TWO: TRANSFORMATIONS

289. "Now, dear," Alden Sibley, NR interview.
289. "The demon Marjorie," ibid.
289. "We decided," Ellie Sibley, NR interview.
289. "a breathtaker," Alden Sibley, NR interview.
289. "had her suspicions," Ellie Sibley, NR interview.
289. "Marjorie was very pleased with her matchmaking," ibid.
290. "That was the generous kind of thing," ibid.
290. "Mother was crazy about him," Dina Merrill, NR interview.
290. "She was a wonderful mother-in-law," Stanley Rumbough, Jr., NR interview.
290. "Mother didn't really discourage," "Dina Merrill Can Always Earn a Living," *Palm Beach Daily News*, October 26, 1975.

291. "I really didn't think I had any choice," Dina Merrill, NR interview.
291. "Oh, it was awful," ibid.
291. "long talking-to," Adelaide Riggs, NR interview.
291. "She was very resentful," Dina Merrill, NR interview.
291. "Miss Hutton made an exquisite picture as a bride," "Miss Hutton, Mr. Rumbough Are Married," *Washington Evening Star*, March 24, 1946.
291. "Everybody had gone to church," Dina Merrill, NR interview.
292. "After high school," Marjorie Durant Dye, NR interview.
292. "At one point," ibid.
293. "Germans were trying," "The Way We Were," *Palm Beach Daily News*, September 30, 1990.
293. "It will no doubt," ibid.
294. "Our beloved 'Sea Cloud,' " *Sea Cloud* 1945 Photo Album.
294. "This initial journey," "Refitted Davies Yacht to Be Here," newspaper unknown, April 15, 1947.
294. "Mother was funny," Adelaide Riggs, NR interview.
295. "Mother used to say," Dina Merrill, NR interview.
295. "what she should and should not do," Adelaide Riggs, NR interview.
295. "ready for blood," ibid.
295. "Deenie started to go," ibid.
295. "it was better than becoming," Marjorie Durant Dye, NR interview.
295. "Well, Granddad could be," Joseph Tydings, NR interview.
296. "not as pleasant," Eleanor Tydings Ditzen, NR interview.
296. "I was kept up half the night," "Mission to Sun Valley," *Time* (March 21, 1955), 19.
296. "Three joyous happy busy years," *Sea Cloud* 1939 Photo Album.
297. "I have never been talked to like that," McCullough, *Truman*, 376.
297. "command their confidence," MacLean, op. cit., 137.
297. "tended to ease up," Bohlen, op. cit., 216.
297. "symbol of the American effort," MacLean, op. cit., 153.
298. "Do come if you can," MacLean, op. cit., 163.
299. "tired of babying the Soviets," Truman, *Harry S. Truman*, 298.
299. "long-term, patient," Boyer et al., op. cit., 979.
299. "Had the message come six months," Kennan, op. cit., 295.
299. "draw the line," Boyer et al., op. cit., 978.
299. "from Stettin in the Baltic," Gilbert, *Churchill*, 866.
299. "certainly not the Liberated," ibid.
300. "actions resulting from Communist philosophy," McCullough, op. cit., 730.
300. "words are quite inadequate," "The Way We Were," loc. cit.
301. "As a result," Marjorie Durant Dye, NR interview.
301. "The largest and probably the most," "54-Room Apartment in Fifth

Avenue House Found Vacant: Little Hope of Renting It," *New York Times,* March 3, 1944.

303. "vocal minority," "Oyster Bay to Hear Plea for University," *New York Times,* July 9, 1947.

303. "We are an American institution," "University Head Deplores Setback," *New York Times,* July 10, 1947.

CHAPTER TWENTY-THREE: THE DUCHESS OF THE DISTRICT OF COLUMBIA

305. "That was one of the most glamorous things," Lady Bird Johnson, NR interview.

305. "sort of a duchess," ibid.

305. "And it was set with gold plates," ibid.

306. "Dear Mrs. Davies," Post Col., Box 25, F. 30.

306. "tested out the macaroons," Fred Korth, NR interview.

307. *golly,* Liz Carpenter, NR interview.

307. "She was very open," Anne Frailey Braverman, NR interview.

307. "Why, she deserves it!," Gerson Nordlinger, NR interview.

307. "That's the Porfirio," ibid.

307. "No, just shaking hands!" Henry Dudley, NR interview.

307. "Jimmy, can you lend me some money?," Vincent Sottile, NR interview.

308. "If anybody could tango," Adelaide Riggs, NR interview.

308. "At that time she'd," Elizabeth Montgomery, NR interview.

309. "You learned to dance," Joe Tydings, NR interview.

309. "sober-faced," B. Beale, "Exclusively Yours: New Type of Gay Party to Be Forthcoming," *Washington Evening Star,* November 6, 1950.

310. "I just love licorice," Elizabeth Montgomery, NR interview.

310. "I must say I don't," Melissa MacNeille Cantacuzene, NR interview.

311. "grabbed up with ill-concealed eagerness," *Washington Sunday Star,* March 20, 1955.

311. "My husband kept saying," Ruth Buchanan, NR interview.

312. "little details like that," Gladys Bendetsen, NR interview.

312. "Had she been born later," Dina Merrill, NR interview.

312. "there was so much interest," Gerson Nordlinger, NR interview.

312. "awed," ibid.

313. "It's all Howard's baby," "Young America Likes It," newspaper unknown, April 28, 1956.

313. "I suppose nothing will ever match," "Tabs for Concert," *Washington Post,* May 25, 1956.

314. "Why take music lessons," "Orchestras," *Time* (May 3, 1963).

314. "I saw him only on account," Post Col., Box 47, Marston interview, February 14, 1966, 5.

315. "overly impressed," Anne Frailey Braverman, NR interview.

315. "Here it is," Ellen MacNeille Charles, NR interview.

315. "Could you please go and tell Joe," Adelaide Riggs, NR interview.

315. "You know, Joe Davies," Gerson Nordlinger, NR interview.

315. "At the end of the evening," Dina Merrill, NR interview.

315. "that man has given me," Betty Beale, NR interview.

315. "As a result," Dina Merrill, NR interview.

315. "I think she felt that she," ibid.

316. "I can't imagine Marjorie swallowing that," Eleanor Tydings Ditzen, NR interview.

317. "He's here," Adelaide Riggs, NR interview.

317. "Why did you put it in his name?" Ruth Buchanan, NR interview.

318. "She took everything," Henry Dudley, NR interview.

318. "She called me up in the bedroom," Vincent Sottile, NR interview.

319. "It has taken great courage," Post Col., Box 22, F. 27, letter of March 1, 1955.

CHAPTER TWENTY-FOUR: VITAL CONTRIBUTIONS

320. "Thus ends a marriage," "The Smart Set: The Davies Story, Pillar to Post," *New York World-Telegram and Sun,* March 1955.

320. "Mr. Davies to whom," "Joseph E. Davies Divorced in West," *New York Times,* March 10, 1955.

320. "a lack of basic, straight thinking," "People, Parting Thoughts," *Newsweek* (March 21, 1955).

320. "as well preserved," "Mission to Sun Valley," *Time* (March 21, 1955).

320. "bitten by the diplomatic bug," "The Smart Set," loc. cit.

321. "the most fabulous hostess in all America," "Marjorie the Magnificent," *Washington Sunday Star,* March 20, 1955.

321. "Grandmother had very strong ideas," Ellen MacNeille Charles, NR interview.

321. "was to turn every place she lived," Liz Carpenter, NR interview.

321. "Mother was not enchanted," Adelaide Riggs, NR interview.

322. "elegance and style," "The Collectors: Riches of the Czars," *Architectural Digest* (January/February 1979).

322. "I bought them at Woolworth's," Elizabeth Montgomery, NR interview.

323. "I really have been quite disgusted," Post Col., Box 18, F. 2, October 17, 1955.

324. "For sheer quality," "A Majestic Garden," *Washington Evening Star,* May 7, 1960.

325. "Don't ever say there's no such thing," "Exclusively Yours: Beauty and Elegance Reign in Mrs. Post's New House," *Washington Evening Star,* May 29, 1957.

325. "is a little less," "Mrs. Post's Party Had a Setting of Splendor," *Washington Post*, July 5, 1957.

325. "refurbishing of Hillwood," "Huge Estates Here Revealed as Cities Within a City," *Washington Post*, August 17, 1961.

326. "My dear, I wondered," "Cereal Heiress Sticks Finger into Civic Pies," *Washington Post and Times-Herald*, June 17, 1956.

326. "three times around the track," Harry Davidson, NR interview.

326. "Why are people so sure," "Marjorie Merriweather Post Says She Won't Remarry," *Washington Daily News*, April 25, 1955.

326. "Grandmother was a romantic," Ellen MacNeille Charles, NR interview.

327. "Mother, were you there?," Adelaide Riggs, NR interview.

327. "to define her life," Roy Meacham, NR interview.

327. "Wealth is a greater responsibility," "America's 10 Richest Women," *Ladies' Home Journal* (September 1957).

328. "could have recognized Post Hall," "Washington Is Talking About . . . ," newspaper unknown, June 3, 1957.

328. "I'll bet that Marjorie," Dr. Gordon Hoxie, NR interview.

329. "Aunt Marjorie was thrilled," the Reverend Julia Sibley, NR interview.

330. "long demonstrated friendship," "Mrs. Post Honored by French," *Washington Evening Star*, November 1, 1957.

330. "Friendship Walk—Hillwood," "Friends Give Mrs. Post Statues and Shrubbery," *Washington Sunday Star*, November 3, 1957.

331. "Friendship outstays," ibid.

331. "Oh, my goodness," Gladys Bendetsen, NR interview.

CHAPTER TWENTY-FIVE: MRS. HERBERT MAY

335. "Walking on fluffy pink clouds," Ellen MacNeille Charles, NR interview.

336. "He was a very attractive person," Adelaide Riggs, NR interview.

336. "He was a charming man," Dina Merrill, NR interview.

336. "I was totally undone," Peggy May Maryn, NR interview.

337. "And she did not talk," ibid.

337. "Don't count on me," Phil May, NR interview.

337. "Grandmother was a romantic," Ellen MacNeille Charles, NR interview.

337. "Money is the least," Phil May, NR interview.

337. "She's the first woman," ibid.

338. "Herb May was a handsome," Henry Dudley, NR interview.

338. "Although I didn't do it intentionally," Betty Beale, NR interview.

338. "Herb had been a widower," Post Col., Box 48, interview, March 1962.

339. "Blue skies," "Herbert Mays Hold Wedding Reception," *Washington Evening Star*, June 27, 1958.

340. "It was like putting the dancers," Mary Day, NR interview.

340. "ever put on a ballet for their guests," "Will Mrs. Post Be Queening Top Tiara?," *Washington Post,* June 16, 1957.

340. "was to be taken seriously," Roy Meacham, NR interview.

340. "She felt a very strong compulsion," Dina Merrill, NR interview.

341. "combined curriculum of dance," Mary Day, NR interview.

342. "Herb, I like this," Chauncy "Tex" Cook, NR interview.

343. "were not constantly filled," Dick Pearson, NR interview.

344. "Mother was terrific like that," Dina Merrill, NR interview.

344. "What the world often saw," Peggy May Maryn, NR interview.

344. "I called her Mother," ibid.

344. "Now, I want you to be married," Jan May, NR interview.

344. "I thought she was a wonderful woman," ibid.

345. "To my new son," Phil May, NR interview.

345. "I felt that I got," ibid.

345. "a much better stadium," Harry Davidson, NR interview.

346. "It's a wonderful field," "It's a Wonderful Field!," *Battle Creek Enquirer and News,* November 3, 1961.

346. "like a fairy tale," Janet Disbrow, NR interview.

348. "Those of us," Post Col., Box 17, F. 34, "Dedication of Flagpole," October 20, 1962.

348. "Margaret was a manager type," the Reverend Julia Sibley, NR interview.

348. "In a sense she decided," Phil May, NR interview.

348. "You mind your business," Dina Merrill, NR interview.

348. "fussed over her," Phil May, NR interview.

349. "Speak up! Don't mumble," Ellen Charles, Melissa Cantacuzene, NR interviews.

349. "She certainly tried every known one," Adelaide Riggs, NR interview.

349. "You don't have to talk so loud," Phil May, NR interview.

CHAPTER TWENTY-SIX: "HER STEP IS FIRM, HER STAMINA DISCOURAGING"

350. "But he was also a charming man," Dina Merrill, NR interview.

350. "People tried to tell her," Estelle Needham, NR interview.

351. "I guess I knew," Eleanor Barzin, NR interview.

351. "You mean, you didn't know?" Dina Merrill, NR interview.

351. "My god," Wright, op. cit., 207.

352. "You can't be unhappy," Phil May, NR interview.

352. "My father learned early on," Peggy May Maryn, NR interview.

352. "She was mortified," Dina Merrill, NR interview.

352. "I want you to know from my heart," Post Col., Box 20, F. 10, September 20, 1963.

353. "I felt no animosity," Peggy May Maryn, NR interview.

353. "There was twice the life force," Roy Meacham, NR interview.

353. "On one hand, she would do," Ellen MacNeille Charles, NR interview.

353. "Gee, you have a nice house," Roy Meacham, NR interview.

354. "And the sweet ones," Marjorie Durant Dye, NR interview.

354. "Marjorie, you could run General Motors," Chauncy "Tex" Cook, NR interview.

354. "I saw a very sad woman," Phil May, NR interview.

354. "I had many lovely things," Gladys Bendetsen, NR interview.

354. "was a mess," Post Col., Box 15, F. 1, May 13, 1964.

355. "looking youthful and charming," "Let's Dance," Washington Post, October 5, 1964.

355. "The tremendous feeling here," "White Tie Indisposed at Ballet," New York Daily News, January 30, 1965.

356. "She was one of the greatest ladies," Fred Korth, NR interview.

356. "the attractive and amusing Korth," "No Nuptial Plans for Marjorie Post," Washington Evening Star, January 31, 1966.

357. "Darling: . . . I'm," Post Col., Box 19, F. 13, undated.

357. "I miss you," ibid.

357. "You should be glad," Post Col., Box 19, F. 13, May 18, 1967, "My dearest Marjorie."

357. "if Fred Korth proposed," Gladys Bendetsen, NR interview.

357. "Look, Mom, why complicate," Dina Merrill, NR interview.

358. "And we were perfectly happy," Fred Korth, NR interview.

358. "wish to show a certain way of life," Dina Merrill, NR interview.

358. "the finest collection of Imperial Russian treasures," "Mrs. Post Serves Tea—for 300," New York Times, May 6, 1966.

359. "This means that the Government's," "Hillwood Estate and Its Furnishings," Washington Sunday Star, December 9, 1962.

359. "To set foot inside," "A World Unique and Magnificent," Life (November 5, 1965).

360. "People have been writing," Post Col., Box 17, F. 16, July 25, 1966.

360. "patrician features," "Mrs. Post Serves Tea—for 300," loc. cit.

360. "At 79," "Mumsy the Magnificent," Time (February 3, 1967).

360. "stood erect and regal," "Orchestra Plays Upbeat Evening for Mrs. Post," Washington Post, March 16, 1967.

361. "is more widely known," "Worthy of a Queen," newspaper unknown, March 17, 1967.

361. "May I have a word?," "Happy Early 80th Birthday, Mrs. Post," New York Times, March 15, 1967.

CHAPTER TWENTY-SEVEN: CAREFUL HOUSEKEEPING

362. "things were getting very much out of focus," Dr. Gordon Hoxie, NR interview.

362. "one of the few entirely undisputed heroes," "Sergeant Chicca Returns," *Marine News* (May 1969).

363. "I'm going to buy you a drink," Rody Cantacuzene, NR interview.

363. "You mean she has all this," Post Col., Box 20, F. 1, memo to Mrs. Post, May 6, 1970.

363. "I wish I could give," ibid.

363. "demonstrated concern," untitled news items, *Washington Evening Star*, March 25, 1972, and October 4, 1969.

364. "I'm so sorry you can't come," Eleanor Tydings Ditzen, NR interview.

364. "she sensed," Nina Rumbough Craig, NR interview.

364. "I'm sending over a watchman," Ellen MacNeille Charles, NR interview.

365. "And for some reason they delivered it," Tony de Bekessy, NR interview.

365. "fast cars," Nina Rumbough Craig, NR interview.

365. "It was very moving," Dick Pearson, NR interview.

366. "She cut me right out of her will," Marjorie Durant Dye, NR interview.

366. "You stand there and greet people," "A Lifetime of Giving," *Palm Beach Daily News*, January 19, 1992.

367. "I have never seen a lady," Henry Dudley, NR interview.

367. "That beautiful never-never land," Johnson, *A White House Diary*, 647.

367. "walked us through," ibid.

368. "ranking with the generosity of Mr. Mellon," "Priceless Gift to the Nation," *Washington Post*, January 18, 1969.

368. "irreplaceable collections," "Mrs. Post Will Donate Estate to Smithsonian," *New York Times*, January 18, 1969.

368. "If we transfer my house," Henry Dudley, NR interview.

369. "like a hundred million," "Mrs. Post Looked Like a Hundred Million," New York *Daily News*, March 16, 1970.

CHAPTER TWENTY-EIGHT: TWILIGHT IN FRIENDSHIP GARDEN

371. "is all too ridiculous," "Mrs. Marjorie Merriweather Post Denies Wedding Rumors," *Palm Beach Daily News*, April 8, 1970.

371. "Fred Korth was still No. 1!," "Still No. 1 . . . ," *Washington Post*, April 10, 1970.

371. "Her poor health became noticeable," Lawrence Lester, NR interview.

371. "four days of entertaining," "Season Ends at Topridge," *Washington Evening Star*, August 25, 1971.

372. "It is so nice to be back," Post Col., Box 20, F. 19, December 22, 1971.

372. "virus," picture caption, *Palm Beach Daily News*, January 1972.

373. "Why, Marjorie, you should be ashamed," Wright, op. cit., 211.
373. "a sad time for everybody," Lawrence Lester, NR interview.
373. "Get me out of here," Marjorie Durant Dye, NR interview.
374. "She smiled when I came in," Dr. Stanley Kuvin, NR interview.
374. "She'll be dead," Marjorie Durant Dye, NR interview.
374. "Gus, I'm home," Adelaide Riggs, NR interview.
375. "I found she had gained weight," Gladys Bendetsen, NR interview.
375. "We just didn't talk about it," Fred Korth, NR interview.
375. "Here, you'd better take that," Alden Sibley, NR interview.
376. "Wait until you see your mother," Adelaide Riggs, NR interview.
377. "this patriot," courtesy of Cliff Robertson. Also "Marjorie Merriweather Post—a Truly Grand and Gentle Lady—Is Remembered in Beautiful Memorial Service," *Congressional Record,* 522-042-34352.
377. "I am making no provision," Last Will and Testament of Marjorie Merriweather Post, Probate Division, Superior Court, Washington, D.C.
378. "I am sure Mother was looking down," the Reverend Julia Sibley, NR interview.
379. "Perhaps the greatest thing about having lots of money," "Marjorie Merriweather Post," editorial, *Washington Star-News,* September 14, 1973.
380. "gave generously of her time," "Mrs. Marjorie Merriweather Post Is Dead at 86," *New York Times,* September 13, 1973.
380. "her ability to give happiness to others," *Congressional Record,* op. cit., 2.
380. "entertained kings and queens," ibid.
380. "great zest . . . instinctive to her," Anne Frailey Braverman, NR interview.
381. "I don't care. I like it," Walter Beach, NR interview; Adelaide Riggs, NR interview.
381. "Everything she touches turns to beauty," "Mumsy the Magnificent," *Time* (February 3, 1967).
381. "there was a gentleness yet firmness," courtesy of Cliff Robertson, and "Marjorie Merriweather Post—a Truly Grand and Gentle Lady . . . ," loc. cit.
382. "how much you learn," Post Col., Box 47, interview, February 13, 1964, 33.

Bibliography

BOOKS

Alpern, Andrew. *New York's Fabulous Luxury Apartments: With Original Floor Plans from the Dakota, River House, Olympic Tower and Other Great Buildings.* New York: Dover, 1975.

Amory, Cleveland. *The Last Resorts.* New York: Harper & Brothers, 1952.

———. *Who Killed Society?* New York: Harper & Brothers, 1960.

Balsam, Consuelo Vanderbilt. *The Glitter and the Gold.* New York: Harper & Brothers, 1952.

Battle Creek 150 Sesquicentennial 1831–1981. Battle Creek: Battle Creek Sesquicentennial Committee, 1980.

Beale, Betty. *Power at Play: A Memoir of Parties, Politicians and the Presidents in My Bedroom.* Washington, D.C.: Regnery Gateway, 1993.

Beard, George M. *American Nervousness.* New York: G. P. Putnam's Sons, 1881.

Becker, Ralph E. *Miracle on the Potomac: The Kennedy Center from the Beginning.* Silver Spring, Md.: Bartleby Press, 1990.

Bigler, Philip. *Washington in Focus: The Photo History of the Nation's Capital.* Arlington, Va.: Vandamere Press, 1988.

Bohlen, Charles E. *Witness to History 1929–1969.* New York: W. W. Norton, Inc., 1973.

Bordin, Ruth. *Frances Willard: A Biography.* Chapel Hill: University of North Carolina Press, 1986.

Boyer, Paul S.; Clifford E. Clark, Jr.; Joseph E. Kett; Thomas L. Purvis; Harvard Sitkoff; and Nancy Woloch. *The Enduring Vision: A History of the American People*, vol. 1, *From 1965.* Lexington, Mass., and Toronto: D. C. Heath and Company, 1991.

Bran, C.C.B. *The National Geographic Society: 100 Years of Adventure and Discovery.* New York: Harry N. Abrams, 1987.

Brinkley, David. *Washington Goes to War.* New York: Knopf, 1988.

Brown, Henry Collins. *Valentine's City of New York: A Guidebook.* New York: Valentine's Manual, 1920.

Caro, Robert A. *The Power Broker: Robert Moses and the Fall of New York.* New York: Knopf, 1974.

Carpenter, Donna Sammons, and John Feloni. *The Fall of the House of Hutton.* New York: Henry Holt, 1989.

Carson, Gerald. *Cornflake Crusade.* New York: Rinehart & Company, 1957.

Catton, Bruce. *Michigan: A History.* New York: W. W. Norton, 1984.

Churchill, Allen. *The Upper Crust: An Informal History of New York's Highest Society.* Englewood Cliffs, N.J.: Prentice Hall, 1970.

Clifford, Clark, with Richard Holbrook. *Counsel to the President: A Memoir.* New York: Random House, 1991.

Coller, Ross H. *Battle Creek's Centennial 1859–1959.* Battle Creek: Battle Creek Enquirer and News, 1959.

Conquest, Robert. *The Great Terror: Stalin's Purge of the Thirties.* New York: Macmillan, 1968.

Cook, Blanche Wiesen. *The Declassified Eisenhower: A Divided Legacy.* Garden City, N.Y.: Doubleday, 1981.

Cowan, Beth Schwartz. *More Work for Mother: The Ironies of Household Technology from the Open Hearth to the Microwave.* New York: Basic Books, 1983.

Curl, Donald W. *Palm Beach County: An Illustrated History.* Northridge, Calif.: Windsor Publications, 1986.

Davies, Joseph E. *Mission to Moscow.* New York: Simon & Schuster, 1941.

Degler, Carl N. *At Odds: Women and the Family in America from the Revolution to the Present.* New York: Oxford University Press, 1980.

Diamonstein, Barbaralee. *The Landmarks of New York*. New York: Harry N. Abrams, 1988.

Dock, Lavinia L.; Sarah Elizabeth Pickett; Clara D. Noyes; Fannie F. Clement; and Anna R. Van Meter. *History of American Red Cross Nursing*. New York: Macmillan, 1922.

Duffy, Christopher. *Red Storm on the Reich*. New York: Atheneum, 1991.

Eagles, Keith David. *Ambassador Joseph E. Davies and American-Soviet Relations 1937–1941*. New York: Garland Publishing, 1986.

Eaves, Charles Dudley, and C. A. Hutchinson. *Post City, Texas*. Austin: Texas State Historical Association, 1952.

Eddy, Mary Baker. *Science and Health with Key to the Scriptures*. Boston: Trustees Under the Will of Mary Baker G. Eddy, 1954, 1975.

Elliott, Frank N. *When the Railroad Was King*. Bureau of History, Michigan Department of State, 1988.

Ewing, Charles. *Yesterday's Washington, D.C.* Miami, Fla.: E. A. Seemann Publishing, 1976.

Federal Works Projects Administration. *The New York Writers Project Guide to the Empire State, American Guide Series*. New York: Oxford University Press, 1940.

Fox, Stephen. *The Mirror Makers: A History of American Advertising and Its Creators*. New York: William Morrow, 1984.

Frank, Judy, and Mary Beth Larrabee, eds. *The Sulgrave Club's First Fifty Years: An Anniversary Album 1932–1982*. Washington, D.C.: 1983.

Freidel, Frank. *Franklin D. Roosevelt: A Rendezvous with Destiny*. Boston: Little, Brown and Company, 1990.

Friddell, Guy, and Wolfgang Roth. *Washington, D.C.: The Open City*. West Germany: Burda GmbH, 1974.

Gilbert, Martin. *Churchill: A Life*. New York: Henry Holt, 1991.

Gill, Brendan. *John F. Kennedy Center for the Performing Arts*. New York: Harry N. Abrams, 1981.

Green, Constance McLaughlin. *Washington: Capital City: 1879–1950*. Princeton, N.J.: Princeton University Press, 1963.

Hathaway, Richard J. *Michigan: Visions of Our Past*. East Lansing: Michigan State University Press, 1989.

Hawes, Elizabeth. *New York, New York: How the Apartment House Transformed the Life of the City (1869–1930).* New York: Knopf, 1993.

Jackson, Shirley. *Palm Beach Houses.* New York: Rizzoli, 1991.

Jacobs, Diane. *Christmas in July: The Life and Art of Preston Sturges.* Berkeley: University of California Press, 1992.

Jensen, Oliver Ormerod; Joan Paterson Kerr; and Murray Belksy. *American Album.* New York: American Heritage, 1968, and Ballantine, 1970.

Johnson, Lady Bird. *A White House Diary.* New York: Holt, Rinehart and Winston, 1970.

Jones, Landon Y. *Great Expectations: America and the Baby Boom Generation.* New York: Coward, McCann & Geoghegan, 1980.

Junior League of City of Washington. *The City of Washington: An Illustrated History,* ed. Thomas Froncek. New York: Knopf, 1977.

Kaiser, Harvey H. *Great Camps of the Adirondacks.* Boston: David R. Godine, 1986.

Keegan, John. *The Second World War.* New York: Viking Penguin, 1990.

Keith, Caroline H. *"For Hell and a Brown Mule": The Biography of Senator Millard E. Tydings.* Lanham, Md.: Madison Books, 1991.

Kennan, George F. *Memoirs 1925–1950.* Boston: Little, Brown and Company, 1967.

Knott, James R. *The Mansion Builders: The Best of the Brown Wrappers, Historical Vignettes of Palm Beach.* 1990.

———. *Palm Beach Revisited: Historical Vignettes of Palm Beach County,* vol. 1, 1987.

———. *Palm Beach Revisited II: Historical Vignettes of Palm Beach County,* vol. 2, 1988.

Krashes, Laurence. *Harry Winston: The Ultimate Jeweler,* ed. Ronald Winston. New York: Harry Winston, Inc., and Gemological Institute of America, 1988.

Lowe, Berenice Bryant. *Tales of Battle Creek.* Battle Creek: Albert L. and Louise B. Miller Foundation, Inc., and the Historical Society of Battle Creek, 1976.

Lowe, David Garrard. *Stanford White's New York.* New York: Doubleday, 1992.

Lutz, Tom. *American Nervousness, 1903: An Anecdotal History.* Ithaca, N.Y.: Cornell University Press, 1991.

Mackay, Robert; Geoffrey L. Rossano; and Carol A. Traynor, eds. *Between Ocean and Empire*. Northridge, Calif.: Windsor Publishing, 1985.

MacLean, Elizabeth Kimball. *Joseph E. Davies: Envoy to the Soviets*. Westport, Conn.: Praeger, 1992.

Major, Nettie Leitch. *C. W. Post: The Hour and the Man*. Washington, D.C.: Press of Judd & Detweiler, Inc., 1963.

———. *Mar-A-Lago*. 1969. Courtesy Hillwood Museum.

Marx, Leo. *The Machine in the Garden: Technology and the Pastoral Ideal in America*. London: Oxford University Press, 1964, 1984.

Massie, Larry B. *Voyages into Michigan's Past*. Au Train, Mich.: Avery Color Studios, 1988.

———, and Peter J. Schmitt. *Battle Creek: The Place Behind the Products, an Illustrated History*. Woodland Hills, Calif.: Windsor Publications, 1984.

Maxtone-Graham, John. *Liners to the Sun*. New York: Macmillan, 1985.

———. *The Only Way to Cross*. New York: Macmillan, 1972.

McCarthy, Kathleen D. *Women's Culture: American Philanthropy and Art, 1830–1930*. Chicago: University of Chicago Press, 1991.

McClellan, Woodford. *Russia: A History of the Soviet Period*. Englewood Cliffs, N.J.: Prentice Hall, 1986.

McCullough, David. *Truman*. New York: Simon & Schuster, 1992.

Mesta, Perle. *Perle: My Story*. New York: McGraw-Hill, 1960.

Miller, Robert B. *Our Town: Yesterday & Tomorrow*. Battle Creek: Albert L. and Louise B. Miller Foundation, 1986.

Numbers, Ronald L. *Prophetess of Health: A Study of Ellen G. White*. New York: Harper & Row, 1976.

Orcutt, William Dana. *Mary Baker Eddy and Her Books*. Boston: Christian Science Publishing Society, 1950.

Peel, Robert. *Mary Baker Eddy: The Years of Authority*. Boston: Christian Science Publishing Society, 1977.

Pipes, Richard. *The Russian Revolution*. New York: Vintage, 1991.

Post, Caroline Lathrop. *Aunt Carrie's Poems*. Battle Creek: C. W. Post, 1909.

Post, Charles William. *I Am Well: The Modern Practice. Natural Suggestion, or, Scientia Vitae*. Battle Creek: La Vita Inn, 1894.

———. *The Road to Wellville.* Battle Creek: Postum Cereal Company, 1926.

Powell, Horace B. *W. K. Kellogg: The Story of a Pioneer in Industry and Philanthropy.* Battle Creek: W. K. Kellogg Foundation, 1989.

Powell, Lyman P. *Mary Baker Eddy: A Life Size Portrait.* New York: Lyman P. Powell, 1940.

Randall, Monica. *The Mansions of Long Island's Gold Coast.* New York: Rizzoli, 1979, 1987.

Riasanovsky, Nicholas V. *A History of Russia,* 4th ed. New York: Oxford University Press, 1984.

Roosevelt, Theodore. *The Works of Theodore Roosevelt, v. 13, Presidential Addresses and State Papers.* New York: P. F. Collier & Son, Publishers, n.d.

Ross, Marvin C. *The Art of Karl Fabergé and His Contemporaries: Russian Imperial Portraits and Mementoes (Alexander III–Nicholas II): Russian Imperial Decorations and Watches.* Norman: University of Oklahoma Press, 1965.

———. *Russian Porcelains.* Norman: University of Oklahoma Press, 1968.

Rossi, Alice S., ed. *The Feminist Papers: From Adams to de Beauvoir.* New York: Bantam, 1974.

Schaeffer, Richard A. *Legacy: Daring to Care: The Heritage of Loma Linda.* Loma Linda, Calif.: Legacy Publishing Association, 1991.

Schaffer, Paul, ed. *An Imperial Fascination: Porcelain, Dining with the Czars, Peterhof,* tr. Robert Whittaker. New York: À la Vielle Russie, 1991.

Schickel, Richard, and Michael Walsh. *Carnegie Hall: The First One Hundred Years.* New York: Harry N. Abrams, 1987.

Sclare, Liisa and Donald. *Beaux-Arts Estates: A Guide to the Architecture of Long Island.* New York: Viking Press, 1980.

Stern, Robert A. M.; Gregory Gilmartin; and Thomas Mellins. *New York 1930: Architecture and Urbanization Between the Two World Wars.* New York: Rizzoli, 1987.

Sturges, Preston. *Preston Sturges,* ed. Sandy Sturges. New York: Simon & Schuster, 1990.

Taylor, Katrina V. H. *Russian Art at Hillwood.* Seattle: University of Washington Press, 1988.

Tindall, George Brown. *America: A Narrative History,* vol. 2. New York: W. W. Norton, 1982.

Truman, Margaret. *Harry S. Truman.* New York: William Morrow, 1973.

Tunis, Edwin. *Wheels: A Political History.* Cleveland: World Publishing Company, 1955.

Van Rensselaer, Philip. *Million Dollar Baby: An Intimate Portrait of Barbara Hutton.* New York: G. P. Putnam's Sons, 1979.

Weiser, Marjorie P. K., and Jean S. Arbeiter. *Womanlist.* New York: Atheneum, 1981.

Weiss, Manny, and Bill Hoffman. *Palm Beach Babylon: Sins, Scams and Scandals.* New York: Carol Publishing, 1992.

White, Norval, and Elliot Willensky, eds. *American Institute of Architects.* New York: Macmillan, 1968.

White, William Chapman. *Adirondack Country.* Syracuse, N.Y.: Syracuse University Press, 1967.

Williams, Robert C. *Russian Art and American Money.* Cambridge: Harvard University Press, 1980.

Wright, William. *Heiress: The Rich Life of Marjorie Merriweather Post.* Washington, D.C.: New Republic Books, 1978.

Ziegfeld, Patricia. *The Ziegfelds' Girl: Confessions of an Abnormally Happy Childhood.* Boston: Little, Brown and Company, 1964.

OTHER SOURCES

Annual Report 1922, Postum Cereal Company Incorporated.

Annual Report 1923, Postum Cereal Company Incorporated.

General Foods Annual Report 1946, General Foods Corporation.

GF 1947 Annual Report, General Foods Corporation.

C. W. Post: A Memorial, Battle Creek, Michigan, Courtesy Kraft General Foods Archives.

Post Collection, Bentley Historical Library, University of Michigan.

Marjorie M. Post letter from Arlington Hotel. December 1, 1933, Kraft General Foods Archives, H. Miscellaneous Hj588 1933.

Ross Coller File, Willard Library, Battle Creek, Michigan.

Clare Chester letter of September 26, 1935. Kraft General Foods Archives.

FDR Library, Hyde Park, New York: Papers of Eleanor Roosevelt. Personal Papers 100. Personal Letters.

FDR Library, Hyde Park, New York: Stephen T. Early Papers.

FDR Library, Hyde Park, New York: PSF Russia 1937–40.

FDR Library, Hyde Park, New York: PPF 1381.

General Foods Family Album, General Foods Corporation, 1948, p. 19.

Frozen Food Age Magazine, "Birds Eye History/Heritage. In the Beginning," August 1987.

Quick Frozen Foods, "Clarence Birdseye: The Man and His Achievements," March 1960.

The Handwriting on the Wall, Postum Cereal Company, 1925.

The Reporter, "Frozen Foods: From the Eskimo to Bing Crosby," October 24, 1950, Kraft General Foods Archives.

The Wellville Post, "Our New York Offices," June 1925.

Index

About the Author

NANCY RUBIN oftens writes about women and social history. Her previous books are *The New Suburban Woman*, *The Mother Mirror*, and *Isabella of Castille* (for which she won the 1992 Author of the Year Award from the American Society of Journalists and Authors). Ms. Rubin has contributed to *The New York Times*, *Business Week's Careers*, *Travel & Leisure*, *Savvy*, *McCall's*, *Ladies' Home Journal*, and other national publications. She teaches journalism at Purchase College, State University of New York. Ms. Rubin lives in New York with her husband, Peter, and is the mother of two grown daughters.

0-595-30146-0